Ethel B. Virtue
September 1943
Personal   Webster City - Iowa

SONOMA
SAN FRANCISCO

SANTA FÉ

SANTA BARBARA
SAN FERNANDO
LOS ANGELES

SAN
DIEGO

ST. AUGUSTI

SAN ANTONIO

MEXICO CITY
VERA CRUZ

ACAPULCO

Cosimini

El Camino Real

UNDERSTANDING OUR
SPANISH–SPEAKING NEIGHBORS

Book One

EDITH MOORE JARRETT
Fillmore High School, Fillmore, California

BERYL J. M. McMANUS
Hollywood High School, Hollywood, California

HOUGHTON MIFFLIN COMPANY
BOSTON · NEW YORK · CHICAGO · DALLAS · ATLANTA · SAN FRANCISCO
The Riverside Press Cambridge

ACKNOWLEDGMENTS

THE authors wish to acknowledge their indebtedness for story material to Francisco García and Antonio Cárdenas of Tepic, Nayarit; to Ezequiel Villaseñor, Tepatitlán, Jalisco; to Lorenzo Gómez Medina, Mazatlán, Sinaloa, and to many other Mexican friends who contributed the charming folk songs of their country.

Appreciation is due to Miss Lilly Lindquist, Supervisor of Foreign Languages, Detroit, Michigan; to Miss Nina Lee Weisinger, Department of Romance Languages, the University of Texas; and to Dr. Jacob Greenberg, Associate Superintendent, New York City, for their reading and helpful criticism of the manuscript. Thanks are due also to Professor G. Rivera of Harvard University for his careful checking of the Spanish text and exercises.

The Riverside Press
CAMBRIDGE : MASSACHUSETTS
PRINTED IN THE U.S.A.

CONTENTS

Page

¡Buen viaje!¹

We who live in the New World are becoming more and more conscious of our neighbors in the Western Hemisphere. Students of your school level in Mexico, for instance, must take two years of English because they live next door to us, for Mexicans realized long ago the importance of learning their neighbor's language. In the same way, it's a wise thing these days for us to study Spanish and to learn to understand our Spanish-speaking neighbors.

Have you ever thought of how far Spain carried her culture in the days of her conquerors and explorers? No matter how you turn the globe, you will always be facing some part of the world where Spanish is spoken. Today the most important Spanish-speaking countries lie in our own hemisphere. Old Spain discovered and colonized most of the new world to the south of us — Mexico, Central America, and except for Brazil, all of South America. As you think of the people who live in those countries, you may be sure that they all have some of old Spain's culture, although you can guess that Peruvians must differ from Cubans, and Bolivians from Argentinians, just as the way they speak the language varies.

Even in our own land we have a great Spanish heritage, for our west and south were first settled and civilized — long before Jamestown — by Spaniards who left us such place names as Florida, San Antonio, Santa Fe, and Los Angeles; gave us fiesta customs and costumes that color every celebration in those localities; and added to our everyday speech such words as hacienda, rancho, patio, burro, and siesta.

How did that Spanish culture reach us? Along *El camino real* ("the King's Highway" or "the Royal Road") for that was the name given to each old trail that led away from Mexico City to Spain's distant colonies. The map shows many *caminos reales* branching from the main road, like a tall palm tree with its base at Mexico City, its sweeping branches spreading to the east as far as St. Augustine, Flor-

---

¹ *Pleasant Journey!*

ida, and to the west even beyond San Francisco, California, while central branches lead into Texas, Arizona, and New Mexico. (See map on the title page.)

Just as those old trails connected Spain with what is now our country, so nowadays the learning of Spanish is a necessary connecting link with our neighbors to the south. Thus, although there really is no "royal road to learning," this new *camino real* will try to lead you smoothly to an appreciation of your own heritage, of a living language, and of the neighbors whose goodwill is so important to us all. In this book we shall learn especially about the common heritage and ways of living of all Spanish-speaking peoples, whether they live in old Spain or in the New World.

A Spanish proverb says that "he who would understand his neighbor must put the head into his house." In the stories you begin to read today, you will do just that. What games do Spanish-speaking young people play? What kind of songs do they sing? What rhymes do most of them know, as we know our "Mother Goose"? Do they celebrate their birthdays, and what do they do at Christmas time?

The answers to all these questions and many more you will find along this road.

El camino real is open before you!

¡*Buen viaje!* Pleasant journey!

El camino real

Young Mexico goes to market on donkey-back.   The white shirts and
trousers still worn by many Indians were designed for them by the Spaniards over four hundred years ago.

Notebook
Every exercise

El burro

*See how many of these words you can guess as you read your
first story in Spanish. Twelve of them are practically like English, and you can find all of them if necessary in the list at the end of
the chapter.*
Guess all you can, to save time and your thumbs!

¿Qué es el burro?[1]
El burro es un animal.
El burro es un animal importante.
¿Es grande el burro?
No, señor (señora, señorita); el burro no es grande.   5
El burro es el animal favorito del hombre pobre.
El hombre pobre usa el burro.
El hombre rico no usa (*does not use*) el burro.
El hombre rico usa el automóvil.
El hombre pobre usa el burro para trabajar.   10
¿Es importante el burro en España?
Sí, señor. El burro es importante en España y en
México.
¿Qué animal usa[2] el hombre pobre?
El hombre pobre usa el burro.   15
¿Qué animal usa el hombre rico?
El hombre rico no usa [*any*] animal. Usa el automóvil.
El automóvil es grande. El burro no es grande.
El automóvil es el vehículo (*vehicle*) favorito del hombre
rico.   20
El automóvil no es el compañero del burro.
El burro no usa el automóvil.

---

[1] An inverted interrogation point at the beginning warns us that a question is
coming. Inverted exclamation points are also used.

[2] You must put in the extra word *does* to make it sound right in English.

Find These Expressions in the Story

1. an important animal
2. it is not large (*it* is in the verb)
3. Is the donkey important
4. in order to work
5. the rich man; the poor man
6. he is the companion
7. of the rich man; of the poor man
8. the automobile is the favorite vehicle
9. he does not use any animal (*he* is in the verb)
10. Is the donkey large?

PREGUNTITAS (*Little Questions*)

Always answer in complete sentences in Spanish, beginning with **Sí, señor** (**señora, señorita**), *or* **No, señor**, *etc., if possible.*

1. ¿Qué es el burro?
2. ¿Es grande el burro?
3. ¿Es importante el automóvil?
4. ¿Quién (*who*) usa el automóvil?
5. ¿Quién usa el burro?
6. ¿Qué animal no es grande?
7. ¿Es grande el automóvil?
8. ¿Qué animal es el compañero del hombre pobre?
9. ¿Es el automóvil el compañero del burro?
10. ¿Cuál (*what*) es el vehículo favorito del hombre rico?

COSAS DE INTERÉS (*Things of Interest*)

1. Position of Descriptive Adjectives

un animal importante, *an important animal*

A Spanish-speaking gentleman was heard to say, "You Americans have such a peculiar way of saying things. Why, you place your adjectives before your nouns, and say, 'a large dog' instead of 'a dog large.'"

What do you learn from his statement?

REMEMBER:	Where are descriptive adjectives placed in Spanish? Descriptive adjectives follow their nouns.

EJERCICIO (*Exercise*) I.   *Write and say in Spanish:*

1. el hombre *poor*
2. el hombre *rich*
3. el burro *large*
4. el animal *important*
5. el compañero *poor*

6. el vehículo *favorite*
7. el animal *large*
8. el compañero *rich*
9. el automóvil *large*
10. el hombre *large*

2. Inverted Order in Questions

¿Es grande el burro? *Is the donkey large?*

Notice how the word order is "inverted" in this kind of question. You must say, "Is large the donkey?"

EJERCICIO II.   *Choose an adjective or noun for each blank and repeat aloud several times so that your ear will become accustomed to the sound:*

1. ¿Es —— el hombre?
2. ¿Es rico el ——?
3. ¿Es —— el automóvil?

4. ¿Es —— el compañero?
5. ¿Es grande el ——?
6. ¿Es pobre el ——?

3. Negative Sentences

el burro no es grande, *the donkey is not large*

To make a sentence negative in Spanish, place **no** before the verb (meaning either *no* or *not*). This sounds peculiar in English: "the donkey no is large."

REMEMBER:	Where does the **no** go? Before the verb.

EJERCICIO III.   *Make these sentences negative and translate them into English:*

1. El hombre rico usa el burro. 2. El burro es grande. 3. El automóvil es importante. 4. El hombre pobre usa el automóvil. 5. El automóvil es grande. 6. El burro es el compañero del automóvil.

4. *Contraction* del

del hombre pobre, *of the poor man*

De *(of)* used with **el** *(the)* becomes **del** *(of the).*

Compare: English: do + not = don't (sometimes)
Spanish: de + el = del (always)

EJERCICIO IV.   *Complete in Spanish:*

1. *of the* hombre *rich*
2. *of the* hombre *poor*
3. *of the* burro *large*
4. *of the* compañero
5. *of the* automóvil
6. *of the* animal *large*

Notice that **de** cannot combine with **un** *(a, an).*   *Say:* de un hombre rico, de un automóvil, de un burro.

PARA PRONUNCIAR (*To Pronounce*)

I. After you have pronounced these words aloud many times, write them from dictation:

a	*e*[1]	*e*[2]	*i*	*o*	*u*
casa	en	ese	mira	como	luna
Ana	les	mesa	piso	solo	fumo
pan	esta	peso	fino	no	una
ala	ser	se	fin	los	¡uf!
la, las	el	le	sin	otro	usa
sala	es	me	mi	con	uno
pasa	esto	pelo	misa	cola	pluma
tan	del	Pepe	sí	cosa	mula

II. Listen carefully as your teacher pronounces these words, then practice them.

1. *h* is never pronounced.

hasta	hay	ha	hora
¡hola!	hoy	habla	¡huy!
ahora	Alhambra	humo	hombre

---

[1] When *e* is followed by a consonant in the same syllable, it is pronounced as in *men.*

[2] When *e* is the last letter in a syllable, it is pronounced more like the *a* in *play* if the y is not pronounced.   (pla-y)

2. *j* is pronounced like a very harsh English *h.*

caja	rojo	julio	paja
jota	ajo	junio	hoja
junto	ojo	¡ja! ¡ja!	hijo

3. *q* is always followed by silent *u.* *qu* has the sound of English *k.*

que   quiso   quiere   queso   quien   queja

4. The sound of *ñ* can be found in the English words *onion* and *canyon.*

año	señor	España	mañana
sueño	niña	español	compañero

5. *rr* and initial *r* are strongly trilled. Try saying *three* as the telephone operator does, *"th-r-r-r-r-ee."*

río	rosa	¡arre!	perro
risa	carro	burro	rápido

Single *r* is less trilled than *rr* and initial *r,* but more clearly pronounced than English *r.*

era	pera	frente	grande (*Growl!*)
mira	mero	tres	presa (*Purr!*)

Final *r* is hard to trill but must never sound like English *r.*

leer	ser	tener	dolor
entrar	estar	por	mirar

6. To pronounce Spanish *t* correctly, put your tongue against your upper front teeth, so low that you could bite it.

t, d, l, and *n* require that same position of the tongue. It is said that Spanish is a "smiling language" because it is much easier to pronounce those four letters if you widen the mouth and tongue by smiling.

roto	tinta	tigre	favorito
tiene	toma	tela	Lupita

7. *b* and *v* are pronounced alike. In the following words neither *b* nor *v* is like any English sound because each is made with the lips slightly open. (Say *b* without closing your lips.) *b* and *v* have this sound when they are in the middle of a word or phrase.

favorito	Cuba	no vamos
mi vaso	dibujo	no sabe
pobre	automóvil	habla

PALABRAS PARA HOY (*Words for Today*) [1]

Most of these words should be learned, for you will meet them over and over again. The numbered words are those most often met in Spanish reading. They are numbered in the order of their importance. Notice how much some of them resemble English.

The italicized English words in parentheses (*accompany*) are not meanings, but words from the same family. They should help you remember the Spanish.

3	el animal	animal	1	no	no; not
	el automóvil	automobile	1	para	in order to
	el burro	donkey	1	pobre	poor (*poverty*)
2	el compañero	companion (*accompany*)	1	¿qué?	what?
1	de; del	of; of the (masc.)	2	rico	rich
1	el	the (masc.)	1	señor	sir
1	en	in; on	1	señora	madam, ma'am
1	es	is; he is; it is	1	señorita	miss
	España	Spain	1	sí	yes
1	grande	large (*grand*)	2	trabajar	to work
1	el hombre	man	1	un	a; an
2	importante	important	2	usa	he uses

[1] Note to teacher: Numbers indicate frequency in Buchanan List: 1 = 1–189; 2 = 190–500; 3 = 501–1000; 4 = 1001–1500.

PARA HABLAR ESPAÑOL (*In Order to Speak Spanish*) [1]

If you wish to begin speaking Spanish right away at every opportunity, you will want to learn these useful expressions, which your teacher will pronounce for you:

FIRST DAY

Buenos días	*How do you do*, or *Good day*
Adiós	*Goodby*, or, used as a passing greeting, like "*hello*"
Con su permiso	*With your permission*, or *Pardon me* (used when passing in front of a person)
Pase usted	*Go ahead*, or sometimes *Come in*
Gracias	*Thank you*
De nada	*You're welcome*

SECOND DAY

See if your name is in this list, and learn to pronounce and spell it if it is. Your teacher will tell you the meanings.

GIRLS		BOYS	
Adela	Juana	Andrés	Jorge
Alicia	Josefa	Antonio	José
Bárbara	Leonor	Arturo	Juan
Beatriz	Lucía	Carlos	Lorenzo
Berta	Luisa	Donato	Luis
Carolina	Margarita	Eduardo	Miguel
Carlota	María	Enrique	Pablo
Dorotea	Marta	Ernesto	Pedro
Elena	Paula	Felipe	Ramón
Emilia	Rosa	Francisco	Ricardo
Engracia	Sara	Guillermo	Roberto
Isabel	Susana	Jaime	Teodoro

Then learn to use:

¿Cómo se llama usted?	*What is your name?*
Me llamo ——, servidor (servidora) de usted.	*My name is ——, at your service.*
¿Cómo está usted?	*How are you?*
Muy bien, gracias.	*Very well, thank you.*
¿Y usted?	*And you?*

[1] Note to teacher: Do not test these expressions at this time, for they will be introduced and drilled later.

THIRD DAY

Learn what to do or say when your teacher uses these expressions in speaking to you:

Levántense ustedes.	*Stand up* (plural command).
Pasen ustedes a la pizarra.	*Go to the blackboard.*
Borren ustedes y siéntense.	*Erase and sit down.*
Está bien *or* **Bueno**	*All right,* or *it's all right,* or *"okay"*
¡Qué cosa!	*The idea!* (when someone makes a mistake)
¿Verdad?	*Isn't that so?*
¡Cuidado!	*Be careful!*

FOURTH DAY

A pupil or the teacher will ask each one of you:

¿Ha preparado usted la lección?   *Have you prepared the lesson?*

Answer with your choice of these expressions:

Sí, señor (señorita, señora)	*Yes, sir (miss, madam)*
Por supuesto	*Of course*
Claro	*Of course*
Seguro	*Sure!* (slang)
Ciertamente	*Certainly*
Sí, ¿cómo no?	*Yes, of course (why not?)*

The teacher will ask:

¿Quién no tiene errores?	*Who has no errors?*
¿Hay preguntas?	*Are there any questions?*
¿Entienden ustedes?	*Do you understand?*

FIFTH DAY

Here are the numbers from one to ten; practice counting things with them:

  uno, dos, tres, cuatro, cinco, seis, siete, ocho, nueve, diez

Here are the names of some colors:

  rojo, *red;* **azul,** *blue;* **amarillo,** *yellow;* **verde,** *green;* **negro,** *black;* **blanco,** *white;* **morado** or **color de violeta,** *purple;* **color de rosa,** *pink;* **color de naranja,** *orange.*

Ask each other this question, pointing out some object:

  ¿De qué color es esto?   *What color is this?*

¡Arre! ¡Burro!

Be sure to guess all the words you can in reading the story.

El burro es el compañero del indio pobre de México.
El burro es el compañero del hombre pobre de España.
Es (*he is*) muy inteligente, porque no desea trabajar.
No desea trabajar porque es muy perezoso.
El burro es muy independiente. No desea andar. Desea **5**
comer.

¡Arre! ¡Burro! Young Spain finds much use for donkeys. This young man, in the old University town of Salamanca, must knock at each house instead of leaving the milk on the doorstep.

Galloway

¿Es (*is it*) agradable usar un burro? Es (*it is*) necesario, pero no es muy agradable. Es necesario usar un burro para trabajar.

10 Es difícil usar un burro con cortesía, porque es muy independiente. Un burro no desea andar rápidamente. Un burro desea andar despacio para comer en el camino. El indio no desea andar despacio. Desea andar rápidamente.

Para usar un burro independiente es necesario decir
15 muchas veces, — ¡Arre! ¡Burro! ¡Arre!

El indio no desea decir — ¡Arre! — muchas veces, pero es necesario. No es posible decir, — ¡Arre! — muchas veces con cortesía.

El burro trabaja mucho en México y en España, porque es
20 el «Fordecito» del hombre pobre.

Find These Expressions in the Story

1. of the poor Indian
2. because he doesn't want to work
3. In order to use a donkey
4. he doesn't want to go
5. he works hard (much)
6. he wants to go slowly
7. because he is very lazy
8. the poor man's Ford
9. Get up!
10. it is necessary to say often (many times)

PREGUNTITAS

Remember to say, **Sí, señor,** *and so forth, in answering the questions.*

1. ¿Qué animal es el compañero del indio?
2. ¿Qué animal no desea trabajar?
3. ¿Desea andar despacio el burro?
4. ¿Desea andar despacio el automóvil?
5. ¿Es agradable usar un burro?
6. ¿Qué desea el burro en el camino?
7. ¿Trabaja mucho el indio en México?
8. ¿Qué animal es el «Fordecito» del hombre pobre?
9. ¿Es necesario comer muchas veces?
10. ¿Es necesario trabajar mucho para comer?
11. ¿Es agradable trabajar mucho en el camino?

12. ¿Es necesario decir, — ¡Arre! — muchas veces en automóvil?
13. ¿Es agradable usar cortesía?   ¿Es necesario?

COSAS DE INTERÉS
5. *Omission of Capitals*

el indio, *the Indian*   **México,** *Mexico*

Many proper nouns in Spanish do not have capitals.
Words on the map are capitalized, but the names of the inhab-
itants are not.   *México* is on the map; *un mexicano* is not.

6. *Meanings of Verb Forms*

desea   **es muy inteligente**
he wants   *he is very intelligent*

Where is the *he?*   It is understood, or "in the verb."

no desea, *he does not want*

Where is the *does?*   It is understood.   Never hesitate to
add or omit a word in English if it sounds better.   No two
languages can follow each other word for word.

EJERCICIO I.   *Write in Spanish:*

1. He does not want to go.   2. He does not use the donkey.   3.
He does not work.   4. He does not want to work.

7. *Punctuation of Quotations*

— ¡Arre!   ¡Burro!   ¡Arre! — *"Get up, you donkey, get up!"*

As you see, Spanish does not use quotation marks where
English does.   The dash is the only warning Spanish gives
that what follows is quoted.

> REMEMBER: A dash in a new paragraph
> means a change of speaker.

Quotation marks (« ») are used for a quotation within a
quotation (where we use single marks), or for coined words
like «*Fordecito.*»

8. *Possessive Case*

es el «Fordecito» del hombre pobre
he is the poor man's Ford

Spanish uses the preposition *de* (*of*) where we use the apostrophe *s* (*'s*) to show possession. Of course the word order must be changed when translating into Spanish.

EJERCICIO II. *Change the English word order of these phrases; then write them in Spanish:*

1. the Indian's donkey (the donkey of the Indian) 2. the man's automobile 3. Mexico's road 4. the animal's companion 5. the companion's animal

REPASITO (*Little Review*)

I. Complete in Spanish:

1. *a* hombre *large*
2. *the* hombre *rich*
3. *a* compañero *poor*

4. *the* burro *lazy*
5. *an* indio *intelligent*
6. *an* animal *necessary*

II. What are the missing words?

1. El —— desea —— en el camino. 2. Muchas veces —— necesario ——, — ¡Arre! ¡Burro! 3. El indio —— usa ——. 4. El burro —— mucho en México. 5. El —— desea andar rápidamente. 6. El —— no desea trabajar. 7. El burro es el —— del hombre ——.

III. Write from dictation the sentences your teacher will read to you.

PARA PRONUNCIAR

I. Repaso (*Review*)

1. *Review the sounds of the vowels by pronouncing these words:*

a	*e*	*i*	*o*	*u*
mapa	pase	río	noche	útil
abra	papel	pie	alto	su

a	e	i	o	u
grande	leer	prisa	sombra	sube
madre	ser	Chile	sol	suelo
padre	creer	misa	sopa	suerte
clase	parte	lindo	loro	punto
gato	de, me	siglo	compro	duro

2. *Practice trilling your r's.* **rr,** initial **r,** and **r** between vowels have a prolonged trill.

¡Arre, burro!	Rosa	rojo	rico
¡Rápidamente!	ropa	tierra	responde

II. Some New Sounds

1. **c** and **g** each have two sounds:

c { (1) **c** before **e** or **i** = **th** as in *thin* (**s** in Spanish America)
(2) **c** elsewhere = **c** as in *cat*

g { (1) **g** before **e** or **i** = harsh **h** as in *Hey!*
(2) **g** elsewhere is hard as in *gun.*

Pronounce these words, being sure to give the correct sound:

c		g	
camino	capitán	inteligente	largo
dice	toca	gana	regalo
como	cierto	coge	ángel
veces	centro	pregunta	página
cinco	acá	gas	golpe
necesario	lección	general	gente

2. **ch** is pronounced as in *church.*

mucho	chico	muchacho	chaqueta	chamaco

3. **z** is pronounced like **th** as in *thin* (**s** in Spanish America).

perezoso	paz	zapato	luz	hizo

4. **s,** with a few exceptions, is like English **s** in *this.*

es	rosas	presente	tres	sesos
usa	siete	suelo	sano	suspenso

s before *b, v, d, g, l, m,* or *n* is like English *s* in *rose.*

desde   mismo   detrás de   es bueno   es verde

5. *d* between vowels or at the end of a word is almost like *th* in *though.*

agradable   adiós   nada   cada
rápido   edades   todo   usted

Final *d* is so soft you can hardly hear it.

¿Verdad?   ¿Sabe usted?   ¿Qué edad?   Es Madrid.

6. *y* is pronounced like Spanish *i* when alone or final; otherwise it is like English *y* in *you.*

hay   y   yendo   yace
muy   tú y yo   mayor   ¡Ay, caray!

PALABRAS PARA HOY

2 **agradable**	agreeable, pleasant	**México**	Mexico (spelled **Méjico** in Spain and other Spanish-speaking countries)
2 **andar**	to go (with no destination)		
¡Arre!	get up! (used for animals)		
2 **el camino**	road	1 **mucho**	much
2 **comer**	to eat	1 **muchas veces**	many times, often
1 **con**	with	1 **muy**	very
con cortesía	with courtesy	2 **necesario**	necessary
1 **decir**	to say	**perezoso**	lazy (**flojo** often used in Mexico)
2 **desea**	he wants (*desires*)		
despacio	slowly	1 **pero**	but
3 **difícil**	difficult, "hard"	1 **porque**	because
el Fordecito	Mexican popular name for a Ford	2 **posible**	possible
		3 **rápidamente**	rapidly
independiente	independent	2 **trabaja**	he works
el indio	Indian	2 **usar**	to use
inteligente	intelligent	1 **y**	and

¡Vámonos!

Juanito es un muchacho de México.   Es un muchacho grande, y también es simpático.

Juanito tiene una hermana.   La hermana se llama Rosita. Rosita no es grande.   Rosita es una muchacha bonita.   También es (*she is*) una muchacha simpática.   Los hermanos son (*are*) simpáticos. 5

Juanito tiene un burro también.   El burro se llama Pícaro. Se llama Pícaro porque es perezoso y no desea trabajar. Pícaro siempre desea comer en el camino.

Los dos muchachos desean ir[1] al mercado.   Pícaro no desea 10 ir al mercado con Juanito y Rosita, pero es necesario.   Pícaro lleva las frutas[2] de Juanito y las flores de Rosita.   Pícaro no desea llevar las frutas y las flores.   Pícaro desea comer las frutas.   Desea comer las flores también.

Rosita desea ir con Juanito y Pícaro.   Rosita tiene flores 15 del jardín (*garden*).   Desea (*she wants*) vender las flores.   Los dos muchachos desean vender mucho.   Siempre es necesario trabajar mucho para comer.   Los muchachos trabajan (*work*) mucho.

Juanito dice, — Pues, ¡vámonos, Rosita!   ¡Arre, Pícaro! 20 Es necesario ir al mercado para vender las frutas y las flores. No es posible vender las frutas en el camino.   ¡Vámonos!

Rosita dice, — Sí, Juanito.   ¡Vámonos!   Es necesario trabajar.   Es necesario ir al mercado con las flores y las frutas. 25

Y ¿qué dice Pícaro?   Pícaro no dice nada (*anything*). ¡Tiene un bocado (*mouthful*) de flores!

[1] *Ir* means *to go* (in or to); *andar* means *to go* (with no destination given). Spanish-speaking people use words much more precisely than we do in English. They don't say "*to go* home"; they say "*to return* home."   They say "*to enter* the house," not, "*to go* into the house."

[2] Spanish-speaking people usually say "fruits," instead of "fruit," as we do.

Roberts

¡Vámonos, Rosita! On the way to market, the Indian girl stops to look at the stone serpents carved by her ancestors no one knows how many centuries ago.

Find These Expressions in the Story

1. a pretty girl
2. she is a "nice" girl
3. in order to sell the fruit
4. he is "nice" too
5. Well, let's go!
6. it is necessary to work hard (much)

7. they want to go to the market
8. he wants to eat the flowers
9. Rosie's flowers
10. Johnny's fruit

11. The brother and sister are "nice."
12. her name is Rosie (she is called Rosie)

COSAS DE INTERÉS

9. Gender of Nouns

All Spanish nouns, even names of things, are either masculine or feminine in gender.

> REMEMBER: Masculine nouns usually end in *o*: *el camino*
> Feminine nouns usually end in *a*: *la muchacha*

Nouns ending in *ión* or *d* are also usually feminine. If a noun has some other ending and common sense can't tell you its gender, you must learn it.

el automóvil (*m.*)   **el animal** (*m.*)   **la flor** (*f.*)

EJERCICIO I. *What gender are these nouns and how do you know?*

1. mercado
2. señor
3. fruta
4. flor
5. lección (*lesson*)
6. muchacha
7. muchacho
8. burro
9. hermana
10. verdad (*truth*)
11. hombre
12. señora
13. cortesía
14. «Fordecito»
15. salud (*health*)

10. Definite Article "the"

masculine { el (s.) / los (pl.) }   feminine { la (s.) / las (pl.) }

There are four words meaning *the* (definite article), and we must use the one of the same number and gender as its noun.

el burro
los burros } masculine

la hermana
las hermanas } feminine

EJERCICIO II. *Give the proper definite article with these nouns:*

1. —— compañero	5. —— señora	9. —— señor
2. —— hermana	6. —— flores	10. —— muchachos
3. —— hermano	7. —— hermanas	11. —— frutas
4. —— señorita	8. —— hombre	12. —— muchachas

11. Agreement of Adjectives

Adjectives that end in *o* change the *o* to *a* when they are used with feminine nouns. We say adjectives "agree" with their nouns. Noun and adjective endings often "match" exactly:

la señorita bonita, *the pretty girl*

> REMEMBER: Adjectives always agree with their nouns in gender and number.

12. Agreement and Position of Adjectives

Adjectives must agree with their nouns no matter where they stand in the sentence: *Juanito es simpático; Rosita es simpática.*

EJERCICIO III. *Give the proper letter (o or a) for the ending of these adjectives and prove your answer.* (They often "match.")

1. El burro no es bonit — (*o* or *a?*). 2. Rosita es bonit —. 3. Es la fruta favorit —. 4. El hombre es perezos —. 5. La señora es ric —. 6. Rosita tiene un compañero simpátic —.

13. Adjectives Not Ending in o

Some adjectives that end in neither *o* nor *a* have the same form for both masculine and feminine genders: *el burro grande, la señora grande.*

Most numbers do not change: **dos muchachas,** *two girls.*

EJERCICIO IV. *Complete these sentences in Spanish:*

1. El hermano es *large*.   2. La hermana es *large*.   3. El hombre
es *poor*.   4. La señora es *poor*.   5. Desean un compañero *intelligent*.
6. La muchacha es *independent*.

14. *Plural of Nouns and Adjectives*

Nouns and adjectives ending in *o, a,* or *e* form the plural by
adding *s*:

<table>
<tr><td>los caminos bonitos</td><td>los hombres pobres</td></tr>
<tr><td>las hermanas simpáticas</td><td>las frutas bonitas</td></tr>
</table>

Nouns and adjectives ending in a consonant form the plural
by adding *es*:

<table>
<tr><td>los animales</td><td>difíciles</td></tr>
<tr><td>los automóviles</td><td>los jardines (*the gardens*)</td></tr>
</table>

> REMEMBER: To make nouns or adjectives
> plural add *s* or *es*.

A noun or adjective with a written accent on the last syllable usually drops it in the plural: *el jardín, los jardines.*

EJERCICIO V. *Make these expressions plural* (Remember
that articles and adjectives must agree with their nouns.):

1. el burro grande   2. la muchacha simpática   3. el jardín bonito (How about that accent?)   4. la flor grande   5. la señorita bonita   6. el hombre pobre   7. el animal agradable   8. la cortesía
necesaria (*Cortesía* keeps its accent.)

15. *Contraction* al

al mercado, *to the market*

Do you remember that *de + el* (*of the*) = *del?*   In the same
way:

> REMEMBER: *a + el* (*to the*) = *al*

The forms *a la, a los,* and *a las* do not change.

EJERCICIO VI. *Write in Spanish:*

1. to the boy
2. of the donkeys
3. of the animal

4. of the girl
5. to the market
6. to the roads

7. to the sisters
8. to the brother
9. of the fruit

PREGUNTITAS

1. ¿Es grande Rosita?
2. ¿Es simpática Rosita?
3. ¿Desean Juanito y Rosita ir al mercado?
4. ¿Desea Pícaro ir al mercado?
5. ¿Qué desea Rosita vender en el mercado?
6. ¿Qué desea Juanito vender en el mercado?
7. ¿Es posible vender las frutas en el camino?
8. ¿Qué lleva Pícaro?
9. ¿Es bonito Pícaro?
10. ¿Son simpáticos los hermanos?

PARA PRONUNCIAR

I. Repaso

Pronounce these words:

fruta	hermano	poco	goma
quinto	señora	Juanito	mercado
escribe	roto	escena	escoge
pizarra	techo	primo	raza

II. New Sounds

1. *ll* is pronounced like the *lli* in *William*. (Spanish-American pronunciation omits any sound of *l* and pronounces it like the *y* in *you*.)

llama	calle	sillón	ellas
lleva	silla	llegar	me llamo

2. You have already learned that *b* and *v* are pronounced alike. In these words they have the sound of *b* as in *boy*, because they follow *m* or *n* or begin a breath group. (*n* before *v* or *b* becomes *m*.)

bonito	hombre	un vaso	¡Vida mía!	tan bien
¡Ven acá!	¡Vámonos!	¡Bueno!	¡Vete!	¡Basta!

REPASITO

I. *What words do you think are missing?*

1. Los —— desean ir al ——. 2. Juanito tiene un —— y una ——. 3. Pícaro desea —— las flores en el ——. 4. Rosita es una muchacha ——. 5. Es necesario —— mucho para ——. 6. Juanito es —— y es —— también.

II. *¿Verdad o mentira?* (*Truth or lie?*)

1. Rosita desea comer en el camino. 2. Los muchachos trabajan mucho. 3. Juanito es un muchacho de España. 4. Pícaro lleva flores al mercado. 5. Pícaro dice, — ¡Vámonos, Rosita!

PALABRAS PARA HOY

1	**a**	to	1 **los muchachos**	children *or* boy and girl (or boys)
	al	to the (*m.*)		
	bonito, bonita	pretty	**Pícaro**	Rascal (used as a proper noun)
2	**desean**	they want *or* wish		
1	**dice**	he *or* she says (from **decir**)	1 **pues**	well; then
1	**dos**	two	**Rosita**	Rosie (nickname for **Rosa,** Rose)
2	**la flor**	flower (*floral*)		
	(*pl.*), **las flores**		1 **se llama**	his, her, *or* its name is
3	**la fruta**	fruit		
1	**el hermano**	brother	1 **el señor**	gentleman, Mr.†
1	**la hermana**	sister	1 **la señora**	lady, Mrs.†
1	**los hermanos**	brother and sister (or brothers)	1 **la señorita**	young lady,† Miss
1	**ir**	to go (in or to)	1 **siempre**	always
	Juanito	Johnny, Jack (nickname for **Juan,** John)		**simpático**	congenial, pleasant, "nice" (*sympathetic*)
1	**la;** (*pl.*), **las**	the (*f.*)	1 **también**	also, too
1	**lleva**	he, she, *or* it carries, takes	1 **tiene**	he, she, *or* it has
			1 **una**	a, an (feminine form of **un**)
	el mercado	market		
1	**el muchacho**	boy	1 **vámonos**	let's go
1	**la muchacha**	girl	3 **vender**	to sell (*vendor*)

† New meanings.

En el camino

PRESENT TENSE FIRST CONJUGATION MODEL		
ganar, *to earn*		
EXAMPLE	ENDING	MEANING
Singular		
gano	**o**	I earn, am earning, do earn
ganas	**as**	thou earnest, *etc.*
usted gana	**a**	you (*polite*) earn, *etc.*
gana	**a**	he, she, or it earns, *etc.*
Plural		
ganamos	**amos**	we earn, *etc.*
ganáis	**áis**	you (*familiar*) earn, *etc.*
ustedes ganan	**an**	you (*polite*) earn, *etc.*
ganan	**an**	they earn, *etc.*

All verbs ending in **-ar** have these endings for the present tense. You will find more about them in the COSAS DE INTERÉS section.

Juanito and Rosita on the way to market meet Pablo, an acquaintance, who is also going to market with his donkey loaded with sugar cane.

JUANITO — Buenos días,[1] Pablo.

PABLO — Buenos días, Rosita y Juanito.

[1] Stop! Listen! Look! There is a list of expressions at the end of each vocabulary (PALABRAS PARA HOY). Often these expressions, called idioms, cannot be translated word for word. In reading a new story save time by looking at this list frequently.

Country roads in Mexico, like those in Spain, have much burro traffic. Wood-gatherers load their donkeys in the shadow of Popocatépetl, the great volcano, and take the wood to market to sell.

ROSITA — Muy buenos días, Pablo.   ¿Cómo está usted?

PABLO — Muy bien, gracias.   ¿Y ustedes?

JUANITO — Muy bien, gracias.   5

ROSITA — ¿Va usted al mercado, Pablo?

PABLO — Sí, Rosita.   *Deseo* ir al mercado para vender mi caña (*sugar cane*).

ROSITA — Su burro de usted *lleva* la caña, ¿verdad?

PABLO — Sí, mi burro *lleva* la caña.   ¿Qué *lleva* su burro de   10
usted, Juanito?

JUANITO — Mi burro *lleva* mis frutas y las flores de Rosita.

ROSITA — Mis flores son bonitas, ¿verdad?

PABLO — Sí, Rosita; son muy bonitas.   ¿*Desean* ustedes
15 vender las frutas y las flores en el mercado?

ROSITA — Sí, *deseamos* vender mucho en el mercado.   *Deseamos* ganar mucho dinero.   ¿Cómo se llama su burro de usted, Pablo?

PABLO — Mi burro se llama Negrito.   ¿Cómo se llama su
20 burro de ustedes?

ROSITA — Nuestro burro se llama Pícaro.   Es un burro muy bueno.

PABLO — ¿*Ganan* ustedes mucho dinero con sus (*your*) frutas?

25 JUANITO — Sí; algunas veces *ganamos* dos pesos.

ROSITA — ¿Gana usted mucho con su caña?

PABLO — Sí, Rosita.   Algunas veces *gano* un peso con mi caña.   ¿*Desean* ustedes [*some*] caña?

ROSITA — Muchas gracias, Pablo, pero usted *desea* vender
30 su caña.

PABLO — Sí, pero siempre *deseo* dar caña a mis amigos, también.

ROSITA — (*Toma* la caña.)   Gracias, Pablo.   Usted es (*are*) muy bueno.

35 PABLO — De nada, Rosita.

JUANITO — (*Toma* la caña.)   Su caña de usted es muy buena.   Muchas gracias, Pablo.

PABLO — De nada, Juanito.

JUANITO — ¿*Desea* usted frutas?   Siempre *deseamos* dar
40 frutas a nuestros amigos.

PABLO — (*Toma* las frutas.)   Sus frutas de usted también son muy buenas.   Gracias, Juanito.

JUANITO — De nada, Pablo.

PABLO — Es necesario ir al mercado, ¿verdad?

45 JUANITO — Sí, es necesario ganar nuestro dinero.

ROSITA — ¡Cuidado, Pablo!   Negrito *desea* comer nuestras frutas también.

JUANITO }
PABLO } — ¡Arre!   ¡Burro!

50 ROSITA — ¡Vámonos!

Find These Expressions in the Story

1. Your sugar cane is very good.
2. Thank you very much
3. You're welcome
4. we earn two dollars
5. sometimes I earn a dollar
6. Look out (careful), Paul!
7. Our donkey's name is
8. My donkey's name is
9. he wants to eat our fruit
10. my flowers are pretty
11. to my friends; to our friends
12. Are you going to the market?
13. Good morning.
14. How are you?
15. Very well, thank you (thanks).
16. Do you want [*some*] fruit?

COSAS DE INTERÉS

16. *First Conjugation Verbs*

Look back at the model verb at the beginning of the chapter. Note that before you can conjugate a verb, you must remove the last two letters (*-ar*), which are called the infinitive ending. The "infinitive" in any language names the verb without telling *who* or *when*. An infinitive in English always begins with *to*: *to wish, to read, to work, to play*. The last two letters in a Spanish infinitive correspond to the *to* in English.

> REMEMBER: How many letters must you remove from the infinitive before you can conjugate the verb? The last two, always.

EJERCICIO I. *Can you answer these questions?*

1. What is "conjugating a verb"? 2. What is the "stem" of ganar? How do you know? 3. Say the endings alone. 4. What vowel is used most in these endings? Can you guess why? 5. Do all *-ar* verbs have the same endings? 6. Which form has a written accent and where? 7. How do you translate each verb form?

Are you wondering why there are two second person forms? Here is the answer:

Spanish can say *you* (either singular or plural) in two ways. The first is a familiar way (*thou* in singular, and *you* in plural), used in speaking to relatives, good friends, and servants (people with whom one is "familiar").

The second way, with **usted** or **ustedes**, is a polite or formal *you*, used in speaking to strangers, acquaintances, or superiors. Notice that **usted** accompanies what is really a third person verb form, instead of the second person. It once was **vuestra merced**, *your grace*, but became shortened with use.

Don't try to use the familiar form yet; we shall be using the polite **usted** almost entirely.

> When you want to say *"you,"*
> REMEMBER: what do you say?
> **Usted.** (pl., **ustedes**)

When you learn the verb endings and can use them, you will know how to conjugate hundreds of verbs, all alike.

EJERCICIO II. *Conjugate the following verbs orally like* **ganar.**

llevar   usar   trabajar   pasar (*to pass*)   desear

EJERCICIO III. *Using the same verbs, give these forms in Spanish:*

1. I carry, he uses, we work, they pass, he desires
2. he carries, I use, they work, you pass, they desire
3. I work, we use, you carry, he passes, you desire

17. Possessive Adjectives, Short Forms

mi	my
tu	thy
su	his, her, its, your (*polite*)
nuestro	our
vuestro	your (*familiar*)
su	their, your (*polite*)

EJERCICIO IV. *Answer these questions:*

1. Since these words are adjectives, will they have to agree with the nouns they modify? (*Of course!*)
   Say: my flowers; our fruit.

2. Which one of these possessive adjectives has several meanings?
3. What's the difference between *su burro* and *su burro de usted?*
Is the *de usted* necessary in order to change the meaning?

REMEMBER: When you want to say *"your,"* what do you say?
Su[1] —— *de usted* (*ustedes*).

4. *Say:* his money; your money

18. Su *and its Meanings*

Su has six possible meanings. With all its explanations, it looks like this:

Singular

su (burro) { de él, his (donkey)
de ella, her (donkey)
de usted, your (donkey) }

Plural

su (burro) { de ellos, their (donkey)
de ellas, their (donkey)
de ustedes, your (donkey) }

When *su* is used in a sentence with the subject *usted,* it almost automatically means *your* without the explanation *de usted.* (There is already one *usted* in the sentence.)

usted gana su dinero   *you earn your money*

Translate: ¿Gana usted su dinero?   ¿Gana Juan su dinero?

EJERCICIO V.   *Write* (be sure the adjectives agree with their nouns):

1. *his* compañero	6. *my* hermano	11. *his* dinero
2. *your* compañero	7. *my* flores	12. *her* dinero
3. *our* camino	8. *his* fruta	13. *your* dinero
4. *our* hermana	9. *his* flores	14. *their* dinero
5. *our* hermanas	10. *your* flores	15. *our* dinero

[1] The proper form of the article, *el* (*la, los, las*) is sometimes used.

PREGUNTITAS

I. 1. ¿Qué dice Juanito a Pablo?
2. ¿Qué dice Rosita a Pablo?
3. ¿Qué desea ganar Juanito?
4. ¿Cómo se llama el burro de Pablo?
5. ¿Gana Juanito mucho dinero con sus frutas?
6. ¿Desea Juanito dar frutas a su amigo Pablo?
7. ¿Desea Pablo dar caña a sus amigos?
8. ¿Desea Negrito comer frutas también?

II. 1. ¿Desea usted comer sus flores?
(*Whose flowers?* See section 18.)
2. ¿Gana usted dos pesos?
3. ¿Lleva usted flores a sus amigos?
4. ¿Ganamos nuestro dinero en el camino?
5. ¿Usa usted su dinero en el mercado? (*Whose money?*)
6. ¿Tiene mucho dinero un hombre rico?
7. ¿Tiene mucho dinero un hombre pobre?
8. ¿Cómo se llama su automóvil de usted?

REPASITO

¿Verdad o mentira?

1. Rosita tiene dos burros. 2. Negrito lleva caña al mercado.
3. Un amigo muchas veces dice, — Buenos días. 4. Pícaro desea tomar las frutas para comer. 5. Juanito es el hermano de Negrito.
6. Un automóvil es el compañero de un burro. 7. Los muchachos hablan (*speak*) siempre con cortesía. 8. Los burros se llaman Pablo y Negrito. 9. Rosita es la hermana de Juanito.

PARA PRONUNCIAR

I. Repaso
1. *Review in Chapters 1 and 3 the sounds of* **b** *and* **v;** *then pronounce these expressions.* Your teacher will tell you what they mean if you are curious.

d after n, nn, l = d ʌ initial

Son veinte.	la bandera (*the flag*)
Me voy también.	lavandera (*the washerwoman*)
Es una violeta.	¡Viva México!
¡Vaya usted!	Vivo en Burgos.
¡Vámonos!	Dame un besito.
¡Ven acá!	Dame un abrazo.
Hablaba bien.	Es tan bueno.
No sabía bien.	Es bueno y barato.

2. *Review the sounds of* **t** (*Chapter 1*) *and* **d** (*Chapter 2*). Be sure you pronounce **t, d, l,** and **n** with the tongue low against the front teeth. Try the English way of saying each letter, then the Spanish, listening to the difference. Don't forget to smile when you pronounce them the Spanish way!

La letra es importante.	Andan a la aldea.
Comen durante el día.	Tratan de leerlo.
Luego levántese usted.	Traen unas tortillas.
No gana en la lotería.	No notan el nombre.
Déme usted el dinero.	Todos han aprendido mucho.
Los loros no leen el libro.	Están detrás de la tienda.

Mexican donkeys work hard, but so do their masters.

Black Star

II. The Last New Sound

x between vowels is pronounced somewhat like **gs**. Before a consonant it is like **s**. The *x* in *México* is an exception, for it is from the Aztec.

examen	exagere	extra	explicar
exacto	éxito	sexto	exclamar

PALABRAS PARA HOY

Hereafter you will find that new groups of words used in the story are listed as *Expressions* at the end of the vocabulary.

1 **el amigo**	friend, (*m.*)	1 **nuestro, -a**	our
1 **la amiga**	friend, (*f.*)	3 **el peso**	a Mexican coin
1 **bien**	well		normally worth
1 **bueno, -a**	good		about 33 cents
2 **¡cuidado!**	be careful, look		in our money
	out!	1 **son**	they are (plural
1 **dar**	to give		of **es**)
1 **dos**	two	1 **su, sus**	his, her
2 **el dinero**	money	1 **su ——— de**	
2 **ganar**	to earn (*gain*)	**usted, ustedes**	your
2 **gracias**	thanks, thank you	1 **tomar**	to take
	(*grateful*)	1 **usted, ustedes**	you (polite)
1 **mi, mis**	my	1 **¿verdad?**	isn't that so?
muchos, -as	many		Doesn't he?
Negrito	Little black one,		Aren't they?
	"Blackie," (used		Isn't it? etc.
	as a proper noun)	**Pablo**	Paul

EXPRESIONES † (*Expressions*)

*algunas veces	sometimes	¿cómo está usted?	How are you?
*buenos días	How do you do,	de nada	You're welcome
	Good morning,		(*for nothing*)
	Good day		(**no hay de que**
¿cómo se llama?	What is the name		is also used)
	of	¿va usted?	are you going?

† Note to teacher: Idioms starred are from the first 200 of Keniston's *Spanish Idiom List* and should therefore be included in the pupil's active vocabulary.

A Roman bridge over a thousand years old has much the same construction as the modern one in the background that King Alfonso ordered built around 1920, when he was trying to modernize his country.

cruelly cold. The south, to earn its modern nickname of "Sunny Spain," has always had a tropical climate that has encouraged a "mañana" (*tomorrow*) attitude and grown fruits to drop in people's laps. The central high plateau, true, has always been hot and dry in summer and cold and bleak in winter, but within its mountains have always been hidden valuable minerals that for three thousand years have tempted people from far away.

Thus even long ago, although travel by sea or land was ever a gamble with death, venturesome souls from one country after another somehow found Spain tempting and wanted it for themselves. Blond Celts from the north first wandered in by land and stayed to mingle with the dark, hairy Iberians who lived there at the dawn of history. Daring and inquisitive Phoenicians rowed their little galleys from the far end of the Mediterranean and stopped over in Spain on their way north to the British Isles. Then followed brave Carthaginians, cultured Greeks, efficient Romans, destructive Vandals, cruel Visigoths;

and lastly, tolerant, wise, and beauty-loving Moors.   Thus, Spain
came to be a country of romantic traditions, blended of ancient customs, medieval grandeur and modern ideas; a land of contrasts with
its many old and new civilizations, just as it has always been with its
varied kinds of climate and soil.

Many of Spain's early settlers came in through Cádiz, Western
Europe's oldest seaport (although Málaga will argue about that); for
there, three thousand years ago, the Phoenicians founded for themselves a trading post.   If it were possible for you to motor south
through Spain today, say from Madrid to Gibraltar, you'd probably
detour toward the west as you approached the Mediterranean and
follow the road signs that point toward Cádiz.   Pyramids of salt glis-
tening in the hot sunlight would dot the flat land on either side of the
highway as you neared the white city on its little island; then the road
would enter the man-made causeway, squeeze through the ancient
city gate, and lead you into the old, old town.

Tight little Moorish streets would threaten your hubcaps, and
people would have to step into doorways to let you pass.   Everywhere your eyes would be blinded by the sapphire sparkle of the sea
in the background and sunlight on buildings apparently whitewashed
only the day before.

There would be nothing now, of course, to remind you of the original founders of Cádiz, although if you investigated you would hear
of Phoenician tombs unearthed there not so long ago; and you might
even find an enormous Phoenician bathtub, carved from stone, in a
museum.

For three hundred years those industrious people kept this little
trading post and worked inland to found other cities, mining the rich
silver and copper deposits they discovered in the interior.   No doubt
they made many modest fortunes for themselves, for they sent home so
much silver that for the first time in history it became more common
than gold.

At last, being businessmen, not statesmen, the Phoenicians began
to have trouble ruling their valuable possession, and made a bad mistake.   They asked the people of wealthy Carthage, originally one of
their own colonies in North Africa, to come over and help them, which
the Carthaginians politely did.   But these allies knew a good thing
when they saw it, and when the dust of battle had cleared away, the
Carthaginians, instead of the Phoenicians, ruled the land.   They called
it "Span," which means "hidden land," for they were so anxious to

Galloway

The great stone aqueduct at Segovia still carries the town water, although it was built by the Romans about the year 100 A.D. without the help of mortar to hold its heavy stones together.

keep this treasure for themselves that they scuttled their own ships on the way to "Span" when suspicious Roman sails on the horizon seemed to be following them.

The Greeks, in the meantime, twenty-five hundred years ago, had founded the same sort of colonies on the northern Mediterranean coast of Spain, bringing with them their sculptures, coinage, and architecture, and sending home the customary contributions to help swell the Greek treasury. But all of these colonizers, Phoenicians, Carthaginians, and Greeks, had no thought of organizing and developing Spain as a country. Their towns were centers of wealth produced for the motherland, their people content to enrich themselves at Spain's expense.

Then the Romans, their Empire growing beyond anything the western world had yet seen, proceeded to exterminate the Carthaginians, and after years of bitter struggle, plowed under the mother city of Carthage. They had already found their victim's colonies in Spain, and stubbornly spent two hundred years conquering the peninsula, a project which ambitious Julius Caesar wound up so thoroughly in 58 B.C. that all together Spain was a Roman colony for six hundred years, over three times as long as our own country has been a nation.

There the Spanish language came into being, based upon the Latin of the conquerors, enriched by the Greek and Phoenician and Iberian (and later the Arabic) that the people of the peninsula were using, growing up into a modified Latin that soon differed far more from the original mother tongue than our American does from London English. We call Spanish a Romance language — coming from the Romans — and if you ever study French, Italian, Portuguese, or Rumanian, you will find them, too, related branches of the mother Latin, changed as each wandered into a different land far from home.

What Rome conquered, she made into Roman soil. In addition to the language, she brought a longer period of peace and better laws into the peninsula than it had ever known before. Roman soldiers had conquered the Greeks, but Greek ideas of beauty and culture had conquered Rome, so she brought them with her to enrich life in Spain. She built roads that have lasted to this day, great stone aqueducts that still carry water just as they did eighteen hundred years ago, and heavy stone bridges that now bear the latest models in rubber-tired traffic. There's no doubt about it; Rome was the colonizer that civilized and united the people she found there, so thoroughly that even

Modern Madrid, built late in Spain's history as compared with other cities, has everything! Trees protect pedestrians from summer heat, and
subways carry them to their homes.

after her downfall her barbaric conquerors could not help absorbing
the culture of their victims.

How the Roman Empire ended in 476 A.D. is too long a story to tell
here, but centuries after famous Spanish rulers had helped make successful Roman history, and Spanish poets had contributed to Roman
literature, and Spanish barbers had beautified Roman dandies, the
great Empire finally came to its end. Barbarous invaders who gave
us our word "vandalism" had gradually come down from the north,
and ruled clumsily and cruelly. Then the Visigoths "of tangled hair
and tattered furs" had sacked Rome and taken her colonies in 409 A.D.,
and for three hundred years Spain was an unhappy land, her culture
at a standstill. At last, in 711, the treachery of a vengeful Spanish
noble brought in the Moors to conquer cruel Roderick, the last Gothic
king, and the second great chapter of Spain began.

Interesting Books to Read

Iberians: SEDGWICK, HENRY: SPAIN, A SHORT HISTORY, ch. I. ELLIS, HAVELOCK: THE SOUL OF SPAIN, ch. II.

Cádiz: NEXÖ, MARTIN ANDERSON: DAYS IN THE SUN, pp. 14–22. "ADVENTUROUS SONS OF CADIZ," NATIONAL GEOGRAPHIC, August, 1924.

Phoenicians: SEDGWICK, ch. I.

Carthaginians vs. Romans: TAPPAN, EVA: STORY OF THE ROMAN PEOPLE, pp. 72–97.

Romans: SEDGWICK, ch. II. PECK, ANNE M., *and* MÉRAS, E. A.: SPAIN IN EUROPE AND AMERICA, ch. II.

Goths: SEDGWICK, chs. III and IV.

Old Spain: CALLCOTT, FRANK: WHEN SPAIN WAS YOUNG (all).

Hillside villages of southern Spain always have a color scheme of red, white, and green, from their tile roofs, whitewashed walls, and gnarled old olive trees that grow everywhere.

Sawders

Cosas de la escuela

There are many new words in this story, but there is nothing else difficult. Remember to guess all you can and don't forget to look for the new expressions in the special section at the end of the chapter.

Vamos a la escuela. Nuestra escuela es muy grande y bonita. También es muy buena. Tiene muchas clases. Ésta (*this*) es la clase de español. Aquí estudiamos el español.

Nuestra profesora es la señorita ———. Ella habla muy 5 bien el español. Deseamos aprender el español como nuestra profesora, porque ella es nuestra amiga.

En nuestra escuela hay muchas ventanas. También hay muchas puertas. Todas las ventanas son grandes, pero no entramos por las ventanas. Entramos por las puertas como 10 los alumnos buenos.

Hay muchas pizarras y una bandera roja, blanca y azul. Las pizarras son negras, pero la bandera tiene colores muy bonitos. Es nuestra bandera.

Usamos lápiz o pluma para escribir en el papel blanco. Los 15 lápices[1] son de muchos colores: amarillos, verdes o rojos. Las plumas son de todos los colores también. Mi pluma es amarilla. La pluma de Arturo es azul. ¿De qué color es su pluma de Vd?

Preparamos todas las lecciones en nuestros libros para 20 hablar muy bien el español, como nuestra profesora. Es necesario trabajar mucho porque el español es difícil. Algunas veces el inglés es difícil también.

Llevamos nuestros libros a la clase, también nuestras plumas y nuestros lápices. Algunas veces llevamos flores 25

---

[1] Nouns or adjectives ending in z change z to c before adding -es.

a la clase para la profesora, pero los alumnos no llevan flores
para obtener (*to get*) buenas notas (*grades*).   Es agradable
llevar flores a la profesora, pero no es necesario.

Pasamos (*we pass* or *go*) a la pizarra para escribir la lección.
30 Un día la profesora no mira, y Carlos no escribe la lección.
Escribe en la pizarra un verso (*verse*).   Es para su amiga,
Dolores.   Aquí tiene Vd. el verso.   El verso dice:

<blockquote>
La rosa es roja,
la violeta azul;
el azúcar es dulce,
y también tú.
</blockquote>

35

Al fin la profesora mira la pizarra y lee (*reads*) el verso de
Carlos.

— Muchas gracias, Carlos, — dice la profesora.   — Vd.
40 tiene un verso muy bonito.   Es un verso para su profesora de
Vd., ¿verdad?

— No, señorita, — dice Carlos.   — El verso es para
Dolores.

Y Carlos se pone (*becomes*) muy rojo, porque toda la clase
45 mira el verso.

Dolores se pone muy roja, también; y ella borra (*erases*)
el verso rápidamente.

¡Qué cosa!   ¡Pobre[1] Dolores!

Find These Expressions in the Story

1. we take (carry) flowers to class
2. She speaks Spanish very well.
3. One day the teacher isn't looking
4. like our teacher
5. a red, white, and blue flag
6. Here is the verse.
7. Charles becomes very red
8. The idea (what a thing)!
9. sugar is sweet
10. It is a verse for your teacher, isn't it?
11. What color is your pen?
12. we want to learn Spanish
13. We go to school.
14. Arthur's pen is blue.
15. All the windows
16. the teacher looks at the blackboard
17. the pens are of all colors
18. all the lessons in our books

[1] *Pobre* has two meanings in Spanish just as *poor* has in English.

This modern school in Mexico City is an example of Mexico's present-day interest in education. More schools have been built in recent years than ever before. The track shown here is only a small part of a vast playground.

PREGUNTITAS

1. ¿Qué tiene nuestra escuela?
2. ¿Qué estudiamos aquí?
3. ¿Qué tiene colores muy bonitos?
4. ¿Es difícil el español?
5. ¿Es difícil el inglés también?
6. ¿Es necesario llevar flores a las profesoras?
7. ¿Usa Vd. su pluma para escribir en la pizarra?
8. ¿Entramos por las ventanas?
9. ¿Qué escribe Carlos en la pizarra?
10. ¿Es el verso para la profesora?
11. ¿Borra Carlos el verso?
12. ¿Es roja como la rosa la pluma?
13. ¿Tiene Carlos una amiga?
14. ¿Lleva Vd. flores a sus amigos?
15. ¿Hay una bandera en nuestra escuela?
16. Nuestra bandera es bonita, ¿verdad?
17. Toda la clase mira el verso de Carlos, ¿verdad?
18. ¿Es agradable obtener buenas notas?

PARA PRONUNCIAR

Practice these words to review the sounds of Spanish letters.
Do not worry about their meanings.

CONSONANT SOUND	a	e	i	o	u
b, v	{ bala vaso	bebe vela	bicho vivo	bota voto	burro vuelo
k	cama	queso	quise	como	cura
th (or s)	zanja	cena	cine	zona	zurzo
ch	chasco	cheque	chico	choza	chula
d (Smile!)	dan	den	dicho	dos	duro
f	falta	fecha	fila	fonda	fuma
g	gas	guerra	guía	goma	gusto
j (h sound)	{ jarro	gente jefe	gitano Jijona	jota	justo
h (letter)	hasta	hecho	hijo	hora	humo
l (Smile!)	lana	leche	Lima	loma	lujo
ll	llama	lleva		llora	llueve
m	mala	mesa	mira	moro	muro
n (Smile!)	nata	negro	nido	nota	nudo
ñ	piña	muñeca	meñique	señor	ceñudo
p	papá	pero	pipa	pollo	pulso
r	rama	renta	rima	rojo	ruso
rr	pizarra	carrera	barril	carro	arruga
s	santo	sello	siglo	sopa	suma
t (Smile!)	tanto	techo	tinta	tonto	tuyo
x	examen		exijo		
Before a consonant:		extranjero		extremo	exclamo
y	{ ya ¡caray!	yerno rey	y	yo soy	yugo muy

REPASITO

*I. These Spanish words should remind you of some English
words which are similar in appearance, although they do not have
exactly the same meanings.   What are they?*

compañero	verde	negro	profesora
libro	azul	blanco	flor

escribir	pluma	bandera	estudiar
grande	nota	vender	ganar
pobre	mirar	alumno	gracias
al fin	día	ventana	simpático

II. Make a list of fourteen words found in this chapter which are associated with school.

puerta, ventana, pizarro mesa, bandera, libro, pluma carta - lápiz - alumno - maestro - papel - lección - clase. profesora

JUEGOS (Games) DE REPASO

I. A pupil points out objects in the room and asks the class, — *¿Qué es esto (this)?* The class should reply, — *Es la puerta,* etc.

II. A pupil points out a colored object and asks a classmate, — *¿De qué color es esto?* The classmate answers, — *Es de color rojo,* etc. Then the second pupil asks someone else the same question about a different object.

Schoolboys of Toledo, Spain, earn money outside of school hours by delivering water to homes which do not have it. The clay jugs hold about three gallons.

Galloway

III. As many pupils as possible go to the board, and when the teacher says, — ¡*Ya!* (*ready, go*) they see which one can be the first to write in Spanish a list of ten objects in the classroom, using the article *a* or *the*.

Then each pupil moves one place to the right, corrects spelling if necessary, and adds an adjective to each noun. (What's the catch?)

Then each moves to the right again and writes the meaning of the phrases he finds, correcting previous work if necessary.

Then each moves back to his own list to see what has happened to it.

PALABRAS PARA HOY

amarillo, -a	yellow	3 estudiar	to study (*studio*)
3 aprender	to learn (*apprentice*)	1 hablar	to speak
1 aquí	here	1 hay	there is, there are
Arturo	Arthur	3 el inglés	English (nearly always used with the article)
3 el azúcar	sugar		
3 azul	blue (*azure*)		
2 blanco, -a	white (*blank*)	1 mirar	to look at (*mirror*)
Carlos	Charles	2 negro, -a	black
2 el color	color	1 o	or
1 como	like (Remember ¿*cómo?* means *how?*)	4 obtener	to obtain, to get
		1 para	for (new meaning)
		1 por	through
1 el día	day (*m.*)	3 preparar	to prepare
2 dulce	sweet	3 rojo	red
Dolores	Spanish girl's name	la rosa	(the) rose
1 ella	she	1 todo, -a	all
1 entrar	to enter	1 tú	thou (you, familiar)
1 escribe	he writes	1 un, -a	one (new meaning)
1 escribir	to write (*scribe, scribble*)	1 vamos	we go
		1 Vd.	abbreviation of usted
1 el español	Spanish (nearly always used with the article)	3 verde	green (*verdure*)
		la violeta	(the) violet

PALABRAS DE LA ESCUELA

el alumno	pupil (*m.*)	1 el libro	book (*library*)
la alumna	pupil (*f.*)	1 el papel	paper
la bandera	flag (*banner*)	la pizarra	blackboard
3 la clase	class	3 la pluma	pen (*plume*, quill pen)
3 la escuela	school		
el lápiz	pencil;	la profesora	teacher (lady)
pl., lápices		1 la puerta	door (*portal*)
la lección	lesson;	3 la ventana	window (*ventilate*)
pl., lecciones			

EXPRESIONES

a la clase	to class	la clase de español	Spanish class
a la escuela	to school		
*al fin	at last, finally (*finish*)	¿de qué color es?	What color is it, *or* what color is —?
*aquí tiene Vd.	here is, here you have (polite way to say it)	hablar muy bien el español	to speak Spanish very well
		¡Qué cosa!	The idea (what a thing)!

CAPÍTULO **6**

¿Cuánto sabe usted?[1]

If you have learned everything you have had so far, you will be able to read these stories without looking up anything, for the only new words are translated for you, or you can guess them.

JUANITO Y EL AUTOMÓVIL

Test your knowledge of both English and Spanish by putting this story into English and punctuating it correctly. What does each dash mean?

[1] How much do you know?

Carlos tiene un automóvil y Juanito tiene un burro.   Un día Carlos dice a su amigo, — Buenos días, amigo.   ¿Cómo está Vd.?

— Muy bien.   ¿Y Vd.?

5   — Bien, gracias.   ¿No desea Vd. usar mi automóvil para ir al mercado?   Es un «Fordecito», pero anda rápidamente.

— Gracias, amigo, — dice Juanito.

Juanito desea usar el automóvil.   Entra en el automóvil y grita (yells), — ¡Arre, «Fordecito»!

10   Pero el automóvil no anda.   Entonces (then) dice a su amigo,

— Su automóvil de Vd. es perezoso.   No desea trabajar. No deseo ir en automóvil.   Prefiero (I prefer) mi burro.

GEORGE SMITH Y EL INDIO

Read this true story and answer the questions at the end.

George Smith no es mexicano.   Es un muchacho inteligente de California.   Algunas veces va (he goes) a México en automóvil a pasar muchos días con sus amigos.   Habla español con sus amigos mexicanos.   Desea aprender a hablar

5   muy bien el español.

En los caminos de México ve (he sees) muchas cosas interesantes.   Ve los burros que (that) trabajan en el camino o van al mercado con los indios.   George no tiene un burro, porque no hay muchos burros en California.   Para George es

10   muy interesante ver (to see) pasar los burros.

Ve que los indios trabajan mucho.   Siempre llevan mucho al mercado, y sus burros llevan mucho también.   Los pobres burros llevan tanto (so much) que algunas veces apenas (hardly) es posible ver los animales.

15   Un día George ve en el camino un burro con su compañero, un indio inteligente.   Van al mercado para vender la caña del indio.   El indio y su burro van muy despacio por el camino, porque el burro lleva tanta caña que es difícil ver el pobre animal.

20   George mira el burro y dice al indio, — Los pobres burros trabajan mucho en México, ¿verdad?

El indio mira a ¹ George, mira su burro, y dice, — Pero al
fin (*after all*), muchacho, son burros,² ¿verdad?
George se pone muy rojo. ¡Es verdad! ¡Son burros!

1. How does George go to Mexico? 2. What is there in Mexico
that he does not often see at home? 3. How much of a load do the
donkeys often carry? 4. Does the Mexican Indian believe that donkeys are supposed to work hard? 5. What does the Indian think of
George's idea?

REPASO DE VOCABULARIO

EJERCICIO I. *Read these statements aloud. If one is true, say*
verdad; *if it is false,* say **mentira.** *Think carefully, because
some may be tricky.*

1. El burro siempre anda rápidamente.
2. El compañero del automóvil es el burro.
3. Los alumnos ganan mucho dinero en la escuela.
4. En la clase usamos plumas o lápices para escribir.
5. Es necesario llevar flores a la profesora para obtener buenas
   notas.
6. Es necesario trabajar para ganar dinero.
7. En el camino hay muchos automóviles.
8. En la clase de español estudiamos y hablamos.
9. Para trabajar, los indios de México usan burros.
10. En el mercado hay flores y frutas.
11. Algunas veces los alumnos son perezosos.
12. El hombre pobre gana mucho dinero.
13. Carlos no dice, — ¡Arre! — a su automóvil.
14. Nuestra bandera es roja, blanca, y amarilla.
15. En la clase hay un burro.
16. La bandera de México es roja, blanca y verde.
17. Las violetas y las rosas son flores bonitas.
18. Hablamos rápidamente el español, pero hablamos despacio el
    inglés.
19. No deseamos comer las flores.
20. Todas las muchachas de la clase son bonitas. (*¡Cuidado!*)

¹ Do not translate the *a*.
² *son burros* is a kind of pun, for it also means they are dumb.

REPASO DE LAS COSAS DE INTERÉS

Give the missing words. If you have forgotten any, you can find them in the COSAS DE INTERÉS sections of Chapters 1–4, to which the numbers in parentheses refer.

1. Descriptive adjectives usually —— their nouns in Spanish. In English they —— their nouns. (§ 1)
2. Nouns or adjectives ending in a consonant add —— to form the plural. (§ 14)
3. In written conversation, each dash in a new paragraph means a change of ——. (§ 7)
4. Nouns that are feminine take —— for *the*. (§ 10)
5. Nouns that end in —— are usually masculine. (§ 9)
6. Nouns that end in ——, ——, or —— are usually feminine. (§ 9)
7. —— always agree with their nouns in gender and number. (§ 11, 12)
8. *de + el* = ——   (§ 4)
9. *a + el* = ——   (§ 15)
10. You must always remove —— letters from an infinitive before conjugating the verb. (§ 16)
11. An infinitive in English always begins with ——. (§ 16)
12. To make a sentence negative, put *no* —— the verb. (§ 3)
13. At the end of a first conjugation verb, —— means *I*; —— means *they*; —— means *we*; —— means *he, she,* or *it*. (p. 22)
14. When you want to say *you*, say ——, and use the —— person verb with it. (§ 16)

EL EJERCICIO HACE MAESTRO (*Practice Makes Perfect*)

EJERCICIO I. *Tell what each of these verbs means.* Watch the endings. Remember that with a verb you usually read backwards.

1. uso   2. llevamos   3. desean   4. Vd. gana   5. ¿gana Vd.? 6. no deseo   7. no trabajamos   8. trabaja (*two possible subjects*) 9. ¿miran?   10. ¿pasa? (*two ways*)   11. preparar   12. no estudio 13. ¿ganan?   14. ¿no gana Vd.?   15. ¿trabajan Vds.?   16. no trabaja (*two ways*)   17. estudian   18. hablan   19. habla (*two ways*)

EJERCICIO II. 1. *Translate in three ways:* hablo, miran, usamos. 2. *Translate in two ways:* no hablo, no trabajamos. 3. *Translate in two ways:* ¿usan?, ¿estudia Vd.?

EJERCICIO III. *Choose an adjective from List (b) to describe each noun in List (a).* When you say them be sure (1) to put the adjective in the correct place, and (2) to have it agree with the noun. (The adjectives are all listed in the masculine singular.)

(a)		(b)	
el hombre	las frutas	bonito	rico
el libro	las flores	rojo	pobre
los compañeros	la pluma	inteligente	amarillo
los muchachos	la bandera	grande	simpático
la hermana	el español	bueno	negro
		agradable	difícil

EJERCICIO IV. *Now make sentences out of your phrases by putting in* **es** *or* **son** (el hombre rico; el hombre es rico). Does the adjective remain the same?

EJERCICIO V. *Translate the words in English.* They are adjectives and must agree with their nouns.

1. *my* lápiz
2. *his* libros
3. *our* bandera
4. *my* escuela
5. *your* hermana
6. *my* flores
7. *your* jardín
8. *our* dinero
9. *our* notas
10. *our* papeles
11. *his* pluma
12. *her* pluma
13. *your* pluma
14. *their* pluma
15. *our* pluma

EJERCICIO VI. *Change what words you need to in these sentences in order to make them true:*

1. Nuestra bandera es roja, verde y negra. 2. Pablo toma las flores de Juanito. 3. Las alumnas entran por las ventanas. 4. Estudiamos en el camino. 5. Yo estudio en la ventana. 6. Es necesario llevar flores a la profesora. 7. Dolores se pone muy blanca. 8. La profesora escribe un verso en la pizarra. 9. Pícaro desea comer el dinero de Juanito. 10. El muchacho pobre de España muchas veces tiene un automóvil.

PARA PRONUNCIAR

I. Accent

Do you understand what we mean by accent or stress? The divisions of words are called syllables. If a word has more than one syllable, some part of that word is going to be pronounced more emphatically than the rest. Take the English word *refuse*, for example. If we emphasize the first syllable, like this: *refuse*, we mean *rubbish* or *worthless matter;* if we emphasize the second syllable, like this: *refuse*, we mean *to decline* or *reject.* In other words, we accent or stress the word according to the meaning we have in mind.

In Spanish there are definite rules for accent, which always tell us how to pronounce words. Here they are:

1. Words ending in a *vowel* or *n* or *s* are stressed on the next to the last syllable. (You may say those letters "throw" the accent back one syllable.)

Can you guess why *n* and *s* are the chosen letters?

me-sa	*cla*-se	*la*-do	*ha*-bla	a-*pren*-de
me-sas	*cla*-ses	*la*-dos	*ha*-blan	a-*pren*-den

2. Words ending in a *consonant* other than *n* or *s* are stressed on the last syllable.

es-cri-*bir*   pa-*pel*   ver-*dad*   hos-pi-*tal*   re-*loj*

3. Words which are exceptions to these rules always have a written accent (′) which tells you how to pronounce them.

le-ván-te-se   au-to-mó-vil   lec-ción   ar-tí-cu-lo

II. Syllabication

1. In general, each word has as many syllables as it has vowels and diphthongs.[1] In dividing words into syllables, single consonants, *ch, ll,* and *rr* begin a syllable. With the possible exception of the last one, all syllables will, therefore, end in a vowel or diphthong. With the possible exception of the

[1] *a, e, o* are strong vowels; *i* and *u* are weak. Any combination of a strong vowel and a weak vowel or of two weak vowels is called a diphthong.

first syllable or of a strong vowel following another strong vowel, all syllables will begin with a consonant, *rr, ch,* or *ll.*

> ge-ne-ral   bu-rro   mu-cho   e-lla

2. Two consonants are divided, one going with the preceding syllable, the other with the following syllable. (Remember that *ch, ll,* and *rr* count as single consonants because they represent a single sound.) If there are three, the last two generally go with the following syllable.

> lec-ción   in-de-pen-dien-te   le-gum-bre   sor-pren-der

3. However, the combination of a consonant plus *l* or *r* is generally not separated.

> a-rre-glan-do   a-pli-ca-do   a-gra-da-ble   a-pre-su-rar-se

4. Two strong vowels do not combine to form a diphthong, but form separate syllables. (A weak vowel is strong when it has a written accent.) *Pronounce carefully:*

> de-se-o   ca-ca-o   tra-en   lo-or
> le-en   le-a-mos   ma-es-tro   le-í-ais

EJERCICIO I. *Copy the words in the vocabulary of Chapter 5 in three columns according to the rules, following the model. Then underline the stressed syllables and pronounce carefully.*

Words ending in a *vowel, n* or *s*	Words ending in other *consonant*	Exceptions to rules
1. amarillo	1. aprender	1. aquí

Juegos de muchachos

HELPFUL HINT: *You will find some verb endings in this story slightly different from those you know.   Look at section 19 and you will understand them.*

In this play polite forms of verbs are used, although Spanish-speaking children would use the familiar form in talking together. We will not try to use both verb forms too soon.

Cuatro muchachas y tres muchachos desean jugar a la escuela. Lupita[1] *es la profesora, y Rosita, Lola, Margarita, Pablo, Juanito y Arturo son los alumnos.*

[1] *Lupita* is an abbreviation and nickname for *Guadalupe*, a very popular name for either boys or girls especially in Mexico, where the Virgin of Guadalupe is the patron saint.

Lola, or *Lolita,* is the nickname for *Dolores.*

Boys play bullfight in almost any Spanish-speaking country.   The "bull" seems to have downed his bullfighter, while the *picador* "on horseback" is trying to attract his attention away from the victim.

Black Star

LUPITA — Buenos días, alumnos.

LOS ALUMNOS — Buenos días, señorita profesora.

LUPITA — Hoy vamos a cantar. Aprendemos a cantar «Buenos propósitos» (*"Good Intentions"*). Arturo, Vd. va a leer las palabras.

ARTURO — Yo no deseo leer las palabras. No leo bien.

TODOS LOS ALUMNOS — Sí, Arturo, Vd. lee muy bien.

LUPITA — Sí, todos leemos bien.

ARTURO — Bueno, leo las palabras. (ARTURO *lee*.)

BUENOS PROPÓSITOS [1]

Gra-cias te da-mos, oh buen Dios por-que po-de-mos hoy can-tar
Te pro-me-te-mos, oh Señ-or si-empre con-ten-tos tra-ba-jar

por-que po-de-mos tra-ba-jar por-que te-ne-mos luz y a-mor.
lue-go ju-gar y des-can-sar pen-san-do en to-dos con a-mor.

LUPITA — ¿Ahora saben Vds. las palabras?

TODOS LOS ALUMNOS — Sí, señorita profesora. Sabemos las palabras.

LUPITA — Vds. aprenden muy bien. Ahora vamos a cantar. (*Todos cantan*.)

LUPITA — Ahora tenemos que dar la lección de aritmética. Pablo, Vd. tiene que contar desde uno hasta diez.

[1] See how much of the song you can read or guess already. To find out how good you are, compare your guess with the translation given in the Repasito on page 59.

It is a song children of Mexico often sing as they start the school day. Notice how words are linked when one word ends and the following word begins with a vowel. This is always done in speaking; in reading poetry or in singing it is especially necessary.

PABLO — No es muy difícil contar. Uno, dos, tres, cuatro, cinco, seis, siete, ocho, nueve, diez.

LUPITA — Muy bien. Ahora, Rosita, Vd. tiene que contar
20 desde diez hasta veinte.

ROSITA — ¿Tengo que contar?

LUPITA — Sí, Rosita.

ROSITA — Bueno. Diez, once, doce, trece, catorce — (*Ella no sabe.*)

25 TODOS LOS ALUMNOS — ¡Quince!

ROSITA — — quince, diez y seis, diez y siete, diez y ocho, diez y nueve, veinte.

LUPITA — Vd. sabe contar muy bien. Ahora, Juanito, ¿cuántos son cinco y siete?

30 LOLA — Señorita profesora, ¡Arturo tiene mi lápiz!

ARTURO — No tengo el lápiz de ella. Pablo tiene su lápiz.

LUPITA — Pablo, Vd. tiene que dar el lápiz a Lola. No es el lápiz de Vd. Es de Lola.

PABLO — Pero ella tiene dos lápices y yo deseo uno.

35 LOLA — Bueno. Yo no deseo más el lápiz. Ahora es de Pablo.

LUPITA — Vd. es muy buena, Lola. Ahora, Margarita, dígame Vd., ¿cuántos días tiene la semana?

MARGARITA — La semana tiene siete días, que son domingo,
40 lunes, martes, miércoles, jueves, viernes y sábado.

LUPITA — ¿Vamos a la escuela los sábados, Juanito?

JUANITO — No, señorita; vamos a la escuela los lunes, los martes, los miércoles, los jueves, y los viernes.

ARTURO — Y muchas veces jugamos a la escuela los sába-
45 dos. Hoy es sábado y yo no deseo jugar a la escuela.

LUPITA — ¡Cuidado, Arturo! Dígame Vd., si las manzanas valen cuatro por tres perras grandes,[1] ¿cuánto vale una manzana?

---

[1] The copper five and ten *céntimo* coins of Spain are popularly called *perras chicas* (*little dogs*) and *perras grandes* (*big dogs*), because on one side there is a lion which could be mistaken for a dog.

A "big dog," at par, is worth less than two cents in our money and it is usually worth much less than that.

ARTURO — Cuatro por tres perras; tres por dos perras; dos por una perra, y una por nada. Pues una manzana no vale nada.   50

LUPITA — ¡Qué cosa! Rosita, si Vd. tiene nueve manzanas y come cuatro, ¿qué tiene Vd.?

ROSITA — Si tengo nueve manzanas y como cuatro, tengo dolor de estómago.   55

TODOS LOS ALUMNOS — ¡Ja, ja, ja!

LUPITA — ¡Qué cosa! Vamos a tener una lección de geografía. Lola, dígame Vd. los nombres (*names*) de seis animales de África.

LOLA — Dos leones y cuatro tigres.   60

TODOS LOS ALUMNOS — ¡Ja, ja, ja!

LUPITA — No deseo jugar más a la escuela. ¿Quién desea jugar al «Déme pan y queso»? [1]

TODOS LOS ALUMNOS — ¡Yo! ¡Vámonos! (*Todos van a jugar al «Déme pan y queso».*)   65

Find These Expressions in the Story

1. Let's sing today (*or* We are going to sing today)
2. from one to ten
3. you have to count
4. You know how to count very well.
5. I haven't her pencil.
6. It isn't your pencil.
7. it's Paul's

8. we play school on Saturdays
9. Then one apple isn't worth anything.
10. I don't want to play school any more.
11. we go to school on Mondays
12. I don't want the pencil any more.

[1] **Déme pan y queso** (*Give me some bread and cheese*) is a game Spanish-speaking children play, just as we play "Pussy wants a corner" except for the words. The answer to «**Déme pan y queso**» is «**Allá es más tieso**» (*Over there it is harder*), instead of "Go to your next door neighbor."

COSAS DE INTERÉS

19. Second Conjugation Verbs

PRESENT TENSE SECOND CONJUGATION MODEL leer, to read		
EXAMPLE	ENDING	MEANING
Singular		
leo	o	I read
lees	es	thou readest
Vd. lee	e	you read
lee	e	he, she, reads
Plural		
leemos	emos	we read
leéis	éis	you (*fam.*) read
Vds. leen	en	you read
leen	en	they read

EJERCICIO I. *Can you answer these questions?*

1. What vowel do you find most of the way through this conjugation instead of the *a* we had before? Why?

2. Why are *-ar* verbs called first conjugation and *-er* verbs called second conjugation?

3. How do you find the stem of any verb? (Present tense.)

4. Do you think all *-er* verbs have the same endings?

5. Have you noticed in your reading any verbs with *-ir* endings? Of what conjugation do you suppose those are?

EJERCICIO II. Learn the endings for the second conjugation and you will be able to conjugate all the regular *-er* verbs in the Spanish language. *Now see if you can do these exercises:*

1. *Conjugate orally like* **leer** (Be sure to take off those last two letters first!):

aprender, *to learn*   **comer,** *to eat*
prometer, *to promise*   **vender,** *to sell*

2. *Now tell what these forms of the above verbs mean:*

aprenden   Vds. venden   ella promete   Vd. come   comen
vendemos   Vd. aprende   yo prometo   comemos   prometen

20. *Present Tense of* Tener

The verb *tener* has the same regular second conjugation endings, but has some irregular stem changes. You will learn more about this kind of verb later.

tener, *to have* (irregular)

Singular		*Plural*	
tengo	I have	**tenemos**	we have
tienes	thou hast	**tenéis**	you have
Vd. **tiene**	you have	Vds. **tienen**	you have
tiene	he, she has	**tienen**	they have

Notice that **tener que** is an idiom meaning *to have to* or *must:* **tengo que leer,** *I have to read.*

EJERCICIO III. *Find eight forms of* **tener** *in the story and make each singular form plural and each plural form singular.*

PREGUNTITAS

I. 1. ¿Quién tiene que contar desde uno hasta diez?
2. ¿Cuánto vale una manzana?
3. ¿Saben cantar bien los alumnos?
4. ¿A qué van a jugar Lupita y sus amigos de ella?
5. ¿Quién es la profesora en la lección?
6. ¿Es muy difícil la aritmética?
7. ¿Cuántos días tiene la semana?

II. 1. ¿Desea Vd. aprender a cantar «Buenos propósitos»?
2. ¿Cantan Vds. algunas veces en la clase?
3. ¿Saben Vds. jugar al «Déme pan y queso»?
4. Cuente Vd. (*count*) desde uno hasta veinte.
5. Dígame Vd. los días de la semana.
6. ¿Lee Vd. bien en español?
7. ¿Tienen lápices verdes todos los alumnos?
8. ¿Tiene Vd. que comer?
9. ¿Tiene Vd. que estudiar en la escuela?
10. ¿Tiene Vd. que escribir su lección algunas veces?

REPASITO

I. Fill out these sentences by changing the italicized infinitives to the proper form. Remember that some are **-ar** verbs and some are **-er**. What difference will that make?

1. Arturo *leer* las palabras.   2. Los alumnos *saber* contar bien.
3. Yo *tener* mucho dinero.   4. Pablo y Arturo no *desear* jugar a la escuela.   5. Lupita no *comer* cuatro manzanas.   6. Nosotros (*we*) *trabajar* los sábados.   7. Pablo y Juanito no *vender* fruta en el camino.
8. Rosita *tener* que contar desde diez hasta veinte.   9. Yo no *comer* en la clase.   10. Nosotros (*we*) *estudiar* para leer la lección.

II. Here are some arithmetic problems. What do they say?

1. cinco y —— son doce
2. ocho y —— son once
3. —— y nueve son trece
4. tres y cuatro son ——

5. dos y —— son cinco
6. once y —— son veinte
7. —— y doce son diez y ocho
8. trece y seis son ——

III. Match the letter and number of the sentences that mean the same.

1. Es de Lola.
2. Ahora vamos a cantar.
3. No deseo más el lápiz.
4. Una manzana no vale nada.
5. Todos leemos bien.
6. ¿Cuántos días tiene la semana?
7. Vds. aprenden muy bien.

a. I don't want the pencil any more.
b. One apple isn't worth anything.
c. How many days are there in the week?
d. You (*pl.*) learn very well.
e. Let's sing now.
f. We all read well.
g. It's Lola's.
h. The week has seven days.
i. Now we are going to count.

IV. If you can write these sentences correctly in Spanish, you may be very proud, because English to Spanish translation is the most difficult exercise of all.[1]

1. The teacher: Good morning, pupils.   What day is today?
2. Rosita: It is Wednesday.   3. The teacher: Yes, it is Wednesday and we are going to sing.   4. The class sings.   5. The teacher: Now we have to work.   Juanito, how much is five and seven?   6. Juanito:

[1] To the teacher: This exercise is optional.

Five and seven are fifteen. 7. The teacher: Be careful! 8. Juanito: Miss, I have to write the numbers (*números*) and I don't have my pencil. 9. The teacher: Who has Juanito's pencil? 10. Lola: I have a red pencil, but it is not Juanito's. 11. The teacher: Well then, Juanito, you must write on the blackboard. 12. Lola: The idea!

V. Here is the translation of the song, «Buenos propósitos». Did you guess it all?

Good Intentions
Thanks we give Thee, oh kind Lord,
Because today we can sing;
Because today we can work;
Because we have light and love.

We promise Thee, oh Lord,
Always happily to work;
Then to play and rest,
Thinking with love of everyone.

PARA PRONUNCIAR

Here is a list of words whose meanings will be clear to you. The similarity between English and Spanish is usually due to (1) Spanish "borrowing" of English words, (2) English "borrowing" of Spanish words, or (3) common Latin origin.

Copy and mark the accented syllable in each of the following words, then practice pronouncing them. Be careful not to allow your English pronunciation habits to interfere. These are really harder for most beginning students to pronounce than are unfamiliar words, because the English pronunciation is already fixed in the mind.

administración	brutal	charlatán	elefante
admirable		chocolate	entrar
agricultura	carácter		espacio
animal	celestial	defecto	especial
	centro	democrático	
banquete	civil	dental	familiar
brillante		deplorable	fatal

formal
fotografía

general
generoso
gloria
gratitud

honesto
horrible
hotel
humano

imaginar
importante
independiente

lección
legal
liberal

majestuoso
mamá
metal
mosquito

nacional
natural
necesario
negativo

oficial
olivo

oportunidad

paciente
posible
presidente
pronunciación
provincial

radio
recepción
refrigerador
religión

secreto
sentimental
sentimiento

serpiente

telegrafiar
territorio
tigre
tolerar

uniforme
universal
urgente

vainilla
valor
violento
voluntario

PALABRAS PARA HOY

1 **ahora** — now
3 **aprender a** — to learn to
  la aritmética — arithmetic
1 **bueno** — all right (new meaning)
2 **cantar** — to sing (*chant*)
2 **contar** — to count
1 **¿cuánto, -a?** — how much? (*quantity*)
1 **¿cuántos, -as?** — how many?
1 **desde** — from (used with hasta)
  la geografía — geography
1 **hasta** — to (used with desde)
1 **hoy** — today
  ¡ja! ¡ja! — ha! ha!
  el juego — game

2 **leer** — to read (*legible*)
  el león — lion
  pl., **leones**
  la manzana — apple
  Margarita — Margaret
1 **más** — more, any more
  nada — nothing
1 **la palabra** — word
1 **por** — for, in exchange for (new meaning)
1 **¿quién?** — who?
1 **saber** — to know, to know how to
4 **la semana** — week
1 **si** — if
1 **tener** — to have
  el tigre — tiger
2 **valer** — to be worth (*value*)

Los días de la semana

el domingo, Sunday, on Sunday
los domingos, on Sundays
el lunes, Monday
el martes, Tuesday

el miércoles, Wednesday
el jueves, Thursday
el viernes, Friday
el sábado, Saturday

Notice that the days of the week do not begin with capitals in Spanish.

Los NÚMEROS (*the numerals*)

cero	zero	ocho	eight	quince	fifteen
uno	one	nueve	nine	diez y seis	sixteen
dos	two	diez	ten	diez y siete	seventeen
tres	three	once	eleven	diez y ocho	eighteen
cuatro	four	doce	twelve	diez y nueve	nineteen
cinco	five	trece	thirteen	veinte	twenty
seis	six	catorce	fourteen	veinte y uno	twenty-one
siete	seven				

EXPRESIONES

dígame Vd., tell me (polite command)

el dolor de estómago, stomach ache

jugar al *or* **jugar a la,** to play (a game)

dar la lección, to recite the lesson

no vale nada, it isn't worth anything

señorita profesora (a polite form of address)

*tener que, to have to, must

*vamos a, we are going to *or* let's (followed by infinitive)

van a (*pl.* of **va**), they go to *or* are going to

CAPÍTULO **8**

¿Quién soy yo?

HELPFUL HINT: *See section 25 to help you read these expressions of time.*

Son las dos y media de la tarde. Todos los alumnos de la clase trabajan. Ellos estudian mucho y aprenden mucho. En la clase de español escriben cartas.

LA PROFESORA — Bueno, niños.   Vds. son muy aplicados.
Vds. escriben cartas buenas, ¿verdad?

ARTURO — Yo escribo una carta buena.

CARLOS — Mi carta es buena también.

5   ROSITA (*Ella es muy simpática.*) — Todos escribimos buenas
cartas.   Deseamos recibir notas buenas.

LA PROFESORA — Sí, es verdad.   Son las dos y media.[1]
Tenemos media hora más.   Vamos a jugar, porque hoy es
viernes.   Muchas veces jugamos los viernes.   ¿Desean Vds.
10   jugar hoy?

TODOS LOS ALUMNOS — Sí, sí, señorita.   ¿A qué vamos a
jugar?

LA PROFESORA — Vamos a jugar al «¿Quién soy yo?»[2]

LOS ALUMNOS — ¡Bueno!

15   LA PROFESORA — ¿Quién desea salir primero?

MARGARITA y CARLOS — ¡Yo deseo salir primero!

LA PROFESORA — Carlos va a salir.   (*Él sale.*)   ¿Quién va a
ser él?

LOS ALUMNOS — ¡Carlos va a ser Vd.!

20   LA PROFESORA — Bueno.   Rosita, dígale Vd. que entre (*to
enter*).

ROSITA (*Ella va a la puerta.*) — Pase Vd., Carlos.

CARLOS — Con su permiso.

CARLOS — ¿Soy grande?   LA CLASE — No.   CARLOS — ¿Soy
25   rico?

LA CLASE — No.   CARLOS — ¿Soy perezoso?   LA CLASE —
No.

CARLOS — ¿Soy aplicado?   LA CLASE — ¡Ya lo creo!

CARLOS — ¿Soy simpático?   LA CLASE — Sí.

---

[1] We are in an American school in this story.   In Spain and most of the Spanish-
American countries pupils usually go to school until five in the afternoon because
they have had a very long lunch hour.   (Chapter 10 tells about it.)   In many
places they attend school on Saturdays, and usually girls and boys go to separate
schools.

[2] "Who am I?"   One person goes out of the room and the class decides that
he is to be someone in the class or any person everyone knows.   On returning,
the one who is "it" asks questions that can be answered by *yes* or *no* until he
guesses who he is supposed to be.

Black Star

School is out for an impromptu fiesta in a Spanish town. The dancers snap their fingers sharply instead of using castanets, and the guitar furnishes lively music.

CARLOS — A ver (*Let's see*). No soy rico. No soy grande. 30
No soy perezoso. Pero soy aplicado y simpático. ¿Soy
hombre? LA CLASE — No.

CARLOS — ¿Vivo en nuestro pueblo? LA CLASE — Sí.

CARLOS — ¿Soy importante? LA CLASE — Sí.

CARLOS — ¿Soy muchacho? LA CLASE — No. 35

CARLOS — ¿Estudio en nuestra escuela?

ALGUNOS ALUMNOS — Sí. OTROS ALUMNOS — No.

CARLOS — ¿Soy niña? LA CLASE — No. CARLOS — ¿Soy
señorita?

40   LA CLASE — Sí.   JUANITO — Y muy simpática. (*Él mira a¹ la profesora.*)

LA PROFESORA — Gracias, Juanito. Favor que Vd. me hace.

CARLOS — Ya caigo (*I catch on now*). ¿Soy la profesora?

45   LA CLASE — Sí. LA PROFESORA — Vd. es muy inteligente, Carlos.

LA CLASE — ¡Ja, ja, ja!

Ahora sale Margarita. Ella es un señor muy importante y rico del pueblo. En dos minutos ella adivina (guesses) *quien es.*

50 *Pero ahora son las tres.*

LA PROFESORA — ¿Qué hora es, niños?

LA CLASE — Son las tres. Pero nuestro juego es interesante. Deseamos jugar más.

LA PROFESORA — No. Hoy no. Vds. tienen que trabajar

55 en casa.

LUIS — Nosotros tenemos que salir ahora, pero mañana yo deseo salir primero.

CARLOS — No tenemos clases mañana, porque es sábado.

JUANITO — El juego es muy interesante.

60   LUIS — ¡Ya lo creo! CARLOS — ¡Vámonos!

TODOS LOS ALUMNOS — Adiós, señorita profesora.

LA PROFESORA — Adiós, niños. Hasta el lunes a las nueve en punto. (*Los alumnos salen.*)

Find These Expressions in the Story

1. is going to leave
2. Yes, indeed.
3. Come in, Charles.
4. I am not big.
5. at nine o'clock sharp
6. it is three o'clock
7. You flatter me.
8. I want to go out first.
9. Not today.
10. We have (a) half hour more.
11. Do you want to play
12. You have to work at home.

¹ Don't try to translate the *a*. You'll learn more about this use of *a* in the next chapter.

COSAS DE INTERÉS

21. Third Conjugation Verbs

Verbs whose infinitives end in -ir are different from the -er verbs in only two forms.

Look at this model carefully and see what the differences are:

PRESENT TENSE THIRD CONJUGATION MODEL escribir, *to write*		
EXAMPLE	ENDING	MEANING
escribo	o	I write
escribes	es	thou writest
Vd. escribe	e	you write
escribe	e	he, she writes
escribimos	imos	we write
escribís	ís	you (*fam.*) write
Vds. escriben	en	you write
escriben	en	they write

Which persons of -ir verbs differ from -er verbs?
What are the endings for these two forms?

EJERCICIO I. *Conjugate:*

    recibir, *to receive*   vivir, *to live*
    abrir, *to open*   salir,[1] *to leave, go out*

EJERCICIO II. *Try to conjugate three verbs at a time.* You will have to think fast and carefully to do it.

    Hablar, leer y escribir el español.
    (Say: *I speak, read, and write Spanish*, etc.)

EJERCICIO III. *Tell what these forms mean.* Remember that each may be said in more than one way in English. There are forms from all three conjugations. *Watch the endings!*

---

[1] The first person singular of *salir* has an extra letter. It resembles *tener: tener, tengo; salir, salgo.* The rest of *salir* is regular.

1. abrimos	8. salgo	15. deseo
2. recibe	9. cantan	16. abre
3. Vd. desea	10. escriben	17. recibimos
4. ¿desea Vd.?	11. tengo	18. Vds. aprenden
5. leemos	12. sale	19. cantar
6. ¿tenemos?	13. Vd. usa	20. responder (*Guess!*)
7. vivimos	14. trabajan	21. no escribo

22. Present Tense of Ser

Here is a very useful and very irregular verb, *ser*, *to be*, which is as peculiar in Spanish as in English. In Spanish, after removing the last two letters, there isn't much left. No wonder it is irregular!

ser, *to be*

Singular		*Plural*	
soy	I am	somos	we are
eres	thou art	sois	you (*fam.*) are
Vd. es	you are	Vds. son	you (*pl.*) are
es	he, she, or it is	son	they are

EJERCICIO IV. *Conjugate the verb* **ser** *in these expressions:*

ser rico (-a) ser alumno (-a)
ser inteligente no ser perezoso (-a)

23. Subject Pronouns

You have already noticed several of these words in your reading.

SUBJECT PRONOUNS			
Singular		*Plural*	
yo	I	nosotros, -as	we
tú	thou	vosotros, -as	you (*fam.*)
usted (Vd., V.)	you (*pol.*)	ustedes (Vds., V.V.)	you (*pol.*)
él	he	ellos	they (*m.*)
ella	she	ellas	they (*f.*)

EJERCICIO V. *See if you can answer these questions:*

1. Which pronoun is used very frequently? Why? 2. Why are subject pronouns usually not needed? 3. What is the difference between *soy* and *yo soy*? 4. Why must you use a pronoun in the following: *Carlos y Lola cantan; canta bien?*

Check your answers with the information in section 24.

24. Uses of the Subject Pronouns

1. The subject pronouns are used (1) for emphasis, (2) for clearness, and (3) when there is no verb stated.

(1) Emphasis: **Yo soy.**
(2) Clearness: **Carlos y Lola leen.   Él lee bien.**

(There is no way to tell whether it is Carlos or Lola who reads well unless *él* is used.)

(3) Alone: **¿Quién desea salir?   Yo.**

2. The subject pronouns are not ordinarily needed, because the verb ending tells who is concerned.

3. **Vd.** and **Vds.** are generally used for politeness, as well as for clearness, since the verb ending for *you* is the same as that for *he* and *she* or *they*.

EJERCICIO VI. *Give the proper subject pronouns:*

1. Lupita y Arturo tienen lápices. —— tiene un lápiz rojo y —— tiene un lápiz amarillo. 2. —— deseamos jugar. 3. Señorita, —— es muy simpática. 4. ¿Quién tiene mi lápiz? ——. 5. ¿Quién tiene mi libro, Carlos o Rosita? ——. 6. —— son aplicados, pero —— son perezosas.

25. Telling Time

When you read the story, did you notice how to say, "It is three o'clock" and "What time is it?"

Instead of talking about the time, Spanish-speaking peoples talk about the *hour* (*la hora*), so always say *la* or *las* with the number.

Read these expressions carefully:

1. ¿Qué hora es?	What time is it?
2. Es la una.	It is one o'clock.
3. Es la una y cinco.	It is five minutes past one.
4. Son las dos.	It is two o'clock.
5. Son las dos y veinte.	It is twenty minutes past two.
6. Son las dos menos veinte.	It is twenty minutes of two.
7. Son las dos y cuarto (*or* quince).	It is a quarter (fifteen minutes) past two.
8. Son las dos y media.	It is half past two.
9. Son las dos en punto.	It is exactly two.
10. ¿A qué hora?	At what time?
11. A las dos.	At two o'clock.
12. de la mañana	A.M.
13. de la tarde (*afternoon*)	P.M.
14. de la noche (*night*)	P.M.

REMEMBER: Use $\begin{cases} la \\ las \end{cases}$ with a number for telling time.

EJERCICIO VII.   *Now answer these questions:*

1. How do you say *past*? (*What is it you really say?*)
2. How do you say *of*? (*What is it you really say?*)
3. Which is always told first, minute or hour?
4. When do you say *la*; when *las*?
5. How do you say *at* in telling time?

In many European and Spanish-American countries the hours are counted up to 24. It is thus possible to say, "It is fourteen o'clock." Any number over 12 is P.M. time, so subtract 12 to find out what it means to you. If an invitation read «*a las veinte,*» at what time would you go?

The clock face on page 69 reminds you to say *y* with the minutes when the long hand is *coming down,* and to say the *next* hour with **menos** when the long hand is *going up.*

Es la –
Son las –

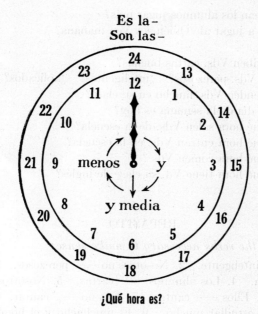

¿Qué hora es?

EJERCICIO VIII. *Read these in Spanish:*

1. It is 9:30.
2. It is 11:50.
3. It is 12:20.
4. It is 1:15 (*two ways*).
5. It is 15:30.
6. It is 8:40.

7. At 1 A.M.
8. At 3 P.M.
9. At 6:30 A.M.
10. At 17:40 (*Why isn't it necessary to say* A.M. *or* P.M.?)

PREGUNTITAS

I. 1. ¿Qué escriben los alumnos?
2. ¿Qué hora es?
3. ¿Es simpática Rosita?
4. ¿A qué va a jugar la clase?
5. ¿Quiénes (*who, plural*) desean salir?
6. ¿Quién sale primero?
7. ¿Es interesante el juego?

8. ¿Desean los alumnos jugar más?
9. ¿Van a jugar al «Quién soy yo» mañana?

II. 1. ¿Escriben Vds. cartas buenas?
2. ¿Son Vds. perezosos? ¿inteligentes? ¿aplicados?
3. ¿Aprenden Vds. mucho en su clase?
4. ¿Qué día de la semana es hoy?
5. ¿A qué hora salen Vds. de la escuela?
6. ¿A qué hora entran Vds. en la escuela?
7. ¿A qué hora comen Vds.?
8. ¿A qué hora tiene Vd. su clase de inglés?

REPASITO

I. Supply the verbs necessary to make sense:

1. Yo —— inteligente. 2. Nosotros no —— perezosos. 3. Carlos
—— la lección. 4. Los alumnos —— cartas. 5. Nosotros —— en
un pueblo. 6. Ellos —— cantar. 7. Ella no —— cantar. 8. Nosotros —— que estudiar mucho. 9. El muchacho y el hombre ——.
10. Vd. —— bien.

II. Tell what each of these means at the end of a verb:

1. -an	4. -o	7. -emos
2. -e	5. -imos	8. -amos
3. -en	6. -a	9. -as

*III. Match these phrases by choosing one from List (a) to go
with each phrase in List (b).*

(a)	(b)
1. No vivimos	a. de la escuela.
2. Aprendemos	b. en un automóvil.
3. Comemos	c. mucho.
4. Los alumnos saben	d. en España.
5. Carlos entra	e. muchas veces.
6. Los alumnos salen	f. muchas palabras.
	g. por la ventana.
	h. a las doce.
	i. por la puerta.

IV. *Translate:*

1. I do not have to study. 2. I am not [a] pupil. 3. I am a rich man. 4. I sing on the radio (*la radio*) on Thursdays and I earn much money. 5. I receive many letters from you (*pl.*) and your friends. 6. I do not have a burro, but I have many horses (*caballos*). 7. Who am I?

V. *Juegos de repaso*

Play the game «*¿Quién soy yo?*»

Now play the game backwards. The person who is "it" asks *¿Quién soy yo?* and each person addressed must tell him something about himself, such as *Vd. es grande, Vd. vive aquí,* and so forth, until he can guess his identity.

PARA PRONUNCIAR

I. Vowel Combinations (Diphthongs)

A, e, and *o* are called strong vowels; *i* and *u* are called weak vowels. The combination of any strong and any weak vowel or of two weak vowels is called a diphthong. The strong vowel or the second of two weak vowels always receives greater emphasis, unless a written accent is used (*hacia, hacía*).

When the weak vowels *i* and *u* begin the combination, they have the sounds of *y* and *w,* respectively.

Pronounce these combinations and the words containing them:

ai, ay	traigo	caigo	baile	hay
au	automóvil	pausa	causa	autor
ei, ey	disteis	peine	rey	maguey
eu	deuda	Europa	reunión	feudo
oi, oy	sois	oigo	hoy	doy
iu	diurno	ciudad	viuda	triunfo
ui, uy	ruina	cuidado	muy	huy
ia	hacia	India	hacía	gracias
ua	incongrua	cuando	Paraguay	acentuar
ie	ciento	bien	sienta	viendo
ue	suelo	bueno	muero	duermo
io	rubio	violeta	comercio	adiós
uo	monstruo	continuo	continúo	cuota

PALABRAS PARA HOY

2 abrir	to open	1 menos	minus, less
3 adiós	good-by	4 el minuto	minute
1 alguno, -a	some	1 el niño	child, boy
aplicado, -a	industrious (applied)	1 nosotros, -as	we
		1 otro, -a	another, other
2 la carta	letter	1 primero, -a	first (primer, primary)
1 cuarto	quarter, fourth		
1 de	from (new meaning)	2 el pueblo	town
1 ellos, -as	they	2 recibir	to receive
1 entrar en	to enter (en used with an object)	1 salir de	to leave, go out of (de used with an object) (sally forth)
1 hasta	until (new meaning)		
1 la hora	hour, time		
4 interesante	interesting	1 ser	to be
Luis	Louis	2 la tarde	afternoon
1 la mañana	morning	1 vivir	to live (revive, vivacious)
1 mañana	tomorrow		
2 medio, -a	half	1 vosotros	you (fam. pl.)

EXPRESIONES

*a las nueve	at nine o'clock	en punto	exactly, sharp
¿A qué hora?	at what time?	favor que Vd. me hace	you flatter me, thank you for the compliment
con su permiso	pardon me (said when passing in front of someone)		
		pase Vd.	come in
de la mañana	A.M.	¿Qué hora es?	What time is it?
de la tarde	P.M.	*son las dos	it is two o'clock
de la noche	P.M. (after sundown)	*son las dos y media	it is two thirty
dígale Vd.	tell him (polite command)	*¡Ya lo creo!	I should say so! Yes, indeed! Of course!
*en casa	at home		

Spain's Heritage · II

Arcos de la Frontera, near Seville, is one of the towns that belonged first to Moors and then to Spaniards in their centuries-long war.   Can you find the Moorish patio of each house?   Note, too, the flat roofs which serve as back yards.

Picture a great tidal wave of dark-skinned Mohammedans — Arabs, Berbers, Moors — in the year 711 A.D., sweeping from North Africa across the Strait of Gibraltar into Spain, reaching, in a few years, up to the farthest northwest corner. There the wave turned to recede; for, when for the first and only time the Moors [1] attacked the little mountain cave of Covadonga in Asturias, to which the last unconquered Spaniards had retreated with their treasures, such a volley of stones and trees rolled down upon them from the cliffs that they gave up and went back, content, no doubt, to know that all the rest of Spain was theirs, at any rate. But from that little cave in Asturias started the counter attack of the Reconquista, and in its honor, nearly eight hundred years later, the title of Prince of Asturias was selected as that to be given to the first-born son of any Spanish king.

By 801 the Spanish had reconquered most of Castilla la Vieja (so called because it had so many castles), while the Moors had settled themselves firmly in the sunny south, which was to be theirs for nearly seven hundred years more.

But before that great Moorish wave had been swept back to Africa, Spain had become a different country, once more happy and prosperous as in the Roman days, although there was always fighting going on somewhere along the wavering line between the Moslem south and the Christian north. Many little towns to this day have "de la Frontera" attached to their names, which means that, being on the frontier, they belonged first to one side and then to the other.

During that time southern Spain became one of the best places in the world for human beings. Old ways of living became Moorish ways, which were pleasant and cultured. Courtesy took the place of barbarian crudeness, and the rule of the Moors was easy. Their laws were few, their taxes light, and their tolerance allowed any religion. They even bought from their subjects the churches they wished to use as mosques, instead of confiscating them as they could have done. Schools and universities were opened, to which came students from all over Europe, and artists and writers were encouraged. City after city took on the Moorish appearance which lasts to this day, for it was the Moors who laid out narrow streets so the buildings would shade them, put patios within the houses for privacy and beauty, hung wrought-iron lace balconies outside door-like windows, and built flat roofs to serve as back yards.

[1] The name "Moors" is often loosely applied to all those Mohammedan peoples —Arabs, Berbers, and Moors — who came into Spain at that time.

In the patios of the Alhambra the Moors put mirror pools to reflect the marble stucco of the lacy walls. The Court of the Myrtles (*above*) is one of the most beautiful.

These people, who "built like giants and finished like jewelers," were far ahead of the Spaniards in architecture at that time. Beauty, they thought, should be within a building instead of on the outside where it might not be appreciated by the passersby. So without, their architecture was massive and simple, but within, there was no limit to their exquisite decoration. The best example of their art, which no visitor to Spain ever misses, is the great fortified palace of the sultans at Granada, known as the Alhambra.[1] To decorate its halls, Moorish builders took white marble, ground it to powder, made plaster of it, and stuccoed the inner walls six inches thick. Then painstaking sculptors with delicate tools carved that marble plaster into deep, intricate designs which stood out from the wall like a layer of thick lace. Even from the domed ceilings dripped stalactites of plaster lace which took years to carve. Then they gilded all this, or tinted it in deep reds, blues, greens, and browns; colors which have lasted all these seven hundred years.

With more mouths in Spain to feed than ever before, more food had to be raised, and the Moors helped solve that problem by inventing

[1] The stories in Chapters 32 and 37 are legends about the Alhambra.

In Granada, the last Moorish stronghold, a ravine spanned by old stone bridges divides the city from the gypsy quarter. Along the stone-paved street gypsies and their donkeys go to town.

Keystone

A blindfolded mule turns the *noria* to irrigate a field in Valencia. Clay jars, fastened to an endless chain, dip into the deep slot of the well and bring up the precious water.

the silo and by building aqueducts to carry water for irrigating the warm and thirsty land. Where there was no water to be brought from a distance, they introduced Egyptian wells, called *norias*, which still irrigate the fields with their home-made bucket pumps. Many a little boy even now spends lazy days keeping his blindfolded mule turning the crude wooden wheel with its endless chain of clay jars which dip into the deep slot of the well.

Because the Moors loved water, having come from desert lands where it was precious, they built luxurious playing fountains or mirror pools in all their patios to cool the air and please the eye. They even had baths in their homes and public baths in all the towns, in an age when the rest of Europe thought bathing a penance!

But with all their wisdom and culture, they had their weakness, for they lacked real teamwork in their methods of government; and gradually the growing Christian kingdoms on the north pressed farther and farther south until Granada became the Moors' last stronghold. Some think the northern climate had hardened the Spaniards, as the tropical "mañana" atmosphere of the south had softened the Moors. At any rate, Boábdil, the last Moorish ruler, could have saved them even then if he had not been so weak; but after plotting against his own father and letting the Christians plunder the country around Granada, he finally had to leave his beloved Alhambra to triumphant Ferdinand and Isabella, and in 1492, Spain's Moorish chapter was finished.

Guides at the Alhambra say that turbaned, white-robed Moors still come, as tourists, to see the proud palace of their ancestors. As they read the graceful Arabic inscriptions carved into the lacy stucco of its lovely walls, tears run down their cheeks, and they say, "Some day we shall have it back again."

That is why the Moors were exiled from Spain, for their conquerors' fear of that very thing was so great that even yet it lives in many proverbs, and in the old, old dance of the Christians and the Moors. Round, doorless watch towers still stare coldly across at Africa all

Round, doorless watch towers, although no longer in use, still stare coldly across at Africa all along the Mediterranean coast, as in the days when Spain feared the Moors' return.

Galloway

along the coast from Huelva to Gerona, and though they are abandoned now, their crumbling stone still speaks eloquently of that long struggle between the Christian Cross and the Mohammedan Crescent.

Now you know of what stuff the Spaniard is made; how in his veins flows the blood of many races with their daring and culture, their cruelty and courtesy, their wisdom and weaknesses; all mingled and mellowed by Father Time in the sunshine of the peninsula's melting pot. This is the formula that made the Spaniard; the old, old recipe that can never be used again.

Spanish sayings about Moors

A más moros, más ganancia. *"The bigger the battle, the bigger the booty."* Said by El Cid.

A moro muerto, gran lanzada. *"For a dead Moor, a great lance-thrust."* "Who's afraid of the big, bad wolf" idea.

Ya no hay moros en la costa. *"The coast is clear."*

Hay moros y cristianos. *"There's an argument going on."*

Moros van, moros vienen. *"Someone is 'seeing things.'"*

Interesting Books to Read

Moors: SEDGWICK, HENRY: SPAIN, A SHORT HISTORY, chs. IV, V, VI, pp. 133–34, p. 167. ELLIS, HAVELOCK: THE SOUL OF SPAIN, ch. XI. VAN LOON, HENDRIK: GEOGRAPHY, pp. 131–35. PECK, ANNE M., *and* MÉRAS, E. A.: SPAIN IN EUROPE AND AMERICA, pp. 17–27, 173, 228–29.

Spanish language: TANNER, LAWLER *and* RILEY: ADVENTURES IN LANGUAGE, pp. 172–82.

In the patio of La Mesquita Cordobans fill their clay jugs at the thousand-year-old Moorish fountain under the orange and olive trees.

Así es la vida

¿Desea Vd. ir a la plaza esta tarde? Pues, venga Vd. conmigo. Todos van a la plaza, porque es el corazón de la vida
pública de cada pueblo de España.[1]
  Aquí tiene Vd. la plaza. ¡Qué bonita! Es una clase de
jardín grande, ¿verdad? Mire Vd. los árboles y las flores. 5
También hay una fuente, muchos bancos, y algunas estatuas
antiguas de hombres famosos. Esta plaza muchas veces se
llama «el jardín»; y lleva el nombre de aquella estatua antigua
cerca de la fuente.[2]
  Son las cinco de la tarde. Es la hora en que todos salen de 10
sus casas para venir a esta plaza y para ver aquí a sus amigos.[3]
  ¡Mire Vd. a aquellas criadas! Cada una tiene que cuidar
a dos o tres niños;[4] y ellas hablan a sus amigas en los bancos,
mientras los niños, muy contentos, juegan (*play*) entre los
árboles. Algunos niños juegan al escondite entre los bancos, 15
y otros juegan al «Déme pan y queso».

[1] People who live in small towns of all Spanish-speaking countries consider
their plaza or "garden" a place to be visited almost every day. Sometimes there
are several plazas, but there is always one more beautiful and popular than the
others.
  Many of the towns founded by the Spaniards in the southwest of the United
States still have the old plazas.

[2] The fountain, sometimes very elaborate, is for use as well as beauty, for the
poor people who do not have running water piped to their houses must go to the
fountain for all their water. There are often public hydrants around the town
for this purpose, too.
  The statues are of the country's heroes, and in Mexico one sees Father Hidalgo
and Benito Juárez represented most often, while all over South America Simón
Bolívar, Antonio Sucre and José de San Martín ride prancing bronze horses.
Your teacher will tell you what each did for his country.

[3] Meals consist of breakfast, dinner, and supper in most Spanish-speaking
countries, and supper is served very late (around nine or ten o'clock), so there is
plenty of time for a stroll around the town "garden" after school or work before
going home.

[4] The nurses or servants of the better-class children bring them to play each
afternoon, and of course the poor children are there at all hours.

Spain's most modern city, Barcelona, has old-style fountains and statues contrasting with its modern office buildings. Strollers must pay to sit on the chairs in the plaza.

Hay otras criadas con aquellas señoritas bonitas, porque las muchachas no salen de la casa solas. No es costumbre. Los señores que pasan miran a las señoritas porque son muy

20 bonitas, pero no hablan con ellas (*them*), porque no es costumbre.

¡Tenga Vd. cuidado! Esa señora cerca de Vd. desea pasar. Ella va a la fuente para llevar agua a su casa. Es necesario llevar agua así, porque no hay agua corriente en todas las

25 casas de los pueblos pequeños. Los pobres tienen que trabajar mucho para llevar agua a sus casas.

¡Oiga Vd! ¡Hay música! Aquellos músicos tocan y cantan para ganar dinero. Dé Vd. una moneda (*coin*)[1] a cada

---

[1] In Mexico the coins would be *centavos* (*cents*), and the musicians would probably carry guitars and violins. The municipal band that plays on Sundays is often in uniform and of course expects no *centavos*.

uno, porque la música es muy buena.   También hay música
aquí los domingos.   Hay una banda que toca muy bien.   30

Pero si algunas veces no hay músicos que tocan, siempre
hay pájaros que cantan en estos árboles, y siempre hay la
música de los niños contentos con sus juegos.   Y las estatuas
antiguas ven a todos, saben todo lo que pasa, y no dicen (*say*)
una palabra.   Así es la vida en los pueblos pequeños, donde   35
(*where*) la plaza es el corazón del pueblo....

Venga Vd.   Es hora de ir.

Find These Expressions in the Story

1. Here is the plaza.
2. it isn't done (customary)
3. It's five P.M.
4. to care for two or three children
5. to see their friends here
6. they look at the young ladies
7. that lady near you
8. those pretty young ladies
9. Such is life
10. Listen!   There is music!
11. Look at those servants!
12. Be careful!
13. How pretty!
14. they know what happens

COSAS DE INTERÉS

26. The Demonstrative Adjectives (*Adjectives which show, point out, or demonstrate*)

Singular		Plural	
este, esta	this	**estos, estas**	these
ese, esa	that	**esos, esas**	those
aquel, aquella	that	**aquellos, aquellas**	those

Spanish has one *this* and two *thats*, which often correspond
to first, second, and third persons.   The "key words" are
este, ese, aquel.

REMEMBER:	1. *este*, this (*which I have*)
	2. *ese*, that (*which you have*)
	3. *aquel*, that (*which anyone else has*)

Aquel also means *that distant*, or *over there*.

EJERCICIO I. *Conjugate* **Yo tengo este dinero,** *changing the demonstratives as necessary for the meaning.*

EJERCICIO II. *Substitute for the English the Spanish form of the demonstrative adjectives.* (Why does each adjective have four forms?)

1. Yo tengo *this* bandera. 2. Rosita tiene *that* lápiz. 3. Juan tiene *those* libros. 4. Nosotros vivimos en *this* casa. 5. Vds. viven en *that* casa. 6. *Those* criadas hablan en la plaza. 7. *That* niño juega en el jardín. 8. Vd. lee *that* papel.

EJERCICIO III. *Name the things in the room, using the correct forms of the demonstrative adjectives according to the location of each in respect to yourself.*

27. Polite Commands

You have had these commands, all polite forms:

tenga Vd. *have*		**oiga Vd.** *listen, listen to*	
venga Vd. *come*		**dé Vd.** *give* (**déme Vd.,** *give me*)	
mire Vd. *look, look at*		**pase Vd.** *come in, pass*	

Here is the formula for making your own polite commands:

1. Take the first person singular of the present tense (if it ends in *o*):

tengo   miro   salgo

2. Remove the *o* and add the "opposite vowel"[1] and *Vd.*:

tenga Vd.   mire Vd.   salga Vd.

3. To make commands plural, add *n* and *s*:

tengan Vds.   miren Vds.   salgan Vds.

This rule will always hold for polite commands if the first person ends in *o*. If it does not, you must learn the command form.

Notice that the pronoun *Vd. follows* its verb in a command.

---

[1] The vowel used most in conjugating -*ar* verbs is *a*; the vowel used most in conjugating -*er* and -*ir* verbs is *e*. Therefore the "opposite vowel" for an -*ar* verb is *e,* and for an -*er* or -*ir* verb is *a.*

	Formula for Polite Commands
REMEMBER:	First person singular present tense, minus *o*, plus opposite vowel, plus *Vd.*

EJERCICIO IV. *Make polite commands from these verbs, using the formula:*

1. pasar	4. cantar	7. llevar	10. mirar
2. escribir	5. aprender	8. abrir	11. tener
3. leer	6. vivir	9. salir	12. ver (§ 29)

28. The " Personal a "

Did you notice the extra word in several sentences of the story?

para ver aquí *a* sus amigos, *to see their friends here*

When the direct object of a verb is a definite person or a proper noun, Spanish puts in an extra, untranslatable *a*.

Every *a* is not a "personal *a*," for it often means *to*.[1] Remember that if it's untranslatable, it's probably a personal *a*.

REMEMBER:	*Veo a Juan.* *I see John.*

EJERCICIO V. *Practice on the* "personal *a*":

1. Find the five "personal *a*'s" in the story.
2. Find *a* used five times where it is not personal, and explain why each cannot be a "personal *a*."

EJERCICIO VI. *Put a* "personal *a*" *in each sentence which requires one.*   (Not all of them do.)

1. Vemos —— los niños. 2. Vemos —— los árboles. 3. La criada tiene que cuidar —— dos muchachas. 4. Los señores miran —— las señoritas bonitas. 5. Las señoritas miran —— las flores.

---

[1] *A* means *at* only in telling time and in some idioms. *En* is usually used otherwise: *en casa,* at home; *en la escuela,* at school.

29. Present Tense of Ver

ver, *to see* (slightly irregular)

Singular		Plural	
veo	I see	**vemos**	we see
ves	thou seest	**veis**	you (*fam.*) see
Vd. ve	you see	**Vds. ven**	you see
ve	he, she sees	**ven**	they see

EJERCICIO VII.   *Can you answer these questions?*

1. Which form of *ver* is irregular?   How?

2. Which form usually accented has no accent?   Why?   (It is only one syllable, which is too short to need an accent.)

3. Will this verb often take a "personal *a*"?   Why?

4. Conjugate *ver*, using a different proper noun as the object of each form.   (*I see Mary, you see Rosie*, etc.)   What's the catch?

PREGUNTITAS

I. 1. ¿Cuál (*what*) es el corazón de cada pueblo pequeño?

2. ¿Qué hay en la plaza?

3. ¿Juegan las criadas entre los árboles?

4. ¿Miran las señoritas a los señores?

5. ¿Por qué (*why*) no hablan los señores con las señoritas en la plaza?

6. ¿Qué lleva esa señora que está (*is*) cerca de Vd.?

7. ¿Por qué es necesario llevar agua de la fuente?

8. ¿A qué hora es costumbre ir a la plaza?

II. 1. ¿Canta Vd. para ganar dinero?

2. ¿Hay plaza en su pueblo de Vd.?

3. ¿Vamos a cantar en la clase?

4. ¿Tiene Vd. muchas criadas en casa?

5. ¿Desea Vd. cuidar a dos o tres niños?

6. ¿Sale Vd. solo (-a) de la casa?

7. ¿Hay agua corriente en su casa de Vd.?

8. ¿Ve Vd. a muchos amigos en la plaza?

9. ¿Tiene Vd. un nombre famoso?

10. ¿Lleva Vd. agua de la fuente?

REPASITO

I. *Which word does not belong in each list?*

(a)	(b)	(c)	(d)	(e)
el sábado	la plaza	el alumno	rojo	dé Vd.
el miércoles	los árboles	el camino	veinte	venga Vd.
el corazón	los pájaros	la escuela	azul	oiga Vd.
el viernes	la semana	el papel	amarillo	Vd. ve
el domingo	la fuente	la pizarra	blanco	mire Vd.

II. *Change the infinitive to the proper verb form:*

1. Arturo, ¡*tener* cuidado! 2. Lolita, ¡*mirar* la lección! 3. Margarita, ¡*salir* de la clase! 4. Vd. *tener* esos lápices. 5. Yo *ver* a muchos amigos. 6. Nosotros *abrir* la puerta para entrar.

III. *Make plural each word possible:*

1. Yo veo la palabra en aquel papel. 2. Vd. lee su lección en esta clase de español. 3. Salgo de mi casa a las cuatro de la tarde. 4. ¡Tenga Vd. cuidado en el camino! 5. El miércoles tengo que ir al pueblo. 6. Cante Vd. para ganar dinero. 7. Esa pluma verde es de Vd. 8. ¡Oiga Vd. la música!

Musicians play in Mexico's plazas on Sundays. Their gold-braided *charro* suits are the traditional costumes of entertainers. Smaller groups, playing stringed instruments, are called *mariachis*.

Emilio Amero

IV. If this sounds like a first grader's reading lesson, remember that you *are* in the first grade in Spanish! *Translate:*

1. What do you see? 2. I see a garden. 3. It is a big garden.
4. Look! There are flowers in this park. 5. I see the children near
the fountain. 6. Listen! The children are talking. 7. Do you see
that boy (*over there*)? 8. He is talking with his friend. 9. That girl
(*over there*) is very pretty. 10. It is six o'clock and the children have
to leave the park. 11. Come! We must go.

REPASO DE PRONUNCIACIÓN

Here is a list of the places where Spanish is spoken. Sometimes the Spanish spelling differs from the English, and the pronunciation will differ greatly. *Pronounce in Spanish:*

EL PAÍS	LA CAPITAL	LOS HABITANTES
España	Madrid	español
México (Méjico)	México	mexicano (mejicano)
Nicaragua	Managua	nicaragüense [1]
Guatemala	Guatemala	guatemalteco
Honduras	Tegucigalpa	hondureño
El Panamá	Panamá	panameño
El Salvador	San Salvador	salvadoreño
Costa Rica	San José	costarricense
Colombia	Bogotá	colombiano
El Ecuador	Quito	ecuatoriano
El Perú	Lima	peruano
Chile	Santiago	chileno
Bolivia	La Paz	boliviano
La Argentina	Buenos Aires	argentino
El Uruguay	Montevideo	uruguayo
Venezuela	Caracas	venezolano
El Paraguay	Asunción	paraguayo
Cuba	La Habana	cubano
Santo Domingo	Ciudad Trujillo	dominicano
Puerto Rico (*U.S.A.*)	San Juan	puertorriqueño
Filipinas (*U.S.A.*)	Manila	filipino

[1] The two dots (*diaeresis*) on the *ü* mean that it is to be pronounced.

PALABRAS PARA HOY

2 **el agua** †	water (*f.*)	1 **ese, -a**	that (near you)
2 **antiguo, -a**	old (*antique*)	**la estatua**	statue
1 **aquel**	that (over there)	1 **este, -a**	this
(*pl.*) **aquellos**	those	3 **famoso, -a**	famous
3 **el árbol**	tree (*arbor*)	3 **la fuente**	fountain
1 **así**	so, thus	3 **el jardín**	garden
el banco	bench	2 **mientras**	while
la banda	band	3 **la música**	music
1 **cada**	each (invariable)	3 **el músico**	musician
1 **cerca de**	near (to)	2 **el nombre**	name (*nominate*)
3 **la clase**	kind (new meaning)	**el pájaro**	bird
		1 **pasar**	to pass; to happen
1 **conmigo**	with me	1 **pequeño**	small
3 **contento, -a**	happy, contented	2 **la plaza**	"square," park
1 **el corazón**	heart	1 **¿por qué?**	why?
3 **corriente**	running (*current*)	2 **público, -a**	public
3 **la costumbre**	custom	1 **que**	who, which, what, that
2 **el criado**	servant (*m.*)	2 **solo, -a**	alone
2 **la criada**	servant, maid (*f.*)	2 **tocar**	to play (musical instruments)
3 **cuidar**	to take care of	1 **venir**	to come
1 **entre**	among, between	1 **ver**	to see (*view*)
el escondite	hide and seek	2 **la vida**	life

EXPRESIONES

así es la vida	such is life	**no es costumbre**	it isn't done, isn't the custom
es hora de	it is time to		
lo que	that which, what	**¡qué bonita!**	how pretty!

ÓRDENES (*Commands*)

dé Vd.	give	**tenga Vd. cuidado**	have a care, be careful
mire Vd.	look at, look		
oiga Vd.	listen, listen to	**venga Vd.**	come

† Feminine nouns beginning with stressed *a* or *ha* take *el* instead of *la* because it sounds better. Compare the English *an apple*, used instead of *a apple*.

La hora de la siesta

As you read the following story, notice the new verbs.

Es la una. Los niños vuelven de la escuela. Los padres vuelven de su trabajo. En las tiendas empiezan a cerrar las ventanas y las puertas.[1] Todo el mundo va a volver a casa para la comida y para la siesta. Desde la una hasta las tres y
5 media es la hora de la siesta en muchos países de habla española.

En la plaza aquellos niños cuentan el dinero que tienen. No van a la escuela. Algunos niños pobres no pueden ir a la escuela. Algunas veces no quieren ir, pero muchas veces
10 tienen que trabajar para vivir. Éste vende periódicos; ése vende flores; aquél vende chicle (*gum*) americano. No ganan mucho dinero.

Mire Vd. a aquel hombre sentado (*seated*) a la sombra de un árbol en la plaza. Empieza a comer. No vuelve a casa
15 porque vive lejos del pueblo. Después de comer[2] duerme a la sombra de aquel árbol.

Vamos a acompañar a estos niños. Entramos en la casa. Las criadas preparan la comida. A las dos empezamos a comer. Comemos mucho. Mientras comemos, los niños
20 hablan de las cosas de la escuela. El padre habla del negocio que tiene.

Después de la comida vamos al patio. El padre lee el periódico. La madre duerme. La criada duerme también pero ella no viene al patio. Nosotros también leemos o hablamos
25 o dormimos. Los niños juegan al escondite. Después de

---

[1] Big corrugated iron shutters are pulled down over the windows and doors whenever the stores are closed, so it is impossible even to "window-shop" during *siesta* time.

[2] **Después de comer,** *after eating.* In Spanish the infinitive form of the verb must be used after a preposition. (Section 50)

jugar se sientan (*they sit down*).   Éste lee un libro; ése escribe una carta; aquél piensa en un examen.

A las tres empiezan a salir.   El padre vuelve a su tienda. Algunas veces la madre va a visitar a sus amigas.   La criada no puede salir porque tiene que trabajar.   Los niños vuelven a la escuela.   A las tres y media todo el mundo trabaja otra vez, los niños en la escuela, los hombres en las tiendas o en las oficinas.   Pueden trabajar más porque han descansado (*they have rested*).   Las madres no tienen que trabajar porque tienen muchas criadas.   ¿No quiere Vd. empezar a trabajar también?

¡Qué buena es la siesta!

Siesta time in Taxco, Mexico, finds streets almost deserted, stores closed, and everyone hurrying home for a long lunch "hour."

Black Star

Find These Expressions in the Story

1. they are beginning to close
2. the money that they have
3. they cannot go to school
4. that one over there sells gum
5. in the shade of that tree
6. We enter (in) the house.

7. After dinner we go
8. After playing, they sit down.
9. he thinks about an examination
10. she doesn't come to the patio

COSAS DE INTERÉS

30. Radical-Changing Verbs

Did you notice that all the new verbs in this chapter had similar changes?   Study these models and notice the changes.

PRESENT TENSE RADICAL-CHANGING MODELS					
volver (ue), *to return*			pensar (ie), *to think*		
	EXAMPLE	STEM		EXAMPLE	STEM
	vuelvo	vuelv		pienso	piens
	vuelves	vuelv		piensas	piens
Vd.	vuelve	vuelv	Vd.	piensa	piens
	vuelve	vuelv		piensa	piens
	volvemos	volv		pensamos	pens
	volvéis	volv		pensáis	pens
Vds.	vuelven	vuelv	Vds.	piensan	piens
	vuelven	vuelv		piensan	piens
POLITE COMMANDS					
vuelva Vd., vuelvan Vds.			piense Vd., piensen Vds.		

EJERCICIO I.   *Answer these questions.   Check your answers by the explanation which follows.*

1. Where do the changes occur?
2. In what places are there no changes?
3. Does the same verb always have the same change?
4. Are the endings changed in any way?

5. If you met a strange verb with **-ue** in the stem, what would you expect to find in the infinitive?

6. If you met a strange verb with **-ie** in the stem, what would you expect to find in the infinitive?

Explanation: Many verbs in Spanish have a **-ue** or **-ie** change in the stem. These are called radical-changing verbs because "radical" means "stem" in Spanish and, as you have seen, they are stem-changing verbs. The endings are the same as usual.

In word lists or dictionaries the change is marked after the verb like this: (**ue**) or (**ie**).

REMEMBER:

Stem vowel $\begin{cases} o > ue \\ e > ie \end{cases}$

First and second persons plural never change.

EJERCICIO II.   *Para adivinar* (*To guess*)

1. *Tell what the infinitive of each form is.*   (If *o>ue,* then *ue<o;* if *e>ie,* then *ie<e.*)

1. cuesta	4. encuentra	7. defienden
2. confiesan	5. Vd. comienza	8. prefiero
3. pueden	6. mueve	(*3d conj.*)

2. *Tell what each of the forms in the previous exercise means, watching the ending as usual.*

EJERCICIO III.   *Using subject pronouns, conjugate these verbs used in the story:*

1. poder	3. dormir	5. volver	7. jugar [1]
2. cerrar	4. querer	6. pensar	8. empezar

EJERCICIO IV.   *Give commands with these verbs, using them in sentences:*

1. contar	3. dormir	5. volver
2. pensar	4. cerrar	6. mover

[1] *Jugar* is the only verb with a *u>ue* change. In old Spanish it was *jogar* instead of *jugar.*

EJERCICIO V. *Make these forms plural:*

1. juego   3. Vd. duerme   5. ella no puede   7. pienso
2. quiere   4. vuelvo   6. él cuenta   8. Vd. empieza

31. Demonstrative Pronouns

The demonstrative pronouns are like the demonstrative adjectives which you have learned, except for the written accent. They must agree with the nouns they replace.

No quiero | este libro. | (*adj.*)   **Quiero** | esta rosa. | (*adj.*)

No quiero | éste. | (*pron.*)   **Quiero** | ésta. | (*pron.*)

When you write the accent, think of it as adding "one" to the meaning of the word.

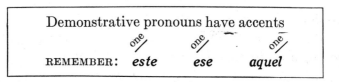

Demonstrative pronouns have accents

REMEMBER: *este*   *ese*   *aquel*

EJERCICIO VI. *Translate these expressions, then give the demonstrative pronoun to replace each one and translate again:* (**este árbol,** *this tree;* **éste,** *this one*)

1. este juego   5. esas señoritas   9. esta fuente
2. esa señora   6. aquel niño   10. aquella puerta
3. estos bancos   7. ese alumno   11. aquellos amigos
4. estas casas   8. aquellas cartas 12. esos pájaros

EJERCICIO VII. *What are the correct demonstrative pronouns?*

1. Yo tengo este libro; Vd. tiene ——; Carlos tiene ——.
2. Yo deseo esta flor; Vd. desea ——; Lola desea ——.
3. Yo cierro estas ventanas; Vd. cierra ——; Juanito cierra ——.
4. Yo leo estos periódicos; Vd. lee ——; Arturo lee ——.
5. Yo cuento estas casas; Vd. cuenta ——; Pablo cuenta ——.
6. Yo juego con —— niños; ella juega con ——.

32. Present Tense of Ir and Venir

ir, *to go*		venir, *to come*	
voy	vamos	vengo	venimos
vas	vais	vienes	venís
va	van	viene	vienen

POLITE COMMANDS

vaya Vd., vayan Vds.   venga Vd., vengan Vds.

EJERCICIO VIII. *Answer these questions:*

1. What second conjugation verb does *venir* resemble? 2. Why does *ir* have to be irregular? 3. What preposition is used frequently with *ir*? 4. What may *vamos a* mean in addition to its ordinary meaning? 5. Where is *venir* regular? 6. Can you use the formula for making polite commands with both these verbs?

EJERCICIO IX. *Tell what each form means; then give the plural in Spanish:*

1. vengo	3. Vd. va	5. va	7. voy
2. Vd. viene	4. ¿va Vd.?	6. viene	8. ¡venga Vd.!

EJERCICIO X. *Complete these sentences in Spanish:*

1. *I go* a casa. 2. *We come* a la escuela los lunes. 3. Carlos *goes* a la puerta. 4. El burro *is going* al mercado. 5. *¡Go* a la tienda! 6. *¡Come* conmigo! 7. *They don't go* con sus amigos. 8. *He is going* a trabajar. 9. *¿Are you coming* con Carlos? 10. *Let's* a cantar. 11. *We are going* a cantar. 12. *I don't come* a la escuela los sábados.

33. Verbs with Prepositions

1. *Read these sentences carefully:*

Arturo empieza a estudiar.	**empezar a,** *to begin to*
Los alumnos aprenden a leer.	**aprender a,** *to learn to*
El hombre no va a trabajar.	**ir a,** *to go to*
Mi amigo viene a hablar.	**venir a,** *to come to*
El hombre no puede trabajar.	**poder,** *to be able to*
El hombre no quiere trabajar.	**querer,** *to want to*

Before a following or dependent infinitive, some verbs in

Spanish require a preposition, which is not translated to English. You must learn the prepositions with the verbs.

2. You have had four verbs that take certain prepositions before a following object.

Piensa en el examen.	**pensar en**	*to think of* or *about*
Entra en la casa.	**entrar en**	*to enter* (*in*)
Juegan al escondite.	**jugar a**	*to play* (*at*)
Sale de la clase.	**salir de**	*to leave* (*from*)

EJERCICIO XI. *Find examples of dependent infinitives in the story. Name the four verbs you have had that take **a** before the infinitive.* (Three are used in this chapter; one was given in Chapter 7.)

EJERCICIO XII. *Complete these sentences in Spanish.* Don't forget to use an extra word if it is needed with the verb you are using.

1. *I begin to* trabajar.
2. *I cannot* trabajar.
3. *I am going to* trabajar.
4. *I want* trabajar.
5. *I come to* trabajar.
6. *I learn to* trabajar.
7. *I have to* trabajar. (How do you say *to have to?*)

EJERCICIO XIII. *Change the verbs in the preceding sentences so that the subjects are* **we, he, you.**

PREGUNTITAS

I. 1. ¿Cuál[1] (*what*) es la hora de la siesta?
    2. ¿A dónde va todo el mundo?
    3. ¿Quién vive lejos del pueblo?
    4. ¿Quiénes preparan la comida?
    5. ¿A qué hora comen?
    6. ¿A dónde van después de la comida?
    7. ¿Qué lee el padre?
    8. ¿A qué hora salen todos?
    9. ¿A dónde va el padre?
    10. ¿Quién no puede salir?

[1] *Cuál* is used with *ser* in questions except when a definition is required; then *qué* is used.

II. 1. ¿Vuelve Vd. a casa para comer?
    2. ¿A qué hora come Vd.?
    3. ¿Quién prepara la comida en su casa de Vd.?
    4. ¿Lee Vd. el periódico?
    5. ¿Tienen chicle los alumnos?
    6. ¿Trabaja su padre de Vd. en una oficina?   ¿en una tienda?
    7. ¿Visita Vd. a sus amigos algunas veces?
    8. ¿Quiere Vd. dormir?
    9. ¿Duermen los alumnos en esta clase?

REPASITO

I. Here is a list of words to use in testing your mastery of several points. (*1*) *Put the correct form of the definite article with each word.* (*2*) *Now use the correct form of any color with each.* (*3*) *Finally make each of the expressions plural.* Example: violeta, la violeta blanca, las violetas blancas.

1. rosa	5. estatua	9. puerta
2. papel	6. lápiz	10. pájaro
3. casa	7. banco	11. bandera
4. automóvil	8. flor	12. pluma

II. Give the appropriate verbs:

1. Los hombres —— en el pueblo. 2. Los muchachos —— en la escuela. 3. Las criadas —— en las casas. 4. La banda —— en la plaza. 5. Los niños —— en el patio. 6. Carlos —— a su amigo. 7. Los alumnos —— notas buenas. 8. La criada —— a la casa.

III. ¿Sabe Vd. (can you) *leer este chiste* (joke)?

Un niño modesto

— Papá, yo no quiero ir a la escuela.
— Pues es necesario ir a la escuela para ser inteligente.
— Yo no quiero ser inteligente.... Yo quiero ser como Vd.

IV. Translate:

1. I leave the house at eight o'clock. 2. I return home at half past three. 3. I cannot (*am not able to*) return at twelve o'clock because we don't have a siesta hour in this town. 4. It is not the custom. 5. In Spain and in Mexico from one to half past three is the siesta

hour.   6. Everybody returns home.   7. The children eat and sleep
or read.   8. This one reads a book, that one reads the newspaper.
9. At three o'clock the pupils begin to return to their classes.   10.
They study from three to four or five o'clock.

PARA PRONUNCIAR

I. More about *g, j, c*

   1. Review the sounds of *g* and *c* (Chapter 2).   *Then pronounce these words:*

a	gas	coja	jarra	casa
e	guerra	coger	gente	queso
	general		jefe	cesta
i	guitarra	cogido	gimnasio	quien
	gitano		jirafa	cinco
o	golpe	cojo	joven	cosa
u	gusto	junto	junio	cura

   2. *Think before you answer these questions:*

     (1) What is the rule for the pronunciation of *c* in
Spanish?

     (2) What is the rule for the pronunciation of *g* in
Spanish?

     (3) Why is the plural of *bloc* spelled *bloques?*

     (4) Why are *cojo* and *coja* spelled with a *j* instead of *g?*

     (5) How is *u* pronounced in *gue* and *gui?*

     (6) Why is the *u* necessary in *gue* and *gui?*   If
omitted, what sound do you have?

     (7) What do the two dots mean in *güe* in a word like
vergüenza?

II. *z*

With a few exceptions, *z* is never written in Spanish followed
by *e* or *i.*

   1. *Compare the Spanish spelling of these words with the
English.*   Why is *c* used instead of *z?*   Pronounce
both lists.

bronze	**bronce**	zephyr	**céfiro**
zero	**cero**	zinc	**cinc**
zebra	**cebra**	zeal	**celo**

2. *Pronounce these words and explain the plural forms:*

feliz	felices	vez	veces
luz	luces	lápiz	lápices
cruz	cruces	raíz	raíces

III. A Puzzle

Can you read this?   (Pronounce all letters with their Spanish sounds and see what you are saying.)

Juai ariu somín tumí?   Iu meicmi uantu crai.

PALABRAS PARA HOY

2 **acompañar**	to accompany	**la oficina**	office
americano, -a	American	1 **el padre**	father (*paternal*)
1 **aquél**	that, that one	2 **el país**	country (a nation)
aquélla (*f.*)			
2 **cerrar (ie)**	to close	**el patio**	patio, courtyard
la comida	dinner, meal	1 **pensar (ie)**	to think, intend
1 **después de**	after	1 **pensar en**	to think about or of (*pensive*)
1 **¿a dónde?**	where? (with a verb of motion)	**el periódico**	newspaper (*periodical*)
2 **dormir (ue)**	to sleep (*dormant, dormitory*)	**poder (ue)**	to be able, can
2 **empezar a (ie)**	to begin to	2 **querer (ie)**	to wish, to want
1 **ése, -a**	that, that one	**la siesta**	afternoon nap
1 **éste, -a**	this, this one	**la tienda**	store
el examen	examination	2 **el trabajo**	work (from *trabajar*)
2 **lejos (de)**	far (from)		
1 **la madre**	mother (*maternal*)	3 **visitar**	to visit
el negocio	business (*negotiate, negotiations*)	1 **volver (ue)**	to return (*revolve*)

EXPRESIONES

*a casa, home (with verb of motion)

a la sombra, in the shade

¡qué bueno! How good! How nice!

de habla española, Spanish-speaking

*otra vez, again (another time)

*todo el mundo, everybody

El día del santo

Pablito y su madre están (*are*) en casa. Pablito se sienta cerca de su madre para jugar con un calendario, pero no sabe leer los nombres de los meses porque él es muy pequeño. Su madre, la señora Muñoz, canta en voz baja mientras remienda
5 (*mends*) la ropa de su hijo. La señora canta:[1]

PRIMAVERA

Hoy las go - lon - dri - nas pla - ti - can-do es - tán,

es que pri - ma - ve - ra ha lle - ga - do ya.

Hoy los pajaritos vienen a cantar;

es que primavera ha llegado ya.

Hoy las florecitas vienen a bailar;

es que primavera ha llegado ya.

---

[1] This is another school song of Spanish-speaking children, called "Spring." See how much of it you can read or guess, then compare with the translation in the Repasito.

Al fin Pablito pregunta, — ¿Qué canción es ésa, mamá? 10

— Se llama «Primavera,» hijito, — contesta la madre.

— ¿Es primavera ahora? — desea saber Pablito.

— No, Pablito. Ahora es verano.

— Pues, ¿cuál es la fecha? No sé leer este calendario

Y Pablito se levanta y lleva el calendario a su madre. 15

— Hoy es miércoles, el primero de julio.

— ¡Ay (*oh*), qué bueno! — exclama Pablito. — En el mes
de julio viene el día de Carmen, y es el cumpleaños de mi
amiga Carmen Rodríguez.[1]

— Sí, el día de Carmen es el diez y seis de julio. ¿Piensas 20
dar un regalo a tu amiguita?

— Sí, mamacita. Cuando Carmen celebra el día de su
santo, siempre le llevo (*take to her*) un regalo muy bonito.

— ¿Sabes cuál es el día de tu santo? — pregunta la señora
Muñoz con una sonrisa. 25

— ¡Ya lo creo! — exclama Pablito. — Como me llamo Pablo,
así mi cumpleaños es el día de San Pablo, el quince de enero.
Siempre viene mi cumpleaños en el invierno. ¿Puedo yo celebrar mi santo también?

— Sí, hijito; si eres un niñito muy bueno y la palomita no 30
escribe tu nombre en la lista (*list*) negra.[2]

— ¡Pero voy a ser muy bueno, mamacita! ¡No quiero
tener mi nombre en la lista negra! Y quiero invitar a todo el
mundo para celebrar mi santo. Y todos van a darme (*give
me*) regalos. 35

— ¡Huy, hijito! — dice la señora con sorpresa (*surprise*).

---

[1] A Spanish-speaking person celebrates his Saint's Day instead of his birthday,
although they are usually the same day. For example, a boy born on August
tenth would probably be named Lorenzo (*Laurence*). If he were born on some
other day and still named Lorenzo, he would celebrate August tenth instead of,
or as well as, his actual birthday.

Such a system makes it easy to remember friends' "birthdays," especially
when stores and florists' shops take advantage of it by advertising, "Don't forget
your gift for Carmen" (or Pablo, or whatever Saint's Day it is).

You will find the traditional serenade for Saint's Days in Chapter 12.

[2] Naughty children are sometimes threatened with the "black list," which
means that *la palomita* has put their names down for no gifts.

We say "a little bird told me"; Spanish-speaking people say "the little dove
told me."

In a sidewalk toy shop Pablito's friends will find gifts for his Saint's Day. Corrugated iron shutters are pulled down over show windows during *siesta* time, and only sidewalk *puestos* are open.

— No es bueno pensar en los regalos que vas a recibir. No es costumbre. Es necesario pensar en el regalito que vas a dar a tu amiguita. ¿Qué quieres comprar para Carmen?

40 — Bueno, mamacita, — contesta Pablito. — Quiero dar a Carmen una cosa muy buena, porque ella es mi amiguita favorita. Creo que voy a darle (*give to her*) un, — un, — ¡una escopeta (*gun*)!

— ¿Una escopeta para una niñita? ¡Qué cosa! — exclama

45 la señora con una sonrisa. — ¿Por qué no llevas un pañuelo bonito a Carmen?

— Bueno, — dice Pablito, muy triste (*sad*). — Pero ¡todavía creo que una escopeta es un regalo muy bueno, muy bueno! [1]

---

[1] *muy bueno, muy bueno.* Such words are often repeated in everyday speech.

34-5

Find These Expressions in the Story

1. It is called "Spring," sonny.
2. if you are a very good little boy
3. I want to invite everybody
4. It is necessary to think about the little gift
5. her son's clothes

6. Carmen's day is the sixteenth of July
7. she is singing in a low voice
8. Oh, how nice!
9. As my name is Paul
10. Wednesday, July first
11. I don't know how to read
12. he gets up

COSAS DE INTERÉS

34. Diminutives

Here are some familiar words which end in *-ito* (*-a*) or *-cito* (*-a*): *Negrito, Rosita, Pablito, Lupita, Fordecito, señorita, repasito, preguntitas.*

As you have noticed, these "diminutive endings" mean small or "little," or merely add an affectionate or pleasing idea to the word. They are used a great deal in spoken Spanish, especially by women and children.[1]

EJERCICIO I. *Remove the final vowel, if there is one, add -ito* (*-a*) *and the definite article to these words, and translate:*

1. árbol
2. animal
3. libro
4. burro
5. papel
6. hermana
7. carta
8. cosa

35. Dates

el primero de julio, *July first*   **el dos de julio,** *July second*

Use the cardinal numbers (*dos, tres, cuatro,* etc.) for dates except for *first*, which is ***primero***. The number always comes before the month.

[1] Here are some popular usages of diminutives: *en un momentito, in just a moment; papacito, daddy; todito, absolutely everything; abuelita, granny; palomitas de maíz* (*little doves of corn*), *popcorn,* or *popcorn ball; ahorita, right now.*

EJERCICIO II. *Say:*

1. the first of January
2. August fifteenth (the fifteen of August)
3. Nov. 20th
4. the fourth of July
5. May fifth
6. Dec. 12
7. April 8
8. June 17th
9. February second
10. September 16
11. March 1

36. Definite Article with a Title

la señora Muñoz canta, *Mrs. Muñoz is singing*

When a title (*señor, señora, profesor,* etc.) is used with a name, the definite article must precede it, except when speaking to the person named. (*Buenos días, señora Muñoz.*)

EJERCICIO III.   *Name all your teachers, giving the proper title* (**señor, señora, señorita**) *and article with their names* (**la señorita Jones,** *etc.*).

EJERCICIO IV.   *Say in Spanish,* "Good morning, Miss (or Mr.) ——," *to one of your classmates. After answering in the same way, he will then greet another.*

EJERCICIO V.   *Complete in Spanish:* (Watch out for the article!)

— Buenos días, *Mrs.* Rodríguez.   ¿Cómo está (*how is*) *Mr.* Rodríguez?   ¿Vive aquí *Professor* Juan García?

— No, *Mr.* Moreno.   No sé donde vive *Professor* García.   Su hermana, *Miss* García, vive en el pueblo.

— Gracias, *Mrs.* Rodríguez.   Adiós.

— Adiós, *Mr.* Moreno.

37. Present Tense of Saber

saber, *to know, know how to, understand*

sé	sabemos
sabes	sabéis
sabe	saben

What is irregular about this verb?
Can you make a polite command from the first person?

38. *Reflexive Verbs*

Compare the literal meanings of these expressions with the commonly used form:

se sientan	(*they seat themselves*)	they sit down
se llama	(*he calls himself*)	he is called, his name is
me llamo Pedro	(*I call myself*)	my name is

These verbs are called reflexive because their action is directed ("reflected") back to the subject. Spanish has more reflexive verbs than English, and they may always be recognized in the infinitive form by the *se* which is attached to them: *sentarse, llamarse, levantarse.*

In conjugating these verbs, the proper reflexive pronoun (*me, te, se; nos, os, se*) must precede each form.

PRESENT TENSE REFLEXIVE MODEL			
sentarse (ie), to sit down (*seat oneself*)			
me siento	I sit down	**nos sentamos**	we sit down
te sientas	thou sittest down	**os sentáis**	you sit down
Vd. se sienta	you sit down	**Vds. se sientan**	you sit down
se sienta	he sits down	**se sientan**	they sit down
POLITE COMMANDS			
siéntese Vd.		**siéntense Vds.**	

EJERCICIO VI.   *Answer these questions:*

1. How do you recognize a reflexive verb?   2. What are the six reflexive pronouns?   3. What do they really mean?   4. Do you always use that exact meaning in translating the verb form?   5. Where do the reflexive pronouns stand in relation to (a) the conjugated verb, (b) the infinitive, (c) the command?

EJERCICIO VII.   *Conjugate like* **sentarse** *the reflexive verbs* **llamarse** (*to be called*) *and* **levantarse** (*to get up, arise*).   Remember that if you leave out the reflexive pronouns the verb is entirely wrong.

The subject pronouns may be used also (*yo me llamo*, etc.), but are not required. Why?

EJERCICIO VIII. *Supply the proper reflexive pronouns:*

1. —— llamo Pablito. 2. El niño —— sienta en el banco. 3. —— llamamos Pedro y Lupita. 4. Carmen —— levanta a las siete. 5. ¿Cómo —— llamas, niño? 6. —— llamo Luis, servidor de Vd. (*at your service*).[1]

PREGUNTITAS

I. 1. ¿Cuándo celebra Pablito el día de su santo?
2. ¿Escribe la palomita en la lista negra los nombres de los niños buenos?
3. ¿Quién quiere una escopeta, Pablito o Carmen?
4. ¿Cuándo vienen a cantar los pajaritos?
5. ¿Quiere Pablito recibir muchos regalos en su cumpleaños?
6. ¿Es un pañuelo un regalo bueno para una niñita?
7. ¿En qué mes viene el día de Guadalupe? (Dec. 12)
8. ¿Quiere todo el mundo celebrar el día de su santo?
9. ¿Qué piensa Pablito dar a Carmen?
10. ¿Cuál es la fecha?

II. 1. ¿Sabe Vd. el día de su santo?
2. ¿Trabaja Vd. mucho en el verano?
3. ¿Quiere Vd. tener su nombre en la lista negra?
4. ¿Sabe Vd. leer el calendario?
5. ¿Qué desea Vd. recibir el día de su cumpleaños?
6. ¿Cuándo es el día de su cumpleaños de Vd.?
7. ¿A qué hora se levanta Vd.?
8. ¿Cuáles son los nombres de los meses en español?
9. Diga Vd. (*say*) los nombres de las cuatro estaciones.

---

[1] This polite phrase, or a similar one, is always used when telling one's name. A tourist in Mexico, knowing no Spanish, marveled at the fact that all the children, when she asked them, seemed "to have the same last name." What was it she didn't understand?

REPASITO

I. *Is your Saint's Day listed?*

1. El día de Margarita es el diez de junio. 2. El día de Juan es el quince de marzo. 3. El veinte y tres (*twenty-third*) de febrero es el día de Pedro. 4. El cuatro de septiembre es el día de Rosa. 5. El día de Lupita es el doce de diciembre.

II. *Give polite commands, singular and plural, of these verbs:*

1. vender	4. mirar	7. contar (ue)
2. cerrar (ie)	5. escribir	8. salir
3. abrir	6. venir	9. ver

III. *Conjugate in the present tense:*

ser, tener (ie), salir, querer (ie), poder (ue), ir, venir (ie), saber, levantarse

IV. *Complete in Spanish:*

1. *that* puerta (*over there*)	4. *those* americanos (*over there*)
2. *these* palabras	5. *that* carta (*yours*)
3. *this* pájaro	6. *those* amigos (*yours*)

V. *Supply the proper words and translate:*

1. My name is ——. 2. My father's name is Mr. ——. 3. My birthday is the ——. 4. Today is the —— of ——. 5. It is —— o'clock. 6. I sit down and begin to study my lesson. 7. I don't know these words very well. 8. I have to study more. 9. Then (*entonces*) tomorrow when the teacher asks, "Do you know those words," I can answer, "I should say so!"

VI. *Here is the translation of* «*Primavera*»:

Today the swallows are chattering;
The fact is that spring has already come.

Today the little birds are coming to sing;
The fact is that spring has already come.

Today the little flowers are coming to dance;
The fact is that spring has already come.

PALABRAS PARA HOY

el año	year	invitar	to invite
1 ayer	yesterday	1 levantarse	to get up, rise
el calendario	calendar	1 llamarse	to be called,
la canción	song (*chant*)		named
3 celebrar	to celebrate	mamá	mama; **mamacita,**
2 como	as (new meaning)		more affection-
2 contestar	to answer		ate way to say
1 la cosa	thing		it
1 creer	to believe (*creed,*	1 el mes	month
	credit)	la paloma	dove
1 ¿cuál?	which, what	la palomita	little dove
(*pl.*) ¿cuáles?		el pañuelo	handkerchief
1 cuando	when; ¿cuándo?	2 preguntar	to ask
	when?	el regalo	gift
el cumpleaños	birthday	el regalito	little gift
la estación	season	3 la ropa	clothes, clothing
3 exclamar	to exclaim	2 el santo	saint, Saint's Day
1 el hijo	son	2 sentarse (ie)	to sit down
hijito	sonny	la sonrisa	smile
¡huy!	Oh, oh! (exclama-	1 todavía	still, yet
	tion of surprise,	1 ya	already, now
	often spelled **uy**)		

Los meses del año:

enero, January	**mayo,** May	**septiembre,** September
febrero, February	**junio,** June	**octubre,** October
marzo, March	**julio,** July	**noviembre,** November
abril, April	**agosto,** August	**diciembre,** December

Las estaciones del año:

3 **el invierno,** winter	4 **el verano,** summer
la primavera, spring	**el otoño,** autumn

Expresiones

¿cuál es la fecha?, what is the date?
*en voz baja, in a low voice

1 me llamo (see reflexive verbs), my name is, I call myself
*es que, the fact (idea) is that

SPANISH PRONUNCIATION

In comparison with many other languages, Spanish is very phonetic. By that we mean that the spelling and pronunciation are closely related. If you learn the sounds of the letters and the rules for accent, you can pronounce anything. Also, the spelling becomes quite simple for you. Have you ever been bothered by such words in English as *do, dew, due; to, too, two;* or *cent, sent, scent?* Then take the word *read.* You say "Read to me," and "I read it yesterday." Even more confusing to a foreigner are the words *reed* and *red,* which sound like *read.* In Spanish you will not be bothered by such things.

Spanish is spoken in many countries. In each country there are variations in pronunciation. A Cuban has a different intonation from a Colombian or a Mexican. An Argentinian has a different pronunciation and style of speech from a Chilean. In Spain itself the pronunciation and manner of speech of the Castilians (from Central Spain) differs greatly from that of the Andalusians (from Southern Spain). We find the same thing true in our own language. An Englishman does not pronounce English the way an American does. Even within our own country we can recognize Southerners, New Yorkers, Texans, New Englanders, and others by their manner of speech. However, we all understand each other.

The difference extends at times to words. Compare a few English words with their American equivalents.

ENGLISH	AMERICAN	ENGLISH	AMERICAN
to let	to rent	tram	street car
luggage	baggage	chemist	druggist
cinema	motion pictures	lift	elevator
shop	store	lorry	truck

Now compare some words in Spanish:

	CASTILIAN	MEXICAN	
string beans	judías verdes	ejotes	
banana	banana	plátano	guineo (Cuban)
tray	bandeja	charola	

	CASTILIAN	MEXICAN	
corn	maíz tierno	elote	
suitcase	maleta	petaca	valija (Guatemalan)
chops	chuletas	costillas	
bedroom	alcoba	recámara	dormitorio (South
eggs	huevos	blanquillos	American)
store	almacén	tienda	
peanuts	cacahuete	cacahuate	maní (Cuban)
store window	escaparate	aparador	
ticket	billete	boleto	
peas	guisantes	chícharos	alberjas (Cuban)
block (city)	manzana	cuadra	

Despite these differences all Spanish-speaking peoples understand each other just as do all English-speaking peoples.

Spanish pronunciation is often classified as Castilian or Spanish-American. Castilian is spoken in the province of Castile in Spain. It has come to be the accepted pronunciation for orators, actors, and teachers. The pronunciation used in the Americas is called Spanish-American. It differs from Castilian mainly in the sounds of *z, ce, ci,* and *ll.* Are you wondering why there is a difference? The answer is that living languages are constantly changing just as styles change. Only the dead languages, that is, the languages that are no longer spoken, remain the same. The *conquistadores* (conquerors) and early colonists left Spain in the sixteenth century, and the Spanish that is spoken in Spain has changed since then. The Spanish that is spoken in the New World has changed even more due to the influence of the languages of the natives and of later immigrants from other countries, but the basic language remains the same though pronunciation and individual words may vary.

If we were teaching English, we should try to teach a standard pronunciation and not that of any one locality. Educated Spanish-speaking people in every country speak alike, for differences in pronunciation are more marked among people of little education. Therefore in learning good Spanish we shall try to learn a standard pronunciation and vocabulary.

¿Cuánto sabe usted?

You should not have to look up anything in order to read this story. When you answer the questions at the end, point out the part of the story that proves you are right.

EL SANTO DE PABLITO

Al fin llega (*arrives*) el día del santo de Pablito. La palomita no tiene su nombre en la lista negra, y su madre dice que puede celebrar su santo.

El quince de enero, este año, es sábado. Pablito y sus amiguitos no tienen que ir a la escuela, y todos van a la casa de Pablito a las tres de la tarde. Sus madres o sus criadas acompañan a los niños, porque los niñitos no van solos por las calles (*streets*). No es costumbre.

Breaking the piñata is the traditional game for birthday parties — and always at Christmas — in Mexico. The blindfolded boy gets three strikes while the rest swing the *piñata* out of his reach.

Charles D. Jarrett

Cuando llegan (*arrive*) todos los niños a la casa de Pablito, le
10 (*to him*) dan sus regalos y dicen, — Felicidades,[1] Pablito.
Pablito, muy contento, contesta, — Muchas gracias.
Las señoras se sientan en la sala (*living room*) para platicar
(*chat*), pero los niños no se sientan. Ellos van al patio y em-
piezan a jugar, y las criadas, que tienen que cuidar a los niños,
15 acompañan a todos.
— ¿A qué vamos a jugar hoy? — pregunta Pablito.
— Queremos jugar primero a «Las Casitas de Alquilar,»[2]
— contesta Carmen.
— ¡Bueno! — exclaman todos, y empiezan a jugar a «Las
20 Casitas de Alquilar.»
También juegan a «La Comba,»[3] a «La Momita,»[4] y a la
«Naranja Dulce.»[5] En todos estos juegos tienen que cantar
canciones, pero es fácil, porque todos saben las palabras.
Mientras juegan a la «Naranja Dulce,» la madre de Pablito
25 sale de la casa con una piñata[6] preciosa para los niños.
— ¡Ay, qué bonita! — exclaman todos.
En la piñata hay dulces y naranjas para cada uno. Los
niños rompen (*break*) la piñata con mucho gusto, y comen los
dulces y las naranjas. Después de tener la piñata, los niños y
30 sus madres comen pasteles (*pastries*) y toman chocolate.
Después de comer, es hora de irse (*go away, leave*), y todos los
amiguitos de Pablito vuelven a casa. Son las siete de la noche

---

[1] *Felicidades, congratulations.* Say this to your friend on his birthday instead
of "Many happy returns."

[2] *Las Casitas de Alquilar, Little Houses to Rent*, is another game like "Pussy
Wants a Corner."

[3] *La Comba, skipping rope.* Spanish-speaking children know many verses
to say as they skip, just as we do.

[4] *La Momita, Blindman's Buff*, is played as we play it except that the one who
is "it" may demand "noise" or "silence" while he tries to catch someone.

[5] *Naranja Dulce, Sweet Orange*, is a simple singing game of small children.
They dance in a circle around one child, who points as they stop, and the one he
indicates must step inside the circle and be embraced.

[6] *una piñata preciosa, a "darling" piñata*, is a large clay jar, covered with bright-
colored paper, and filled with nuts, fruits, and candies. The children hang it up
by a cord, and one who is blindfolded tries to strike it with a cane and break it.
Then everyone scrambles to get all the goodies he can.

Piñatas are occasionally made for birthday parties, but are always used at
Christmas time in Mexico.

cuando salen. Otra vez dicen a Pablito, —Felicidades. Nos divertimos mucho (*we had a good time*) esta tarde.

El día del santo es muy interesante, ¿verdad?

35

1. Why was Paul allowed to have a party on his birthday? 2. Why did the children's mothers or maids accompany them? 3. What games did they play and where? 4. What had Paul's mother made for the party? 5. What did the children do with it? 6. What refreshments were served? 7. What do people of Spanish-speaking countries say for a birthday greeting?

REPASO DE VOCABULARIO

EJERCICIO I. There are no new words in this paragraph. *See how quickly you can read it with understanding.* You should be able to read it in two minutes or less and know what you have read.

En España y en México hay muchos caminos buenos. Hay algunos automóviles en los caminos pero también hay muchos burros. Los hombres pobres van al mercado con sus burros. Llevan frutas, flores, y otras cosas para vender. En todos los pueblos hay un mercado grande. Venden muchas cosas en este mercado. Otros hombres trabajan en las oficinas o en las tiendas. Los niños van a la escuela. Muchas veces los niños van a una escuela y las niñas van a otra. Después de las clases los niños juegan en la plaza o en los patios de sus casas. Algunos niños pobres venden periódicos.

EJERCICIO II. Your teacher will dictate the paragraph to you. There are 100 words. *See how high a score you can make. Remember to put in those accents!*

EJERCICIO III. *Name in Spanish:*

seis colores	tres animales	cuatro juegos
siete días	cuatro regalos	tres cosas en la plaza
dos frutas	ocho cosas en la clase	tres estaciones
dos flores	cinco verbos	doce meses

114 EL CAMINO REAL

EJERCICIO IV. *Describe each of these in a complete sentence:*

1. el burrito
2. un alumno de la clase
3. una alumna de la clase
4. la profesora (¡*Cuidado!*)
5. el calendario
6. el regalo para Carmen
7. nuestra bandera
8. el azúcar
9. su hermano de Vd.
10. su amigo de Vd.

EJERCICIO V. *Give the opposites of these words in Spanish:*

1. rico
2. grande
3. invierno
4. venir
5. abrir
6. aplicado
7. este
8. hijo
9. padre
10. más
11. imposible
12. verdad
13. la tarde
14. lejos de
15. entrar en
16. sentarse

EJERCICIO VI. *As the teacher calls on you, act out these sentences. Tell what you are doing (in Spanish, of course!).*

1. ¡Abra Vd. la puerta! 2. ¡Cierre Vd. la ventana! 3. ¡Pase (*go*) Vd. a la pizarra! 4. ¡Escriba Vd. la fecha en la pizarra! 5. ¡Diga Vd. a la clase el presente del verbo *sentarse*! 6. ¡Escriba Vd. el presente del verbo *ser* en la pizarra! 7. ¡Lea Vd. lo que hay en la pizarra! 8. ¡Pase Vd. su libro a otro alumno!

EJERCICIO VII. *Read these problems in Spanish. Practice for speed.* You might have a contest to see which row can give them the most rapidly.

Models:
$$2 + 2 = 4 \qquad \text{dos } \textbf{y} \text{ dos } \textbf{son} \text{ cuatro.}$$
$$3 - 1 = 2 \qquad \text{tres } \textbf{menos} \text{ uno } \textbf{son} \text{ dos.}$$
$$3 \times 3 = 9 \qquad \text{tres } \textbf{por} \text{ tres } \textbf{son} \text{ nueve.}$$

$4 \times 4 = 16$	$5 \times 2 = 10$	$20 - 15 = 5$	$11 + 8 = 19$
$5 + 6 = 11$	$10 \times 2 = 20$	$9 + 8 = 17$	$5 + 4 = 9$
$10 + 3 = 13$	$17 - 5 = 12$	$9 \times 2 = 18$	$3 \times 2 = 6$
$9 - 6 = 3$	$7 + 8 = 15$	$9 - 2 = 7$	$10 - 6 = 4$
$18 - 2 = 16$	$7 \times 2 = 14$	$14 - 6 = 8$	$10 - 8 = 2$

REPASO DE COSAS DE INTERÉS

Look up the section numbers if you have forgotten any of these.

1. Name the subject pronouns. (§ 23)
2. Which have both a masculine and a feminine form? (§ 23)

3. Give three uses of the subject pronouns. (§ 24)
4. Why are they not usually essential? (§ 24)
5. Give the endings of second conjugation verbs (§ 19); of third. (§ 21)
6. What changes do radical-changing verbs have? Where? (§ 30)
7. List the irregular verbs you have studied. Conjugate them. (§ 20, § 21, § 22, § 29, § 32, § 37)
8. How are polite commands made? (§ 27)
9. What is the "personal *a*"? Give an example. (§ 28)
10. Give the feminine and both plural forms of **este, ese, aquel.** (§ 26)
11. Name some verbs that require a preposition before a following infinitive. (§ 33)
12. List all the verbs you know that have a preposition before a following object. (§ 33)
13. When do you say **señora Muñoz** and when do you say *la señora Muñoz?* (§ 36)
14. What is a reflexive verb? Conjugate **levantarse.** (§ 38)

SABER ES PODER (*Knowledge is Power*)

EJERCICIO I. *Give the correct form of the infinitives in italics in the following sentences:*

1. Yo *ser* alumno. 2. Ella *ser* profesora. 3. Ellos *salir* de la clase. 4. Vd. *tener* mi lápiz. 5. Él no *venir* a la clase. 6. El niño *dormir*. 7. Nosotros *querer* trabajar. 8. Carlos no *poder* ir. 9. Carlos y yo *abrir* nuestros libros. 10. ¿Qué *tener* Vd.?

EJERCICIO II. *What are the missing words?*

1. Veo —— mi amigo. 2. Los alumnos empiezan —— cantar. 3. Entro —— la tienda. 4. Quiero este libro; no quiero ——. 5. —— llamo Pablo. 6. ¿Qué hora es? —— —— dos. —— —— una. 7. ¿Quién entra? ——. (*Give a pronoun.*) 8. —— sentamos en la clase. 9. El hombre tiene —— trabajar. 10. Aprendemos —— hablar español. 11. Mis amigos salen —— la clase.

EJERCICIO III. *Give the correct form of the verb in each command:*

1. ¡(*ir*) Vd. a la puerta!
2. ¡(*tener*) Vd. cuidado!
3. ¡(*leer*) Vd. el libro a Juanito!
4. ¡No (*cantar*) Vd.!
5. ¡(*mirar*) Vd.!

6. ¡(*cerrar*) Vds. sus libros!
7. ¡(*contar*) Vd. hasta veinte!
8. ¡(*venir*) Vd.!

EJERCICIO IV. *Give demonstrative or subject pronouns to replace the following:*

1. este automóvil, ——
2. Rosita, ——
3. Rosita y Lola, ——
4. Juanito y Luis, ——

5. Carlos y Lupita, ——
6. esa niña, ——
7. aquella tienda, ——
8. estos hombres, ——

EJERCICIO V. *Read in Spanish, following this model:*

8:00 A.M., *May 2,* **el dos de mayo a las ocho de la mañana**

1. 2:15, Jan. 14
2. 9 A.M., May 3
3. 10:00, July 1

4. 9 P.M., Dec. 20
5. 11:45, Feb. 12
6. 1 P.M., May 17

7. 7:30, Aug. 13
8. 5:05, Sept. 15
9. 20:30, Nov. 6

PARA PRONUNCIAR

Here is the Spanish alphabet:

a, be, ce, che, de, e, efe, ge, hache, i, jota, ka, ele, elle, eme, ene, eñe, o, pe, cu, ere, erre, ese, te, u, ve, ve doble, doble uve, equis, i griega, zeta.

The letters *k* and *w* are used only in borrowed words. *Ch, ll, ñ,* and *rr* are considered separate letters. (Notice the arrangement of the general vocabulary.)

When you can say the alphabet, have a spelling match in Spanish.

LAS MAÑANITAS (*The Dawn Serenade*)

If you lived in Mexico, you would probably learn this song before any other, for it is used as a serenade on people's birthdays or Saint's Days, usually at four o'clock in the morning. School children sing it beneath their teacher's window, young fellows sing it for their sweethearts, and army officers have the

Mexican music is popular in our own country as well as below the Río Grande. These musicians serenade the diners in the Spanish patio of a restaurant in Mexico.

whole army band play it for their friends. No one knows how old it is or who composed it, and it has a different version almost every time it is sung.

LAS MAÑANITAS

Arr. by E. M. JARRETT

És - tas son las ma - ña - ni - tas que can - ta - ba el Rey Da -

vid y a las mu - cha-chas bo - ni - tas se las can - ta - ba a - sí. Des -

pier - ta, mi bien, des - pier - ta, mi - ra que ya a - ma - ne - ció, ya los

pa - ja - ri - tos can - tan, ya la lu - ne se o - cul - tó.

1. Éstas son las mañanitas
   que cantaba el Rey David,
   y a las muchachas bonitas
   se las cantaba así.

Coro:
  ¡Despierta, mi bien, despierta!
  ¡Mira, qué ya amaneció!
  Ya los pajaritos cantan,
  ya la luna se ocultó.

2. ¡Qué bonitas mañanitas!
   Parece que va a llover.
   Así estaba la mañana
   cuando te empecé a querer.

3. Amapolita adorada
   de los llanos de Tepic,
   si no estás enamorada,
   enamórate de mí.

These are the morning-songs
That King David used to sing,
And to the pretty girls
They were sung like this.

Chorus
Awake, my love, awake!
Look, the dawn has already come!
Already the little birds are singing,
Already the moon has gone down.

What pretty early mornings!
It looks as if it may rain.
So it was on the morning
When I began to love you.

Beloved little poppy
Of the plains of Tepic,
If you aren't in love (already),
Fall in love with me.

Andalucía, Home of the Conquerors

The Giralda Tower at Sevilla is Moorish, but Christians added the weathervane, called "Faith," that tops it. They also built the great cathedral beside it — Spain's loveliest.

Sawders

It was from the south of Spain that the *conquistadores* started their march through our history books and into our lives, bringing us the Spanish culture that still colors our southwest.

From that region of Spain called Andalucía, or from provinces bordering it, came most of the bold conquerors and hardy explorers. Later, wealthy nobles left southern Spain to settle enormous grants of land given them by a king who casually dealt out the new territory to his favorites by setting a finger on an inaccurate map. If the Americas had been settled by sturdy, hard-working Basques from the wooded green hills of the north of Spain, or by proud, dignified Castilians from the high, dry central plateau, our history books might have a different story to tell. As it is, when we say "Spain," most of us picture the sunny southern part, for that is the land that is responsible for much of our Spanish culture.

Spain as a whole is not a very large country. Its area is only a little greater than that of California, which means that a diagonal airline between San Sebastián on the north and Cádiz on the south would be only about five hundred and fifty miles, which we could fly non-stop in about three hours. Then, across the country from Valencia on the Mediterranean straight west to the Portuguese border would be only about three hundred and seventy-five miles, a matter of a little over two hours.

Since the best way to get a good idea of the geography of any country is from the air, as many travelers can testify these days, suppose we take an imaginary plane journey over the home of the *conquistadores* to see what we can see, with a guide to tell us stories as we go. No doubt we shall be able to appreciate their courage even more when we see the pleasant home they left to come to an unknown land where all sorts of hardships awaited them.

Suppose we start south from Madrid, the capital that sits like a great green spider in the center of a tawny web of roads stretching across the high, dry central plateau. We watch the dry brown plains of La Mancha [1] gather up into the Sierra Morena, and as we fly over that cactus-studded mountain range with its metallic green and red and orange ridges, we see them melt down again into rolling plains, but plains now richly colored with the silver-gray of olive orchards and the deep, dark green of orange groves, for we are within sight of Córdoba. As we look down we see many red-tile-roofed ranch houses nestling

[1] Don Quijote made his famous stand against the windmill in La Mancha, which is the common name for the province of Ciudad Real.

Hard-working Basques come down from the wooded green hills of the north of Spain to fish along the Cantabrian coast. They are the people of Spain who on the whole look most like us.

among the orange trees, each one of freshly whitewashed stucco, and each one pierced by a Moorish patio. This is the Spain, says our guide, that many think the only one, a land of sunshine, bright blue sky and flowers; of dark-eyed señoritas, of oriental culture and languorous living with its singing and music of guitars. This is Andalucía, land of romance, the part of Spain that has always stolen the whole country's publicity.

Just below the white, tree-filled city flows the sluggish, muddy Guadalquivir River with its little boats. Across it, like some gray, prehistoric animal, lies the heavy stone bridge the Romans built fifteen hundred years ago. Our guide points out beside the river the great rectangle of the Mezquita, a Moorish mosque a thousand years old, built where once a Roman temple stood.

The smooth Guadalquivir, gradually widening, leads us to fly on above orange orchards and vineyards, pepper trees and palms, over the fields where swift Miura bulls snort and charge vainly at the passing shadow of our plane as if daring us to come down and face them. Some day every one of those high-spirited animals will make his last fierce stand in the bull ring, perhaps in Sevilla, perhaps across the sea in Mexico or South America. The colors that will fly from the dart in his shoulder will tell that he is from the Miura farm, and crowds will cheer and bullfighters grow even more wary as they face the pawing beast.

When finally we look away from the galloping bulls toward our destination, we see ahead of us the shining tip of the tall Giralda Tower that marks Sevilla, its colored tiles flashing in the sunlight. Beneath it lies the city that is "more Spanish than Spain." How our guide gesticulates as he tries to tell us all at once of the charms of Sevilla! It is another Andalusian city of dark eyes, restless fans and castanets; of haunting Moorish music and saucy gypsy dances. It is a city of

Spain's Andalucía is covered by our airplane trip.

contrasts, too; of aged monuments to the past and billboards of the present. Donkey carts or shiny black, horse-drawn victorias idle side by side with powerful limousines along the wide Avenida de las Delicias, following the stone-banked river. Modern ocean liners call for olive oil, oranges, and wine, docking beside the ancient Moorish Torre del Oro which once saw the *conquistadores* set sail, and which received the riches brought back by the "Silver Fleets" of the Golden Age.

Much as we want, as any tourist, to stay in Sevilla, we follow the "Great River" fifty miles on down to the Atlantic, hovering for a moment over familiar little white Cádiz — the "Ship of Stone," as the Romans called it. Then we turn southeast to see the stern British Rock of Gibraltar, its great cliff facing toward the land, and not, as we had supposed, toward the sea. Ten miles away, across the Strait, loom the black-browed cliffs of Africa, faced by the Spanish mountains that come down to the coast. As we turn northeast, we see that where the hills are not dry and brown as Spain's mountains so often are, they bristle with dark green cork oaks whose naked white trunks and limbs have been stripped of their thick, spongy bark.

The highway below us winds through the coastal hills toward Málaga, its narrow line often seemingly plastered like an elongated mud-dauber's nest on the steep cliffs. A thousand feet below the road, in the blue Mediterranean, fishermen in tiny boats are gathering in their seines. Here shallow ravines are a bright pink with the wild oleander that clusters along their dry watercourses, while the deeper valleys opening to the sea are green with waving sugar cane, and there date palms and bananas ripen. Grapes grow on terraced mountain sides, and those white patches we see are sanded spots where the purple or green clusters are laid to be turned by the sun into raisins for the world.

Hugged by the coastal mountains, the seaport of Málaga is protected from the cold north winds blowing off the snowy Sierra Nevada. In peace times, ships of all nations come to this harbor to carry off Andalucía's fruits, almonds, olive oil and cork; and the famous fishermen of the town put out from here in their little painted boats, some old and some new.

Now we must leave the blue Mediterranean, and climbing higher than we have since we left Castilla, we turn west toward Granada, lying three thousand feet high in the lap of the snow-capped Sierra Nevada. Below the old gray city with its towering cathedral lies the

Narrow streets, cobblestoned and winding, were laid out in Moorish fashion by the Spaniards who brought their culture to the New World.

Crops grow on terraced mountain sides along the Mediterranean, for Spain must use all her land. Modern highways covering most of the country were built under Alfonso XIII, the late king.

Granada's cathedral, where Ferdinand and Isabella are buried, towers over the old gray city that lies in the lap of the snowy Sierra Nevada. Below Granada the sweeping plain fades into blue distance.

sweeping plain, flat and fading into the blue distance.   Above the town, on a green, wooded hill, cluster the stern, red-brown buildings of the Alhambra.   They are squarish and solid-looking, but we know already what jewel-like beauty is hidden within them.   Across the ravine from the Alhambra, the cactus-studded hillside is dotted with bare white spots that we know surround the cave doors of the Spanish gypsies; and above the whole scene rises the snowy Sierra Nevada, cooling the summer breezes for the sleepy town.   In the great cathedral there rest also the bones of Ferdinand and Isabella, the «Reyes católicos» who rode proudly into Granada that day in 1492 when Boábdil "wept like a woman" for the lost kingdom he could not "hold like a man."

If we were to fly on to the north, we should leave the Andalusian provinces, for they make up most of the south of Spain, and that region is after all the most important one to us.   So we end our journey here, in that pleasant Spanish land that sent its culture across the sea to the New World and as far as ships could sail.

Interesting Books to Read

Basques: CANFIELD, DOROTHY: BASQUE PEOPLE (all).   GALLOP, RODNEY: A BOOK OF THE BASQUES (all).   MERCEIN, ELEANOR: BASQUERIE (all).   PECK, ANNE M., *and* MÉRAS, E. A.: SPAIN IN EUROPE AND AMERICA, pp. 90–95, 189–90.

Córdoba: PECK *and* MÉRAS, p. 20.   LAUGHLIN, CLARA E.: SO YOU'RE GOING TO SPAIN, ch. IV.   PHILLIPS, HENRY ALBERT: MEET THE SPANIARDS, ch. XIX.

Sevilla: PECK *and* MÉRAS, p. 19, p. 71.   LAUGHLIN, ch. V.   PHILLIPS, chs. XVI, XVII, XVIII.   BAEDEKER: GUIDE TO SPAIN AND PORTUGAL, pp. 389–421.

Granada and the Alhambra: ELLIS, HAVELOCK: THE SOUL OF SPAIN, ch. XI.   PHILLIPS, ch. XV.   BAEDEKER, pp. 332–63.   LAUGHLIN, ch. III.   NEWMAN, EDWARD: SEEING SPAIN AND MOROCCO, pp. 103–20.

Ferdinand and Isabella: LAUGHLIN, p. 69 f., pp. 80–84.   SEDGWICK, HENRY: SPAIN, A SHORT HISTORY, chs. XV and XVI.   WILBERFORCE, ARCHIBALD: NATIONS OF THE WORLD: SPAIN, pp. 146–54.   PECK *and* MÉRAS, pp. 28–37.

Boábdil: LAUGHLIN, p. 70 f.

En el mercado[1]

Es domingo. Todo el mundo va al mercado. ¿No quiere
Vd. ir también? El mercado está cerca de la plaza. Todo el
mundo va al mercado para comprar o vender algo. ¿Ve Vd.
aquel edificio grande? Es el mercado. Dentro del edificio
5 hay muchos puestos. Pero el edificio no es bastante grande y
hay puestos también en las calles delante del edificio, detrás
del edificio, y al lado del edificio.

Vamos a entrar. Los vendedores de flores están a la
derecha. Hay violetas, rosas, y otras clases de flores. ¡Qué
10 bonitas son! Detrás de los puestos de flores están las legumbres. Al lado de aquellos puestos están las frutas. Todas
están en montones (*piles*) muy pequeños. Queremos algunas
manzanas y hablamos al vendedor del tercer puesto.

— ¿Quieren Vds. algo? — pregunta él.
15 — ¿Cuánto valen éstas? — (Hay tres en el montoncito.[2])
— Seis centavos, señor.
— Es demasiado. Tres centavos.
— No, señor. ¡Mire Vd. qué buena fruta es! Pero como
es Vd., puede llevarse (*to take away*) las manzanas por cinco.
20 — No. Cuatro centavos, no más.
— Bueno. Las manzanas son de Vd.

Damos cuatro centavos al vendedor y él nos[3] da las manza-

[1] Markets like this one are more typical of the Spanish-American countries
than of Spain. Sunday is always the big market day. People come from miles
around with their merchandise, often starting in the middle of the night in order
to reach the market in time to be ready for the day's business. In districts where
telephones, radios, and newspapers are scarce, market day is a social as well as a
business event.

[2] Guess what this word means.

[3] Notice the position of this word. You must reverse the English order. You
will learn more about this in the next chapter.

Any Mexican market is always surrounded by vendors who spread their wares upon the ground. On Sundays everyone comes in from the country to buy, sell, and gossip.

nas. En los países de habla española es necesario regatear (*bargain*). No es costumbre pagar el primer precio.

Detrás del puesto de las legumbres están los vendedores de carne. Hay muchas moscas (*flies*) aquí porque no tienen ni refrigeradores[1] ni abanicos (*fans*) eléctricos.[1]   25

Ahora vamos a la izquierda. Hay puestos de cestas, de ropa, de libros, y de otras cosas. No veo ningún puesto de dulces.[2] ¿Dónde están los dulces? El vendedor de dulces está cerca de la puerta. Después de comprar (*buying*) algunos, hablamos al vendedor. Tiene dos hijos. Uno está en el mercado y vende dulces también.   30

— No gana mucho dinero, — nos dice el padre, — pero es un buen muchacho. Mi otro hijo, Juanito, es pequeño. Va a la   35

---

[1] Guess this word. Spanish sometimes borrows words from English, making a few changes in pronunciation. English borrows words from Spanish, too, as you will notice from time to time.

[2] *Sweets* are *candies*, of course.

escuela pero no aprende mucho.   Es perezoso y no quiere estudiar, pero no es un mal muchacho.

Pasamos a la calle.   Fuera del edificio hay más puestos. Todo el mundo vende o compra algo.   Mire Vd. a aquellos dos
40 niñitos que duermen encima de aquel banco que está al lado del edificio.   Un perro duerme debajo del banco.   Creo que es el perro de los niñitos.   La madre de los niños vende algo a aquella señora.   La señora tiene una cesta grande para llevar las cosas que compra.   Hablan mucho porque la señora no
45 quiere pagar el primer precio.   Quiere regatear (*bargain*).

El mercado es interesante, ¿verdad?   Pero ya son las doce y media y tenemos que volver a casa para comer.   Podemos volver al mercado otro día para ver más.

Find These Expressions in the Story

1. is near the plaza
2. in front of the building
3. beside the building
4. How much are these?
5. It is too much.
6. The apples are yours.
7. he gives us the apples
8. the first price
9. I don't see any candy stall.
10. A dog is sleeping under the bench.

COSAS DE INTERÉS

39. Present Tense of Estar

estar, *to be*

estoy	I am		estamos	we are
estás	thou art		estáis	you are (*fam.*)
Vd. está	you are	Vds. están	you are (*pol.*)
está	he, she, it is		están	they are

Why must you be particularly careful to accent the forms *está* and *estás* correctly?   What meaning do you give to these two words by accenting them on the first syllable?

40. Uses of Ser *and* Estar

You have had two verbs meaning *to be*.   Though the English meaning is the same, each verb is used in a special way. *Ser* tells what kind of person or thing is meant; *estar* tells how the person or thing is at the moment. Study these examples carefully.

SER	ESTAR
1. Tells *who* or *what:*	1. Tells *where:*
¿Quién es? Es Juan.	¿Dónde está? Está en casa.
¿Qué es? Es una cesta.	Estamos en la clase.
2. Describes *permanent* conditions:	2. Describes *temporary* conditions:
El hielo (*ice*) es frío (*cold*).	El agua está fría.
3. Tells *what kind of:*	3. Tells *how:*
Es una niña bonita.	¿Cómo está Vd.? Estoy bueno.
Es un hombre rico. Es rico.	Estamos contentos.
La ventana es grande.	La ventana está abierta (*open*).

In these examples notice how the meaning changes when the verb is changed:

Juanito es malo.
Johnny is bad (character).

Juanito está malo.
Johnny is ill (now).

Lola es buena.
Lola is good (character).

Lola está buena.
Lola is well (in good health).

REMEMBER: *Ser* { Who, what? / What kind of? } *Estar* { How? / Where? }

EJERCICIO I. *Conjugate the verbs in these expressions:*

1. estar en la clase   2. ser alumno[1] (*Watch the plural!*)

EJERCICIO II. *Read these sentences aloud. Give the reason for the use of* **ser** *or* **estar** *each time.*

1. ¿Dónde está su amigo de Vd.? 2. ¿Quién es su amigo de Vd.? 3. Es el mercado. 4. El mercado está en un edificio grande. 5. Somos americanos. 6. Estamos en América. 7. Mi amigo es un

[1] Notice that the indefinite article is generally omitted before an unmodified predicate noun: *es alumno,* he is a student.

muchacho grande. 8. Mi amigo no está aquí. 9. La niña está contenta. 10. Las flores son bonitas.

EJERCICIO III. *Use the correct verb in the following sentences:*

1. Hoy *is* lunes. 2. Los niños *are* en la calle. 3. ¿Dónde *is* mi libro de español? 4. ¿*Is* éste su libro de Vd.? 5. El hombre *is* cerca de la puerta. 6. No *they are* aquí. 7. Tiene que *to be* aquí a las diez. 8. Va a *to be* profesora. 9. La bandera *is* encima del edificio. 10. *We are* sus hermanos. 11. Queremos *to be* ricos. 12. Él *is* malo (*ill*).

EJERCICIO IV. *Put these sentences into Spanish:*

1. Where are you?
2. Who are you?
3. What is it?
4. They are friends.
5. My book is on the bench.
6. Who is Juanito?
7. He is my friend, but he isn't here now.
8. How are you?

41. Some Prepositions to use with Estar

When telling place or position you often need to use prepositions. Several have two or more parts, as in English when you say "far from" or "in front of."

PREPOSITIONS OF PLACE

encima de
on, upon, over, on top of
delante de
in front of, before (*position*)
cerca de
near, near to
dentro de
in, within, inside (of)
al lado de
beside, at the side of

debajo de
under, beneath
detrás de
in back of, behind
lejos de
far from
fuera de
without, outside of

EJERCICIO V. *Answer these questions in complete sentences:*

1. ¿Dónde está la profesora? 2. ¿Dónde están los alumnos? 3. ¿Está Juanito cerca de la profesora? 4. ¿Está Rosita lejos de la profesora? 5. ¿Está Vd. cerca de la profesora? 6. Dónde está la pizarra? 7. ¿Dónde está la bandera? 8. ¿Dónde están las ventanas? 9. ¿Dónde está la puerta? 10. ¿Dónde están los libros? 11. ¿Dónde está Vd. (*in relation to four different people*)?

Courtesy of Helen B. Durfee

In a typical puesto Aztec love of symmetry is shown by the neatly balanced piles of dried peppers spread out to sell. Three kinds are laid out here in graduated sizes.

42. Adjectives with Shortened Forms

un(o), **-a,** an, one	**mal**(o), bad
primer(o), first	**algun**(o),[1] some
tercer(o), third	**ningun**(o),[1] no, none, not any
buen(o), good	

[1] When the *o* is dropped it becomes necessary to write the accent: *algún, ningún.* Why? (See *Accentuation,* section 155.)

A few common adjectives in Spanish drop the *o* when used before a masculine singular noun. Alone or after the noun they keep the *o*, and with the feminine and plural forms they keep their endings. You have already used *uno* in this way. Say *uno* in counting, or, for example, *tengo uno*, but say *un libro, un lápiz, una cosa.*

EJERCICIO VI. *Find in the story five examples of shortened adjectives.*

EJERCICIO VII. *Translate these sentences carefully, noticing the forms of the adjectives:*

1. Es un buen muchacho. Es bueno. 2. Es un mal muchacho. Es malo. 3. Un mal hombre no trabaja. 4. Los hombres buenos trabajan. 5. No tiene ningún dinero. 6. El primer día es domingo y el tercero es martes. 7. Un niño estudia, y uno no estudia. 8. El primer mes es enero; la primera estación es la primavera.

EJERCICIO VIII. *Supply the correct form of the adjective given in parentheses.* Remember to drop the *o* if you are using it before a masculine singular noun. Of course you will give the regular feminine and plural endings if the sentence demands it.

1. No veo la —— palabra. (primero)
2. ¿Sabe Vd. el —— verbo? (primero)
3. ¿Cómo se llama el —— muchacho? (tercero)
4. Carlos es perezoso; no es ——. (malo)
5. No hay muchachos —— en esta clase. (malo)
6. — Arturo es un —— muchacho. — No, no es ——. (malo)
7. — ¿No tiene Vd. —— lápiz? — No, no tengo ——. (ninguno)
8. No hay —— puesto de dulces en el mercado. (ninguno)
9. El —— mes es marzo. La —— estación es el otoño. (tercero)
10. Carlos es mi —— amigo. (bueno)

PREGUNTITAS

I. 1. ¿Dónde está el mercado?
    2. ¿Hay puestos dentro del edificio?
    3. ¿Dónde hay puestos también?
    4. ¿Es grande el edificio?

An outdoor sarape shop displays hand-woven Indian blankets from all parts of Mexico. Colors vary from those of natural wools to gaudy reds, greens, and blues.

5. ¿Dónde están los puestos de flores?
6. ¿Por qué no pagamos el primer precio?
7. ¿Por qué hay muchas cestas?
8. ¿Dónde está el vendedor de dulces?
9. ¿Quién es Juanito?
10. ¿Dónde duermen los niñitos?

II. 1. ¿Cómo se llama un hombre que vende algo?
2. ¿Tenemos puestos en nuestros mercados?
3. ¿Hay muchos puestos en nuestros mercados?
4. ¿Es necesario regatear en nuestras tiendas?
5. ¿Paga Vd. el primer precio en nuestras tiendas?
6. ¿En qué edificio está Vd. ahora?
7. ¿Duerme Vd. debajo del banco?
8. ¿Qué prefiere Vd. comer: dulces o legumbres?
9. ¿Cuántos centavos tiene Vd. hoy?
10. ¿Qué va Vd. a comprar con su dinero?

REPASITO

I. Give the meanings of these forms.   Give two meanings for those marked (2).

1. soy	8. vive (2)	15. ¿pregunta Vd.?
2. no tengo	9. quiero	16. me levanto (2)
3. ¿viene Vd.? (2)	10. contestan (2)	17. ¡levántese Vd.!
4. compramos (2)	11. recibimos	18. nos sentamos
5. piensa en	12. ¡vaya Vd.!	19. cierra (2)
6. ir	13. ¡pregunte Vd!	20. pago
7. ¿no creen Vds?	14. Vd. pregunta	21. estamos

II. Put these expressions into Spanish:

1. John's house (*the house of John*) 2. the boy's book 3. the boys' book (*What difference does the position of the apostrophe make in English?*) 4. my sister's friend 5. this meat 6. that man (*over there*) 7. We see our friends. (*Remember the "personal a."*) 8. My mother is at home. (*You're telling where she is.*) 9. a good book (*two ways*)

III. Interrogative Words

1. *Tell the meanings of these words.* Notice that they all have accents.

1. ¿qué?
2. ¿cómo?
3. ¿cuándo?
4. ¿por qué?
5. ¿cuál, cuáles?
6. ¿dónde, en dónde, a dónde?
7. ¿cuánto, cuánta?
8. ¿cuántos, cuántas?
9. ¿quién, quiénes?
10. ¿a quién, a quiénes? (*whom, to whom*)

2. *Choose an interrogative word for each of these sentences:*

1. ¿—— tiene Vd.?
2. ¿—— no va él?
3. ¿—— está el perro?
4. ¿—— sabe Vd.?
5. ¿—— habla Vd.?
6. ¿—— salen Vds.?
7. ¿—— se llama el hijito?
8. ¿—— clase de flor es?
9. ¿—— es la fecha?
10. ¿—— meses hay en el calendario?
11. ¿—— tiene mi libro?
12. ¿—— entra el hombre?

IV. Act out these commands as they are given. You will show your comprehension by the speed with which you act.

1. Ponga Vd. el lápiz encima del libro; cerca del libro; lejos del libro; dentro del libro.
2. Ponga Vd. el lápiz a la derecha del libro.
3. Ponga Vd. un papel debajo del libro.
4. Ponga Vd. el libro debajo del banco.
5. Ponga Vd. el libro delante de Vd.; detrás de Vd.; al lado de Vd.
6. Diga Vd. (*say*) el nombre de un alumno cerca de Vd.; lejos de Vd.

V. Write in Spanish:

1. Today is Sunday and we are going to the market. 2. Where is the market? It is near the plaza. 3. It is eleven o'clock and everybody is there. 4. Who is that man (*over there*)? He is Johnny's father. 5. He sells fruit in the third stall to the left. 6. I am going to buy some apples. Look! These are good. 7. I see my friend near the door of the building. 8. Hello, Charles, how are you? 9. Very well, thank you. Are you buying something? 10. Yes, but I do not pay the first price because it isn't the custom.

VI. ¿Sabe Vd. leer este chiste?

Entre alumnos

Juanito — ¿Debo (*ought I*) decir que Montevideo es en la Argentina o está en la Argentina?

Pablo — Montevideo está en la Argentina, por supuesto (*of course*).

Juanito — No, señor. No es posible decir que Montevideo está en la Argentina.

Pablo — ¿Por qué no?

Juanito — Porque Montevideo está en el Uruguay.

PALABRAS PARA HOY

1 algo	something	4 el edificio	building (*edifice*)
2 al lado de	beside, at the side of	1 estar	to be (where)
1 bastante	enough	2 fuera de	outside of, without
2 la calle	street	la legumbre	vegetable (*legume*)
2 la carne	meat (*carnivorous*)	1 mal (-o, -a)	bad (*malicious, malady*)
el centavo	cent		
la cesta	basket	1 ni ... ni	neither ... nor
3 comprar	to buy		(used with **no** before the verb)
3 debajo de	under, beneath, below	1 ningún (-o, -a)	no, none, not ... any
2 delante de	in front of, before	1 nos	us
3 demasiado	too much, too	2 pagar	to pay (for)
1 dentro de	in, within, inside	3 el perro	dog
3 detrás de	behind, in back of	3 el precio	price
2 los dulces	candy (new meaning)	el puesto	stall
		1 tercer (-o, -a)	third
3 encima de	on, upon	el vendedor	seller (*vendor*)

EXPRESIONES

*a la derecha, to the right, at the right
*a la izquierda, to *or* at the left

Una carta de mi amigo

Tepic, Nayarit, México,
2 de agosto de 19—.

Querido amigo Carlos,

Aquí estoy al fin en Tepic, una ciudad pequeña de México. Tepic es una ciudad colonial,[1] con casas antiguas, una plaza 5 bonita, una iglesia hermosa, y gente muy simpática.   Vivo en el Hotel Imperial, donde tengo un cuarto muy grande, con balcón (*balcony*) y una vista encantadora (*charming*) de la plaza y de las torres (*towers*) altas de la iglesia.   Las miro muchas veces, porque son tan hermosas contra aquel cielo 10 azul.

Tengo muchos amigos aquí.   Antonio Herrera es mi amigo favorito, y le llamo mi «cuate» (*pal*).   Le veo todos los días. Lolita, su hermana, es muy bonita; y la veo a ella todos los días también.   Me invitan a su casa algunas veces cuando dan 15 una «tamalada,»[2] y voy con mucho gusto.

¿Sabe Vd. lo que es una tamalada?   Pues es una cena de tamales de muchas clases, y los comemos con buen apetito. También nos dan café con leche[3] (*milk*), y lo tomamos con azúcar y mucha leche.   No lo tomamos sin leche, porque está 20 muy cargado (*strong*).

Las comidas que me dan en el hotel son muy buenas. Cuando me siento a la mesa, primero me dan una sopa buena.

---

[1] A "colonial city," in Mexico, is one founded by the Spaniards three or four hundred years ago, when Mexico was a Spanish colony.
What things mentioned in this letter from Mexico would you expect to find in Spain?   (*Tamales*, beans, *tortillas*, and mangos are not found in Spain.   Otherwise the letter could have been written from Spain instead of Mexico.)

[2] A *tamalada* is a "*tamal supper*," at which several kinds of *tamales* form the main course.   There are sweet ones, as well as "hot" ones; both being mainly of cornmeal, and indescribable if you've never eaten them.

[3] Typical Mexican coffee is the blackest, strongest brew you can imagine, so it's no wonder they use at least half hot milk with it.

Charles D. Jarrett

Charles D. Jarrett

Street scene in Tepic, Mexico, shows fruit vendor, idlers, shoppers, and waiting taxis. Arcades like these surround almost every plaza.

Looking across the plaza from the hotel gallery, Frank can see the cathedral towers standing out against the bright blue sky.

La como con mucho gusto. Entonces me dan un plato
25 después de otro, de carnes y de legumbres. Al fin me dan frijoles (*beans*) con tortillas,[1] y después (*afterwards*) hay frutas — mangos, plátanos (*bananas*), y piña (*pineapple*) fresca. La piña es muy dulce, y la como con canela (*cinnamon*). Así la comen los mexicanos.
30 Me dicen los mexicanos que «es mejor comer que ser cristiano,»[2] y creo que es verdad, porque si no comemos, morimos.
Voy aprendiendo (*I am learning*) las costumbres de México,[3] porque los mexicanos son muy corteses y yo quiero serlo (*to be*

[1] Boiled beans warmed-over by frying, accompanied by *tortillas* (flat, freckled, cornmeal pancakes baked on top of the stove) are the inevitable fifth course of any small-town Mexican meal.

[2] "It is better to eat than to be a Christian," perhaps a frank admission that we're all better citizens with a full stomach than without.

[3] The social customs of all Spanish-speaking countries are much the same, and many courteous expressions are used.

Do you know which people, Spanish-speaking or English-speaking, are supposedly the more polite?

so) también. Cuando me levanto de la mesa, digo a los sen- 35
tados (*those seated*), — Buen provecho. — Y ellos me contestan, — Muchas gracias.

También digo, — Con su permiso, — cuando paso delante
de alguien, y él me contesta, — Pase Vd.

Digo, — Salud, — cuando alguien estornuda (*sneezes*); y él
me contesta, — Gracias. 40

Cuando Antonio me presenta a sus amigos, no dice mi
nombre; al contrario, yo lo digo, y el otro dice su nombre también. Así es muy fácil aprender a presentar a los amigos en
español. Pero hay otras cosas que no sé decir, y algunas veces
tengo mucha vergüenza. Entonces Antonio me dice lo que 45
debo decir.

Esta carta ya es muy larga. Ahora la doy al cartero (*postman*), y Vd. la recibirá (*will receive*) pronto. Escríbame Vd.
una carta larga, y dígame todas las noticias (*news*).

Sin más por ahora, quedo de Vd. atto., afmo. y S.S.,[1] 50

Frank Stuart.

P.D. Aquí me llaman Paco.[2]

F.S.

Find These Expressions in the Story

1. I look at them often
2. I call him my "pal."
3. one dish after another
4. They invite me to their home (*house*)
5. I remain, yours truly,
6. When I get up from the table
7. Write me a long letter
8. when I pass in front of anyone (*someone*)
9. I see her every day, too.
10. they give us coffee
11. other things that I don't know how to say
12. he tells me what I ought to say

[1] *quedo de Vd. atto., afmo. y S.S.* (*quedo de Vd. atento, afectísimo y seguro servidor*), I remain, yours truly (*your attentive, very affectionate and constant servant*).

[2] *Francisco* (*Frank*) has as many nicknames as our William: *Paco, Paquito, Pancho, Panchito, Frasco, Frasquito, Frascuelo, Currito,* and *Currín.*

COSAS DE INTERÉS

43. *Present Tense of* Dar, Poner, *and* Decir

dar	poner	decir (i)
to give	*to put* or *place*	*to say* or *tell*
doy	pongo	digo
das	pones	dices
da	pone	dice
damos	ponemos	decimos
dais	ponéis	decís
dan	ponen	dicen

POLITE COMMANDS

dé Vd.	ponga Vd.	diga Vd.
den Vds.	pongan Vds.	digan Vds.

44. *Direct Object Pronouns*

The little words are the ones that cause the difficulties in Spanish, for the long ones can often be guessed. Weren't you puzzled over *las miro muchas veces* and *la veo todos los días* in the letter?

The *las* and *la,* with their new meanings, came from this list:

DIRECT OBJECT PRONOUNS			
Singular		*Plural*	
me	me (*Indirect:* to me)	**nos**	us (*Indirect,* to us)
te	thee (*Indirect:* to thee)	**os**	you (fam.) (*Ind.,* to you)
le	him	**los**	them (*m.*)
lo	it (*m.*)	**las**	them (*f.*)
la	her, it (*f.*)		

EJERCICIO I. *Answer these questions:*

1. Which of these direct object pronouns look just like the definite articles?

2. What other list of pronouns starts just like this one?

3. What is the difference in meaning between direct and indirect object pronouns?

4. Which persons of these pronouns have both direct and indirect meanings for the same form? (You will have the third person indirect forms later.)

EJERCICIO II: *Notice these sentences:*

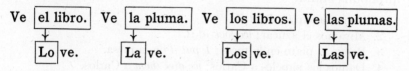

1. Which of the pronouns used are just like the definite articles?

2. Which definite article can you not use over again as a direct object pronoun?

3. How would you say *it*, meaning *la sopa; el dinero?*

4. How would you say *them*, meaning *las niñas; los hermanos?*

EJERCICIO III. *Translate these expressions:*

escríbame Vd., la tomo, la vemos, nos ve, me dicen, déme Vd. el plato, póngalos Vd. en la mesa

45. Position of Object Pronouns (*Direct, indirect and reflexive*)

When you conjugate reflexive verbs (remember *sentarse?*), where do the reflexive pronouns stand?

All object pronouns, direct, indirect, and reflexive, precede a "conjugated" verb form (finite verb): *me levanto, lo como, me sirven.*

> REMEMBER: Object pronouns stand before a "conjugated" verb.

EJERCICIO IV. *Complete in Spanish:* "he sees me, he sees thee, he sees him," *etc.*

EJERCICIO V.   *Find in Frank's letter five examples of object pronouns which precede their verbs, and tell whether the pronouns are direct, indirect, or reflexive.*   (Indirect object pronouns mean *to* or *for*.)

EJERCICIO VI.   *Complete these sentences.*   Where do those pronouns stand?

1. Como la carne; *I eat it.*[1]
2. Miramos el azúcar; *we look at it.*
3. Pongo el plato en la mesa; *I put it* en la mesa.
4. Damos los papeles a Carlos; *we give them* a Carlos.
5. Dicen las palabras a Juan; *they say them* a Juan.
6. Veo a María; *I see her.*   (*What becomes of the "personal a"?*)
7. Vemos a Pablo; *we see him.*
8. Ven a Pablo y a María; *they see them.*
9. Me ven; *they see us* también.

46. Object Pronouns with Affirmative Commands

You have had some polite commands used with pronouns:

escríbame Vd.	*write me*	**déme Vd.**	*give me*
dígame Vd.	*tell me*	**siéntese Vd.**	*sit down*

Where do the pronouns stand with these commands?   Is this like the English order?

> REMEMBER: Object pronouns follow and are attached to affirmative commands.

There is also a new accent to add.   To tell where to put it, count the vowels backward, and if there are three, write the accent upon the third vowel.

Example: **Dígame Vd.**[2]

3 2 1

---

[1] The English "I eat it" sounds as peculiar to Spanish-speaking people as their "it I eat" does to us.

[2] *Déme Vd.*, although it has only two vowels, has an accent because *dé Vd.* already had one.   What's the difference between *dé Vd.* and *de Vd.*? How would you make *dígame Vd.* plural?

EJERCICIO VII. *Write carefully:*

1. put it; write it (*la palabra*)   2. tell me   3. tell us   4. eat them (*las frutas*)   5. look at it (*la cena*)   6. give us   7. sit down   8. get up

PREGUNTITAS

I. 1. ¿Dónde está Paco?
2. ¿Qué clase de ciudad es Tepic?
3. ¿Dónde está Tepic?
4. ¿Qué es una «tamalada?»
5. ¿Qué comen en el hotel?
6. ¿Son muy corteses los mexicanos?
7. ¿Por qué es fácil presentar a los amigos en español?
8. ¿Cuándo tiene Paco mucha vergüenza?
9. ¿Quiénes creen que «es mejor comer que ser cristiano?»
10. ¿Tiene México costumbres como las (*those*) de España?

II. 1. ¿Tiene Vd. «cuates» en México?
2. ¿Toma Vd. café con leche?
3. ¿Come Vd. muchos frijoles con tortillas?
4. ¿Invita Vd. a sus amigos a una «tamalada» muchas veces?
5. ¿Tiene Vd. mucha vergüenza cuando no sabe la lección?
6. ¿Qué debemos decir cuando nos levantamos de la mesa?
7. ¿Cuándo debe Vd. decir, — Con permiso?
8. ¿Cuándo debe Vd. decir, — Salud?

REPASITO

I. Add diminutive endings (-ito, -a) to these words after removing the last vowel:

plato, mesa, pañuelo, frijoles, sopa (*The last two, with diminutive endings, are waiters' slang!*)

II. Give the correct form of **ser** *or* **estar:**

1. Aquí *I am.* ¿Quién *is it?*   2. Pablito y su madre *are* en casa. 3. El día de mi santo *is* el quince de agosto.   4. ¿Dónde *is* Paco? *He isn't* aquí.   5. La sopa *is* en el plato.   6. El número *is* encima de la puerta.   7. Paco y Carlos *are* amigos.   8. Una tamalada *is* una cena de tamales.   9. Carmen *is* una niña muy hermosa.

III. Change verbs, pronouns, and possessive adjectives to the first person where possible (Yo estoy en Tepic, *etc.*)

Frank está en Tepic. Antonio le llama «Paco.» Ve a sus amigos todos los días.[1] Va a una tamalada y come con mucho gusto. Va aprendiendo las costumbres. Cuando se levanta de la mesa, dice, — Buen provecho. —— Sus amigos le contestan, — Gracias. —— Antonio le presenta a sus amigos, y algunas veces Paco no sabe lo que debe decir en español.

IV. Change the word order in these phrases so you can use the long form instead of the shortened form of the adjective:

1. después del primer mes
2. cerca de un mal niño
3. en el buen café
4. al lado del tercer mexicano
5. lejos de algún pajarito
6. ningún pañuelo (*accent?*)

V. Conjugate these "old friends" in the present tense and give the polite commands if possible:

1. tener (ie) 2. ir 3. venir (ie) 4. volver (ue) 5. salir 6. ser
7. ver 8. saber

VI. Give in Spanish the correct forms of these verbs:

1. nosotros *come*
2. ellos *see*
3. yo *know*
4. ella *goes*
5. Vd. *have*
6. yo *leave*
7. Juan y yo *return*
8. ¡*come* Vd.!
9. ¡*Go* Vds.!
10. yo *am*
11. ella *says*
12. él *has*

VII. Write in Spanish:

1. Tell me, do you have your book today? 2. All right, then you can write these sentences without mistakes. 3. Put your book on top of the table. 4. Is this your pencil? Use it. 5. If you have a pen, use it. 6. Do you know all the words? If not, learn them. 7. I see a word that is not in the lesson. Do you see it? 8. It isn't in the PALABRAS PARA HOY because it is too easy. 9. We study the words and we learn them. 10. We study the verbs and we learn them also.

VIII. ¿Sabe Vd. leer estos chistes?

Es muy fácil

— ¿Sabe Vd. en qué calle vive Pepe (*Joe*)?

[1] See story.

— Sí, pero no sé el número (*number*) de su casa.

— Hombre, eso (*that*) no es importante.   El número está encima de la puerta.

El pobre perro

— Dígame Vd.   ¿A dónde va Vd. tan de prisa (*fast*) y tan enfadado (*angry*)?

— Busco mi perro, y si no le encuentro (*find*) le mato (*kill*).

PALABRAS PARA HOY

1 **alguien**	anyone, someone	1 **los**	them
2 **alto, -a**	high (*altitude*)	**el mango**	mango, a tropical
el apetito	appetite		fruit with a person-
3 **el café**	coffee		ality all its own
la cena	supper	1 **me**	me; to me
2 **el cielo**	sky (*celestial*)	2 **la mesa**	table
1 **la ciudad**	city	**mexicano, -a**	Mexican (spelled
2 **contra**	against		**mejicano** in Spain
cortés	courteous		and other Spanish-
(*pl.*) **corteses**			speaking countries)
2 **el cuarto**	room	1 **morir (ue)**	to die (*morgue*)
1 **deber**	ought to, must	1 **nos**	us; to us
1 **entonces**	then	4 **el plato**	plate, dish
3 **fácil**	easy (*facility*)	1 **poner**	to put, place
3 **fresco, -a**	fresh	2 **presentar**	to present, introduce
2 **la gente**	people	2 **pronto**	soon, quickly
1 **hermoso, -a**	beautiful	3 **querido, -a**	dear
3 **la iglesia**	church	3 **la salud**	health (often used
1 **la**	her; it (*f.*)		as an exclamation)
1 **las**	them (*f.*)	1 **sin**	without
2 **largo, -a**	long	**la sopa**	soup
1 **le**	him	**la tamalada**	**tamal** supper
1 **llamar**	to call	1 **tan**	so
1 **lo**	it (*m.*)	2 **la vista**	view

EXPRESIONES

buen provecho, may it benefit you (polite expression used when leaving the table)

con mucho gusto, with the greatest of pleasure (One often hears con todo gusto.)

P.D. (Posdata), postscript (like our *P.S.*)

tener (mucha) vergüenza, to be (very much) ashamed

*al contrario, on the contrary

*todos los días, every day

La carta del tío Pepe [1]

El tío Pepe vive en Murcia en España. Ha pasado la vida felizmente allí. Ha trabajado mucho pero no ha ganado mucho. Sin embargo cree que la vida es buena y siempre es feliz.

5 El tío Pepe nunca ha ido a la escuela. No sabe leer ni escribir. Tiene un hijo en América. Cuando recibe una carta de su hijo no sabe leerla. Tiene que ir al escribiente público [2] del pueblo. En todos los pueblos de España hay un escribiente público porque hay mucha gente que no sabe leer ni 10 escribir. El escribiente lee las cartas que recibe la gente. También escribe las respuestas.

Muchas veces tiene su mesa cerca de la plaza. Algunas veces tiene allí una máquina de escribir que usa para escribir las cartas. Generalmente es una máquina antigua. Todo el 15 mundo le mira cuando escribe y dice, — ¡Miren Vds.! ¡Qué rápidamente escribe con aquella máquina! Es una maravilla, ¿verdad? (La verdad es que no escribe ni maravillosamente ni rápidamente.)

Un día el tío Pepe ha recibido una carta y va a ver 20 al escribiente. — Buenos días, don [3] Pablo, — le (to him) dice.

---

[1] Though *tío* means *uncle*, the title is not necessarily limited to relatives. An older person whom everyone knows and likes may be called "Uncle John" or "Aunt Mary" in Spanish as well as in English.

Pepe, *Joe*, is a nickname for **José,** *Joseph*.

[2] In Mexico these scribes are called *evangelistas*. Their biggest business is probably that of writing love letters, for which they charge a *tostón*. *Tostón* is Mexican slang for fifty *centavos* (about ten cents in our money).

[3] *Don* (*masc.*) and *doña* (*fem.*) are used with first names. There are no English meanings for these words. *Señor, señora, señorita* are used with last names only. In formal address sometimes both are used, if both names are being given. For example, *Carlos Fernández* may be addressed or referred to in these ways: *señor Fernández* or *don Carlos* or *señor don Carlos Fernández*.

— Buenos días, — contesta don Pablo cortésmente. —
¡Qué contento está Vd. esta mañana, tío Pepe!

— ¡Ya lo creo que estoy muy contento!   He recibido una
carta de mi hijo, Juanito.   Quiero saber lo que dice la carta.   25
Hágame Vd. el favor de leerla.

— Con mucho gusto, — contesta don Pablo, y la lee al tío
Pepe.

Cuando la ha leído, el tío Pepe dice, — ¿Quiere Vd. leerla
otra vez?   Quiero saberla muy bien.   Tengo que decir a mi   30
esposa lo que dice la carta.

Entonces don Pablo la lee muy despacio.   Al fin el tío Pepe
dice, — Creo que ya la he aprendido.   (El tío Pepe no sabe
leer ni escribir, pero sin embargo es muy inteligente y tiene una
buena memoria.)   El tío Pepe paga a don Pablo y vuelve a   35
casa.

Under the arcade that surrounds the plaza of almost every Spanish town,
the public letter-writers sit at their typewriters.   Both business and
social letters come their way.

Sawders

Después de entrar en la casa, lee la carta a su esposa, doña María, y la lee correctamente.   Al saber que el tío Pepe ha recibido una carta de América, todos los vecinos vienen para
40 verla y para saber lo que dice el hijo.   Entonces el tío Pepe lee la carta varias veces.   Ya la sabe de memoria.

Al quedarse solos otra vez, su esposa le pregunta, — ¿Vas a escribir la respuesta hoy?

— No.   No es bueno escribir algo sin pensar.   Antes de
45 escribir la carta, tenemos que pensar en lo que deseamos decir a Juanito.   Después de decidir, yo iré (*I shall go*) a ver a don Pablo y él escribirá (*he will write*) la carta.

Después de decir esto, el tío Pepe y su esposa empiezan a hablar de las cosas que van a decir a su hijo en América.

Find These Expressions in the Story

1. He has worked hard (much)
2. I am very pleased (contented)
3. he has never gone to school
4. he writes neither marvelously nor rapidly
5. he cannot read it
6. He doesn't know how to read nor write.
7. He knows it by heart now.
8. don Pablo answers courteously
9. How happy you are
10. Please read it.
11. I think I have learned it now.
12. After entering the house
13. On knowing
14. without thinking

COSAS DE INTERÉS

47. The Past Participle

INFINITIVE		PAST PARTICIPLE	
trabajar	*to work*	trabajado	*worked*
aprender	*to learn*	aprendido	*learned*
vivir	*to live*	vivido	*lived*

The past participle in English is made by adding -*ed* to the infinitive.   However, there are many irregular verbs in English, such as *go, gone; run, run; sing, sung; see, seen.*

The past participle is formed in Spanish by adding **-ado** or **-ido** to the stem of the verb.

> **Past Participle**
>
> REMEMBER: Stem + $\begin{cases} \textbf{\textit{-ado}} \text{ (-ar verbs)} \\ \textbf{\textit{-ido}} \text{ (-er, -ir verbs)} \end{cases}$

Used as a verb, a past participle must always have a helper. (See section 48.)

EJERCICIO I.   *Give the past participles:*

1. hablar	4. tomar	7. ser	10. vender
2. comprender	5. comer	8. estar	11. comprar
3. usar	6. ir	9. tener	12. cantar

EJERCICIO II.   *Translate the past participles you wrote in Ejercicio I.   Which are irregular in English?*

48. The Present Perfect Tense

PRESENT PERFECT TENSE MODEL			
usar	*to use*		
haber usado	*to have used*		
he usado	I have used	**hemos usado**	we have used
has usado	thou hast used	**habéis usado**	you have used
Vd. ha usado	you have used	**Vds. han usado**	you have used
ha usado	he has used	**han usado**	they have used

EJERCICIO III.   *Answer these questions:*

1. What is the helping (auxiliary) verb?   2. What does it mean? 3. What is the ending for past participles of the first conjugation verbs?   4. What is the ending for past participles of second and third conjugation verbs?   5. Does the ending of the past participle change? 6. What changes to indicate person?   7. What is the difference between *haber* and *tener?*   8. What is the present tense of *haber?*

The present perfect tense is a compound (*two-part*) tense used as in English.   It is formed by using the auxiliary verb, **haber** (*to have*), with the past participle, which never changes its form.   All verbs form the present perfect tense like the model.

Nothing may come between the auxiliary verb and the past participle. Example: *Vd. no lo ha mirado.* *¿No lo ha mirado Vd.?*

HELPFUL HINT: Both *haber* and *tener* mean to have, but *haber* is like a crutch. It never goes about alone, but always supports or helps a past participle.

REMEMBER: To have { *haber* — A helping verb
tener — Possession, ownership

EJERCICIO IV. *Conjugate these verbs in the present perfect tense:*

1. cantar
2. aprender
3. recibir
4. estar
5. tener
6. ir

EJERCICIO V. *Translate these forms:*

1. he acompañado
2. ha cerrado
3. hemos comido
4. han contado
5. Vd. ha dado
6. Vds. han deseado
7. ¿ha entrado?
8. ¿han empezado Vds.?
9. ¿ha dormido Vd.?
10. ¿han vivido?
11. no he estudiado
12. no hemos sabido
13. ha tenido
14. he ido
15. ha leído
16. no ha creído
17. se ha levantado
18. nos hemos sentado
19. han vendido
20. ha venido
21. ¿lo ha comido?
22. ¿hemos cerrado?

EJERCICIO VI. *Put the verbs in Ejercicio V in the present tense.*

EJERCICIO VII. *Give these forms in Spanish:*

1. I have studied
2. Have you studied?
3. we have visited
4. he has worked
5. they have taken
6. she has not played
7. he has had to go (*tener que*)
8. I have not received
9. Have you prepared?
10. you have learned

EJERCICIO VIII.   *Use the correct form of* **haber** *or* **tener** *in these sentences:*

1. Carlos —— dos hermanas.   2. Nosotros —— que ir a la escuela.
3. ¿—— aprendido Vd. mucho?   4. Los niños —— jugado en la calle.
5. ¿Dónde —— estado Vd.?   6. ¿Qué —— Vd.?

49. Formation of Adverbs

perezoso, lazy	**perezosamente,** lazily
rápido, rapid	**rápidamente,** rapidly
feliz, happy	**felizmente,** happily
cortés, courteous	**cortésmente,** courteously

In English what do you add to an adjective to make an adverb?   What is the Spanish equivalent of English *-ly*?

Notice the first two examples carefully.   Do you see that the feminine form of the adjective, if it has one, is used to form the adverb?

EJERCICIO IX.   *Form adverbs from these adjectives and translate:*

1. correcto	3. posible	5. bonito	7. dulce
2. exacto	4. independiente	6. necesario	8. rico

50. The Infinitive with Prepositions

EJERCICIO X.   *Find seven examples in the story of a preposition followed by an infinitive.   Translate each.   How must the infinitive be translated to make it sound right in English?*

REMEMBER: After a preposition use the infinitive form of a verb.
Its English meaning usually ends in *-ing.*

EJERCICIO XI.   *Complete these expressions in Spanish:*

1. al *saying* esto   2. después de *saying* esto   3. sin *saying* esto
4. al *seeing*   5. después de *leaving*   6. antes de *using*   7. sin *knowing*
8. Hágame Vd. el favor de *close* la puerta.

51. Object Pronouns with the Infinitive

Translate these model sentences:

1. Don Pablo lee la carta.
2. Don Pablo la lee.
3. Don Pablo la ha leído.
4. Léala Vd., don Pablo.
5. Don Pablo va a leerla.
6. Don Pablo va a sentarse.

Where are the object pronouns placed in Spanish?
What are two exceptions to the general rule?

REMEMBER:
> Object pronouns stand before the verb except with
> (1) affirmative commands, (2) infinitives

EJERCICIO XII. *Replace the italicized words with pronouns:*

1. El tío Pepe no sabe leer *la carta*. 2. María quiere leer *la carta*.
3. Voy a comprar *los dulces*. 4. El vendedor va a vender *los dulces*.
5. El niño quiere leer *el libro*. 6. Carlos no ha estudiado *la lección*.
7. Tiene que estudiar *la lección*. 8. Escriba Vd. *la carta*. 9. Aprendemos a hablar bien *el español*. 10. Los alumnos empiezan a cantar *la canción*.

52. Present tense of Hacer

hacer, *to do, to make*

hago	hacemos
haces	hacéis
hace	hacen

POLITE COMMANDS

haga Vd.	hagan Vds.

EJERCICIO XIII. *Give the correct forms of* **hacer:**

1. Yo lo —— bien. 2. No quiere —— lo. 3. ¡—— lo Vd. otra vez! 4. Ella no lo ——. 5. No ha querido —— lo. 6. Nosotros lo —— con mucho gusto. 7. ¿Qué —— los niños? 8. María lo —— felizmente.

EJERCICIO XIV. *Answer in Spanish.* You cannot answer with the verb used in the question. *Example:* What is he doing? He is working.

1. ¿Qué hace Vd. en la escuela?   2. ¿Qué hacen los alumnos aplicados?   3. ¿Qué hacen los pájaros?   4. ¿Qué hace un escribiente público?   5. ¿Qué hace una criada?   6. ¿Qué van Vds. a hacer después de esta clase?   7. ¿Qué hace una banda?   8. ¿Qué hace Vd. antes de ir a la escuela?   9. ¿Qué hace Vd. ahora?   10. ¿Qué hace la gente en el mercado?

PREGUNTITAS

I. 1. ¿Dónde vive el tío Pepe?
    2. ¿Ha ganado mucho?
    3. ¿Por qué no ha aprendido a leer?
    4. ¿Dónde está su hijo?
    5. ¿Cómo se llama el escribiente público?
    6. ¿Dónde está su mesa?
    7. ¿Qué usa para escribir?
    8. ¿Por qué está contento el tío Pepe?
    9. ¿Cómo se llama la esposa del tío Pepe?
   10. Al saber que el tío Pepe ha recibido una carta de América, ¿quiénes vienen para verla?

II. 1. ¿Tiene Vd. una máquina de escribir?
     2. ¿Sabe Vd. escribir a máquina?
     3. ¿Ha aprendido Vd. mucho en la escuela?
     4. ¿Ha aprendido Vd. a leer y a escribir?
     5. ¿Tiene Vd. una buena memoria?
     6. ¿Escribe Vd. rápidamente?   ¿correctamente?
     7. ¿Ha comido Vd. hoy?
     8. ¿Han estudiado Vds. la lección?
     9. ¿Está Vd. contento (-a) hoy?

REPASITO

I. Give the meanings for each of these forms:

1. pongo	8. ha dormido	15. soy
2. se sienta	9. ¿ve Vd.?	16. voy
3. me quedo	10. salgo	17. hago
4. ha celebrado	11. llamar	18. hemos comprado
5. da	12. llamarse	19. sé
6. ¡venga Vd.!	13. me he sentado	20. Vds. van a tener
7. duermen	14. estoy	21. ¡siéntese Vd.!

II. Give a related English word (cognate) for each of these Spanish words. The word must be similar in sound and meaning, but need not be an exact translation.

1. vender	6. escribir	11. ventana	16. pensar
2. periódico	7. vivir	12. primero	17. antiguo
3. mirar	8. edificio	13. bandera	18. dormir
4. carne	9. negocio	14. estudiar	19. año
5. pluma	10. vecino	15. valer	20. esposa

III. Use the correct form of **ser** *or* **estar:**

1. Don Pablo y doña María *are* vecinos.   2. Nosotros *are* contentos hoy.   3. Carlos *has been* in América.   4. Los libros *are* encima de la mesa.   5. *It is* las seis.   6. Juanito *is* un buen muchacho.   7. El perro *is* un animal inteligente.   8. ¿Dónde *is* el mercado?

IV. Answer in Spanish, using a pronoun in place of nouns that are direct objects. Example: ¿Tiene Vd. el lápiz?   Sí, señorita, lo tengo.

1. ¿Escribe Vd. la carta?   2. ¿Sabe Vd. los verbos?   3. ¿Ve Vd. a Juan?   ¿a los alumnos?   ¿a las muchachas?   4. ¿Tiene Vd. el dinero?   5. ¿Ha estudiado Vd. las palabras?   6. ¿Ha estudiado Vd. la lección?   7. ¿Nos ve la profesora?   8. ¿Ha dado Vd. el libro a su amigo?   9. ¿Ha comido la manzana?   10. ¿Comen los burros las manzanas?

V. Write in Spanish in the form of a letter, supplying the date and salutation.

1. I am going to write my first letter in Spanish.   2. I have to write this letter with [a] pen because I have not learned to type.   3. I am studying Spanish in school.   4. We read, write, and talk in Spanish.   5. Sometimes we play and sing in Spanish, too.   6. The teacher talks to us in Spanish.   7. If she does not talk rapidly, we understand her.   8. This week we have studied (*los*) verbs.   9. I know them because I have studied my lesson.   10. Write to me and tell me what (*lo que*) you are doing.   11. I remain, yours truly (*See Chapter 14*), Mary Rodríguez.

VI. ¿Sabe Vd. leer estos chistes?

Pregunta importante

— ¿Cómo se llama la estación (*station*) que hemos pasado?
— No sé, hijo.
— ¡Pues es lástima (*pity*), porque Juanito se ha quedado allí!

¿A cuál quiere ver?

— ¿Está en casa el señor Fernández?
— Hay dos hermanos; ¿por cuál pregunta Vd.?
— Por el que (*the one who*) tiene una hermana en Tepic.

PALABRAS PARA HOY

1 allí	there	2 generalmente	generally
1 antes de	before (*anteroom*)	1 haber	to have (auxiliary verb)
1 al año	year (*annual*)		
correctamente	correctly	la máquina	machine
cortésmente	courteously	la máquina de	
decidir	to decide	escribir	typewriter
el escribiente	scribe, letter-writer	4 la maravilla	marvel
		4 maravillosamente	marvelously
2 la esposa	wife (*spouse*)	María	Mary, Marie
1 esto	this (neuter pronoun; refers to an idea or previous statement)	2 la memoria	memory
		1 ni	nor (alone)
		1 nunca	never
		1 quedarse	to remain, to stay
2 feliz	happy (*felicity, felicitate*) (used with ser)	1 la respuesta	answer, reply
		1 el tío	uncle
		el vecino	neighbor (*vicinity*)
2 felizmente	happily		

EXPRESIONES

*al + infinitive, on *or* upon — ing
de memoria, by heart, from memory
escribir a máquina, to type

*hágame Vd. el favor de + infinitive, please
*sin embargo, nevertheless, however
varias veces, several times

El premio gordo¹

El señor don Jorge Cárdenas ve en la calle a su amigo, el señor don Alberto Rojas, después de una ausencia muy larga. Los dos señores están muy contentos de verse (each other).

DON JORGE — ¡Hola (*hello*), don Alberto! ¡Venga Vd. acá! ¿Cómo está Vd.?²

DON ALBERTO (*Al abrazar* [embracing] *a su amigo.*)³ — ¡Hombre, qué contento estoy de verle a Vd. otra vez! No
5 le he visto a Vd. desde aquella tamalada en casa de los Herrera.⁴ Y no me ha escrito⁵ ni una palabra durante su ausencia.

DON JORGE — Es que he estado muy ocupado (*busy*) con mis negocios, y no he podido escribir fácilmente. ¿Ha estado Vd.
10 bien?

DON ALBERTO — Sí, gracias. ¿Y Vd., y su señora, y los hijitos?

---

¹ *El premio gordo, the big prize.* National lotteries are customary in all Spanish-speaking countries, and tickets are sold in shops as well as everywhere on the streets. The big prize is as much as a hundred thousand dollars, and there are many smaller prizes each time.

Nowadays, big drawings are often broadcast over the radio, with musical selections at intervals during the calling of the winning numbers.

The lottery is advertised in all the papers and in street signs, so one never forgets it. Can you read these advertisements?

«La Fuente de la Fortuna Tiene Para Vd. $100,000»

«¡Hágase Rico! ¡Sacuda Vd. (*shake*) Esa Perra (*dog's*) Suerte!»

«Hacemos Hogares (*homes*) Felices» — Lotería Nacional

² Don Jorge and don Alberto, being old friends, would be more likely to address each other in the second person (¿*Cómo estás?*), but we need practice on the polite form!

³ A Spanish *abrazo* (*embrace*) is customary between men as well as between women. They rest their chins on each other's shoulders and pat each other affectionately on the back, then shake hands afterward.

⁴ *los Herrera.* We say "*the Herreras*"; but in Spanish, family names are never made plural.

⁵ *Vd.* is understood, but omitted because of the needless repetition.

One-twentieth of a lottery ticket that was not the lucky number. This piece, from the National Lottery of Mexico, would have won ten thousand *pesos* (about $2000) if the numbers had only been right!

DON JORGE — Todos están muy bien, gracias. Y Vd. está tan gordo como siempre. No ha perdido[1] ni un «kilo.»[2]

DON ALBERTO — Ni Vd. tampoco. Y sin embargo no soy tan gordo como Vd. 15

DON JORGE — No, pero yo soy más alto que Vd.

DON ALBERTO — Sí, desde niño siempre ha sido Vd. más alto que yo. Pero, ¿qué ha hecho Vd. con aquel sombrero de ala ancha (*wide-brimmed*) que llevaba (*you used to wear*)? 20

DON JORGE — Lo he dado a mi criado y he comprado éste nuevo. ¿No ha sabido Vd. la noticia (*news*)? He ganado el premio gordo en la lotería.

DON ALBERTO — ¡Verdad! ¡Felicidades (*congratulations*)! Vd. es más afortunado que yo, porque yo nunca he ganado ni 25 un centavito. Ahora va Vd. a ser más rico que Enrique Ford. Así es la vida.

DON JORGE — ¿Sabe Vd. por qué nunca ha ganado[1] el premio gordo? Pues, es que no ha comprado bastantes billetes de lotería. 30

[1] *Vd.* is understood, but omitted because of the needless repetition.

[2] *un «kilo,»* slang for *kilogramo*; a unit of weight (2¼ lb.) of the metric system, which is used in all Spanish-speaking countries. People weigh themselves by *kilos* instead of *pounds*.

DON ALBERTO — Pero no he deseado perder más dinero.

DON JORGE — Exactamente. Pues, yo, al contrario, siempre he tenido la costumbre de comprar el primer billete que me han ofrecido (*offered*) en la calle, y así he salido muy bien.
35 He ganado tres premios. El premio más pequeño fué (*was*) de cinco duros, y el premio más grande fué de cincuenta mil duros. Ésa fué la mejor suerte que he tenido.

DON ALBERTO — Vd. es el hombre más afortunado del mundo. Yo he salido peor, porque al gastar mi dinero en
40 billetes, lo he perdido. No pienso comprarlos más.

DON JORGE — Como Vd. quiera (*as you like*). «He dicho.»[1] Pero en cuanto a mí (*as for me*), yo voy a comprarlos. Allá va un vendedor de billetes. ¡Psst![2] ¡Hombre, venga Vd. acá!

45 VENDEDOR (*Desde lejos.*) — Allá voy, señores. (*Viene el vendedor.*) ¡Miren Vds! Estos números van a salir. Este 13931 (trece mil novecientos treinta y uno) debe ser afortunado. También tengo este número 5341 (cinco mil trescientos cuarenta y uno), que suma (*adds up to*) trece.[3]

50 DON JORGE — Bueno, favor de darme un cachito (*piece*)[4] de cada número. (*Da el dinero al vendedor.*)

VENDEDOR — Buena suerte, señor.

DON JORGE — Gracias. (*A don Alberto, con una sonrisa.*) ¿No quiere Vd. hacerse rico?

55 DON ALBERTO — Yo voy a hacerme rico sin comprar billetes de lotería.

DON JORGE — Pues, tengo que ir a la oficina. Adiós, amigo. Hasta la vista.

[1] *He dicho,* in this case, *I have spoken*; or in other words, *I've said my piece.* Instead of saying "Thank you" to the audience at the end of a speech, a Spanish orator says *He dicho,* and sits down.

[2] *¡Psst!* This is the informal Spanish way to attract the attention of a friend or a servant.

[3] Numbers that read the same backward as forward are often considered lucky in buying lottery tickets, as well as those whose digits total 13 or 21. Everyone has his own pet method of selecting the number that he is sure will win.

[4] *un cachito,* slang for one tenth or one twentieth of a lottery ticket; each number being divided into ten or twenty parts which may be sold together or singly. Of course, a person holding one twentieth of the winning number gets only one twentieth of the prize.

DON ALBERTO — Adiós, don Jorge.

(*Se va don Jorge por la derecha, mientras el vendedor se va por la izquierda.*) 60

DON ALBERTO (*Al pensar en el premio gordo que ha ganado su amigo.*) — ¡Psst! (*Al vendedor.*) ¡Hombre! ¡Véndame Vd. esos billetes!

Telón (*curtain*)

Find These Expressions in the Story

1. how glad I am to see you again!
2. at the Herrera's
3. I am taller than you
4. You are as fat as ever (always)
5. I have not been able to write easily
6. I have never won even a penny
7. Neither have you.
8. Good luck
9. Upon thinking about the big prize
10. Haven't you heard the news?
11. you are going to be richer than
12. There goes a vendor
13. The smallest prize
14. Come here, man!
15. the luckiest man in the world
16. I am coming (there)

COSAS DE INTERÉS

53. Irregular Past Participles

Here are some useful verbs with their irregular past participles. Notice that they all end in *-to* or *-cho*.

abrir	to open	abierto	opened (open)
decir	to say or tell	dicho	said or told
escribir	to write	escrito	written
hacer	to make or do	hecho	made or done
morir	to die	muerto	died (dead)
poner	to put or place	puesto	put or placed
ver	to see	visto	seen
volver	to return	vuelto	returned

EJERCICIO I. *Use the past participles given above with the "helping verb" to form these expressions:*

1. I have spoken (*said*)
2. we have seen
3. they have put
4. he has died

5. you have seen
6. she has returned
7. I have made or done
8. we have written

54. Comparison of Adjectives

There are two ways to compare adjectives in English:

POSITIVE	COMPARATIVE	SUPERLATIVE
1. new	newer	newest
2. important	more important	most important

The second method is used with longer adjectives. It is the one used to compare almost all adjectives in Spanish.

nuevo	más nuevo	el más nuevo
importante	más importante	el más importante

These adjectives follow and agree with their nouns as usual, and, of course, the article precedes the noun in the superlative form:

el libro más nuevo, *the newest book*
la niña más bonita, *the prettiest girl*

Sometimes the possessive adjective takes the place of the definite article in the superlative, since, of course, both cannot be used:

mi libro más nuevo, *my newest book*

EJERCICIO II. *Say in Spanish:*

1. the most industrious pupil
2. the sweetest fruit
3. my "nicest" friend

4. her newest hat
5. the most beautiful houses
6. the tallest boys

After a superlative, use *de* instead of *en* for *in:*

la niña más bonita *de* la escuela
the prettiest girl in *the school*

In comparison, *than* is usually expressed by *que:*

Vd. es más alto que yo, *you are taller than I*

Comparison of equality is expressed by *tan* . $^{(adj.)}$. *como:*

Vd. es tan alto como yo, *you are as tall as I*

Two common adjectives are compared irregularly in Spanish as well as in English:

bueno, *good*   **mejor,** *better*   **el mejor,** *best* [1]
malo, *bad*   **peor,** *worse*   **el peor,** *worst*

Two common adjectives, *grande* and *pequeño,* may be compared either regularly or irregularly, but with a difference in meaning:

Regular (*referring to size*):

grande, más grande, el más grande
pequeño, más pequeño, el más pequeño

Irregular (*referring to age*):

grande, mayor (*older*), **el mayor** (*oldest*)
pequeño, menor (*younger*), **el menor,** (*youngest*)

EJERCICIO III. *Compare these adjectives in Spanish and English.* (Watch the gender and number!)

bonito, blanca, contentos, agradables

EJERCICIO IV. *Complete these sentences in Spanish:*

1. Yo no soy *as* gordo *as* Vd. 2. Vd. es *larger than* yo, pero yo soy *older than* Vd. 3. Lupita es la niña *happiest in* la clase. 4. Mi tío *richest* vive en la ciudad. 5. Nosotros no somos *richer than* Enrique Ford. 6. Los alumnos *best* se levantan para dar la lección. 7. Don Alberto tiene la *worst* suerte. 8. Hemos comprado *the newest book in* la tienda.

55. Direct Object Pronoun "You"

no le he visto a Vd., *I have not seen you.*

The third person direct object pronouns *le,* him; *los,* them; *la,* her; *las,* them; are also used to mean *you* (*polite*), usually with the addition of *a Vd.* after the verb for clearness and politeness.

---

[1] These adjectives are irregular in English, too; for we cannot say *good, gooder, goodest.* *Mejor* and *peor* often precede their nouns.

EJERCICIO V. *Say:*

1. I see you, John.
2. I see you, Dolores.

3. We see you, gentlemen.
4. We see you, ladies.

The "personal *a*" is not used in these sentences, for the *a* with *Vd.* is merely part of the prepositional phrase *a Vd.*

56. Inverted Word Order

We are accustomed to putting the subject after the verb in a question:

¿Ha escrito Vd. la carta?
Have you written the letter?

We also often find the subject after the verb when there is no question, particularly after an adverb or adverbial phrase:

Siempre ha sido Vd. más alto que yo.
You have always been taller than I.

57. Aquí, acá; allí, allá

¡Venga Vd. acá!, *Come here!*
Allá va un vendedor, *there goes a vendor.*

Aquí and *acá* both mean *here,* but *acá* must be used with a verb of motion (*go, come*).

In the same way, *allá, there,* must be used instead of *allí* with a verb of motion.

58. Difference between Venir and Ir

Ir means *to go* and *venir* means *to come;* but we often find *go* used in Spanish where *come* sounds better to us. The reason is that *venir* should be used only when it means *to come toward the speaker.* We cannot say in Spanish, "Are you coming to the party tomorrow?" because we aren't at the party now.

When a Spanish servant answers a call, he doesn't say, "I am coming," for he is not moving *toward himself*; instead, he must say — *Allá voy, "I am going there."*

PREGUNTITAS

I. 1. ¿Ha visto don Alberto a su amigo desde la tamalada?
    2. ¿Por qué no ha escrito don Jorge muchas cartas?
    3. ¿Es don Alberto más gordo que don Jorge?
    4. ¿Cuál de los dos es más alto?
    5. ¿Por qué no ha ganado don Alberto el premio gordo?
    6. ¿Qué contesta el vendedor cuando don Jorge le llama?
    7. ¿Cómo va don Alberto a hacerse rico?
    8. ¿Qué números deben ser afortunados?
    9. ¿Qué billete ha comprado don Jorge siempre?
   10. Al fin, ¿qué hace don Alberto?

II. 1. ¿Es Vd. más gordo que sus amigos?
    2. ¿Quiere Vd. ser más rico que Enrique Ford?
    3. ¿Ha perdido Vd. mucho dinero en la calle?
    4. ¿Ha estado Vd. bien durante la semana?
    5. ¿Qué contesta Vd. cuando alguien le llama?
    6. ¿Quiere Vd. gastar su dinero en billetes de lotería?
    7. ¿Quién es el alumno más inteligente de la clase?
    8. ¿Quién ha vuelto a la escuela después de una ausencia muy larga?
    9. ¿Ha abierto Vd. una carta de su padre?

REPASITO

I. Supply the proper prepositions, if any:

1. Salimos —— la casa a las nueve —— la noche. 2. Los señores miran —— las señoritas en la plaza. 3. Las señoritas miran —— la fuente en la plaza. 4. Vienen —— comprar ropa nueva. 5. Pablito quiere —— dar un regalito a Carmen. 6. La gente aprende —— cantar aquella canción. 7. Pedro no desea entrar —— la clase todavía.

II. Complete these sentences in Spanish. (Watch the verb forms.)

1. Paco sale de la casa al *seeing me.* 2. Después de *winning* el premio, voy a la ciudad. 3. Pablo *has lost* el dinero y tiene que trabajar más. 4. Varias veces *I have* perdido este sombrero. 5. Alberto no puede aprender sin *studying.* 6. Luis nunca come antes de *going* a la escuela.

III. Make all the changes that are necessary in these sentences to make them true.

1. El tío Pepe siempre ha ido a la escuela.
2. Los mexicanos toman café con crema (*cream*).
3. Hay puestos en la calle lejos del mercado.
4. No es costumbre pagar el tercer precio en el mercado.
5. Es costumbre dar premios a los amigos en su santo.
6. Una escopeta es un buen regalo para una niñita.
7. En España una casa generalmente tiene una plaza en el centro.
8. En algunos pueblecitos los ricos[1] tienen que llevar agua a sus casas.
9. Los lunes generalmente hay música en la plaza de cada pueblecito.
10. Los norteamericanos son más corteses que los españoles.

IV. Give the opposites of these words in Spanish:

1. más	6. encima de	11. aquí	16. adiós
2. mejor	7. alguno	12. gastar	17. ganar
3. delante de	8. malo	13. algo	18. antiguo
4. cerca de	9. abierto	14. algunas veces	19. muere
5. voy	10. vuelto	15. entrar en	20. compramos

V. Choose a cast to put on the play El premio gordo *for the class.*

VI. Write in Spanish:

1. Come here, Louise. I see you. 2. Where is your friend? I haven't seen him today. 3. He is the tallest boy in our class, but he is not as tall as Arthur. 4. Have you written the lesson for today? Yes, I have written it. 5. What are you going to do after school? 6. I have to go home. My mother is not at home and I have to work. 7. Have you bought a ticket for the dance (*el baile*)? 8. Yes, I have bought it, but I don't want to go. I prefer to study. 9. The idea! Who wants to study when there is a dance? 10. Well, I have to go. Until I see you again.

[1] Adjectives are often used without their nouns: *the rich, the poor.* (Section 114.)

VII. ¿Sabe Vd. leer estos chistes?

Es hora de irse

— ¡Señor!   ¡Vd. se ha sentado encima de mi sombrero nuevo!
— ¿Ya tiene Vd. que irse?

Un alumno moderno

La profesora — Todos han escrito ocho o diez páginas (*pages*) sobre (*about*) la leche, y Vd. ha escrito solamente (*only*) cuatro renglones (*lines*).

El alumno — Es que yo he escrito sobre la leche condensada.

VIII. Dos refranes (proverbs)

Perder con gloria no es perder.

Libros y amigos, pocos (*few*) y buenos.

PALABRAS PARA HOY

2	abierto	open, opened	Jorge	George
1	acá	here (with verb of motion)	el kilogramo	kilogram
			la lotería	lottery
	afortunado, -a	lucky, fortunate	1 el mayor	oldest
	Alberto	Albert	1 mejor	better (adj. or adv.)
1	allá	there (with verb of motion)	el menor	youngest (*minor*)
4	la ausencia	absence	1 mil	thousand
	el billete	ticket	1 muerto	died, dead
1	cincuenta	fifty	1 el mundo	world
1	desde	since (new meaning)	1 ni	not even (new meaning)
1	dicho	said, told	1 nuevo, -a	new
2	durante	during	2 el número	number, numeral
2	el duro	dollar (Spanish)	1 peor	worse (adj. or adv.)
	Enrique	Henry	1 perder (ie)	to lose (*perdition*)
1	escrito	written	el premio	prize (*premium*)
2	ganar	to win (new meaning)	1 puesto	put, placed
4	gastar	to spend (money)	1 saber	to find out (new meaning)
	gordo, -a	fat; big (prize)	el sombrero	hat
1	hacerse	to become, "get"	2 la suerte	luck
1	hecho	done, made	1 vuelto	returned

EXPRESIONES

desde niño, since a child
*en casa de, at the home of
estar muy contento de, to be very
  happy to
*favor de + infinitive, please (short-
  ened form of Hágame Vd. el
  favor de)
hasta la vista, until I see you again,
  good-by

más —— que, more —— than, *-er*
  added to English adjective
*ni Vd. tampoco, nor you either,
  neither have you
salir (muy) bien, to come out (very)
  well (in lottery, grades, etc.)
tan —— como, as —— as

CANCIÓN DE LAS GAVIOTAS DE NAYARIT

This West Coast song of Mexico, supposedly about seagulls, seems to be concerned mainly with love!

Arr. by E. M. JARRETT

1. Ya las gaviotas tienden su vuelo
   abren sus alas para volar;
   andan buscando nidos de amores,
   nidos de amores no encontrarán.

Now the seagulls begin their flight,
They open their wings to fly;
They are looking for love nests,
(But) love nests they will not find.

2. Dime, negra, ¿por qué no me amas?
   ¡Tú eres mi vida, mi bienestar!
   Dame un abrazo, dame un besito,
   vente conmigo, vamos al mar.

Tell me, darling, why don't you love me?
You are my life, my well-being!
Give me a hug, give me a little kiss,
Come with me down to the sea.

3. ¡Cómo brilla tu pelo negro,
   como las olas al reventar!
   Miles de conchas tiene la arena,
   miles de perlas tiene la mar.

How your black hair shines,
Like the waves as they break!
Thousands of seashells has the sand,
Thousands of pearls has the sea.

4. ¡Cuán bonito es tener amores
   en esta tierra que Dios formó!
   Dame un besito con tu boquita
   para vivir más contento yo.

How wonderful to be in love
In this land which God made!
Give me a kiss with your little mouth
So I may live more happily.

Spain Comes to America · I

In Tenochtitlán, the Aztec capital, stood a pyramid as high as an eighteen-story building and covering thirteen acres. The Spaniards destroyed it, but this one, even higher, still stands.

Galloway

I. México *1521 Cortez*

GOLD! Treasure! Adventure!

In the plazas of Sevilla in the early sixteenth century there was talk of little else.

"That Hernán Cortés sent back two shiploads of treasure from his Mexico last week!"

"And did you hear how Francisco Pizarro had a great room filled with gold as high as he could reach in that strange Perú he just conquered?"

"¡*Pues sí!* And they say the Indians he found there used sheets of silver and gold to cover their temple walls inside and outside, too!"

"The Torre del Oro [1] is running over with gold, and more ships are arriving every month!"

Gold! Treasure! Adventure!

Columbus, financed by Ferdinand and Isabella the same year they drove the Moors from Spain, had indeed solved the mystery of the great ocean and thrown open a glorious new world. Every young man with the money to pay his passage or a way to earn it shipped for that fascinating country. Every nobleman with a drop of adventure in his veins took his family and moved to one of the great land grants given him by a king who had never seen them. Every returning sailor had tales to tell of strange people, of tropical fruits and flowers, of fabulous wealth in the west.

Mexico, conquered in 1521 by Spanish Cortés "for gold and God," blossomed with boom towns that sprang up overnight wherever there was ore to mine. One gold rush followed another, and occasionally a young fellow who had left Spain with nothing suddenly became a millionaire, just as three hundred years later, a California prospector sometimes "struck it rich."

Little hillside Guanajuato alone sent King Philip II so much bullion that in 1557 he gratefully sent over Spain's oldest madonna, a little wooden image of the Virgin Mary that, hidden in a damp cave near Granada for over eight hundred years, had miraculously survived the whole Moorish occupation.

Spain had not been the first to travel the seas in search of gold, glory, or new trade routes. Portugal, next door, had begun some

---

[1] The old Moorish tower on the bank of the Guadalquivir River in Sevilla became the customs house which received the gold brought by the "Silver Fleet" from the New World.

years before under her Prince Henry the Navigator, who was probably the first person ever to carry on exploration in a systematic manner.

Then Portuguese Magellan, disappointed in the meager reward given him by his own country, offered to sail under the Spanish flag of Charles I. With his hardy Basque pilot, Sebastián del Cano, he started the voyage that brought the first ship around the world, to limp into Cádiz in 1522, although Magellan himself had not lived to tell the tale.

About the same time, Ponce de León, who wanted never to grow old, found his Florida; Balboa discovered his Pacific Ocean on the other side of the narrow Isthmus of Panama; Cortés reached his Mexico, and Pizarro, imitating him, conquered the Incas of Perú. Spain was definitely on the map, and gold poured into her treasury. To twenty countries she gave her language and customs, and at one time collected taxes from all of them. That, indeed, was Spain's Golden Age in more ways than one, for at home her art and literature flourished, her industries rivaled her foreign commerce, and she became for a time the most powerful nation on earth.

Mexico, when independent young Cortés first reached there, was not a place of wandering Indians living in wigwams like our own American

Genuine relics of Aztec days are still found in Mexico. The little portrait heads and the ancient clay jug were plowed up in a cornfield; the Aztec calendar bowl and idols are tourist trophies.

Charles D. Jarrett

"Los reyes católicos" always refers to Ferdinand and Isabella, although all the rulers of Spain were Catholic. Here they are painted upon a three-foot plate from the famous Talavera factory in Spain.

redskins. Instead, the blond conqueror found an astounding civilization. The Aztecs had built Tenochtitlán, their capital city, in a shallow lake in obedience to a sign their tribe had long sought.[1] There Cortés found neat stone or adobe houses facing on stone-lined canals where gay canoes and barges floated. The roofs were flat, with flowers growing upon them; corn and carnations, beans and pansies grew intermingled on floating gardens made of pine logs from the mountains.

The nobles wore over their robes full-length capes of cotton cloth covered with the tiny iridescent blue-green feathers of hummingbirds' breasts. Their jeweled gold bracelets, anklets, and necklaces made Spanish eyes glitter, for here was the booty they coveted.

Moctezuma, the Aztec emperor, had fresh fish brought every day from the sea three hundred miles away. Wrapped in great green leaves, it had been passed from one swift Indian runner to another like the baton in a modern relay. Moctezuma could receive news of his well-trained army in any part of his empire by these same mes-

---

[1] The Mexican flag, with its emblem of an eagle, cactus, and rattlesnake, tells the legend of the Aztecs' long search.

sengers, who brought him great sheets of colored sketches in fanlike folds that told him the details of any event as clearly as our Sunday comics tell a story.

Luxurious palaces and treasure-filled temples with huge stone idols adorned the city, and there were even zoos, and an aviary. The great central market, where small silver disks and quills of gold dust served for money, furnished a meeting place where everyone might exchange his handicrafts or garden produce. Each vendor had a little *puesto* with his fruits or vegetables neatly stacked in symmetrical little piles, as the Indians still like to see them.

Into this lake city with its four great causeways rode haughty Cortés, unhindered by the wondering Aztecs who stood by without raising a hand against him. How did this happen? Three lucky circumstances made it possible for Cortés, with six hundred men and a few horses — animals never before seen in America — to conquer these brave, intelligent, and well-armed people. In the first place, strangely enough, Cortés was helped by a girl, an Aztec maid called Malinche in her own language and Marina in Spanish. She had been sold as a slave to the Mayan Indians of Yucatán, where she had learned the Mayan language. At the same time, two Spaniards ship-wrecked on the coast of Yucatán had learned Mayan, so between them and pretty Marina, Cortés was able to talk to the Aztecs. Of course Marina promptly fell in love with the handsome *conquistador*, and it was she who gave him much information that helped him in his campaign.

The second piece of luck which fell to the Spaniard, although it was engineered by his own cleverness, was that he was able to ally himself with the Aztecs' old enemies, the Tlaxcalans, who were delighted to help even such peculiar strangers conquer their hated neighbors.

The third circumstance, and the explanation for the unexpected welcome, was due to pure luck and superstition; and without it, Cortés probably never could have succeeded. Ages before, according to the tribal legends of the Aztecs, there had ruled among their short, dark people a tall, fair god with blond beard and blue eyes, called Quetzal-cóatl. It is possible that he had been a venturesome shipwrecked Viking, worshiped by the superstitious Indians just because he was so different from them; but at any rate, he had been their leader and teacher for many years. At last, however, the jealousy of the high priests had caused him to leave; but as he went, he had told his people solemnly that some day he would return.

The Temple of Quetzalcóatl, a pre-Aztec pyramid near Mexico City, is decorated with carved stone rattlesnakes, because the Fair God's name means "Feathered Serpent."

You can guess the feelings of Moctezuma when his messengers brought him pictures of these strangers descending upon him, for among them were tall, fair men with blond beards! Was one of these Quetzalcóatl? Or were they all his descendants? In either case, to try to fight them would be hopeless. So poor, puzzled, superstitious Moctezuma rode forth bearing gifts to welcome them as they approached his city, when a word from him before they had even left Vera Cruz could have annihilated the entire six hundred.

The story of Cortés' conquest of Mexico is a bloody one, as the tale of any conquest must be, with cruelty, treachery, and greed running through it. There was that terrible massacre of dancing, unarmed Aztecs as they celebrated a May festival. There was the capture of poor broken-hearted Moctezuma and his tragic death when one of his own subjects stoned him as he stood upon Cortés' palace wall trying to calm the infuriated Indians. There was the "Sad Night" when the Spaniards fled from the lake city along a causeway with their portable bridge which failed to work, followed by howling Aztecs who captured alive every man they could catch for their temple sacrifices. The fleeing Spaniards were so burdened with treasure that soldier after soldier sank as he tried to swim the canals, until dead bodies formed a bridge over which the rest could cross. The *ahuehuete* tree where Cortés sat down and wept for his comrades after that battle four hundred years ago still stands in Mexico City, with street cars clanging past it now and tourists coming to stare.

Finally there came the inevitable end of the Aztec empire, and with it the Spanish torture of brave Cuauhtémoc, Moctezuma's successor, who refused to tell where all the Aztec treasure had been hidden, even when his feet were rubbed with oil and roasted over glowing coals.

After the conquest was all over and colonization began, Tenochtitlán became Mexico City, and Spaniards intermarried with Indians, forming what we now call the Mexican people. Then it was that Cortés built the first city hall in North America, as well as hundreds of churches and cathedrals to substitute the Christian religion for idol worship and human sacrifices. There a university was founded over eighty years before our Harvard, and from Spain's new colony a stream of gold poured into her treasury.

At this point the story flows over into the history of our own country, for from the Mexican capital went out more explorers who gave Spanish names to what is now all our southwest, and from there the kindly *padres* set forth on foot along *el camino real* to found the California missions and to educate the North American Indians.

Thus you see how it happens that, behind the present-day Spanish atmosphere of our own southwestern states, lie the sixteenth-century

Temple sacrifices are thought to have been made on this huge stone, now in the National Museum in Mexico City. Aztecs always fought to bring their enemies back alive, to use in their rites.

Keystone

Galloway

Under this ahuehuete tree Cortés sat down and wept for his lost comrades four hundred years ago. It still stands in Mexico City, with traffic flowing around it.

quest for gold and its companion spirit of adventure. They had brought Spain to America, and Spain had come to stay.

Interesting Books to Read

Aztecs: RICHARDS *and* LANDÁZURI: CHILDREN OF MEXICO (all). EMBREE, EDWIN: INDIANS OF THE AMERICAS, p. 13, pp. 53–84. SPINDEN, HERBERT: ANCIENT CIVILIZATIONS OF MEXICO, ch. IV.

Mayas: MAGOFFIN *and* DAVIS: THE ROMANCE OF ARCHEOLOGY, ch. XII. CHASE, STUART: MEXICO, ch. III, pp. 26–36. MORRIS, ANN AXTELL: DIGGING IN YUCATÁN (all).

Tenochtitlán: SPINDEN, pp. 207–19. RICHARDS *and* LANDÁZURI, chs. II to V. SPENCE, LEWIS: MYTHS AND LEGENDS, MEXICO, PERU, pp. 29–31.

Moctezuma: RICHARDS *and* LANDÁZURI, p. 70. BIART, LUCIEN: THE AZTECS: HISTORY, MANNERS, CUSTOMS, ch. V.

The Conquest: RICHMAN, IRVING: THE SPANISH CONQUERORS, ch. IV. CHASE, ch. IV. RICHARDS *and* LANDÁZURI, chs. VII, VIII, IX. SPINDEN, pp. 22–30. PECK, ANNE M., *and* MÉRAS, E. A.: SPAIN IN EUROPE AND AMERICA, pp. 55–61.

Lo que lleva el español bien vestido

You will find several words in this story and hereafter which are similar to English in meaning as well as in form. When you meet such a word, guess! These words will not be given in PALABRAS PARA HOY *because you can guess them easily and should not waste time needlessly by looking up meanings. Make your head save your thumbs!*

Casi todo el mundo viste más o menos a la europea en España y en los otros países de habla española. Es verdad que hay prendas (*garments*) regionales, pero la ropa ordinariamente se parece mucho al traje europeo o norteamericano.

5   Los hombres españoles del norte (*north*) del país [1] llevan boina (*beret*) [2] en vez de sombrero. Los campesinos llevan blusa de obrero (*smock*) de color obscuro. Ésta es más larga que una camisa. Los artistas de nuestro país la usan algunas veces.

10   Casi todos los campesinos, grandes o pequeños, llevan zapatos hechos a mano. Los llaman alpargatas,[3] y generalmente son blancas o negras. Así, vestido de blusa larga sin corbata, pantalón de color obscuro, con la boina en la cabeza y las alpargatas en los pies, el campesino está listo (*ready*)

15 para su trabajo.

El traje de las españolas del norte se parece al nuestro (*ours*), aunque muchas veces usan vestido negro, o falda negra con blusa de color más claro (*light*). Las mujeres más pobres

---

[1] Some people of the north of Spain are called Basques.

[2] A beret is a small visorless cap with a little cloth tab where we'd put a button. The style is becoming popular in this country, and the French have worn navy blue ones for years.

[3] *Alpargatas* are something like canvas tennis shoes, except that the flat soles are of hemp rope. They are tied around the ankle by tapes, cost about twenty cents a pair, and are good for about three months' steady wear. Of course the aristocrats never wear *alpargatas*!

Basque farmers wear the typical beret, smock, and *alpargatas* of northern Spain. Fat, cream-colored oxen wear over the yoke a silky goatskin dyed pink or yellow.

también llevan alpargatas, con medias de algodón (*cotton*); y miran curiosamente los zapatos de tacón (*heel*) alto de las turistas. Las españolas generalmente tienen los pies y las manos más pequeños que las norteamericanas. Las mujeres de los pueblecitos también creen muy curioso el sombrero de moda que llevan las turistas, porque ellas mismas (*themselves*) casi nunca han llevado sombrero. Se ponen un velo negro para cubrir la cabeza. Lo llevan cuando salen a la calle o cuando van a misa (*mass*), porque las mujeres tienen que cubrirse la cabeza en una iglesia católica.

No es necesario describir el traje que se lleva en Madrid, porque como en cualquier capital del mundo, se sigue (*one follows*) la moda corriente (*current*) y las tiendas se parecen a las (*those*) de París.

People of Toledo put a great deal of heavy, bright-colored embroidery on their fiesta costumes, which are no longer in daily use.

Peasant fiesta costumes of the past made Spain very colorful. The embroideries, laces, and jewelry were often handed down in a family for generations.

Cuando nosotros pensamos en el traje de España, generalmente pensamos en aquella falda ancha de color vivo y de
35 muchos volantes (*ruffles*), con blusa ajustada (*tight*), mantón
de Manila (*Spanish shawl*) y mantilla de encaje.[1] Pues no
tenemos razón, porque aunque es verdad que éste es el traje
de la española, se usa solamente en Andalucía, y entonces
solamente durante las fiestas.

40 Cuando la española lleva la mantilla en vez del velo negro,
usa en el pelo una peineta (*high comb*). Desde la niña de seis
años hasta la mujer de cincuenta años o más, muchas veces
lleva también una rosa o un clavel (*carnation*) rojo sobre (*over*)
la oreja izquierda. Y desde niña, cada mujer del sur (*south*)
45 de España, donde hace mucho calor en el verano, casi siempre
lleva en la mano un abanico bonito. ¡Con qué gracia (*grace*)
lo abre y lo cierra! Pero no lo usa porque tiene calor; es que
quiere ocultar (*hide*) o mostrar (*show*) aquellos ojos negros [2]
y aquella cara bonita con la boca de carmín y los dientes como
50 perlas.

El compañero de la señorita vestida así lleva un traje tan
bonito como el de ella (*hers*). Tiene una chaqueta corta y
negra, bordada de oro (*gold*) o plata (*silver*); una corbata
grande de color vivo; pantalón ancho, bordado también; y en
55 la cabeza un sombrero cordobés.[3] Nunca lleva boina. Con
su guitarra, el andaluz (*Andalusian*) vestido así sirve perfectamente para adornar un calendario norteamericano, pero
no se ve ordinariamente en las calles de Sevilla.

Es que todo el mundo va adoptando (*is adopting*) las modas
60 de París; y pronto, todos, en cualquier parte del mundo, nos
pareceremos unos a otros (*will look like one another*).

[1] A lace *mantilla* may be white or black, the former for Sundays and *fiestas*,
the latter for daily use. Draped over one of those high, tortoise-shell combs, it
makes a pretty frame for a pretty face. Except for *fiestas*, a plain black veil without the comb takes the place of the lace *mantilla*, although a dramatic red rose behind the ear is everyday equipment in Andalusia for everyone from little sister
to grandmother.

[2] You should see a Spanish girl use her fan! In fact, in the language of love a
great deal can be said silently by a graceful fan and two sparkling Spanish eyes!

[3] A Cordovan hat is of stiff black felt, wide-brimmed and shallow-crowned; the
hat we always see used in the theater to represent Spain.

Find These Expressions in the Story

1. What the well-dressed Spaniard wears
2. they have almost never worn hats
3. they wear handmade shoes
4. the tourists' high-heeled shoes
5. as in any capital of the world
6. they put on a black veil
7. the six-year-old little girl

8. a red carnation over her left ear
9. where it is very hot in the summer
10. she almost always carries a fan in her hand
11. they have smaller hands and feet
12. the women have to cover their heads

Basque policemen of the north of Spain wear the familiar beret with their colorful uniforms. Basques are often handsome people.

Black Star

COSAS DE INTERÉS

59. *Articles of Clothing and Parts of the Body*

con la boina en la cabeza, *with his beret on his head*
las alpargatas en los pies, *his shoes on his feet*

The definite article is ordinarily used instead of the possessive adjective with articles of clothing and parts of the body.

usan vestido negro o falda negra
they wear black dresses or a black skirt

Since a person wears only one dress or one skirt at a time, Spanish-speaking people, when referring to such articles of clothing, use only the singular form of the word. In like manner they use the singular form in speaking of parts of the body: ***para cubrir la cabeza,*** *to cover their heads* (only one head apiece!).

EJERCICIO I.   *Complete in Spanish:*

1. Nos ponemos *our shoes.*   2. Nos ponemos *our hats.*   3. Las mujeres se cubren *their heads* con *black veils.*   4. Los campesinos llevan *long blouses* sin *neckties.*   5. Algunas españolas llevan una rosa sobre *their left ears.*   6. Las señoritas tienen los *teeth* como perlas, pero no llevan *hats.*   7. Los hombres españoles llevan *berets* en *their heads.*   8. Casi todo el mundo lleva alpargatas en *their feet.*

60. *More About Adjectives*

los pies y las manos más pequeños
smaller hands and feet

When one adjective modifies (*describes*) two or more nouns, it must be plural in form even if each noun itself is singular. (One and one are two!) If any one of the nouns is masculine, the adjective must be masculine plural; but if they are all feminine, it must be feminine plural.

una chaqueta corta y negra, *a short, black jacket*

When two adjectives describe the same noun, they usually follow it and are connected by **y.**

EJERCICIO II.   *Use the adjectives in these phrases to describe the nouns following them.   Be sure to put the adjectives in their proper places.*

1. (*grande, negro*) los perros   2. (*blanco*) el sombrero y la boina
3. (*obscuro*) la blusa y la corbata   4. (*rojo*) la rosa y el clavel   5.
(*gordo, alto*) una mujer   6. (*bonito*) las señoras y las señoritas   7.
(*nuevo, hermoso*) los abanicos

61. Past Participles Used as Adjectives

zapatos hechos a mano, *hand-made shoes.*

Hecho is a past participle, but like any other participle, it may be used as an adjective when it is not used with a helping verb.   *Vestido* is often used in this way, and has also become a noun, meaning *dress* or *suit.*

EJERCICIO III.   *Change the infinitive to the proper form of the past participle:*

1. una señorita *vestir* así   2. una mantilla *llevar* en la cabeza
3. un abanico *usar* para ocultar la cara   4. un calendario *adornar*
con (*by*) un andaluz (*Andalusian*)   5. la cabeza *cubrir* con un velo

62. Idioms with Tener

Tener is used to form many idioms.   Here are the ones we have already met:

tener que	to have to
tener dolor de estómago (cabeza, dientes)	to have a stomach- (head-, tooth-) ache
tener vergüenza	to be ashamed (have shame)
tener razón; no tener razón	to be right (have reason); to be wrong
tener —— años	to be —— years old
tener los pies pequeños	to have small feet (used with any part of the body)
tener cuidado	to be careful
tener calor	to be warm (living beings only; for weather use **hace calor**)

tener la bondad de   please (to have the kindness to)

tener hambre; sed   to be hungry; thirsty

EJERCICIO IV. *Supply suitable words with each form of* **tener**:

1. El alumno tiene —— de —— porque ha estudiado demasiado. 2. Las españolas tienen las —— más pequeñas que las norteamericanas. 3. ¿Cuántos —— tiene Pepe? Tiene quince ——. 4. Usamos los abanicos cuando tenemos ——. 5. Si creemos que la mantilla nunca se usa en Andalucía, no tenemos ——. 6. El niño que no sabe la lección debe tener ——.

PREGUNTITAS

I. 1. ¿Qué lleva en la cabeza el hombre del norte de España?
2. ¿Qué lleva el campesino en los pies?
3. ¿Lleva sombrero la española generalmente?
4. ¿Qué llevan las turistas en la cabeza?
5. ¿Por qué llevan velo las españolas cuando van a misa?
6. ¿Por qué no es necesario describir el traje de Madrid?
7. ¿Usan las señoritas el abanico porque tienen calor?
8. ¿Cuándo es costumbre llevar la mantilla?
9. ¿Lleva boina el andaluz vestido para una fiesta?

II. 1. ¿Sabe Vd. usar un abanico como una española?
2. ¿Ha llevado Vd. una rosa roja sobre la oreja izquierda?
3. ¿Ha visto Vd. una boina alguna vez (*ever*)?
4. ¿Lleva Vd. zapatos blancos cuando hace calor?
5. ¿Cuándo tiene Vd. más calor, en el verano o en el invierno?
6. ¿Viste Vd. trajes de moda?
7. ¿Cuántos años tiene Vd.?
8. ¿Hace mucho calor hoy?
9. ¿Tiene Vd. razón siempre?

REPASITO

I. Draw a picture of a person and label in Spanish all the parts of the body and articles of clothing that you know.

II. Conjugate each of these verbs in both the present and present perfect tenses:

ser, ver, decir (i), morir (ue), vestirse (i), ponerse, hacer

III. Write in Spanish:

1. We have to put on our jackets and our hats. 2. You are right. Where have I put my hat? 3. I don't know. I haven't seen it. 4. Your hat is very pretty. 5. Thank you, but your hat is prettier. 6. Well, let's go. Be careful. Give me your hand. 7. Although I am smaller than you, you have smaller feet than I. 8. I have big feet. I am ashamed. 9. Do Spanish women have small hands and feet? 10. Do they wear shoes or *alpargatas*? 11. They wear shoes. The country people wear *alpargatas*.

IV. ¿Sabe Vd. leer estos chistes?

Patatas[1] gratis

— ¿Cuánto vale un biftec (*beefsteak*)?
— Cincuenta centavos.
— ¿Y las patatas fritas (*fried*)?
— Ésas son gratis.
— Pues entonces déme Vd. solamente las patatas.

Es verdad

— Papacito, ¿es verdad que el calor dilata (*expands*) las cosas?
— Sí, hijo. En el verano, cuando hace calor, los días son más largos que en el invierno, cuando hace frío (*cold*).

Es fácil saber

— ¿Cómo sabe Vd. la edad (*age*) de las aves (*fowls*)?
— Por los dientes.
— Pero las aves no tienen dientes.
— Pero los tengo yo.

V. What have you learned about Spanish dress?

1. In what part of Spain do the men wear berets?
2. What do Spanish women in small towns wear on their heads?
3. What kind of clothes would you expect to see in Madrid and Barcelona?
4. What are *alpargatas*?

[1] *Patatas* in Spain; *papas* in Spanish America.

188 EL CAMINO REAL

5. What two articles of clothing worn by tourists seem curious to people in small Spanish towns? Why?
6. Where is the so-called "typical" (calendar-type) Spanish costume seen? When is it worn?
7. What adornment do Spanish women like, young or old?
8. Where is the fan much used? For what unusual purpose is it used?
9. How is the veil worn on festive occasions?
10. What is a *mantilla*? When is the white *mantilla* worn?
11. How does an Andalusian man dress on fiesta days?
12. How does his northern brother dress for work in the fields?

PALABRAS PARA HOY

el abanico	fan	3 la fiesta	festival, holiday
3 ancho, -a	wide	1 llevar	to wear (new meaning)
1 aunque	although		
bordado	embroidered	la moda	style, mode
el campesino	farmer, country person	1 la mujer	woman
		2 obscuro, -a	dark (*obscure*)
2 casi	almost	1 parecerse a	to resemble
3 corto, -a	short	1 ponerse	to put on
2 cubrir	to cover	1 solamente	only
2 cubierto	covered (past part. of cubrir)	2 vestir (i)	to dress (trans. or intrans.)
2 el cuerpo	body	2 vestirse (i)	to dress, get dressed
4 describir	to describe	2 vestirse de	to dress in
1 la española	Spanish woman	2 vivo, -a	bright (*vivid*)
europeo, -a	European		

EL CUERPO

2 la boca	mouth
2 la cabeza	head
el dedo	finger
3 el diente	tooth (*dentist*)
la frente	forehead
1 la mano	hand (*manual*)
1 el ojo	eye
4 la oreja	ear
3 el pelo	hair
2 el pie	foot
la pierna	leg

LA ROPA

la blusa	blouse, shirt
la camisa	shirt
la corbata	necktie (*cravat*)
la chaqueta	jacket
4 la falda	skirt
la media	stocking
el pantalón	trousers (*pantaloons*)
3 el traje	suit or dress
el velo	veil
3 el vestido	suit or dress
el zapato	shoe

EXPRESIONES

a la europea, European style
de moda, stylish
en vez de, instead of
hacer (mucho) calor, to be (very) hot (weather only)
hecho a mano, handmade
se parece mucho a, resembles very much
se lleva, is worn
se usa, is used

*tener —— años, to be —— years old
*tener calor, to be hot (living beings only)
*tener razón, to be right; no tener razón, to be wrong
se ve, is seen
tener hambre, to be hungry
tener sed, to be thirsty
tener la bondad de, please (to have the kindness to)

CAPÍTULO 18

¿Cuánto sabe usted?

Read the story and answer the questions in English to see if you understand it. Remember that you are to guess new words that look like the English.

UN CUENTO (*story*) DE LA LOTERÍA [1]

Muchas personas se han hecho ricas con un billete de lotería, y otras muchas han perdido dinero. Pero en los periódicos todo el mundo ha leído solamente los cuentos de los premios gordos, y así todavía quiere jugar a la lotería. Así es que hay muchas supersticiones en cuanto a (*concerning*) la lotería, 5 y casi todo el mundo cree que él tiene la manera más afortunada de comprar un número. Muchas personas siempre compran el mismo (*same*) número, creyendo (*believing*) que algún día tiene que salir.

[1] This story of Mexico is supposed to be true!

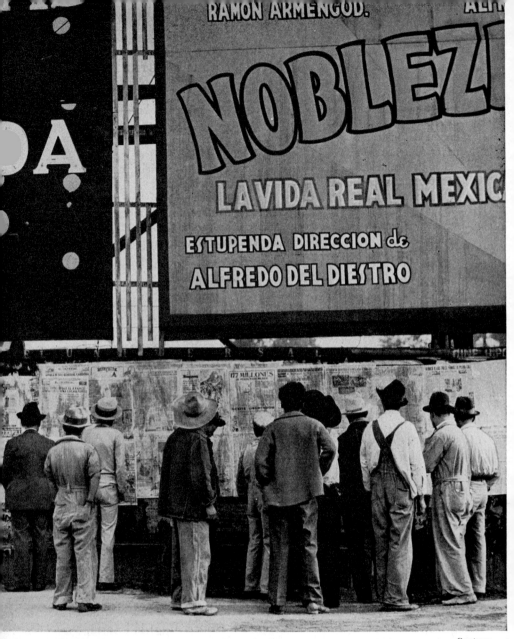

Newspapers are posted in one of the plazas of Mexico City. Lists of winning lottery numbers are also put up so that people may find out quickly how lucky they have been.

Aquí tiene Vd. un buen cuento de una viejecita (*a little old lady*) y su billete. Se dice que es verdad, y a lo menos todo el mundo lo cree. 10

Esta viejecita vive en un pueblo de México, y cada semana ha comprado el mismo número, el 4567. Un día va al centro ("*downtown*") a buscar (*look for*) su número en la lista de premios para saber si ha ganado algo. Hay mucha gente cerca de la lista, y ella no puede verla. 15

Cerca de la viejecita está un forastero (*stranger*) más alto que ella, que ha visto el billete que ella lleva en la mano, y él le dice cortésmente — Señora, si quiere Vd. darme su billete, yo puedo ir a ver si ha ganado algo. 20

La viejecita le da el billete, y en un momentito vuelve el forastero, lo devuelve (*returns*) y dice — ¡Qué lástima! Señora, Vd. no ha ganado nada.

La viejecita vuelve a casa, pero al (*on*) otro día, mientras está otra vez en el centro, mira por casualidad (*by chance*) la lista de premios. ¡Cuánto se sorprende (*surprised she is*) al ver que su número, el 4567, ha ganado el segundo (*second*) premio! Pero al mirar su billete, ve que el mal forastero le (*to her*) ha dado otro en vez del suyo (*hers*), ¡y que él, sin duda (*doubt*), se ha ido (*gone away*) con el segundo premio! 25 30

La pobre viejecita está muy triste (*sad*), pero entonces mira el billete substituido por el forastero, y cuánto se sorprende al ver que este número, que el mal forastero le ha dado a ella, ha ganado el primer premio! 35

¡El mal forastero ha estado tan ansioso (*anxious*) de engañar (*trick*) a la pobre viejecita, que él no ha pensado en mirar su propio (*own*) número en la lista!

Be able to show what part of the story proves your answer:

1. How do many people choose the lottery ticket number they buy? 2. Did the little old lady always buy the same number? 3. Why did she give her ticket to the tall stranger? 4. What did he say she had won? 5. Did he return a ticket to her? 6. What did she discover on the prize list the next day? 7. Where was her original ticket?

8. What ticket did she have? 9. Who won more on the drawing, the little old lady or the tall, wicked stranger? 10. Why hadn't he looked at his own number on the list?

REPASO DE VOCABULARIO

EJERCICIO I. *¿Verdad o mentira?* *See how rapidly you can read these sentences and give the correct answers. Whenever you answer* **mentira,** *change the sentence to make it true.*

1. Los hombres están en casa siempre.
2. Un buen alumno no estudia su lección.
3. Algunos niñitos no se ponen los zapatos en el verano.
4. El perro es más inteligente que el burro.
5. Los perros no aprenden tan fácilmente como los niños.
6. No es posible perder con un billete de lotería.
7. No es posible vivir sin comer.
8. Madrid es la capital de España.
9. Madrid está en México.
10. Es posible ser inteligente sin poder leer.
11. Cuando hace mucho calor nos ponemos la chaqueta.
12. No es posible tener razón siempre.
13. Para recibir muchas cartas tenemos que escribirlas también.
14. Siempre debemos decir la verdad.
15. En España los vendedores de billetes de lotería están en las calles.
16. Vamos a la iglesia los domingos.
17. Tenemos dos manos, una boca, y cuatro pies.
18. El pelo cubre la cabeza.
19. Usamos los ojos para ver.
20. Es mejor vivir que morir.
21. Los pueblecitos son más grandes que los pueblos.
22. En una ciudad hay muchos edificios y mucha gente.

EJERCICIO II. *Name in Spanish (use an article with each noun):*

1. ten articles of clothing 2. ten parts of the body 3. eight things to eat 4. ten common Spanish names (*first names*) 5. six expressions made with *tener*

EJERCICIO III. *What do these expressions mean in English?*
Give the meaning, not a word-for-word translation.

1. hace mucho calor
2. sin embargo
3. hágame Vd. el favor de
4. en vez de
5. al fin
6. algunas veces
7. varias veces
8. otra vez
9. con mucho gusto
10. muchas veces

11. de la mañana
12. favor que Vd. me hace
13. hasta la vista
14. ¡ya lo creo!
15. no es costumbre
16. de habla española
17. al contrario
18. estar muy contento de
19. — Gracias. — De nada.
20. con su permiso

EJERCICIO IV. *Add* **a** *or* **the** *in Spanish to each noun and*
describe with an appropriate adjective, using each adjective only
once. Be sure to give the correct form. Remember there
are some that may stand before the noun.

NOUNS

1. año
2. apetito
3. árbol
4. aritmética
5. café
6. cesta
7. cena
8. cielo
9. ciudad
10. cuarto
11. edificio
12. esposa

13. gente
14. iglesia
15. memoria
16. mes
17. mesa
18. perro
19. ropa
20. tío
21. traje
22. suerte
23. mujer
24. número

ADJECTIVES

1. tercero
2. rico
3. corto
4. primero
5. ancho
6. pobre
7. pequeño
8. perezoso
9. fácil
10. malo
11. largo
12. hermoso
13. grande
14. obscuro
15. feliz

16. nuevo
17. difícil
18. cortés
19. contento
20. bueno
21. bonito
22. antiguo
23. americano
24. alto
25. alguno
26. vivo
27. gordo
28. afortunado
29. ocupado
30. simpático

REPASO DE COSAS DE INTERÉS

EJERCICIO I. *Complete these statements:*

1. The possessive adjectives agree with their ——. (§ 17)

2. The third conjugation present tense endings are ——. (§ 21)
3. *La* or *las* with a number means telling ——. (§ 25)
4. First person singular present tense minus **o** plus the opposite vowel plus —— equals ——. (§ 27)
5. A "personal **a**" must be used before ——. (§ 28)
6. An accent on a demonstrative pronoun (*éste*) means ——. (§ 31)
7. That (*near you*) is translated by ——. (§ 26)
8. In conjugating radical-changing verbs, **e>** —; **o>** —. (§ 30)
9. Radical-changing verbs do not change in the —— persons. (§ 30)
10. Reflexive and direct object pronouns stand before a —— verb. (§ 45)
11. When a title is used with a name, it is preceded by the ——, except when ——. (§ 36)
12. —— is the only ordinal number used for dates. (§ 35)
13. —— on the end of a word means *little*. (§ 34)
14. *To be*, telling *where*, is the verb ——. (§ 40)
15. *To be*, telling *who* or *what*, is the verb ——. (§ 40)
16. Some adjectives drop —— before a —— —— noun. (§ 42)
17. Object pronouns come —— an affirmative command. (§ 46)
18. Object pronouns come —— an infinitive. (§ 51)
19. *To have* is —— when it means *to possess*. (§ 48)
20. *To have* is —— when it is a helping verb. (§ 48)
21. In English, *-mente* means ——. (§ 49)
22. The verb form used after a preposition must be the ——. (§ 50)
23. Irregular past participles end in —— or ——. (§ 53)
24. Regular past participles end in —— or ——. (§ 47)
25. The —— —— is used instead of the possessive adjective when referring to parts of the body or articles of clothing. (§ 59)
26. *-er* at the end of an adjective in English is expressed in Spanish by using —— before the adjective. (§ 54)
27. In comparisons, *as...as* is translated ——...—— (§ 54); *-er...than* is translated ——...——. (§ 54)

EJERCICIO II.   *Now do these:*

1. Name the seven adjectives that have a shortened masculine form. (§ 42)
2. Give the past participles of **morir, hacer, ver, volver, decir, poner, abrir, cubrir, escribir.** (§ 53 or § 148)
3. Give all the direct object pronouns. (§ 44)

¿CUÁNTO SABE USTED? 195

4. Explain the difference in use between **aquí** and **acá;** between **allí** and **allá.** (§ 57)
5. Give the list of possessive adjectives. (§ 17)
6. Say: I see you, Mary; I see you, John. (§ 55)

EJERCICIOS DE REPASO

EJERCICIO I. *Answer in Spanish:*

1. ¿Cuál es más grande, Denver o Nueva York? 2. ¿Quién es el alumno más inteligente de la clase de español? 3. ¿Quién es la alumna más bonita de la clase de español? (*¡Tenga Vd. cuidado!*) 4. ¿Quién es tan alto como Vd.? 5. ¿Quién es más alto que Vd.? 6. ¿Quién es el alumno más alto de la clase? 7. ¿Quién es el hombre más rico del mundo? 8. ¿Quién es más perezoso que Vd.?

EJERCICIO II. *Give the meanings of these verb forms:*

1. pongo	8. sé	15. somos
2. salgo	9. digo	16. ha abierto
3. viene	10. venga Vd. acá	17. puede
4. va	11. viste	18. ha hecho
5. he dicho	12. ha muerto	19. cuente Vd.
6. estoy	13. he visto	20. hemos puesto
7. doy	14. pierde	21. ¿es?

EJERCICIO III. *Give the infinitive for each verb in Ejercicio II.*

EJERCICIO IV. *Read these in Spanish:*

1. Aug. 18	6. At 7 A.M.	11. $10 \times 2 = 20$
2. March 12	7. At 8:45 P.M.	12. $19 - 12 = 7$
3. July 1	8. It is 12:10 A.M.	13. $8 + 7 = 15$
4. Dec. 20	9. It is 1:30 P.M.	14. $18 - 5 = 13$
5. Jan. 19	10. It is 5:30 P.M.	15. $4 \times 4 = 16$

EJERCICIO V. *Give the missing words for these sentences:*

1. Carlos es más alto —— Pablo. 2. Pablo es tan bueno —— Pepe. 3. Llevamos —— zapatos en —— pies. 4. En España se lleva la mantilla en la ——; en América se lleva el ——. 5. Pepe no lleva —— chaqueta hoy. 6. Arturo tiene —— ojos cerrados. 7. Al —— una carta, la leemos. 8. ¡Venga Vd. ——, Lupe! 9. —— Pablo es escribiente. 10. —— señora Fernández es su esposa.

EJERCICIO VI. *Answer these questions, using a pronoun instead of repeating the noun:*

1. ¿Tiene Vd. el libro de español hoy?   2. ¿Ha estudiado Vd. la lección?   3. ¿Quiere Vd. comer los dulces?   4. ¿Ha visto Vd. a su amigo hoy?   5. ¿Ha abierto la profesora la ventana?   6. ¿Lleva Vd. el sombrero en la clase?   7. ¿Sabe Vd. los verbos irregulares?   8. ¿Va Vd. a escribir la carta?

EJERCICIO VII. *Choose the correct verb in these sentences and explain your choice:*

1. Lupita (*es, está*) bonita.   2. Nosotros (*somos, estamos*) contentos. 3. Carlos no ha (*sido, estado*) aquí.   4. ¿Cuál (*es, está*) la fecha? 5. Buenos Aires (*es, está*) la capital de la Argentina.   6. La Argentina (*es, está*) en la América del Sur.   7. Este libro (*es, está*) mío; ¿dónde (*es, está*) el de Vd.?   8. Las rosas (*son, están*) rojas.   9. Don Pablo (*es, está*) escribiente.   10. El puesto de don Pablo (*es, está*) cerca de la plaza.

CAPÍTULO *19*

La fiesta de la cueva

¡Ay, qué bueno!   Los señores de Navarro me han invitado a ir con ellos (*them*) a la Fiesta de la Cueva.[1] No sé nada de las fiestas, porque no he ido nunca a una, y he aceptado con mucho gusto.

[1] *La Fiesta de la Cueva, the Cave Festival.* The thirty-first of July is the day of San Ignacio de Loyola, a Basque saint who is supposed to have lived at one time in a cave above Guanajuato, a picturesque mountain town of central Mexico. The fiesta was originally a religious pilgrimage to his shrine in the cave, but nowadays it is just a big picnic, attended by six or seven thousand people with their lunches and at least three thousand guitars.

In this story you learn the popular superstition connected with the weather of that day, and why the *señoritas* all wear new dresses.

Sawders

Everyone loves a fiesta, and crowds turn out to watch the colorful parades and dances. Some of these Indians are in costume for the dance of the Moors and Christians.

En la plaza de Guanajuato todos hablan de la fiesta. 5
Teresa, la hija mayor de los Navarro, al encontrar a una
amiga suya en la calle, dice, — ¿Va a llover el día de San
Ignacio? ¿Qué piensas?

Su amiga contesta, — ¿Quién sabe? Yo tengo un vestido
nuevecito que llevar. ¿Tienes el tuyo? 10

— Tengo el mío también, — dice Teresa.

Parece que todas las señoritas van a vestirse de ropa nueva
para la fiesta, así no hay nada más importante que el tiempo.

Al fin llega el treinta y uno (*thirty-first*) de julio. Me
15 levanto temprano (*early*), preparo una merienda (*lunch*) para
llevar a la cueva, y salgo a pie con mis amigos. Todos
llevamos sombrero de ala ancha, porque en el verano hace
calor en Guanajuato. Siempre hay sol por la mañana, y no
llueve nunca entonces; pero durante la tarde muchas veces
20 hace viento y llueve mucho. Todos miramos el cielo de vez
en cuando, pero hace buen tiempo. Naturalmente, las señoritas, con los vestidos nuevos, quieren saber si va a llover o no.

No se queda casi nadie en la ciudad. Hasta (*even*) los
vendedores han ido a la fiesta, con sus frutas y bebidas
25 (*drinks*) que vender, porque todo el mundo va a tener hambre
y sed después de subir a la montaña.

Al fin llegamos a «La Hormiguera»[1] cerca de la cueva, y
nos sentamos a la sombra de los arbolitos, aunque nadie está
muy cansado. Tenemos mucho calor, y allí hace más fresco
30 que al sol.

Los tres hijos menores de la familia están muy contentos
porque pueden jugar con sus amiguitos. Los padres hablan
con sus conocidos (*acquaintances*); mientras los jóvenes,
Teresa, y su hermano mayor, David, visitan a sus amigos.

35 Acá viene a visitarnos un joven con una guitarra. Yo no
le conozco, y David nos presenta, porque es un amigo suyo.
Dice, — Quiero presentarle a un amigo mío.

— Pedro Ramos, servidor de Vd., — dice el joven.

— Paco Stuart, — contesto yo. — Tengo mucho gusto en
40 conocerle a Vd.

Teresa no le conoce tampoco, y David le presenta. Pedro
toca la guitarra y canta muy bien, y le escuchamos (*listen*) con
mucho gusto. Al fin Teresa le pregunta, — ¿De quién es esa
guitarra fina?

45 — Es suya y mía,[2] señorita, — contesta Pedro cortésmente.

[1] The open slope on the mountain below the cave is called «*La Hormiguera*,»
the Ant Hill, because from above, it looks very much like one with so many people
swarming over it that one day in the year.

[2] When one admires some possession of a Spanish friend, he always replies, "It
is yours," or "It is at your service." Consequently, Pedro tells Teresa that the
guitar is "yours and mine." Of course one always politely refuses such a gift by
replying, "It couldn't have a better owner."

Parece que Pedro está muy contento de conocer a Teresa.

Poco después de comer nuestra merienda debajo de los arbolitos, alguien dice que hace más frío que antes. Sí, es verdad. El cielo ya no está azul, hace viento, y parece que va a llover pronto. 50

— ¡Qué lástima! — pienso yo. — Aquí están todas estas jóvenes bonitas con los vestidos nuevecitos, y van a mojarse (*get wet*). ¿Por qué no vuelven a casa antes de la lluvia?

Pero no quieren volver, y dentro de poco alguien grita (*cries out*), — ¡Ya viene el agua! — y empieza a llover a 55 cántaros (*"pitchers-full"*).

— ¡Ay, qué lástima! — digo a Teresa. — Vd. va a ponerse (*become*) muy triste ahora, porque ese vestido nuevecito está como una sopa.[1] Es lo que todas las señoritas han temido (*feared*) durante toda la semana. 60

— ¿Yo muy triste? — contesta Teresa con sorpresa. — ¡Pues, no! Parece que Vd. no sabe la costumbre. Es que todas nosotras queremos la lluvia en el día de esta fiesta porque si los vestidos nuevos se mojan (*get wet*), es buena suerte. Es prueba (*proof*) de que vamos a encontrar un novio 65 dentro de un año.

— ¡Verdad! — exclamo. Yo miro la cara alegre (*merry*) de Teresa, y entonces miro a Pedro, su (*her*) amigo nuevo.

— Parece, — pienso yo con una sonrisa, — que este año el novio ha llegado antes de la lluvia. 70

Find These Expressions in the Story

1. I have mine, too.
2. I have never gone to one
3. there is nothing more important than the weather
4. a "brand-new" dress to wear
5. It is always sunny in the morning
6. it is colder than before
7. it seems that it is going to rain soon
8. Whose is that fine guitar?
9. nobody is very tired
10. Teresa doesn't know him, either
11. I know nothing about fiestas
12. it never rains then

[1] *como una sopa*, "*wet as soup.*" What expression would we use?

COSAS DE INTERÉS

63. *The Irregular Verbs* Conocer, Parecer, Traducir

PRESENT TENSE

conocer, *to know*	parecer, *to seem*	traducir, *to translate*
conozco	parezco	traduzco
conoces	pareces	traduces
conoce	parece	traduce
conocemos	parecemos	traducimos
conocéis	parecéis	traducís
conocen	parecen	traducen

POLITE COMMANDS

conozca Vd.	parezca Vd.	traduzca Vd.
conozcan Vds.	parezcan Vds.	traduzcan Vds.

64. *Usage of* Conocer *and* Saber

conocer = to know or be acquainted with (*persons and places*)
saber = to know or have information about (*things*)
saber + infinitive = to know how (*to do something*)

No conoce a mi amigo.   **¿Conoce Vd. bien a París?**
He isn't acquainted with my friend.   *Do you know Paris well?*

Sabemos los verbos.   **Sé tocar la guitarra.**
We know the verbs.   *I know how to play the guitar.*

EJERCICIO I.   *Which verb would you use in each of these sentences?*

1. *I know* a Pedro.   2. — ¿Quién *knows*? — dice el señor.   3. Vd. no *know* la fecha.   4. Tengo mucho gusto en *know* le a Vd.   5. Yo no *know* nada de las fiestas.   6. Teresa *knows* que va a llover.   7. Yo *know* bien a Guanajuato.[1]   8. Lola *knows how* escribir.

[1] Why does Guanajuato need a "personal *a*"?   (See section 28.)

65. Double Negatives

nada, nothing (*anything*)   **ninguno,** none (*not any*)
nadie, no one (*anyone*)   **tampoco,** neither (*either*)
nunca, never (*ever*)

These negative words require *no* before the verb (*no tengo nada*). If they themselves precede the verb, the *no* is not necessary (*nada tengo*). It is more emphatic to put *nada, nadie,* etc., before the verb.

$$\text{No tengo} \left\{ \begin{array}{l} \textbf{nada.} \\ \textbf{ninguno.} \end{array} \right. \quad or \quad \left. \begin{array}{l} \textbf{Nada} \\ \textbf{Ninguno} \end{array} \right\} \text{tengo.}$$

EJERCICIO II.   *Complete each sentence in Spanish; then repeat, using a different word order.*

1. No veo *nothing.*
2. No voy *never.*
3. No leo *none.*
4. Yo no voy *either.*

5. *No one* viene temprano.
6. *Nothing* sabemos.
7. No vemos *no one.*[1]
8. *Never* como demasiado.

66. Long Forms of Possessives

$$\text{Es} \left\{ \begin{array}{ll} \textbf{mío} & \text{mine, of mine} \\ \textbf{tuyo} & \text{thine, of thine} \\ \textbf{suyo } cr \left\{ \begin{array}{l} \textbf{de él} \\ \textbf{de ella} \\ \textbf{de Vd.} \end{array} \right. & \begin{array}{l} \text{his, of his} \\ \text{hers, of hers} \\ \text{yours, of yours} \end{array} \end{array} \right.$$

$$\text{Es} \left\{ \begin{array}{ll} \textbf{nuestro} & \text{ours, of ours} \\ \textbf{vuestro} & \text{yours, of yours} \\ \textbf{suyo } cr \left\{ \begin{array}{l} \textbf{de ellos} \\ \textbf{de ellas} \\ \textbf{de Vds.} \end{array} \right. & \begin{array}{l} \text{theirs, of theirs} \\ \text{theirs, of theirs} \\ \text{yours, of yours} \end{array} \end{array} \right.$$

These long forms of the possessives agree with their nouns just as any adjectives do. They are used with the verb *ser* or after their nouns:

---

[1] *Nadie* takes a "personal *a*" when it is the object of a verb.

¿De quién es el libro?	Es mío.	una amiga mía
Whose book is it?	*It is mine.*	*a friend of mine*

If they are used alone, they must be preceded by the definite article. They agree with their nouns even though the nouns are understood:

No tengo la mía (*referring to* chaqueta).
I don't have mine.
Los nuestros están en la mesa (*referring to* libros).
Ours are on the table.

EJERCICIO III. *Continue:*

1. La casa es mía, la casa es tuya, *etc.*
2. El mío está en la mesa, el tuyo está en la mesa, *etc.*
3. Yo tengo mi libro; tengo el mío, *etc.*

EJERCICIO IV. *Complete in Spanish:*

1. *My* madre no está aquí. 2. *My* padres han ido a la ciudad. 3. No tenemos *our* flores; *ours* están en casa. 4. Las palabras son *yours*. 5. Los vestidos son *theirs*. 6. Tengo *mine* (la ropa). 7. *Mine* (las clases) son fáciles. 8. No es *hers*; es *his*.

67. Que *as a Connective*

frutas que vender	un vestido que llevar
fruits to sell	*a dress to wear*

Que is sometimes used as an untranslatable connective between a noun or pronoun and an infinitive. Say these expressions over several times, until your ear becomes accustomed to the sound of that *que:*

algo que hacer	something to do
nada que estudiar	nothing to study
mucho que comer	much to eat
sombreros que llevar	hats to wear
libros que leer	books to read

68. Hacer *with Expressions of Weather*

hace calor	it is hot
hace frío	it is cold
hace fresco	it is cool
hace viento	it is windy
hace sol (*or* hay sol)	it is sunny
hace buen tiempo	it is good weather
hace mal tiempo	it is bad weather

Hacer is used for invisible weather phenomena. *Haber* (*hay*) is used for visible phenomena connected with weather conditions: *hay polvo, it is dusty; hay lodo, it is muddy; hay neblina, it is foggy,* etc.

Llover (ue), *to rain,* is a regular radical-changing verb, used, of course, only in the third person singular: *llueve, it is raining; ha llovido, it has rained.*

PREGUNTITAS

I. 1. ¿Quién no sabe nada de las fiestas?
    2. ¿Desea Paco ir a la fiesta con los Navarro?
    3. ¿De qué hablan las señoritas en la calle?
    4. ¿Qué van a llevar las jóvenes a la fiesta?
    5. Generalmente ¿hace buen tiempo por la mañana en Guanajuato?
    6. ¿Por qué van los vendedores a la fiesta?
    7. ¿Dónde se sientan todos cuando llegan?
    8. ¿Conoce Pedro a Teresa antes de ir a la fiesta?
    9. ¿Qué sabe hacer muy bien Pedro?
    10. ¿Por qué no vuelven las señoritas a casa antes de la lluvia?
    11. ¿Ha tenido Teresa buena suerte este año?

II. 1. ¿Desea Vd. ir a una fiesta?
    2. ¿Está Vd. muy triste esta mañana (tarde)?
    3. ¿Está Vd. muy cansado al subir a una montaña?
    4. ¿Quiere Vd. encontrar un (-a) novio (-a) dentro de un año?
    5. ¿Es buena suerte si se moja (*get wet*) la ropa nuevecita?
    6. ¿Cuándo hace más calor, — en el verano o en el invierno?
    7. ¿Se levanta Vd. temprano para ir a una fiesta?

REPASITO

I. Supply the proper form of **ser, estar, tener,** *or* **hacer:**

1. Yo *am* muy contento hoy. 2. David *is* cansado al llegar a la Hormiguera. 3. El niño —— diez años. 4. Todos los niños *are* *hungry.* (*¡Cuidado!*) 5. La lluvia *is* buena suerte para las señoritas. 6. *It is hot* esta mañana (weather). 7. Paco *is* triste porque no puede ir a la fiesta. 8. Casi nadie *is* en Guanajuato durante la fiesta. 9. Generalmente *it is* fresco en la primavera. 10. Pedro *is* un joven muy cortés.

II. Use these expressions in sentences, using any form of the verbs:

1. servidor de Vd.	7. tan —— como
2. por supuesto	8. más —— que
3. tener sed	9. tener razón
4. todos los días	10. de la noche
5. en vez de	11. en punto
6. tener —— años	12. hace frío

III. Sort these words into five lists of related subjects (the first five will head your lists):

camisa, pelo, visto, padre, sopa, hijo, carne, abierto, diente, sombrero, mano, vuelto, madre, fruta, café, esposa, escrito, pie, zapatos, falda, cabeza, muerto, leche, dicho, oreja, corbata, hecho, tío, dulces, manzana, boca, media, ojo, blusa, puesto

IV. Write in Spanish:

1. How are you? I am tired. What a pity! 2. Do you have something to do today? 3. No, I have nothing to do. 4. Do you want to go with me? 5. Of course. With the greatest of (much) pleasure. 6. Do you know that girl (*over there*)? 7. Of course. I know her well. She is a friend of mine. 8. It is cold and I don't have a jacket. 9. Here is mine. Take it. 10. Thank you very much. Mine is at home. 11. Have you seen my father? No, I haven't seen him. 12. Whose hat is this? It is mine.

V. ¿Sabe Vd. leer estos chistes?

Nada que decir

Él — Vd. no ha dicho una palabra durante veinte minutos.

Ella — No, porque no he tenido nada que decir.

Él — ¿Nunca dice Vd. nada cuando no tiene nada que decir?

Ella — No.

Él — Bueno. ¿Quiere Vd. ser mi esposa?

¿Quién sabe?

El médico (*doctor*) — ¿Cómo está el enfermo (*sick man*) cuando está solo?

La enfermera (*nurse*) — No sé, doctor. Cuando está solo, no estoy con él (*him*).

PALABRAS PARA HOY

1	**antes**	before	1	**nuevecito, -a**	(nuevo — o + ecito), "brand-new"
3	**cansado, -a**	tired		
1	**conocer**	to know, be acquainted with (persons)	1	**los padres**	parents (new meaning)
1	**de**	about (new meaning)	1	**parecer**	to seem
2	**encontrar**	to meet (*encounter*)	1	**poco**	little (in amount)
1	**joven**	young	4	**la sorpresa**	surprise
	pl. **jóvenes**		2	**subir a**	to climb up
	el, la joven	young man, woman	1	**suyo, -a**	his, hers, your, etc. usually replaced by **de él, de ella,** etc.
1	**llegar**	to arrive		
1	**llegar a**	to reach, arrive at	3	**tampoco**	neither, either
	llover, (ue)	to rain		**Teresa**	Theresa
	la lluvia	rain	1	**el tiempo**	weather
1	**mío, -a**	mine, of mine	2	**triste**	sad
1	**nadie**	no one, anyone	1	**tuyo, -a**	thine
4	**el novio**	sweetheart		

EXPRESIONES

al sol, in the sunshine
*****a pie,** on foot
de ala ancha, wide-brimmed (hat)
dentro de poco, in a short time
¿de quién?, whose
*****de vez en cuando,** from time to time
hace buen tiempo, it is good weather
hace fresco, it is cool (weather)
hace frío, it is cold (weather)

hay (hace) sol, it is sunny
hace viento, it is windy
*****por la mañana,** in the morning (when not telling the exact time)
*****por supuesto,** of course
¡qué lástima!, too bad; what a pity
servidor de Vd., at your service
tener mucho gusto en, to be very glad to
*****todos los días,** every day
*****ya no,** no longer

PATITO, PATITO

This saucy little Mexican folk song is a conversation between two little ducks, one of whom seems rather annoyed. It is sung very quickly; often the singers, just for fun, keep time with their feet in a shuffling step called *zapateado* (forward right, step left beside it; backward right, step left beside it).

Arr. by E. M. Jarrett

La patita:

Pa - ti - to, pa - ti - to co - lor de ca -

fé, si us té no me quie - re pues lue - go ¿por - qué? Ya no se pre -

su - ma que al ca - bo yo sé que us-té es un pa - ti - to co - lor de ca -

El patito:

fé. Me di - jo que sí, ya lue - go que no; e - ra un - a pa -

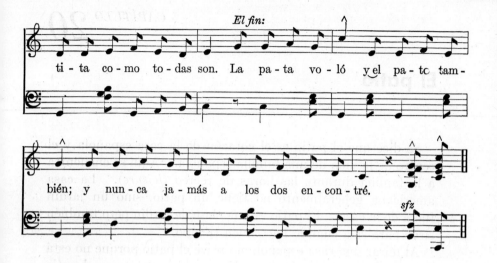

ti - ta co - mo to - das son. La pa - ta vo - ló y el pa - to tam -

bién; y nun - ca ja - más a los dos en - con - tré.

sfz

La patita:	The Little Duck:
Patito, patito	Little drake, little drake,
color de café	The color of coffee,
si usté (d) no me quiere	If you don't like me,
pues luego, ¿por qué?	Well, then, why?

Ya no se presuma	Now don't be conceited
que al cabo yo sé	For after all I know
que usté es un patito	That you're just a little drake
color de café.	The color of coffee.

El patito:	The Little Drake:
Me dijo que sí	You told me yes,
ya luego que no;	Then later said no;
era una patita	You were only a little duck
como todas son.	Like all the rest.

El fin:	Ending:
La pata voló	The duck flew away,
y el pato también;	And so did the drake;
y nunca jamás	And never again
a los dos encontré.	Did I meet the two.

El patio[1]

Se dice que el patio es el corazón de la casa española y el centro de la vida de una familia española. Aquí se encuentra a la familia durante las horas de recreo (*leisure*). La casa americana generalmente no tiene un patio, sino un jardín
5 fuera de la casa. El patio es una clase de jardín pero también sirve para sala cuando hace buen tiempo.

Al mirar una casa española no se ve el patio porque no está fuera de la casa sino dentro. No se puede entrar en el patio desde la calle sin pasar por el zaguán.[2] El patio está en el
10 centro de la casa. Todos los cuartos dan al patio. En las casas grandes algunas veces hay dos o tres patios. Entonces la cocina (*kitchen*) y los cuartos de los criados dan al segundo patio. Las criadas lavan la ropa allí también. Si la familia tiene un automóvil, lo pone en ese patio, porque no hay
15 garage.

El patio generalmente es un lugar muy bonito. La casa del señor López[3] tiene un patio muy grande. En el suelo hay azulejos (*colored tiles*). En las casas más pobres no hay azulejos, sino piedras. En el patio del señor López hay una
20 fuente pequeña con agua corriente en el centro. Cuando se

---

[1] This story describes the typical old-fashioned Spanish-style house that was introduced into Spain by the Moors and which is still found in all Spanish-speaking countries.

[2] The *zaguán* is a passageway leading from the big entrance door or gate through the house into the patio. It is often a driveway by which the family car enters the courtyard.

If the house is near the business district, the part facing the street on either side of the *zaguán* may be rented for shops, while the family lives in the rear or upstairs. Upstairs rooms are always considered the best, because they are not so likely to be damp. (Artificial heat is rare in many "warm" countries, although it is badly needed.)

[3] López is as common a name in Spanish as Smith or Jones is in English. Many surnames end in *-ez*. This ending in old Spanish meant "*the son of*": **López**, *the son of Lope;* **Fernández**, *the son of Fernando;* **Rodríguez**, *the son of Rodrigo*, etc.

ve esta fuente se sabe que el señor López es un hombre bastante rico porque muchas veces no hay agua corriente en las casas españolas. Cerca de la fuente hay plantas con flores de colores muy vivos. Contra las paredes hay más plantas. Hay algunas mesitas y muchas sillas de todas clases. Alrededor del patio hay un pórtico.[1] En el pórtico hay colgadas jaulas (*cages*) con pajaritos que cantan. Encima del pórtico está la galería.[2] Los cuartos del primer piso[3] dan a la galería. Desde la galería se ve el patio y se puede mirar lo que pasa allí.

El patio es un lugar agradable, lleno de luz, colores, y la música de los pájaros. Cuando hay demasiado sol, un criado corre el toldo (*pulls over the awning*) que sirve para cubrir el patio. El toldo da sombra al patio.

Durante la hora de la siesta y por la noche la familia se sienta en el patio. Por la noche el criado descorre (*pulls back*) el toldo y se pueden ver el cielo de azul obscuro y las estrellas. Muchas veces la luna sirve de luz y no es necesario usar la luz eléctrica.

Muchas veces, cuando los amigos visitan a la familia, todos platican (*chat*) allí. Ya no cantan los pajaritos porque se han dormido. Pero alguien toca, y los jóvenes cantan al son (*sound*) de la guitarra. Algunas veces bailan también. Los niñitos juegan al escondite al principio, pero pronto se cansan y se duermen. Si hace fresco, las señoras se ponen el mantón (*shawl*), para protegerse (*protect themselves*) del aire de la noche.

A las once y media la criada entra y ofrece a todos tazas de chocolate[4] con pasteles (*cakes, pastry*). Entonces se despier-

---

[1] A *pórtico* is a kind of veranda encircling the patio, its roof supported by a series of graceful arches. It is sometimes called *el corredor*.

[2] A *galería* is the same as a *pórtico* except that it is above the ground floor. Every room of a typical Spanish house opens upon a *galería*, no matter how many floors there are.

[3] In Spain and other European countries the floors are numbered starting above the ground floor rather than with it. The main floor is the *piso bajo*, then comes the *primer piso* (first floor above the ground; second floor to us), *segundo piso*, etc.

[4] Here is a word English has borrowed from Spanish. Spanish, before that, had borrowed it from the Aztec language.

50 tan los niños en seguida. Ellos se comen todos los pasteles. Al fin los amigos se despiden de la familia y se van a sus propias casas. Todo el mundo se duerme en seguida.

FLOOR PLAN OF A HOUSE IN DURANGO, MEXICO

You can tell from the plan that this house belongs to a well-to-do family. Most Spanish-style houses are rectangular in shape, but the owner of this house bought some of his neighbor's property in order to add the third patio and the *despensa*.

All rooms open on the *pórtico*. On the patio side are large arches with bird cages hanging from the top and an iron railing which supports flowerpots filled with bright-colored flowers, such as camelias, roses, geraniums, and carnations. In the *pórtico* and patio are more potted flowers and shrubs, at least one of which will be a jasmine to fill the night air with its heavy, sweet aroma.

Between the *zaguán* and the *pórtico* is a door of iron grillwork. A glass door separates the *pórtico* of the main patio from that of the second patio.

You will notice that the only rooms that have windows are those facing the street. The other rooms, however, are not dark, as you would expect, having large French doors which let in the light from the patio.

The *asistencia* is a *sala* used by the family to receive their intimate friends, the main *sala* being reserved for formal occasions.

For a long time even the houses of the wealthy did not have running water. In those days the *mozo* carried all the water from the *acequia* (ditch) in the street. For bathing a tin bathtub was placed in the sewing-room and the *mozo* brought in the water a bucketful at a time. All the plants were watered laboriously by the *mozo* in the same way. As one Mexican lady said, "Mexican houses are charming, if you have lots of servants."

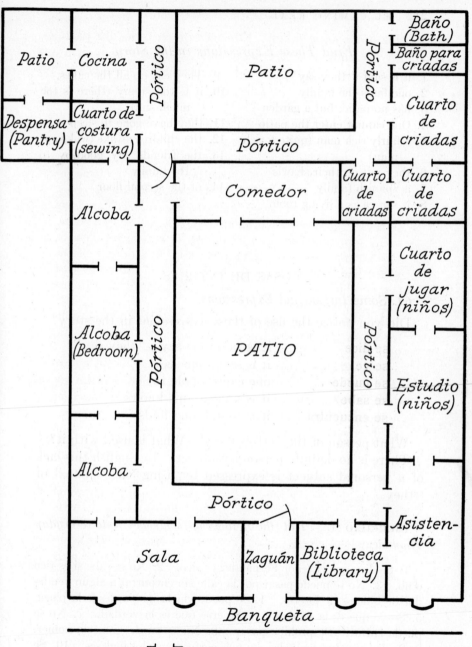

Legend: ⊣⊢ doors ⏝ windows with reja

Find These Expressions in the Story

1. it is said ("they say")
2. one finds the family
3. has no patio, but a garden
4. One cannot enter the patio
5. a fairly rich man (quite a rich man)
6. they put on their shawls
7. a Spanish family
8. it serves as a living room
9. They eat up all the cakes.
10. it is too sunny (there is too much sun)
11. they have gone to sleep
12. the children awake (wake up)
13. the friends say good-by to the family
14. of the second floor

COSAS DE INTERÉS

69. Some Impersonal Expressions

Did you notice the use of these expressions in the story?

se dice	it is said, one says, "they say"
se ve	it is seen, one sees
se puede	one can (is able to)
se sabe	it is known, one knows
se encuentra	it is found, one finds

What person of the verb is used?   What is used with it?
There is no definite person as subject.   In English this lack of a personal subject is expressed by using "it," "one," or "they."

EJERCICIO I.   *Put the following sentences into everyday English:*

1. Se dice que el señor Fernández es rico.   2. No se sabe si es rico o no.   3. No se puede pasar por la calle sin encontrar a algún vendedor de billetes de lotería.   4. Se puede ver la iglesia desde la plaza. 5. Se ve que es la verdad.   6. Se cree que es la verdad.   7. No se puede entrar.   Se prohibe pasar.   8. No se puede vivir sin comer. 9. Se dice que los españoles son más corteses que los ingleses.   10. Se habla en voz baja en la iglesia.

Moors designed patios like this one in Seville when they conquered Spain. Now many houses in Spanish-speaking countries have Moorish patios, with fountains and flowers.

70. *Reflexive Verbs with Changed Meanings*

EJERCICIO II.   *Compare the meanings of these two lists of verbs:*

comer	to eat	comerse	to eat all, to "eat up"
ir	to go	irse	to go away, to go off
poner	to put, to place	ponerse	to put on, become
dormir	to sleep	dormirse	to go to sleep
hacer	to make, to do	hacerse	to become, "get"
llevar	to take or carry	llevarse	to take or carry away
despedir (i)	to dismiss	despedirse de	to say good-by to
llamar	to call	llamarse	to be called or named

EJERCICIO III.   *Conjugate in the present and present perfect:*

irse   ponerse   dormirse

EJERCICIO IV.   *Give the meanings of these expressions:*

1. se duerme (*two meanings*) 2. va 3. se va 4. me llamo 5. se ha dormido 6. me he puesto los zapatos 7. lo come 8. se lo come 9. ¡Póngase Vd. el sombrero! 10. ¡Váyase Vd. en seguida! 11. se han ido

EJERCICIO V.   *Give these verb forms in Spanish:*

1. I am putting on 2. they have gone to sleep 3. I am going away 4. he eats up the soup 5. he gets rich

71. Sino *and* Pero

El lápiz es rojo *pero* la pluma es azul.
El lápiz no es azul *sino* rojo.

Sino and *pero* both mean *"but."*   *Sino* is used in negative sentences.   Think of *sino* as meaning "but on the contrary."

REMEMBER: Use *sino* after a negative when no verb follows.

EJERCICIO VI.   *Use the correct word in these sentences:*

1. No tengo seis manzanas *but* cinco. 2. La casa española no tiene jardín, *but* un patio. 3. Me voy, *but* tengo que volver. 4. Sabe leer, *but* no es inteligente. 5. No son las ocho, *but* las ocho menos diez. 6. El patio no es grande *but* pequeño.

72. Adjectives of Nationality

You have learned that adjectives that do not end in *o* have no special feminine form. There are a few exceptions to this rule. *Find these expressions in the story:*

the Spanish house   A Spanish family   Spanish houses

Contrast these with: **la casa azul, casas azules**

Adjectives of nationality have four forms regardless of the ending.

Singular	Plural
español (masculine)	**españoles** (masculine)
española (feminine)	**españolas** (feminine)
inglés (masculine)	**ingleses** (masculine)
inglesa[1] (feminine)	**inglesas** (feminine)

EJERCICIO VII.   *Give these expressions in Spanish:*

1. the Spanish woman   2. the Spanish town   3. the Spanish city
4. the English dog   5. the English house   6. the American town

EJERCICIO VIII.   *Make plural the expressions given in Ejercicio VII.*

73. More Radical-Changing Verbs

PRESENT TENSE MODEL E > I VERB **servir,** *to serve*	
sirv o	serv imos
sirv es	serv ís
sirv e	sirv en
POLITE COMMANDS	
sirva Vd.	**sirvan Vds.**

A few verbs of the third conjugation (*-ir*) change *e* to *i* in the stem.

[1] An accent on the last syllable is dropped when a plural or feminine ending is added. (See *Accentuation*, section 155.)

Where do the changes occur? Where are there no changes?
What does (*i*) after a verb indicate to you?

EJERCICIO IX. *Conjugate like* **servir:**
> pedir, despedirse (*to say good-by to*), vestirse

EJERCICIO X. *Give the correct form of the verb in the present tense:*

1. Yo *pedir.*
2. Vd. *servir.*
3. Nosotros *despedirse.*

4. La criada *servir.*
5. Lupe *despedirse* de Rosa.
6. La luna *servir* de luz.

PREGUNTITAS

I. 1. ¿Dónde se encuentra la familia durante las horas de recreo?
    2. ¿Tiene jardín la casa española? (*Use* **sino** *in your answer.*)
    3. ¿Dónde está el patio?
    4. ¿Se puede ver el patio desde la calle?
    5. ¿De qué es el suelo?
    6. ¿Qué se ve en el patio?
    7. ¿Es pequeño el patio del señor López? (*Practice with* **sino.**)
    8. ¿Dónde está el pórtico?
    9. ¿Qué se usa para cubrir el patio?
    10. ¿Quiénes se comen los pasteles?

II. 1. ¿Sabe Vd. bailar?
    2. ¿Tiene Vd. un patio en su casa?
    3. ¿Dónde están las estrellas? ¿la luna? ¿el sol?
    4. ¿Sabe Vd. tocar la guitarra?
    5. ¿Se ve el sol por la noche?
    6. ¿Se ve la luna durante el día?
    7. ¿Tienen Vds. luz eléctrica en su casa?
    8. ¿A qué hora se despierta Vd.?
    9. ¿A qué hora se levanta Vd.?
    10. ¿A qué hora se duerme Vd.?

REPASITO

I. ¿Sabe Vd. leer estos chistes?

En una tienda

El vendedor — Éstos son los mejores zapatos del mundo.

El cliente — ¿No tiene Vd. ningunos de clase superior?
El vendedor — Sí.   Aquí tiene Vd. estos otros.

En la calle

Un músico va por la calle y toca la guitarra.   Un policía le interrumpe (*interrupts*) y le dice:
— ¿Tiene Vd. licencia (*permit*)?
— No, señor.
— Pues entonces, acompáñeme Vd.
— Con mucho gusto.   ¿Qué va Vd. a cantar?

II. The following dialogue reviews four pairs of words: **sino** and **pero, conocer** and **saber, ser** and **estar, tener** and **haber.**   *Choose the correct words to replace those in English. Be sure to give the correct forms of each verb.*

Entre dos alumnos

— Buenos días, Carlos.
— Buenos días, Arturo.   ¿Cómo *are* Vd.?
— Muy bien, gracias.   ¿Y Vd.?
— Bien.
— *¿Do you know* Vd. a Juan?
— *I don't know.   ¿Is he* el muchacho grande que acompaña a Carlos muchas veces?
— No.   No *he isn't* grande *but* pequeño.
— ¿Cuántos años *is* él?   (*There is a "catch" to this.*)
— *He is* quince años *but he is* pequeño.   Vd. debe *to know* le porque *he is* en la clase de español.   Se sienta cerca de las ventanas.
— Ah, sí.   Creo que le *I know.   He is* su amigo de Vd., ¿verdad?
— Sí, *he is* mi amigo.   *He is* muy simpático.   *¿Do you know* Vd. donde *he is* ahora?
— No, no *I don't know* donde *he is.*   No le *I have* visto hoy.   ¿Qué quiere Vd.?
— Pues no *I am* contento.   Juan *has* mi libro de español.   Todavía no *I have* estudiado mi lección y vamos a *to have* un examen.   Quiero estudiarla ahora *but* no puedo porque no *I have* mi libro.
— Aquí *is* mi libro.   Tómelo Vd.   Ya *I have* estudiado la lección. *It is* muy fácil.
— ¡Qué bueno!   *But I have* que aprender los verbos.   Muchas gracias.
— De nada.

III. Practice reading the dialogue aloud, putting in the correct forms, until you can read it correctly and rapidly.

IV. Write in Spanish:

1. What does one see in a patio?   2. One sees many things.   3. There are flowers, plants, a fountain, and other things.   4. Where is the patio?   It is inside the house.   5. It is said that it is the heart of the Spanish house.   6. Do we have patios in our houses?   7. Sometimes.   Generally we have a garden in front of or in back of the house. 8. What does one do in the patio?   One can do many things.   9. Do you receive your friends in the garden?   10. No, when my friends visit me, we don't sit in the garden but in the living room.   11. If it is hot, but (it is) not sunny, we sit in the garden.

PALABRAS PARA HOY

2	el aire	air	2	ofrecer	to offer
4	alrededor de	around	3	la pared	wall (*partition*)
4	bailar	to dance	1	pedir (i)	to ask for
4	el balcón	balcony	2	la piedra	stone
	cansarse	to grow weary		el piso	floor, story (level of
3	el centro	center			a building)
3	colgar (ue)	to hang	2	propio, -a	own
3	despedirse		2	sacar	to take out
	de (i)	to say good-by to	4	la sala	parlor, living room
2	despertarse		1	segundo, -a	second
	(ie)	to awake	2	servir (i)	to serve
2	la estrella	star		la silla	chair
4	lavar	to wash (*lavatory*)	1	sino	but
2	el lugar	place	2	el sol	sun (*solar*)
4	la luna	moon (*lunar*)	2	el suelo	floor, ground
2	la luz	light		la taza	cup
2	lleno de	full of, filled with		el zaguán	passageway
1	la noche	night			

OLD WORDS WITH NEW MEANINGS

bastante	fairly, quite	dormirse	to go to sleep
comerse	to eat all ("to eat up")	irse	to go away or off
después	afterward, next, then later	pasar	to happen

EXPRESIONES

al principio, at first
dar a, to face, open on

*en seguida, at once
*por la noche, in the evening, at night

The Inca capital of Cuzco, high in the Andes, was founded four hundred years before Aztec Tenochtitlán.   Buildings were trimmed with gold because gold was considered beautiful and not something to spend.

Galloway

II. Perú

Mexico had been set up under Spanish rule, and Mexico, remember, then included all of southwestern North America. Now where could the venturesome spirits of Spain go in search of new worlds to conquer? No doubt many an ambitious young fellow studied crude maps of the known world like a tourist planning a trip; and one of them, we know now, decided upon a vast, unexplored territory to the south as the next place to be added to the growing list of Spanish possessions.

Did the far-away Incas in their gorgeous, five-century-old capital feel the chill breath of doom sweep over them as Francisco Pizarro cast his eyes southward toward their country? They should have, for from that moment their fate was sealed.

This Francisco Pizarro (his friends probably called him Pancho) was a seventeen-year-old boy herding pigs in Extremadura, the home of Cortés, when Columbus discovered America. Tales of the New World thrilled him, as they did everyone in those days; and when he grew older he left the pigs and sailed with Balboa and the crew that discovered the Pacific Ocean. After that, Pizarro, not so young as he once had been, tried to settle down in Panama to be a farmer, but that sort of life was entirely too dull. From the north came the tale of Cortés' conquest of the Aztecs; from the south came rumors of equally wealthy Indians still unconquered, and memories of his earlier explorations still lingered with the restless farmer. No doubt there was a worried Mrs. Pizarro who begged him not to go, but there was nothing she could do about it.

Finally he left his tropical home, talked the King of Spain into giving him money for ships and supplies, and in 1530 started down the west coast of South America to the country we now call Perú, taking along twenty-seven horses and less than two hundred men.

Following rumors of gold, smelling out treasure like a bloodhound on his victim's trail, Pizarro made his way up to a high valley between two ranges of the Andes, unhindered by the friendly Indians of the coast villages, who had brought him gifts of fruits and vegetables. High in the mountains he found the deep-chested Incas, a powerful tribe of Indians as civilized and intelligent as the Aztecs, with a vast empire that reached from the equator into what is now Argentina; with a capital, Cuzco, that was four hundred years older than Aztec Tenochtitlán.

These "People of the Sun," as they called themselves, had to be ex-

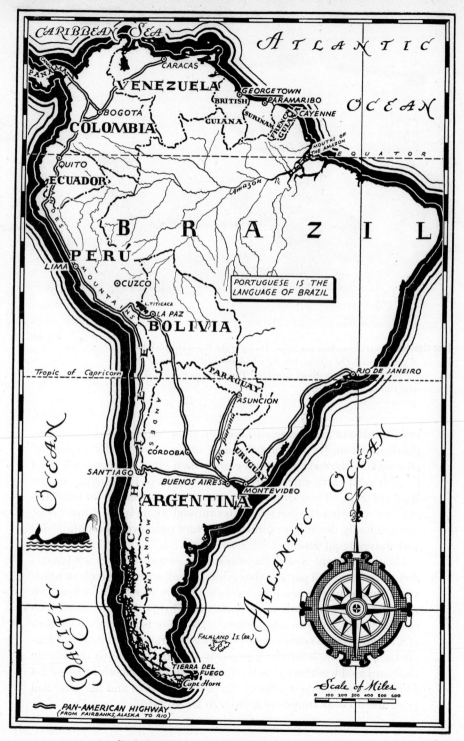

South America has nine Spanish-speaking countries.

Inca stonework puzzles modern masons. How did the Incas cut such huge blocks of granite with the soft metals they had and fit them so well that they could be put together without mortar? These people would tell you it was done with a magic juice.

cellent farmers and masons to raise crops or build cities in such perpendicular country. Along the sides of the steep, rocky Andes ran stone-walled terraces where they grew their crops, each terrace filled in with good earth carried up from the depths of the canyons on the backs of men. Their irrigation system of canals reached for hundreds of miles, carrying the precious water through tunnels, over aqueducts, and gradually down from terrace to terrace until every mountain side was watered and green.

Great mountain roads, the surest sign of any country's advancement, connected all parts of the empire, crossing bridges made of tough vines that swung across deep ravines. There were temples and palaces and homes everywhere, all surrounded by gardens and trees, with fountains and pools to adorn them. Nowhere in history do we hear of a building more beautiful and lavishly decorated with gold and jewels than the temple of the sun god in Cuzco. While to the greedy Spaniard gold was money, to the Incas it was only something beautiful to be used for ornamentation. No wonder Pizarro and his band had been able to hear rumors of it from so far away.

High in the Andes the Incas built stone terraces where they grew their crops, each terrace filled in with earth carried up from the valley floor far below.

No doubt Atahualpa, the Inca (as the people called their ruler), with his army of forty thousand, knew that Pizarro was coming, in the same way that Moctezuma had known of Cortés' arrival. Perhaps it was only native courtesy that made him receive the strangers politely; perhaps it was because so small a group did not alarm him. Certainly luck was with Pizarro, as it had been with Cortés.

As he was received before the golden throne of the Inca, who was holding court in a small town, Pizarro's twenty-seven horsemen made their mounts rear and prance to frighten the assembled Indians, who had never seen such animals before. Then suddenly Pizarro called upon the surprised Emperor to surrender, and when of course Atahualpa refused, the Spaniards attacked viciously, their horses trampling the terrified people and driving them in all directions. Atahualpa himself, left unprotected, was quickly taken prisoner, and the conquest of Perú was practically over.

Atahualpa's people were frantic over his capture. What could they give, they asked, for his ransom? Pizarro's men tried to think of more treasure than there could possibly be. "Fill this great room," said they, "with gold to the height a man can reach."

Then the yellow metal poured in from all over the empire — heavy plates, bowls and vases of hand-wrought gold; necklaces, bracelets, and chains of gold; bands of the precious metal torn from their buildings — and the room was full. But it was all in vain. By that time the Spaniards had decided it would be unwise to free Atahualpa, and the "last Inca," heart-broken and probably glad to die, was finally strangled.

Legends say that many a swift Inca runner, loaded with gold for the ransom and on his way to rescue Atahualpa, heard out on the mountain roads the news of the execution and hid his precious burden on the spot rather than deliver it to the Spaniards.

Ship after ship went back to Spain loaded with loot for the Spanish king, who was congratulating himself for his investment in Pizarro, while Cuzco, the beautiful Inca capital, was destroyed so thoroughly that it has never been rebuilt to resemble its former glory in any way.

Perú then comprised most of the land now included in Argentina, Chile, and Bolivia, so that all these areas were colonized in the following years by venturesome Spanish noblemen who built up large estates or opened mines. As in Mexico, Spanish churches took the place of native palaces and temples, new animals were introduced from Europe, and traders came to make money. Spaniards, Indians, and

The great cathedral was the first building Pizarro planned for Lima. Today his mummified body lies inside it and his bronze statue guards the entrance.

The Plaza de Armas in Lima, Peru, was laid out under Pizarro's personal direction when he decided to found a new city in the country he had conquered.

the Negroes brought from Africa intermingled, and by the time these Latin-American peoples divided into separate independent countries, about a hundred years ago, the population had become a mixture of these races.

Cruel, the *conquistadores* admittedly were, but you must remember that in those days human life was cheap, might made right, and the strong had no mercy on the weak. Although we cannot help regretting the cruelty of the conquest of Perú, we must remember Pizarro as the poor boy who made his place in history because he took to South America the Spanish language and customs that still color most of it, just as Cortés gets the credit for the Spanish atmosphere of Mexico and our own southwest.

Today the old sections of the colonial cities, such as Lima (where Pizarro's mummified body lies in a glass casket in the cathedral for anyone to see), La Paz, and Quito, still look much like old Spain. Their colonial buildings with Moorish patios, balconies, and flat roofs are still standing; their older streets are still narrow and cobblestoned, and their four-hundred-year-old cathedrals still look down upon tree-planted Spanish plazas.

"For gold and God" Spain conquered the Americas, and although they are no longer hers, the spirit of the mother country still lingers in them.

Interesting Books to Read

Incas: MAGOFFIN *and* DAVIS: THE ROMANCE OF ARCHEOLOGY, ch. XIII. SPENCE, LEWIS: MYTHS AND LEGENDS, MEXICO, PERU, ch. VI. ROTHERY, AGNES: SOUTH AMERICA: WEST COAST AND EAST, chs. VII and IX.

Cuzco: ROTHERY, ch. VII. NILES, BLAIR: PERUVIAN PAGEANT, chs. VIII and IX.

Pizarro: NILES, pp. 32–34, ch. VI, pp. 146–48, p. 149. ROTHERY, ch. V. RICHMAN, IRVING: THE SPANISH CONQUERORS, ch. VI.

Atahualpa: NILES, pp. 100–01, 117–18.

CAPÍTULO 21

Los nombres españoles

El cartero acaba de traer las cartas a la casa del señor García. La criada las ha dado a Lola[1] y la niña las lleva a su mamá. La encuentra en el patio.

---

[1] *Lola* is a nickname for *Dolores.* In Spanish-speaking countries girls are frequently named after the Virgin Mary, who has many titles, such as *Virgen de la Soledad* (*Solitude*), *del Refugio, de Dolores* (*Sorrows*), *de la Concepción;* consequently, *Soledad, Refugio, Dolores* (*Lola*), and *Concepción* (*Concha*) become girls' names.

Another common name is *Jesús,* given to both girls and boys. The girl's nickname is then *Susita.*

— ¡Mire Vd., mamacita mía!   Le traigo a Vd. las cartas.

— ¡Qué bueno!   Vamos a ver lo que hay.

— Déjeme Vd. separarlas, — dice Lola.

— Pero tú no sabes[1] leer los nombres, hijita.

— Sí puedo, mamacita.   ¡Oiga Vd.!

Lola empieza a mirar las cartas.   No sabe leer bien porque solamente tiene seis años y medio.   Lee los nombres muy despacio, letra por letra.

— *Ese, ere...* (*Sr.*)   ¿Qué quiere decir esto, mamacita?

— Quiere decir señor.

— Y ¿por qué lo escriben así?

— Es una abreviatura, hijita, una manera corta de escribirlo.[2]

— Ah.   Señor Luis García y... y.. y... No sé esta palabra.   ¿Qué es?

La señora García toma la carta y lee, — Señor Luis García y Sandoval.   Es para tu padre.

— ¿Por qué se dice Sandoval?   No nos llamamos Sandoval.

— Pues Sandoval es el apellido de la madre de tu papá, tu abuela, antes de casarse con tu abuelo.

— Pero todo el mundo le llama «señor García».

— Sí.   Pero cuando se escribe su nombre en cartas o en documentos formales, se usa su nombre completo.

— ¿Por qué?

— Es costumbre, niña.   También es una manera de identificarse.   Hay muchos hombres que se llaman «señor García.» Pero cuando tu papá usa los dos nombres, indica que es el señor García cuya (*whose*) madre se llamaba (*used to be named*) la señorita Sandoval.

— ¡Qué curioso![3]   Entonces Vd. escribe en sus cartas «señora María García y Sandoval,» ¿verdad?

— No.   Mi nombre completo es María Fernández de

[1] Parents address their children with the familiar form.   Often the children, especially when they are very young, address their parents with the polite form.

[2] Other common abbreviations are *señora, sra.; señorita, srta.; don, D.; doña, Da.*

[3] You will notice many words in Spanish with the ending *-oso*.   In adjectives it is often equivalent to the English ending *-ous*.   What do these mean: *generoso, maravilloso, precioso, estudioso, curioso?*

García. Antes de casarme con tu papá me llamaba (*my name used to be*) María Fernández (apellido[1] de mi padre) y Serrano (apellido de mi madre). Al casarme he abandonado el apellido de mi madre y he tomado «de García,» apellido de

40 mi esposo. Cuando una mujer se casa, siempre toma el apellido de su esposo.

— ¿Cómo debo yo escribir mi nombre?

— Tú te llamas Dolores García y Fernández.

— Ah. Ya caigo (*I catch on*). Fernández es el nombre de

45 mi abuelita que vive en Santander.[2] Es su madre de Vd.

— Sí. Y ella se llama María López, viuda[3] de Fernández.

— Y ¿se dice viuda porque es muy vieja?

— No. Se dice viuda porque su esposo, tu abuelo, ha muerto.[4]

50 — Pero es vieja, ¿verdad?

— Sí, es vieja. Tiene setenta y dos años.

— Y ¿cuántos años tiene Vd., mamacita?

— Es un secreto. Después de los treinta, las mujeres nunca quieren contar los años.

55 — Papá me ha dicho que él tiene cuarenta años.

— Sí, es verdad.

— ¿Y mi otro abuelo? Me parece que tiene cien años porque tiene el pelo blanco.

— No. No tiene más que sesenta y nueve años.

60 — ¡Oiga Vd., mamacita! ¿Cómo me llamaré (*will my name be*) yo al casarme?

— Pues ¿quién sabe, hijita? Ahora favor de darme las cartas.

Las cartas han caído al suelo y Lola las recoge (*picks up*) y

65 las da a su madre. La madre empieza a leerlas, y Lola coge (*takes*) su muñeca y dice, — ¡Oye (*familiar command*), muñeca

---

[1] The definite article is generally omitted before nouns in apposition; that is, nouns used parenthetically explaining a preceding noun.

[2] Santander is a city on the coast of Northern Spain near the French border. It has been a fashionable summer resort for wealthy Spaniards.

[3] *Viuda* is abbreviated *vda*.

[4] The Spaniard ordinarily would say "has died" rather than "is dead."

mía! Yo soy la señorita Dolores García y Fernández, pero voy a casarme con el señor Fulano[1] y tú serás (*will be*) la señorita Ana María[2] García y Fulano.

Al oír esto, la señora García se ríe y dice, — ¡Qué cosa, 70 chica!

Pero también se pone (*becomes*) un poco triste, porque piensa que dentro de poco será (*it will be*) verdad.

A Spanish signature usually ends with a *rúbrica* (flourish). Sometimes one who cannot write adopts a *rúbrica* which is as legal as his name. P. Alcaraz adds a graceful one to his name.

En espera de sus apreciables letras me repito su atto. y S.S.

Find These Expressions in the Story

1. The postman has just brought
2. I am bringing you
3. What does this mean?
4. before marrying your father
5. your grandfather has died
6. they never want to count the years
7. Who knows?
8. Listen! (two ways: polite and familiar)
9. she becomes a little sad
10. It seems to me he is a hundred years old
11. How should I write my name?
12. you can't read the names
13. everyone calls him Mr. García
14. He is only sixty-nine years old.
15. I am going to marry Mr. So-and-So
16. On hearing this

[1] *Fulano* is the equivalent of our term "*So-and-So*" when we don't know or recall a definite name. "*Fulano de Tal*" is used as we use the name "*John Doe*."

[2] English says "*Mary Ann*," but Spanish says **Ana María**.

COSAS DE INTERÉS

74. Present Tense of Traer, Caer, Oír

Review the conjugation of *salir* (section 21).   Each of these three verbs has a similar change in the first person singular of the present tense, and therefore in the polite commands.

traer, *to bring*	caer, *to fall*	oír, *to hear*
traigo	caigo	oigo
traes	caes	oyes
trae	cae	oye
traemos	caemos	oímos
traéis	caéis	oís
traen	caen	oyen

POLITE COMMANDS

traiga Vd.	caiga Vd.	oiga Vd.
traigan Vds.	caigan Vds.	oigan Vds.

PAST PARTICIPLES

traído	caído	oído

Notice that the past participles of *traer*, *caer*, and *oír* have written accents like *leer* and *creer*.

75. Present Tense of Reír

The following verb is radical-changing ($e > i$) but it also has to have written accents in many forms. *Reír* is frequently used with the reflexive pronouns, though it is equally correct to omit them.   *To laugh at* is *reírse de.*

reír (i), *to laugh*

río	reímos
ríes	reís
ríe	ríen

POLITE COMMAND	PAST PARTICIPLE
ría Vd.	reído

EJERCICIO I. *Give the verbs in Spanish:*

1. *Juan* laughs, brings, hears, falls, leaves
2. *Yo no* laugh, bring, hear, fall, leave
3. *Nosotros* laugh, bring, hear, fall, leave
4. *Rosa y Lola* laugh, bring, hear, fall, leave
5. *Vd.* laugh, bring, hear, fall, leave

EJERCICIO II. *Give the verbs in Ejercicio I in the present perfect tense:* Juan has laughed, *etc.*

EJERCICIO III. *Complete these commands in Spanish:*

1. ¡No *laugh* Vds.!
2. ¡*Listen* me Vd.!
3. ¡*Bring* me Vd. el libro!
4. ¡*Leave* Vd. en seguida!

76. Cardinal Numbers to 100

10	**diez**	40	**cuarenta**
20	**veinte**	50	**cincuenta**
21	**veinte y un (o, -a)**	60	**sesenta**
22	**veinte y dos**, *etc.*	70	**setenta**
30	**treinta**	80	**ochenta**
31	**treinta y uno**	90	**noventa**
32	**treinta y dos**, *etc.*	100	**cien(to)**

What is the ending equivalent to English *-ty* in the numbers from thirty to ninety inclusive?

When will the *-o* be dropped in *veinte y uno, treinta y uno,* etc.? (Before a masculine noun.)

When will the *-to* be dropped in *ciento?* (Before a noun or *mil, thousand.)*

EJERCICIO IV. *Read these numbers in Spanish:*

75	82	31	26	100
52	43	97	63	15
55	66	77	22	39

EJERCICIO V. *Read in Spanish:*

21 muchachos	1 automóvil
100 casas	100 burros
41 alumnos	1 casa

EJERCICIO VI.　*Count in Spanish:*

1. By tens to 100; by elevens to 99
2. With even numbers from 30 to 60
3. With odd numbers from 69 to 99

PREGUNTITAS

I.　1. ¿Cuántos años tiene Lola?
　　2. ¿Lee fácilmente?
　　3. ¿Qué acaba de hacer el cartero?
　　4. ¿Qué es una abreviatura?
　　5. Escriba Vd. en la pizarra las abreviaturas de *señor, señora, señorita, viuda, doña, don.*
　　6. ¿Cómo se llama el padre de Lola?
　　7. ¿Cómo se llama su madre?
　　8. ¿Cómo se llamaba (*used to be*) su madre antes de casarse?
　　9. ¿Cómo se llama la muñeca de Lola?

II.　1. ¿Cómo debe Vd. escribir su nombre completo en español?
　　2. ¿Cuántos abuelos tiene Vd.?
　　3. ¿Tiene Vd. hambre?
　　4. ¿Cuántos años tiene su abuelo de Vd.?　¿su abuela?　¿su padre?　¿su madre?
　　5. ¿Ríe Vd. mucho?
　　6. ¿Qué apellido tiene Vd.?
　　7. ¿Es Vd. viejo (-a)?　(*Use* sino *in your answer.*)
　　8. ¿Qué hacemos con la boca?
　　9. ¿Ha aprendido Vd. los números?
　10. ¿Cuántas letras hay en el alfabeto?
　11. ¿Tiene Vd. un vestido nuevo?
　12. ¿De qué color es su vestido de Vd.?
　13. ¿Hace calor hoy?
　14. ¿Llueve en el verano?

REPASITO

I. Write your own and your parents' names, using the full Spanish forms.

II. Translate each of these sentences in two ways:

1. No tengo nada. 2. No veo a nadie. 3. No hemos oído nada.
4. No van nunca a la iglesia. 5. No tiene ningún dinero.

III. Complete with the correct form of **ser** *or* **estar:**

1. Nosotros —— contentos. 2. ¿—— Vd. triste hoy? 3. Lola
—— inteligente. 4. Pablo —— un buen muchacho. 5. Guanajuato
—— un pueblo bonito. —— en México. 6. Los pájaros —— en las
jaulas. 7. Los pájaros —— muy bonitos. 8. Yo no —— cansado.
9. He —— cansado. 10. El abuelo —— aquí.

IV. Give the feminine form for each word:

azul	abuelo	cortés
español	inglés	francés (*French*)
esposo	hijo	americano
padre	fácil	criado

V. Conjugate in the present tense:

servir, dormirse, encontrar, saber, pedir

VI. Answer in Spanish:

1. ¿Qué hora es? 2. ¿Qué día es? 3. ¿Cuál es la fecha? 4. ¿Hace
calor? 5. ¿Hace frío? 6. ¿Hace viento? 7. ¿Tiene Vd. hambre?
8. ¿Tiene Vd. razón siempre? 9. ¿Tiene Vd. los pies pequeños?
10. ¿Tiene Vd. las orejas grandes? 11. ¿Se usa un abanico cuando
hace frío? 12. ¿Se pone usted una chaqueta cuando hace calor?
13. ¿Qué se pone usted en la cabeza para protegerse del sol? 14.
¿Llueve ahora? 15. ¿Cuántos años tiene Vd.?

VII. Try this game:

«*Caracoles*» is like the English game "*Buzz.*" Count around the
class in Spanish to 100. Every time you reach 7, a multiple of 7, or a
number containing a 7, say «*Caracoles*» instead of the number.
Every person who says the number when he should say «*Caracoles*»
has to stand up, and the winner is the one who stays seated the
longest.

VIII. Write in Spanish:

1. I have just read a letter from a friend of mine. 2. My friend is

in Mexico.   3. He has studied Spanish in school.   4. Now he speaks it every day.   5. He says that the Mexicans are very pleasant.   6. On Thursdays and Sundays everyone goes to the plaza.   7. In the evening there is music.   8. My friend sits in the plaza in order to hear the music and to look at the people.   9. The families sit on benches around the plaza.   10. The children play in the center of the plaza. 11. The young ladies walk (use **andar**) to the right around the plaza and the young men walk to the left.   12. There are many vendors. They sell newspapers, candies, papers, and other things.

IX. ¿Sabe Vd. leer estos chistes?

Una invitación

—Señor, déme Vd. diez centavos, porque no he comido hoy.
—Ni yo tampoco.
—Pues déme Vd. veinte y vamos a comer juntos (*together*).

Precaución

Él — ¿Quiere Vd. tener un esposo tuerto (*one-eyed*)?
Ella — ¡Claro que no!
Él — Entonces déjeme llevar la sombrilla (*parasol*).

PALABRAS PARA HOY

la abuela	grandmother	2 la letra	letter (of the alphabet)
el abuelo	grandfather		
los abuelos	grandparents	1 levantar	to raise, lift
el apellido	surname	2 la manera	manner, way
1 caer	to fall; *pp.*, **caído**	la muñeca	doll
el cartero	postman	1 oír	to hear, listen
2 casarse (con)	to marry	3 reír	to laugh
chico, -a	little one	reírse de	to laugh at
1 dejar	to let, allow	1 traer	to bring, carry
2 el esposo	husband (*spouse*)	1 viejo, -a	old
		4 la viuda	widow

CARDINAL NUMERALS 10–1000

diez	10	cincuenta	50
veinte	20	sesenta	60
treinta	30	setenta	70
cuarenta	40	ochenta	80

noventa	90	quinientos	500
ciento (cien)	100	seiscientos	600
doscientos, -as [1]	200	setecientos	700
doscientos uno	201	ochocientos	800
trescientos	300	novecientos	900
cuatrocientos	400	mil	1000

EXPRESIONES

acabar de, to have just

*no . . . más que, only (no more than)

*querer decir, to mean

CAPÍTULO 22

Un norteamericano en México

Alfredo está escribiendo una carta a su amigo en los Estados Unidos del Norte. Aquí tienen Vds. la carta.

México, D.F.,[2]
10 de noviembre de 19—.

Querido amigo mío:

Como sabe Vd., estoy aquí en la capital para seguir mis estudios. Hay tantas cosas que ver y que hacer que es difícil encontrar la oportunidad[3] para escribir cartas.

[1] You will learn how to use these numbers in Chapter 28.

[2] *D.F.* stands for **Distrito Federal** (*Federal District*), where Mexico City is located. Compare "Washington, D.C."

Many people go to Mexico City to study in the University of Mexico, which was founded in 1555, sixty-five years before the Pilgrims landed at Plymouth Rock!

[3] Frequently the ending *-ad* or *-dad* is equivalent to the English ending *-ty*. For example: **oportunidad**, *opportunity;* **ciudad**, *city;* **universidad**, *university;* **majestad**, *majesty.*

Vivo con una familia mexicana muy simpática.   Todos me
10 ayudan muchísimo.   El hijo mayor está estudiando el inglés
en el colegio.¹   Quiere hablar conmigo para practicar la
lengua.   No la habla muy bien, aunque está aprendiéndola
rápidamente.   Casi siempre sale muy bien en los exámenes.
Solamente necesita práctica (practice) en hablar.   Todos me
15 dicen que yo hablo muy bien el español, pero creo que es un
favor que ellos me hacen.²   Sé que estoy aprendiendo muchísimo, y siempre trato de hablar español.

He aprendido algo muy curioso.   Todo el mundo me pregunta, — ¿Es Vd. inglés?
20   Al principio yo contestaba (used to answer), — Soy americano.

Pero entonces me preguntaban (would ask), — ¿De Chile,
de la Argentina, o de qué país?

Yo contestaba, — Soy de los Estados Unidos del Norte.³
25   — Ah.   Vd. debe decir que es norteamericano.

Ahora sé que un americano es alguien de un país sudamericano o norteamericano.   Nosotros debemos decir que somos
norteamericanos.

Al saber que soy norteamericano, todo el mundo me pre-
30 gunta, — ¿Conoce Vd. a muchos actores del cine? —   Les
interesan mucho nuestras estrellas del cine.   Quieren ir a ver
las películas norteamericanas aunque generalmente no pueden
entender lo que dicen los actores.   Hay títulos en español que
leer, para entender lo que están diciendo los actores.⁴
35   Muchas veces alguien me dice, — ¿Conoce Vd. al Sr.
Fulano?   Es un pariente mío que vive en los Estados Unidos
del Norte.

---

¹ *Colegio* literally means *college,* but the school is not the same as our college.
It is the secondary school corresponding to our high school plus junior college.
From the *colegio,* students go to the university (*universidad*).

² See the Vocabulary for Chapter 8 if you have forgotten this phrase.

³ The abbreviation is E.E.U.U. or E.U.A.

In Mexico they call our country « *Los Estados Unidos del Norte*» because theirs
is officially « *Los Estados Unidos Mexicanos.*»

⁴ American movies are shown in Spanish-speaking countries just as they are
here, but titles telling what the actors are saying are printed in Spanish at the
bottom of the film.

The University of Seville has been attended by many students from other lands. The "quadrangle" of this university turns out to be circular, with a moat around it.

No saben que nuestro país es grandísimo y que sería milagro (*it would be a miracle*) conocer a aquel individuo.

Estoy asistiendo a algunas clases en la universidad. Me parece que los profesores hablan rápidamente, pero poco a poco estoy acostumbrándome al sonido (*sound*) de la lengua y puedo entenderla bastante bien. 40

Todo el mundo me dice que soy muy simpático. Dicen eso porque trato de hablar su lengua. Nunca he visto gente tan amable como la gente mexicana. Todos quieren ayudarme. 45 Y ¡qué corteses son!

Probablemente Vd. está jugando al fútbol[1] ahora. Aquí

[1] Some words, especially those dealing with American sports, have no equivalent in Spanish because they did not exist in their language until they were copied from ours. Spanish uses our words, changing the spelling to form a sound similar to our pronunciation. You will find a list of some of these words in the *Repasito* this time.

In the same manner we sometimes have to use Spanish words because we have none for certain things of Spanish origin. Examples: *tortilla, tamal, tamalada, mantilla.*

no lo juegan como nosotros, porque juegan al soccer.   En
50 otra carta voy a decirle a Vd. algo del juego español que se
llama «pelota».[1]   Es un juego dificilísimo y rapidísimo.

Pero ahora tengo que acostarme.   Todo el mundo está
durmiendo y yo quiero dormirme también.

Quedo de Vd. atto. afmo. y S.S.[2]

55
Alfredo

Find These Expressions in the Story

1. There are so many things to see
2. a very nice Mexican family
3. he is learning it rapidly
4. I think they flatter me
5. I am learning a great deal (very much)
6. I try to speak Spanish
7. I am from the United States.
8. Our movie actors interest them.
9. what the actors are saying
10. our country is very large
11. It is a very rapid and difficult game.
12. I have to go to bed
13. everyone is sleeping
14. I have never seen such kind people

COSAS DE INTERÉS

77. The Gerund

INFINITIVE	MEANING	GERUND	MEANING
entrar	to enter	entrando	entering
pensar (ie)	to think	pensando	thinking
encontrar (ue)	to find	encontrando	finding
comer	to eat	comiendo	eating
vivir	to live	viviendo	living
dormir (ue, u) III RC [3]	to sleep	durmiendo	sleeping
decir (i) III RC	to tell	diciendo	telling
pedir (i) III RC	to ask for	pidiendo	asking for
ir	to go	yendo	going

1. What is the equivalent of the English -ing for -ar verbs?
2. What is the equivalent of -ing for -er and -ir verbs?

---

[1] *Pelota,* or «*jai alai,*» as it is also called, is a Basque game popular in all Spanish-speaking countries.

[2] For the translation, see the notes to Chapter 14.

[3] "III RC" means "third conjugation radical-changing."

3. To what part of the verb is the ending added?

4. Which radical-changing verbs have a stem change in the gerund?

5. How is the gerund of *ir* irregular?   What would it be if it were regular?   What happens to *-iendo* in rapid speech?

REMEMBER:

(1) *-ing* = $\begin{cases} \textit{-ando (-ar} \text{ verbs)} \\ \textit{-iendo (-er, -ir} \text{ verbs)} \end{cases}$

(2) In *-ir* radical-changing verbs:
Stem *o* > *u;* stem *e* > *i*

Spanish does not allow an unaccented *i* between two vowels. Therefore the *i* of *-iendo* turns to *y* when the stem ends in a vowel.   Example: *leer, leyendo.*

EJERCICIO I.   *Give the gerunds of these verbs.*   (Watch out for III RC verbs!)

trabajar	servir (i)	entender (ie)	pedir (i)
morir (ue, u)	llegar	llover (ue)	conocer
ver	ser	escribir	preguntar
venir (ie, i)	dar	salir	hacer
oír [1]	traer [1]	caer [1]	poner

78. Progressive Form of the Present Tense

PRESENT PROGRESSIVE MODEL

estar estudiando, *to be studying*

estoy estudiando	estamos estudiando
estás estudiando	estáis estudiando
está estudiando	están estudiando

The gerund is used with **estar** to make the progressive form of the present tense.   Both **estudio** and **estoy estudiando** may be translated *I am studying.*   The progressive form emphasizes the idea of progressing or continuing action.

[1] How many vowels?

EJERCICIÒ II.   *Put these verbs in the progressive form:*

1. miro	5. ella pierde	9. no gana
2. Vd. piensa	6. duermen	10. Vd. sube
3. tocamos	7. vende	11. empezamos
4. ayudan	8. Vds. escriben	12. veo

EJERCICIO III.   *Put these verbs in the regular form of the present tense:*

1. está durmiendo   2. están viviendo   3. estoy asistiendo   4. Vd. está oyendo   5. estamos volviendo   6. Carlos está jugando   7. Vds. están aprendiendo   8. está vendiendo

EJERCICIO IV.   *Give the regular and the progressive forms and translate:*

1. cuidar (*I*)   2. bailar (*he*)   3. leer (*they*)   4. gastar (*you*)
5. abrir (*we*)   6. lavar (*she*)   7. llamar (*you, pl.*)   8. recibir (*it*)

79. Object Pronouns with the Gerund

Read these model sentences carefully:

Está trayendo la carta; está trayéndola.
He is bringing the letter; he is bringing it.

Está aprendiendo el español; está aprendiéndolo.
He is learning Spanish; he is learning it.

Me despido; estoy despidiéndome.
I am saying good-by.

1. Where are object pronouns placed with the gerund?
2. Can you apply the "1-2-3-accent" rule to gerunds with object pronouns?   (See section 46.)
3. What is the position of object pronouns with a conjugated verb?
4. What are the three times when object pronouns follow the verb?
5. *Translate and explain word order:* no quiere vernos; lo puedo encontrar; escríbame Vd. una carta; estoy aprendiéndolo; debemos decirlo; todos me preguntan; ¿la conoce Vd.?; quiere conocerla; dígame Vd.; no me diga Vd.

REMEMBER:	Object pronouns precede a verb unless it is: 1. an infinitive 2. an affirmative command 3. a gerund Then they follow and are attached to the verb.

EJERCICIO V. *Use pronouns in place of the italicized nouns:*

1. Lola está oyendo *la música*. 2. El chico está comiendo *la manzana*. 3. Arturo no está usando *el lápiz*. 4. Está escribiendo *la carta*. 5. Juan está leyendo *los verbos*. 6. La criada está lavando *la ropa*. 7. El hombre está vendiendo *el animal*. 8. Lupita está ayudando *a Carlos*.

EJERCICIO VI. *Put these forms into Spanish, saying each one in two ways (regular and progressive). Be careful, for they are all reflexive verbs!*
levantarse

1. I am falling asleep. 2. He is marrying. 3. They are rising. 4. She is washing herself. 5. He is putting on his (*la*) jacket. 6. We are sitting down (*seating ourselves*). 7. You are dressing.

80. Present Tense of Seguir

seguir (i), *to continue* or *follow*

sigo	seguimos
sigues	seguís
sigue	siguen

POLITE COMMAND
siga Vd.

GERUND: siguiendo (*III RC*)
PAST PARTICIPLE: seguido

The letter *u* is silent in *gue* and *gui* unless marked: *güe, güi* (*vergüenza*). The first person singular and commands of *seguir* have to drop the *u* because *u* in *gua* and *guo* is pronounced.

EJERCICIO VII. *Conjugate like* seguir: conseguir (i) (*to attain*), perseguir (i) (*to pursue*).

EJERCICIO VIII. *Say in Spanish:*

1. follow me   2. he continues   3. he has continued   4. we continue   5. she is continuing (*progressive form*)

81. The Absolute Superlative

difícil	difficult	**dificilísimo**	very (most) difficult
mucho	much	**muchísimo**	very much
rápido	fast, rapid	**rapidísimo**	very fast

EJERCICIO IX. *After you have looked at the examples above,
answer these questions:*

1. How may *-ísimo* be translated in English? (*two ways*)   2. To
what is it added?   3. If an adjective ends in a vowel, what must be
done before adding *-ísimo?*   4. Give the feminine singular and plural
and the masculine plural of *muchísimo.*

EJERCICIO X. *Give the absolute superlative for these adjectives and then tell what the form means in English:*

hermoso	contento	vivo	bonito	fácil [2]
alto	importante	gordo	largo [1]	blanco [1]
dulce	inteligente	malo	rico [1]	grande

EJERCICIO XI. *Complete in Spanish:*

1. Es una mujer *very fat.*   2. El libro es *very easy.*   3. Es un juego
very fast (rapid).   4. Los Estados Unidos del Norte es un país *very
large.*   5. Es una costumbre *most curious.*

PREGUNTITAS

I. 1. ¿Dónde está Alfredo?
    2. ¿Qué está haciendo?
    3. ¿Dónde está su amigo?
    4. ¿Quién está estudiando el inglés?
    5. ¿Comó se llama la escuela secundaria de los países de habla
       española?

---

[1] What change in spelling is necessary in order to keep the sound?

[2] Two written accents in the same word are impossible; consequently *a* loses its
accent.

6. ¿Quién necesita práctica en hablar?
7. ¿Qué es un americano?
8. ¿Cómo se llama una persona de los Estados Unidos del Norte?
9. ¿Qué interesa a los mexicanos?
10. ¿Qué país es grandísimo?
11. ¿Cómo es la gente mexicana?
12. ¿Juegan al fútbol en México?

II.   1. ¿Qué aprende Vd. poco a poco?
2. ¿Es Vd. americano?
3. ¿Trata Vd. de hablar español?
4. ¿Está Vd.[1] durmiendo ahora?
5. ¿Es facilísimo el juego de fútbol?
6. ¿Asiste Vd. a la universidad?
7. ¿Asiste Vd. al cine muchas veces?
8. ¿Quién es su actor favorito?

REPASITO

I. What do these endings usually mean?

1. -oso	3. -ando	5. -mente	7. -ísimo
2. -ción	4. -ad	6. -iendo	8. -er

Give three examples of words for each ending.

II. Practice pronouncing these words, which are English words used in Spanish with spelling changes to produce a sound as nearly like the English word as possible. Remember to sound each letter according to Spanish rules for pronunciation.

1. béisbol	4. noquear	7. boicotear	10. suéter, suera
2. líder	5. boxeo	8. mítin	11. biftec
3. nócaut	6. fútbol	9. raquetero	12. flirtear

Guess the meanings. Check your guesses with the list in the footnote.[2]

---

[1] Note the position of *Vd.* in a question with the progressive form of the verb. But: *¿ Está durmiendo Juan?*

[2] 1. baseball 2. leader 3. knock-out 4. to knock out 5. boxing 6. football 7. to boycott 8. meeting 9. racketeer 10. sweater 11. beefsteak 12. to flirt

III. Give commands, using the following verbs. (Example: poner: ¡Ponga Vd. el sombrero en la mesa!)

1. traer	5. quedarse	9. ir
2. salir	6. oír	10. sentarse
3. seguir	7. reír	11. venir
4. levantarse	8. decir	12. leer

IV. Use pronouns in place of the italicized nouns:

1. Voy a escribir *la carta.* 2. No ha recibido *la carta.* 3. ¡Ponga Vd. *el libro* aquí! 4. Necesitamos *el dinero.* 5. La mujer da *las frutas* al hombre. 6. Carlos trata de hablar *el español.* 7. Los alumnos están estudiando *los verbos.* 8. Su padre está leyendo *el periódico.* 9. Su madre está ayudando *a Juanito.* 10. Ha escrito *el nombre.*

V. Write in Spanish, using the progressive form wherever possible:

1. Are you sleeping? No, I am thinking. 2. Do you think with your eyes closed? Sometimes. 3. Tell me, what have you done with my book? 4. It is on the table. Have you read it? 5. No. It is most difficult. 6. Read it, but don't read rapidly. 7. Mary opens the book to page two hundred and fifty and reads to her friend. 8. She is reading in a low voice. 9. Her friend says, "I can't hear you." 10. Mary continues reading. 11. She is tired and puts the book on the table. 12. The girls begin to talk.

VI. ¿Sabe Vd. leer estos chistes?

En un hotel

— ¿Qué precio tienen los cuartos?

— En el primer piso, cinco dólares por día; en el segundo, cuatro; en el tercero. . . .

— ¡Bastante! Este hotel no tiene la altura (*height*) que yo necesito.

Mala suerte

— ¿Con que (*so then*) ha muerto el amigo Pérez?

— Sí, señor; y ciertamente que nunca me consolaré (*I shall console myself*) de su muerte (*death*).

— ¿Tan buenos amigos eran (*you were*) Vds.?

— No; pero me he casado con su viuda.

PAJARILLO BARRANQUEÑO

This is a folk song with the typically Mexican vocal glide
and suddenly loud ending. Each stanza should be sung
twice.

Arr. by E. M. JARRETT

Pa - ja - ri - - llo, pa - ja - ri - llo, pa - ja - ri -
To - ma es - ta . . . . lla - vi - ta de o - ro, a - bre el co -

- llo ba - rran - que - ño, ¡Qué bo - ni - tos o - jos tie - ne, lás - ti -
- ra - zón y ve - rás lo mu - cho que yo te quie - ro, y lo

ma que ten - gan due - - ño! due - ño! . . ¡Ay!
po - co que tú me am - - as. me am - as. . . ¡Ay!

1. Little bird, little bird,
   Little bird of the ravine,
   What pretty eyes it has;
   Too bad they have an owner.

2. Take this little golden key,
   Open my heart and you shall see
   How much I love you
   And how little you care for me.

PALABRAS PARA HOY

Alfredo	Alfred	2 **la lengua**	language (*lingo*)
acostarse (ue)	to go to bed,	1 **muchísimo**	very much
	to lie down	2 **necesitar**	to need (*neces-*
3 **acostumbrarse a**	to become ac-		*sity*)
	customed to	4 **norteamericano,**	from the
4 **amable**	kind (*amiable*)	**-a**	United States
3 **asistir a**	to attend	**el pariente**	relative
3 **ayudar**	to help	**la película**	film
el cine	movies	1 **seguir (i)**	to continue,
	(*cinema*)		follow
1 **entender (ie)**	to understand	**sudamericano,**	South Ameri-
1 **eso**	that (referring	**-a**	can
	to an idea)	1 **tantos, -as**	so many
los Estados Uni-	the United	3 **el título**	title
dos del Norte	States	2 **tratar de**	to try to
3 **el estudio**	study	1 **yendo**	going (gerund
4 **interesar**	to interest		of **ir**)

EXPRESIÓN
*poco a poco, little by little

CAPÍTULO 23

Tres fiestas típicas

Nuestro amigo, Paco Stuart, pasaba cada verano en algún país de habla española, aprendiendo todo lo posible acerca de sus costumbres.   Al mirar el calendario español, podía ver que cada día era el día de algún santo o héroe.   Muchos de
5 estos santos eran tan importantes que era costumbre celebrar su día con una fiesta.   Especialmente era costumbre celebrar

The dance of the Moors and Christians is about to begin in a little Spanish town. The "Moors" wear turbans or fezzes, and the "Christians" wear uniforms.

el día del santo patrón (*patron saint*) de cada pueblecito. Por ejemplo, Paco aprendió (*learned*) que cualquier pueblo llamado San Marcos (*St. Mark*) — en México, en España, o en la América del Sur — celebraba el veinte y cinco de abril, porque 10 éste era el día de San Marcos. En México era también el principio de la estación de lluvias,[1] y la gente creía que sin esta celebración, el santo no iba a traer cosechas (*crops*) buenas.

La fiesta empezaba muy temprano por la mañana con 15 cohetes (*fireworks*)[2] al amanecer (*at dawn*); y durante todo el

---

[1] *la estación de lluvias,* the rainy season. In most of Mexico one does not speak of "winter" or "summer"; the year is divided into the "rainy season" and the "dry season." The rains officially begin on April 25 and then the brown countryside turns green and beautiful, even in the desert country, for it rains nearly every day until October.

[2] On fiesta day the dawn is greeted by a swish and boom of skyrockets which blossom red from the top of the church. Then the bells in the towers add their clanging to the noise, and in a few minutes the dim streets are alive with people coming to the mass which officially begins their fiesta.

This story could have been told just as well in the present tense, for all these things are true today, just as when Paco discovered them. But we wanted to use that new tense!

Girls of Tehuantepec are called the prettiest of Mexico. For their fiesta dance and the Battle of Flowers they carry brightly lacquered gourds.

día había ceremonias, procesiones, y bailes en honor del santo que traía la lluvia. Sus amigos le dijeron (*told*) a Paco que antes era una fiesta puramente religiosa, y que todos iban a

20 la iglesia para rezar (*pray*); pero que hoy día se había convertido (*it had changed*) en algo como una feria (*fair*) con vendedores en las calles y las plazas, y con juegos, rodeos,[1] y música de guitarras y violines por todas partes.

Paco aprendió una cosa curiosa en estas fiestas. Era que

25 muchas veces, hasta en México, se veía la danza de los moros[2]

[1] Any Westerner knows what a *rodeo* is, but Easterners may have to be told that it is a spring round-up for branding the new calves. A fiesta *rodeo* is just for fun, to show the skill of the men at riding and roping. Sometimes it is called a *fiesta de charros*. The word *rodeo* is of Spanish origin.

[2] The Dance of the Moors and Christians is a medieval-appearing performance which represents the Christians' final defeat of the Moors in Spain in 1492; and, strangely enough, it is probably given more often in Mexico than in Spain. One often hears even in modern Mexico the expression «*Ya no hay moros en la costa*» (*the coast is clear*), which still commemorates that age-old Spanish fear of the Moors.

y los cristianos, aunque nunca había habido (*there had been*) moros allí. Paco creía que la historia de España, con sus setecientos años de moros, se veía en aquella costumbre mexicana, porque los mexicanos habían (*had*) adoptado la danza antigua que habían aprendido de los conquistadores hacía 30 muchos años.

Una fiesta famosísima que Paco encontraba en todos los países de habla española era Carnaval, que duraba los tres días antes de cuaresma (*Lent*). Durante esos días, toda la gente se divertía muchísimo, sabiendo que al fin de la fiesta 35 vendrían (*would come*) cuarenta días sin diversiones. En España, Paco aprendió que la celebración más popular de Carnaval se verificaba (*took place*) en Sevilla; mientras que cuando estaba en México, Paco trataba de ir a Mazatlán para aquella fiesta como todos los mexicanos. 40

Cada vez que Paco estaba en Mazatlán durante Carnaval, había en las calles procesiones de gigantones[1] y carros adorna-

---

[1] *Gigantones,* big giants, are over-sized papier mâché figures of people, comical or serious, which are used in many fiesta processions. They are particularly popular in Sevilla at carnival time; in almost any Spanish church one can find many of them stored away between festivals.

Everyone makes cascarones at carnival time, by decorating eggshells and filling them with confetti.

Charles D. Jarrett

dos (*decorated*), con el Rey Momo (*Fun King*) ocupando el
trono (*throne*) de un coche majestuoso.   Más tarde había un
45 «combate de flores» (*Battle of Flowers*) en la avenida principal,
y toda la gente se paseaba por ésta en sus automóviles, tirando
flores al encontrar a sus amigos.   Por la noche cientos de
personas recorrían las calles, vestidas de trajes extravagantes
y llevando caretas (*masks*),[1] riendo, cantando, dando chascos
50 (*playing jokes*) y divirtiéndose muchísimo.   También se
tiraban «cascarones,»[2] y dentro de poco las calles estaban
llenas de confetti.   En los centros sociales había bailes de
carnaval, y todos se divertían hasta muy tarde.

Durante los tres días de Carnaval, Paco siempre tenía la
55 oportunidad de comer toda clase de golosinas (*goodies*) que se
vendían en las calles; y los vendedores se hacían ricos, o al
menos ganaban mucho dinero vendiéndolas.   Así era que
con los ricos y los pobres de cualquier país de habla española
que Paco visitaba, esta fiesta era una de las favoritas.

60 La fiesta más famosa de México, a donde iba Paco muchas
veces, era la (*that*) de la Virgen de Guadalupe, el doce de
diciembre.[3]   Se celebraba durante toda una semana, y hasta
los españoles y los sudamericanos trataban de ir una vez si
podían.   La Virgen de Guadalupe es la santa patrona de la

---

[1] The fun and noise in the streets resemble New Year's Eve merrymaking in
any American city, when "anything goes" and one may be as foolish as he wishes.

[2] *Cascarones*, literally, *big eggshells*, are half the fun of Carnival in Mexico and
South America.   A hole is punched in one end of the egg and the contents shaken
out.   When dry, the shell is decorated with water colors, filled with confetti, and
the hole covered with paper and a fringed frill.   The game is to crush a *cascarón*
on your victim's head before he can do the same to you, of course saying *con su
permiso* as you do it.

Cascarones are also very popular in Mexico on the fifth of May and the sixteenth of September, which are like our Fourth of July.

[3] *La Virgen de Guadalupe* is a picture of a madonna which mysteriously appeared on December 12, 1531, painted neatly in oils upon the blanket of an Indian.
Her fiesta is the grandest one of the year in Mexico, and turns the Villa de Guadalupe (now officially named Villa Madero, but no one calls it that) into a crowded
fair that lasts for a week.   In the very lap of the church are merry-go-rounds,
sideshows, Hula dancers, fortune-tellers, and booths that sell everything from
religious medals to soft drinks; so when the pilgrim has dutifully climbed the
stone steps of the Hill of Tepeyac on his knees, he may enjoy himself in a big way
during the rest of his stay.

Fruit fiesta in Tehuantepec features a parade of girls carrying lacquered gourds of fruits and knickknacks on their heads.

65 república mexicana; y miles y miles de personas iban a su
capilla (*chapel*) para dar las gracias por los favores que habían
recibido durante el año.

Los pobres pasaban días enteros en el camino a pie o en
burro, cada uno llevando algo que vender; y al llegar a la
70 Villa de Guadalupe, vivían en las calles como los gitanos
(*gypsies*), durmiendo, comiendo y vendiendo allí sus mer-
cancías (*merchandise*). Por todas partes se vendían «gorditas
de la Virgen,»[1] calientitas y envueltas en papelitos de colores

---

[1] «*Gorditas de la Virgen*,» "*little fat ones of the Virgin*," are plump little cookies
patted out of stiff, sweet dough and fried right there in the street over a charcoal
brazier. Rolled up in lots of eight or so in bright tissue paper twisted and fringed
at the ends, they contribute color and one of the more pleasant smells to the
crowded fiesta.

Dance of the bull is part of almost any fiesta. The "bull" often runs
through the crowd charging the onlookers, to everyone's amusement.

Black Star

vivos. Los grandes y los chicos las compraban y las comían durante la fiesta. También compraban velas adornadas 75 para ofrecer a la Virgen; y después compraban curiosidades para llevar a casa como recuerdos de su visita.

En la Capilla del Pozo (*Chapel of the Well*), Paco veía muchas veces a los enfermos beber el agua del pozo para curarse; y los sanos (*the well-ones*) la llevaban a casa en una 80 botella para dar a un amigo o pariente que no había podido hacer el viaje. Sus amigos muchas veces le decían a Paco que si bebía (*drank*) del pozo, tendría que (*he would have to*) volver a México algún día; pero la verdad era que Paco volvía de vez en cuando sin haber bebido de esa agua sulfúrea (*sulphur*), 85 porque le parecía que México era un país muy simpático.

Find These Expressions in the Story

1. any little town named St. Mark
2. had changed into something like a fair
3. all the people enjoy themselves very much
4. Paco used to try to go to Mazatlán for that fiesta like all the Mexicans
5. Later there was a Battle of Flowers
6. laughing, singing, playing jokes, and enjoying themselves
7. he often used to see the sick drink the water of the well
8. The poor would spend whole days afoot on the road
9. the rich and the poor of any Spanish-speaking country
10. thousands and thousands of persons would go to her chapel

COSAS DE INTERÉS

82. The Imperfect Tense ("Past Descriptive")

In this story you found a new past tense, called the Imperfect Tense, and used to describe past conditions or to tell of events which happened over and over again. It is very easy to learn because the imperfect stem for every verb in the language except three is the infinitive minus the last two letters. The three exceptions are *ser*, *ir*, and *ver*.

There is one set of endings for *-ar* verbs, and another for *-er* and *-ir* verbs.

IMPERFECT TENSE OF REGULAR VERBS	
-ar verbs: **cantar**	**-er, -ir** verbs: **responder**
used to sing, was singing, sang, (sometimes) *would sing*	*used to answer, was answering, answered,* (sometimes) *would answer*
cant aba	respond ía
cant abas	respond ías
cant aba	respond ía
cant ábamos	respond íamos
cant abais	respond íais
cant aban	respond ían

83. *Imperfect Tense of* Ser, Ir, *and* Ver

THE THREE IRREGULAR IMPERFECTS

ser, *to be*	ir, *to go*	ver, *to see*
era	iba	veía
eras	ibas	veías
era	iba	veía
éramos	íbamos	veíamos
erais	ibais	veíais
eran	iban	veían

EJERCICIO I.   *Answer these questions:*

1. What is the regular imperfect stem?
2. What are the only three verbs irregular in the imperfect tense?
3. What are the regular first conjugation endings? How many accents?
4. What are the regular second and third conjugation endings?
5. What tense do the letters *aba* or *ía* show in an ending?
6. How do you say *used to* in Spanish?
7. Are third conjugation radical-changing verbs irregular in the imperfect?
8. What is the only irregularity about *veía*, etc.?

EJERCICIO II. *Conjugate in the imperfect:*
> estar, dormirse, tener, pagar, poner, irse, ser, ver

84. Use of the Imperfect Tense

The imperfect tense is used for:

1. Past description (*"was —— ing"*):

el sol brillaba	**eran las dos**
the sun was shining	*it was two o'clock*
cantaban los pájaros	**la niña era bonita**
the birds were singing	*the girl was pretty*

2. Repeated past actions; that is, actions done over and over again (*"used to,"* sometimes *"would"*):

de vez en cuando llamaba	**cada vez que pasaba alguien**
from time to time he called	*every time anyone would pass*

> **tocaba el piano todos los días**
> *he used to play the piano every day*

> **jugaba al fútbol los sábados**
> *he used to play football on Saturdays*

EJERCICIO III. *Translate, watching the tenses carefully:*

1. pagamos
2. pagábamos
3. cantan
4. cantaban
5. han cantado
6. ponían
7. vemos
8. veíamos
9. está cantando
10. tenías
11. ella estaba
12. se iba
13. eran
14. yo salía
15. ¡salga Vd.!

85. Imperfect of **Haber**

> **hay dos pájaros aquí,** *there are two birds here*
> **había dos pájaros aquí,** *there were two birds here*

Hay, *there is* or *there are*, is an old form of **haber,** and has no plural. Therefore, when **haber** in the imperfect is used to mean *there was* or *there were*, it has no plural either.

Used as a helping verb, **haber** is conjugated in the imperfect like any **-er** verb, thus forming the past perfect tense. (Chapter 38.)

EJERCICIO IV.   1. *Find three examples in the story of* **había** *used impersonally* (*that is, meaning* there was *or* there were). 2. *Find four examples of* **había** *used with the past participle as a helping verb.*

PREGUNTITAS

(*These questions are asked in the present tense because the answers are still as true as when Paco used to learn about them.*)

1. ¿Por qué hay muchas fiestas en un país de habla española?
2. ¿Qué día se celebra en un pueblecito?
3. ¿Cuándo empiezan las lluvias en México?
4. ¿Qué danza tienen muchas veces en las fiestas?
5. ¿Hay moros en México hoy día?
6. ¿Cuál es una fiesta famosísima en todos los países de habla española?
7. ¿Qué diversiones hay durante Carnaval?
8. ¿Qué son cascarones?   (*Eggshells* are **cáscaras.**)
9. ¿Qué es la Virgen de Guadalupe?   ¿Cuál es su día?
10. ¿Qué llevan los pobres a la Villa de Guadalupe?
11. ¿Cómo viven los pobres durante la fiesta?
12. ¿Por qué van miles de personas a la capilla?
13. ¿Por qué beben los enfermos el agua del pozo?
14. ¿Vuelven muchas personas a México sin beber del pozo?

REPASITO

I. Select from List (*b*) *an opposite for each word or expression in List* (*a*).

(a)

el principio	la luna	enfermo	peor
caliente	el mío	dormirse	morir
temprano	llegar a		
por la mañana	nadie		
contento	nuevo	(b)	
hoy	corto	mujer	quedarse en casa
vender	hombre	viaje	comprar
hacer un viaje	tener calor	vivir	viejo

el fin	alguien	tener frío	salir de
frío	bueno	hambre	ganar
mejor	tarde	el sol	triste
largo	por la noche	nunca	ayer
despertarse	el de Vd.		

II. Here are the idioms we have had with *vez*, *time*. *Select one to complete each of the numbered sentences following them, using each idiom at least once.*

algunas veces, sometimes

muchas veces, often

de vez en cuando, from time to time

otra vez, again

una vez, once

en vez de, instead of

1. Yo compraba mis regalos —— hacerlos. 2. Dígame Vd. ——. 3. Cada mexicano quería ir a la fiesta de Guadalupe al menos ——. 4. Paco comía mucho, pero —— tenía hambre. 5. —— todos compraban «gorditas de la Virgen.» 6. —— no llueve en el día de la Fiesta de la Cueva. 7. —— los indios tenían que hacer un viaje largo para llegar a la fiesta.

III. *Give these verb forms in Spanish.* (Watch the tenses!)

1. he sleeps
2. he was sleeping
3. he used to sleep
4. we make
5. we used to make
6. they give
7. they were giving
8. they have given
9. we used to be (**ser**)
10. I was going
11. I used to go
12. he has brought
13. he was bringing
14. he is bringing (*prog.*)
15. he brings

IV. Write in Spanish:

1. We used to live in the country (*el campo*). 2. In the country there were many animals. 3. We used to have a donkey. 4. His name was Whitey. 5. The donkey was the children's companion. 6. There were lots of (*many*) birds in the country. 7. My little brother used to look for the birds' nests. 8. Fortunately he was little and couldn't climb the trees. 9. On Saturdays we would go to the market. 10. We had to get up early because the market was in town. 11. We always went in (*the*) automobile. 12. The donkey had to remain home then. 13. I can still see him looking at us sadly when we would leave.

V. Answer these questions in English:

1. How did the Dance of the Moors and Christians ever get to Mexico when there are no Moors there?
2. Why is Carnival celebrated so enthusiastically in Spanish-speaking countries?
3. Why do people drink from the Well of Guadalupe?
4. How would the people of a little town, named San José, for instance, know what day to celebrate for its Patron Saint?
5. Why would a Battle of Flowers be very appropriate in Sevilla? (Southern Spain is much like Southern California or Florida.)

VI. Tres chistes para leer si no puede Vd. dormir

Hermanos amables

— No deben Vds. pelear (*fight*), niños. ¿No les han dicho que debemos amar (*love*) a nuestros enemigos?
— No es mi enemigo; es mi hermano.

Un animal bueno

La madre — Vamos a ver, hijita, si sabes cuál es un animal que nos da vestidos y alimento (*food*).
La niña — Yo sé. ¡Es papá!

Un padre rico

Una señora de alta sociedad pide (*asks for*) dinero para sus pobres a (*from*) un banquero riquísimo y éste le (*to her*) da cincuenta duros.
— ¿Cincuenta duros, nada más? Pues, señor, su hijo de Vd. me ha dado doscientos duros.
— Es que mi hijo, señora, tiene la suerte de tener un padre muy rico, y el mío murió (*died*) hace muchos años.

VII. Algunos refranes (proverbs)

Más vale tarde (*late*) que nunca.
No hay rosa sin espinas (*thorns*).
Cortesía de boca, mucho vale y poco cuesta (*costs*).
Más vale el buen nombre que las muchas riquezas (*riches*).
Muchos pocos hacen un mucho.

PALABRAS PARA HOY

4	acerca de	about	1 iba	(imperf. of ir), he, she used to go, was going
4	el baile	dance		
2	beber	to drink (*beverage*)		
4	el carro	car	4 pasearse	to go for a walk, ride, or drive
4	divertirse (ie)	to enjoy oneself		
	divirtiéndose	enjoying themselves	2 el principio	beginning
			3 recorrer	to run through (streets)
3	durar	to last (*endure*)		
4	enfermo	sick (*infirm*)	3 el recuerdo	souvenir
2	entero, -a	whole (*entire*)	3 riendo	(ger. of reír) laughing
3	envuelto	wrapped (*envelope*)		
			1 setecientos, -as	seven hundred
1	era	(imperfect of ser) he, she, it was, used to be	2 tarde	late (new meaning) (*tardy*); más tarde, later
1	éste, -a	the latter (new meaning)	4 temprano	early
1	el fin	end (*finish*)	3 tirar	to throw
1	había	(imperf. of haber) there was, there were; (with p.p.), had	4 la vela	candle
			2 el viaje	trip (*voyage*)
			1 veía	(imperf. of ver), he, she used to see, was seeing
1	hasta	even (new meaning)		

EXPRESIONES

*al menos, at least
*hace (hacía) muchos años, many years ago (tense depends upon tense of main verb)
  hacer el (un) viaje, to take the (a) trip
  hoy día, nowadays

*por ejemplo, for example
*por todas partes, everywhere
  se vendían, were sold
*una vez, once
  todo lo posible, all possible (neuter pronoun referring to a whole idea)

¿Cuánto sabe usted?

Here is a story told in familiar words.   You should be able to read it in four minutes.   Check your understanding of it by the true-false statements at the end.

EL TRAJE DE LOS MEXICANOS

Hay poco que decir acerca del traje de los ricos de México, porque visten como los norteamericanos.   Las señoras ricas generalmente prefieren (*prefer*) vestir de negro, pero todos sus vestidos son muy de moda.   Llevan sombrero en vez de velo

5 en la cabeza, y es un sombrero muy elegante, también.   Antes, muchas iban a París en la primavera o en el otoño para comprar vestidos nuevos, gastando allí mucho dinero.   Hoy día van a Nueva York o a Hollywood.

Practical dark rebozo takes the place of hat and coat for the poorer class woman of Mexico.   Of cotton, it is about a yard wide and three yards long, with fringed ends.

Roberts

Big hats and white cotton suits that look like pajamas are the traditional costume of the Mexican Indian. *Sarapes*, hand-woven woolen blankets, are his overcoat by day and his bedding by night.

El traje de los pobres, como en todos los países, es más pintoresco (*picturesque*), porque no lo compran en Hollywood. 10 Las indias del norte llevan falda y blusa de color obscuro, y rebozo (*scarf*) negro en la cabeza en vez de sombrero. Este rebozo también sirve para llevar al nene (*baby*) y otras cosas. En los pies generalmente no llevan zapatos, sino guaraches (*sandals*), o van descalzas (*barefoot*). En el sur (*south*) las 15 indias llevan ropa de colores más vivos; y se parecen a pájaros tropicales con las faldas rojas, azules, amarillas o verdes.

Antes, sus esposos llevaban muchas veces pantalón y camisa blancos que se parecían a los *pajamas*; aunque hoy día están empezando a usar los «overoles» americanos. ¡Qué 20 lástima! Con el traje blanco, el sombrero de ala ancha, los guaraches y el sarape (*blanket*) de colores vivos, el indio con su burrito era una figura muy pintoresca (*picturesque*) en los caminos de México.

Correct dress for *charro* consists of short jacket, tight trousers, wide hat, and bright *sarape*. Boots are unusual, but the silver-mounted saddle is very typical. *Charros* ride each Sunday morning in Chapultepec Park.

¿Verdad o mentira?

1. Mexican Indians always dress very stylishly. 2. Wealthy Mexican women generally wear black. 3. Wealthy Mexican women often buy their clothes in our country or in Europe. 4. The Indian woman's black scarf serves several purposes. 5. The Indian men often wear white shirts and trousers. 6. Indian women wear broad-brimmed hats. 7. Rich Mexicans dress much as we do. 8. The Indian women of the North wear brighter colors than those of the South.

Companion of the charro is the *china poblana*, with her spangled red and green skirt and embroidered white blouse. She wears the costume only for fiestas or on the stage.

REPASO DE VOCABULARIO

EJERCICIO I. *Finish each sentence with one of the words given in parentheses.*

1. El padre de mi madre es mi (*tío, hermano, abierto, abuelo*).
2. En el cielo por la noche se encuentran la luna y (*las estrellas, las iglesias, el sol, la sala*).
3. En la plaza de un pueblo español se veían árboles, bancos, flores, y (*una piedra, una familia, una fuente, calles*).
4. Una persona que no ha comido va a tener (*hambre, comidas, suerte, hombre*).
5. En las fiestas los españoles tienen la costumbre de cantar, bailar, y (*dormirse, divertirse, despertarse*).
6. Al casarse, una señora abandona el apellido de su (*padre, madre, hijo, pariente*).
7. Cuando hace buen tiempo no (*lluvia, llega, llueve, lleva*).
8. Cuando hace mucho calor, es difícil trabajar sin tener (*razón, color, calor, caliente*).
9. Es necesario tener bastante dinero para (*hacerse viejo, hacer un viaje, tener cincuenta años*).

10. Un señor que vive en los Estados Unidos del Norte se llama un (*sudamericano, americano, norteamericano*).

EJERCICIO II.   *Select the phrase from group (b) which makes the proper ending for each incomplete sentence in (a).*

<table>
<tr><td>(a)</td><td>(b)</td></tr>
<tr><td>1. Todo el mundo le miraba cuando escribía</td><td>a. y S.S.</td></tr>
<tr><td>2. El día de Guadalupe es</td><td>b. en las manos.
c. en la cabeza.</td></tr>
<tr><td>3. Yo iba a ver a don Pablo después de</td><td>d. a máquina.</td></tr>
<tr><td>4. Alguien se hace rico cuando gana</td><td>e. el premio gordo.</td></tr>
<tr><td>5. Una ciudad es más grande que</td><td>f. mi nombre.</td></tr>
<tr><td>6. Las señoritas llevaban una mantilla</td><td>g. — Salud.</td></tr>
<tr><td>7. Cuando paso delante de alguien, digo</td><td>h. comer.</td></tr>
<tr><td>8. Quedo de Vd., atto., afmo.,</td><td>i. un pueblecito.</td></tr>
<tr><td>9. Los señores ricos llevaban zapatos</td><td>j. en los pies.</td></tr>
<tr><td>10. Cuando alguien me presenta a sus amigos, digo</td><td>k. el primer perro.
l. — Con permiso.
m. el doce de diciembre.</td></tr>
</table>

EJERCICIO III.   *Answer in Spanish:*

¿Para qué sirve:
    un viaje, el cartero, la noche, el sol, una taza, un traje, un sombrero?
¿Para qué sirven:
    los ojos, las manos, los pies, los dientes?

REPASO DE COSAS DE INTERÉS

EJERCICIO I.   *Complete these statements:*

1. **Acá** and **allá** are used with verbs of ——.   (§ 57)
2. **Venir** should be used only when it means to come ——.   (§ 58)
3. To compare regular adjectives, use —— and ——.   (§ 54)
4. In comparisons, *than* is translated by ——.   (§ 54)
5. After a superlative, use —— instead of ——.   (§ 54)
6. **Conocer** is to know ——; **saber** is to know ——.   (§ 64)
7. ——, ——, and —— require **no** before the verb when they follow it.   (§ 65)

8. The long forms of the possessives are used after their —— or after the verb ——.   (§ 66)
9. If used elsewhere, these long forms must be preceded by the ——.   (§ 66)
10. —— is often used as an untranslatable connective between a noun or pronoun and an infinitive.   Ex.: *algo* —— *hacer*. (§ 67)
11. In speaking of heat and cold, use —— for weather, —— for living beings, and —— or —— for things.   (§§ 68, 62, 40)
12. *Sino* is used instead of *pero* after a —— with no verb following. (§ 71)
13. Adjectives of nationality have —— forms even if they do not end in *o*.   (§ 72)
14. *Se* is often used with a third person verb without a subject to mean —— or ——.   (§ 69)
15. Gerunds end in —— or ——, which means —— in English. (§ 77)
16. In III RC gerunds, the stem vowel *e>* —— and *o>* ——. (§ 77)
17. In Spanish spelling, there cannot be an unaccented *i* between two ——.   (§ 77)
18. To form progressive tenses, use —— with the ——.   (§ 78)
19. Object pronouns —— the verb unless it is an ——, ——, or ——; then they —— it and are —— to it.   (§ 79)
20. When adding a pronoun to a gerund, it is necessary to count "——, ——, ——, ——."   (§ 79)
21. The ending *-ísimo* on an adjective or adverb means ——.   (§ 51)
22. The *-ar* endings of the imperfect tense are ——.   (§ 82)
23. The *-er* and *-ir* endings of the imperfect are ——.   (§ 82)
24. The only irregular verbs in the imperfect are ——, ——, ——. (§ 83)
25. The imperfect tense usually means "—— ——" or "—— *ing*." (§ 84)

EJERCICIO II.   *Give the list of:*

subject pronouns (§ 23); reflexive pronouns (§ 38); direct object pronouns (§ 44); demonstrative adjectives (§ 26); short forms of the possessives (§ 17); long forms of the possessives (§ 66); seven adjectives which sometimes drop the *o* (§ 42).

REPASO DE VERBOS IRREGULARES

I. Following the model given below, make an outline for each of these verbs:

traer, dar, hacer, dormirse

SYNOPSIS MODEL

INFINITIVE	**salir,** *to leave*
GERUND	**saliendo,** *leaving*
PAST PARTICIPLE	**salido,** *left*
1ST PERSON PRESENT	**salgo,** *I leave*
POLITE COMMAND	**salga Vd.,** *leave!*
1ST PERSON PRES. PROGRESSIVE	**estoy saliendo,** *I am leaving*
1ST PERSON IMPERFECT	**yo salía,** *I was leaving*
1ST PERSON PRESENT PERFECT	**he salido,** *I have left*

Why do we put the polite command beneath the first person singular?

II. Translate these verb forms carefully:

1. hemos hecho
2. cantaban
3. Vd. oía
4. tráigame Vd.
5. no puedo
6. han visto
7. íbamos
8. me voy
9. yendo
10. estamos leyendo
11. oiga Vd.
12. has vuelto
13. dígame Vd.
14. están trayéndolo
15. me comía

III. Give the first person, singular and plural, present tense, of each of these verbs, and the polite commands for each one starred:

1. ir*
2. ser
3. estar
4. poner*
5. dar*
6. tener*
7. venir*
8. salir*
9. conocer
10. hacer*
11. leer
12. saber
13. ver*
14. decir*
15. seguir (i)*
16. traer*
17. caer*
18. oír*

IV. Give the gerund and past participle of each of these verbs:

1. cubrir
2. abrir
3. decir (III RC)
4. morir (III RC)
5. hacer
6. volver

7. ver	10. traer	13. oír
8. poner	11. creer	14. caer
9. escribir	12. leer	15. servir

V. Give the present tense and gerund:

| 1. querer (ie) | 3. contar (ue) | 5. servir (i) |
| 2. mover (ue) | 4. despertarse (ie) | 6. morir (ue, u) |

VI. Conjugate in the present perfect: hacer, volver, contar.

VII. Conjugate in the present progressive: poner, leer.

VIII. Conjugate in the imperfect: saber, dar, ir, ser, ver.

LA COSTUMBRE HACE LEY (*law*)

EJERCICIO I. *How much do you know about Spanish-speaking peoples?*

1. Name the countries where Spanish is spoken.
2. Is Spanish pronounced the same in all of these countries? [1]
3. Are the social customs of all Spanish-speaking countries much alike?
4. Why do the people in the south of Spain have the darkest complexions?
5. In what part of Spain do boys and girls look much like typical Americans?
6. Can a car be driven across the Pyrenees?
7. Where would one find the "typical" Spanish costume that we see on the stage here?
8. Why are fans so popular in Andalucía?
9. What is a "big dog" in Spain?
10. What is always to be found in the center of a typical Spanish town?
11. What is in the center of a typical Spanish home?
12. What Spanish cities are "more Spanish than Spain"?
13. Why do the poorer people carry water from the plaza fountain?

---

[1] A traveler in Sevilla asked the *sacristán* (*sexton*) of the cathedral at what hours he could enter. — *Dehde lah dieh hahta lah doh* — replied the *sacristán* in the typical lower-class Spanish of the south. He meant *desde las diez hasta las dos.* What sound did he leave out?

14. Why do stores close from one to three or four each afternoon?
15. What day do Spanish-speaking people personally celebrate in addition to their birthdays?
16. Are birthday gifts customary?
17. What is a market like in a Spanish-speaking country?
18. What is one of the typical buying and selling customs?
19. Why are there public letter-writers in little towns?
20. Why are national lotteries operated?
21. Do you always call a Spanish-speaking person by what appears to be his last name?
22. Are "Latins" as polite as we are?

EJERCICIO II.   Algo para leer

1. Tres refranes:
   No hay atajo (*short-cut*) sin trabajo.
   Primero son mis dientes que mis parientes.
   Entre la mano y la boca, se pierde la sopa.   (*What do we say?*)

2. Here is a jingle used for "counting out" in children's games, like our "Eenie, meenie, minie, mo."   Why not try it?
   — ¿Quién es éste?
   — Un negrito.
   — ¿Y qué hace?
   — Chocolate.
   — ¿Para quién?
   — Pa' el más bonito.   (*Pa'* = *para*)
   — Bate (*beat*) y bate el chocolate.

Mexico in the Making

Mexico's monument to independence stands on the *Paseo de la Reforma,* once the *Paseo de Carlota.* "Freedom" holds a wreath over Father Hidalgo, who carries the banner of Mexico's patron saint.

Sawders

Not many years ago people in Mexico used to say cynically, "In our country, peace breaks out every now and then." That odd remark will not seem strange to you if you will just glance back over her story, for although the gory conquest by Cortés was over in a few years, there was still much blood destined to be shed before Mexico was to settle down into the modern, progressive country that she is today.

After Cortés, you can count on the fingers of one hand the people who made most of Mexico's history: Father Hidalgo, a priest; Benito Juárez, an Indian; Maximilian and Carlotta, unexpected French Emperor and Empress of a country that had thought itself a republic; and Porfirio Díaz, the Iron Man who had himself "elected" president for thirty years. Four out of these five came to an unhappy end; all of them caused the loss of many lives, and only two of them (Hidalgo and Juárez) have statues erected in their memory throughout the country, which is a good indication of what Mexico, where monuments are numerous, thinks of them.

Going back to colonial times, we find that Spain did not treat her new colony too well. Two hundred and fifty years later, our own ancestors were to complain bitterly about "taxation without representation"; but Mexico, long before, had had even more to protest about in Spain's iron rule of the wealth-producing New World. For almost three hundred years Mexico was to Spain merely a source of income. Kings appointed court favorites as viceroys who, with few exceptions, sailed home from their terms in Mexico with pockets bulging, each leaving behind him a record of cruelty to the natives and of his concern only for the fortune he was collecting for himself. One of the viceroys, to crush the spirit of the people, even forbade them the joyful *jarabe tapatío*, now Mexico's national folk dance, ordering a penalty of two years of imprisonment for the performers and two months for the onlookers!

Finally it was a sixty-year-old priest, Miguel Hidalgo y Costilla, who talked the people of his little parish of Dolores into rebellion after the Spaniards had added the last straw by cutting down the mulberry trees from which the poor were trying to raise silkworms. When Father Hidalgo rang the bell of his little church that early morning on the sixteenth of September of 1810 and gave the famous "Grito de Dolores" (the war cry of "Long live Mexico! Long live independence! Down with the Spaniards! Down with bad government!"), he probably did not realize that he was starting a war between Spain and

Mexico that would last for ten years, and that long before its end he himself would pay the supreme penalty. But that was what did happen, for within a year the brave priest was executed at Chihuahua, and his head placed in an iron cage and hung on the corner of the Castillo de Granaditas in Guanajuato as a warning to those who dared rebel against powerful Spain.

But his spirit went marching on, and, after a long and bloody struggle, Mexico won her independence in 1821, and was ready to begin making her own history.

Mexico then, remember, included all of what is now our own southwest, and it was not long before the United States entered the pages of her story. The war of 1847 is told briefly in our history books, but it is a big, resentful chapter in the Mexican texts. Of course we paid well for the territory — New Mexico, Arizona, and California — that we annexed after the war was over, and for a conqueror to dictate such liberal terms of peace was something which had never been done before. Still, Mexico cannot forget that our flag once floated over Mexico City because there were only cadets, youngsters from the Military Academy, there at the time to defend her capital.

Thus Mexico lost her desert north, already explored and settled by Spaniards and Mexicans, and we gained a part of our country that to this day keeps some of its early Spanish flavor in spite of gold rushes, Horace Greeley![1] and eastern tourists.

Father Hidalgo was Mexico's Washington, and his little church bell is now Mexico's Liberty Bell. Then came a Mexican Lincoln, the Indian Benito Juárez, who had the interests of the poor at heart. He went to work to free them, although they were not slaves in name, from the domination of the aristocrats. The wealthy Conservatives objected to the Reform Laws of Juárez; the middle-class Liberals applauded them. A country divided against itself was an invitation to foreign powers to step in, and France saw the opportunity.

About the time of our own War Between the States, when our North and South were too busy battling to notice what our neighbor below the Rio Grande was doing, France's Napoleon III joined the Mexican Conservatives on the pretext that Mexico had not paid her debts and sent young Maximilian, an Austrian archduke in need of money, to rule the country. The fact that Maximilian insisted upon being "elected" to the job of Emperor betrayed his youth and innocence; but the "election" was favorable, and he and his bride, the beautiful

[1] "Go west, young man!"

Good-natured, blond Maximilian tried hard to be a good Emperor, but a sword hung over his head.

Ambitious Carlotta, with her flashing black eyes and willful mouth, loved being Empress of Mexico.

Belgian Princess Carlotta, entered Mexico to begin a fantastic reign that reads like a fairy tale.

For three years the Mexican capital was the scene of gaiety and festivity unheard of before or since, when the young rulers spent their "allowance" of $141,000 a month on every luxury that caught their fancy. Ambitious Carlotta, with her flashing black eyes, firm little chin and willful mouth, was the "brains" of the pair, but even then her youth and ambition prevented her from realizing until too late what the situation really was. Good-natured, blond Maximilian, with the silky young beard that failed to hide his weak mouth and chin, tried hard in his feeble way to be a good Emperor; but, surrounded by "yes-men," as rulers often are, how was he to know of the sword that hung over his head?

The parties went on. They say Carlotta never wore one of her gorgeous gowns twice; and we do know that she rode in a gold and plate-glass coach decorated with cherubs, and gave a glittering reception each week.   She loved beauty, and commanded that trees be planted in every bare plaza of the country; she had an avenue two hundred feet wide cut diagonally through Mexico City from the heart of the capital to her castle on Chapultepec Hill so that she could watch her beloved Maximilian ride home each day.

Inside the capital everything was lovely, while outside, Mexican guerrilla bands were continually fighting Napoleon's French soldiers, who were getting anxious to go home; and everywhere more and more of the Mexicans who weren't invited to Carlotta's parties muttered ominously at the rule of a foreign country and plotted to get back what was their own.

At about that time, our War Between the States ended, and we looked around to see what had been going on in our neighbor's yard.

Father Hidalgo, a kindly old priest, started Mexico's war for independence with his famous "Grito de Dolores."

Indian Benito Juárez, the stern reformer of Mexico, always tried to better conditions for the poor.

"Paseo de Carlota," Carlotta called the avenue she ordered slashed through Mexico City, but Benito Juárez changed it to *Paseo de la Reforma.* Chapultepec Castle is seen in the distance.

There, in violation of our Monroe Doctrine, sat Maximilian, playing at Emperor. Immediately we sent several businesslike notes to Napoleon III. He took the hint, and back to France went his troops, which was the cue for Maximilian and Carlotta to go, too. But being an Emperor was after all more aristocratic and better paid than being a mere archduke, and the pair decided to stay and rule the country without France's backing. Some say it was Maximilian's ambition that kept them there, but his sister, looking on from faraway Austria, told everybody that it was "that woman" with her love of power who sealed the Emperor's fate by insisting that they stay.

It wasn't long, at any rate, before Carlotta scented the danger that Maximilian did not realize; accordingly, probably against her husband's wishes, she sailed for France to see Napoleon and demand more troops.

That interview must have been embarrassing to the French Emperor, for he had no choice between the veiled orders of the United States and the stormy demands of a beautiful lady with an extensive vocabulary. Carlotta was furious, but still refusing to give up, she went to Rome to see the Pope and ask his intercession. He refused to interfere, and the shock was too much for the high-strung, nervous little Empress.

Something snapped, and Carlotta went mad, to remain so for the rest of her days, living until 1927 a fanciful life of playing at Empress of Mexico in the Belgian castle to which her people took her. Each morning, they say, her servants, playing the parts of court attendants, ambassadors, and nobles, listened to her orders, consulted gravely with the "Mad Empress" on imaginary affairs of State, and let her believe she still ruled her Empire.

Meanwhile, desperate Maximilian let himself be deceived into going to Querétaro, where he expected to find an army to back him, only to be besieged and captured by Mexicans who wanted no Emperor. A brief court martial by Benito Juárez, and the next day Maximilian stood before a firing squad on the Hill of the Bells.

Weak as the young Emperor may have been, no one can say he did not die bravely. He gave each soldier a gold piece, asked forgiveness for his sins against the country, and faced the rifles with head high.

On top of Chapultepec Castle is a roof garden with rosebushes, palms, and orange trees, where Carlotta and her guests used to stroll while conscientious Maximilian worked in his study.

Galloway

Thus ended the French chapter in Mexico, but memories of it remain. To this day one sometimes hears the folk song, "Adiós, Mamá Carlota"; and visitors to Mexico City go on Sundays to see a suite of rooms in Chapultepec Castle, still furnished luxuriously, just as when Maximilian and Carlotta lived in them.   In the National Museum today their gold and glass carriage stands significantly beside the severely plain black one of Benito Juárez, for the days to follow under his stern rule were as proper as his coach, and no doubt equally dull to the wealthy Conservatives who had attended Carlotta's gay parties.

After the death of Juárez, who had been elected President three times, and had always fought with his famous Reform Laws for the good of the down-trodden, came a man who put Mexico before the eyes of the world more than ever before.   Porfirio Díaz, who had helped capture Maximilian, headed a revolt and took command of the country.   For thirty years he was an absolute dictator, conscientiously having himself "elected" now and then, but meanwhile, building railroads, developing mines and oil wells, and encouraging modern industries.   People still talk about the clever way he cleaned up the

Important cities are mainly in the central part of Mexico.

bandits by hiring them to be country policemen on horseback, and about the time he rid himself of an overambitious opponent by graciously appointing him ambassador to a country which had no Mexican Embassy — as the luckless man discovered when he arrived there. Díaz added cast-iron lace bandstands to the plazas that Carlotta had had planted with trees, and ordered the construction of the white marble National Theater that was to sink eight feet into the ground before it was finished, thirty years later.

Opening up the country to foreigners with money to invest put Mexico on the map of international commerce, gave her more peace, law, and prosperity than she had ever known before, and made her the "Treasure House of the World." Still, looking back upon the "good old days of don Porfirio," for which old-timers still sigh, we can see now that he did nothing for the poor. As a result, we find in monument-loving Mexico today no gilded statues of the dictator.

He was eighty years old when in 1911 his resignation was finally demanded by Madero, his unfortunate successor; and, as he sailed for France to end his days, he wept, "My poor Mexico! What will she do without me?"

What she did was just what he anticipated, for, from 1910 to 1920, "The Revolution" swept the land again and again. Men, women, and children were fleeing or fighting for ten years; nothing remained the same as it had been. To this day, roofless, bullet-pitted adobe houses stare sightlessly at the sky, mute reminders of that struggle, while legends and ballads of its heroic names are still to be heard. President after president came into office, eleven in those ten years, some by ballots and some by bullets; and several of them paid with their lives for their brief occupancy of the canopied presidential chair.

Since then peace has slowly come out of chaos, and with the completion of President Cárdenas' Six-Year Plan (1934–1940), a great "bloodless revolution" is found to have taken place. Reforms have begun to better working conditions for the poor, schools have been provided to educate the Indian who had known nothing but misery for four hundred years, and gradually Mexico has taken a long step toward becoming a modern, progressive republic, solving her problems constitutionally and intelligently.

Who knows what great name will be the next to head a modern chapter? Peace, we hope, has "broken out" for a long time to come.

Interesting Books to Read

CAPÍTULO 25

El portal de los Cervantes[1]

«Paz en la tierra hacia los hombres de buena voluntad»

Es la tarde del diez y seis de diciembre, en la sala de los Cervantes. Los tres niños de la familia están preparando el portal para la Navidad. La señora de Cervantes y la criada, Tinita, están ayudándolos. Han puesto dos mesas largas contra la pared de la sala, y sobre ellas han

5 construido de papel montañas (*mountains*), valles, llanos (*plains*),

---

[1] A *portal*, literally, *town gate, arcade,* or *entrance,* has come to mean a whole Nativity scene of little figures representing Mary, Joseph, and the Christ Child, which is found each Christmas in Spanish-speaking homes. It is set up as early as December 16, and stays in place sometimes till February 2. All during the Christmas season people go to see and admire each other's *portales,* for each family, in a spirit of friendly rivalry, tries to make its display the best. Some *portales* are so elaborate that the parents do most of the work, spending months making the tiny figures and houses.

Nativity scenes, which are a necessary part of Christmas in every Spanish-speaking home, are more elaborate in Mexico than in other countries. The cathedral in this one is made of soap!

y desiertos.   Los han cubierto de aserrín (*sawdust*) de colores.¹   Se parece mucho a un paisaje (*landscape*) verdadero.   En el suelo hay una caja grande de cositas para el portal, y Tinita está sacándolas para los niños.

ADELITA (*la hermana mayor*) — Tinita, tráigame Vd.² las figurillas³ de la Virgen María y San José.   10

¹ *aserrín de colores, colored sawdust.*   Dyeing sawdust green, red, and brown is a Christmas job for the children, like our custom of dyeing eggs for Easter.

² Would Adelita really use *Vd.* in addressing the servant?   Of course not; neither would the children use it in speaking to each other, but we must practice our polite commands!   However, we will let *mamacita* use the familiar forms, for we simply can't imagine her using *Vd.* to the children and servants!

³ The little figures of Mary, Joseph, the Christ Child, the Wise Men, and the angel are the center of the scene.   At Christmas time such figures made of clay, lead, or cardboard can be bought in any Spanish-speaking country, while clever people often make beautiful ones of their own.

DOMINGO (*el hermano mayor*) — Y tráigame a mí los animalitos, por favor. Voy a ponerlos aquí cerca del pesebre (*manger*) del Niño Jesús.

15 TINITA (*trayendo las figurillas y los animalitos*) — Aquí los tiene Vd., Adelita.

ADELITA — Gracias. Déle Vd. a él los animalitos. Yo no quiero más que la gente. Miren Vds. ¿Les parece bien poner el San José aquí delante de los tres Reyes Magos (*Wise Men*)?

20 FELIPE — A mí me gusta así.

DOMINGO — Pero a mí no me gusta. Los Reyes son más importantes que el San José, y deben estar más cerca del pesebre (*manger*) que él. ¿Verdad, mamacita?

LA SEÑORA DE CERVANTES — Tienes razón, Domingo.
25 ¿Qué crees tú, Adelita?

ADELITA — No me importa. Los pongo[1] aquí si les gusta a Vds.

FELIPE — Bueno.

DOMINGO — Dénos Vd. los animalitos, Tinita. Felipe y yo
30 vamos a arreglarlos. Quiero poner un perro en este árbol.

TINITA — Aquí los tienen Vds. El burrito de María, dos ovejas, dos vacas, y algunos otros animales. ¡Y miren Vds.! Hay tres camellitos nuevecitos para los Reyes Magos!

LA SRA. DE C. — Su[2] tía Catalina les mandó (*sent*) esos
35 camellos para el portal.

FELIPE — ¡Ay, qué bueno! Tenemos que darle las gracias a la tía Catalina. Nos faltaban camellos. Nuestro portal va a ser preciosísimo este año. Pero, Domingo, ¿no vamos a usar el tren (*train*) con todos los carros? A mí me gusta un
40 tren.

DOMINGO — A mí también. Aquí está, en la caja. Ayúdeme, Felipe, y hacemos un ferrocarril (*railroad*) que llegue (*will reach*) a Belén (*Bethlehem*). (*Los dos niños arreglan el ferrocarril.*)

---

[1] **Los pongo aquí,** present tense, but with a future meaning often found in everyday usage: *I'll put them here.*

[2] In Spanish America the polite plural forms are used instead of the familiar plural, even when speaking to children.

ADELITA — ¿Dónde ponemos el ángel?   Debe estar en el 45
cielo.

LA SRA. DE C. — Eso es fácil.   Lo colgamos por un hilo
(*thread*) sobre el pesebre.   No se ve el hilo, y va a parecer que
el ángel está volando por el aire.

DOMINGO — Entonces yo pongo este aeroplano en un hilo, 50
también.

FELIPE — Mire Vd.   ¿No le gusta a Vd. este gato durmiendo cerca del ratón (*mouse*)?

DOMINGO — ¡Magnífico!   Y vamos a (*let's*) poner un oso
entre las ovejas, y el caballo en el jardín, y —— 55

LA SRA. DE C. — ¡Chis! (*Sh!*) Alguien llama a la puerta.

(*Tinita va a la puerta y la abre.   Entra un joven norteamericano, amigo de los Cervantes, que está haciendo un viaje por
México.*)

LA SRA. DE C. — Buenas tardes, señor Smith.   ¡Cuánto 60
gusto tenemos en verle a Vd.!

EL SEÑOR SMITH — Buenas tardes, señora, y señoritos.
Pasaba por esta calle, y decidí (*I decided*) hacerles una visita.
Parece que Vds. están muy ocupados.   No quiero molestar-
los.[1] 65

ADELITA — ¡Oh, Vd. no va a molestarnos!   Hacíamos
nuestro portal.   Venga Vd. acá a mirarlo.   Acabamos de
arreglarlo.   Está casi completo.   Vd. sabe que un portal es
nuestro «arbolito de Navidad,» ¿verdad?   Representa el
nacimiento (*birth*) del Niño Jesús y todo el campo (*country*) 70
alrededor de Belén.

EL SR. S. — ¡De veras!   Nunca he visto antes un portal.
A ver lo que hay.   ¡Pero, miren Vds.!   ¡Parece que hay
muchos errores!   ¡En esa montaña cubierta de nieve (*snow*)
hay palmeras (*palm trees*), y los osos polares están en el 75
desierto, y los pollos están nadando (*swimming*) en el río!   ¡Y
hay un indio hablando por teléfono, y un aviador trabajando
en el ferrocarril!   ¡No había tales cosas en Belén!

TODOS LOS NIÑOS (*riendo mucho*) — ¡Qué cosa!

---

[1] Why doesn't he add *a Vds.* to explain *los*, as we have been taught to do?

80   ADELITA — ¡No hay errores!   Es que en un portal tratamos
de tener toda clase de contrastes y anacronismos.[1]

   EL SR. S. — ¡De veras!   ¡Qué costumbre tan curiosa!   En
mi país no tenemos nada como esto.

   TINITA (*que cree que este extranjero norteamericano es muy*
85   *curioso*) — Pues, si no tiene Vd. nada como esto, yo digo que
lo que es muy curioso es su país de Vd.

   LA SRA. DE C. — Los dos tienen razón.[2]   Solamente «hay
que bailar al son que se toca.»[3]

Find These Expressions in the Story

1. Give him the little animals.
2. But I don't like it.
3. Your Aunt Catherine sent you those camels.
4. We needed (lacked) camels.
5. there is an Indian talking on the phone
6. I don't care (it doesn't matter to me).
7. Let's see what there is.
8. Come here and look at it.
9. I like a train.
10. Someone is knocking at the door.
11. We have just arranged it.
12. How glad we are to see you!
13. We have nothing like this in my country.
14. That's easy.
15. let's put a bear among the sheep
16. It looks as if (seems) you are very busy.

COSAS DE INTERÉS

86. Indirect Object Pronouns

Here are the rest of the indirect object pronouns that were
mentioned (first and second persons only) in section 44.

---

[1] An anachronism is an error relating to the time of events; for example, there were no airplanes or trains in Bethlehem in Christ's time, so to put them into a Nativity scene is an anachronism.

[2] *Los dos tienen razón, you (two) are both right.*

[3] Any Spaniard feels that he can settle an argument definitely by a shrug of the shoulders and a fitting proverb.

INDIRECT OBJECT PRONOUNS			
Singular		*Plural*	
me	to me	nos	to us
te	to thee	os	to you
le —— a Vd.	to you	les —— a Vds.	to you (*pol.*)
le —— (a él)	to him	les —— (a ellos)	to them (*m.*)
le —— a ella	to her	les —— a ellas	to them (*f.*)

Notice that the third person forms are alike for either gender; therefore they often need explanations to make them clear. (Remember the explanations used for *su?* These are the same except that they use *a* instead of *de,* for all indirect object pronouns mean *to.*)

Le doy los animalitos.
I give the animals to him, her, you.

Le doy los animalitos a ella.
I give the animals to her.

EJERCICIO I.   *Answer these questions:*

1. What preposition with its object may explain the indirect object in English?

2. Do indirect object pronouns have both masculine and feminine forms?

3. Then how do you know whether *le* means *to him, to her,* or *to you?*

4. What belongs in the blanks between *le —— a Vd.,* etc.?

5. Where do indirect object pronouns stand in the sentence? (Give the complete rule.)

6. Why are the explanations *a él,* and *a ellos* given in parentheses?

7. Can you use the explanation *a ella* without the *le?* (You can't have an explanation if there's nothing to explain!)

8. In the expression *déme Vd.* (*give me*) is the *me* a direct or an indirect object pronoun?

EJERCICIO II.   *Translate:*

1. Le doy el lápiz.   2. Le doy a ella la carta.   3. Les traigo a Vds. los zapatos.   4. Nos da las corbatas.   5. Les digo la fecha.   6. Déles Vd. a ellas el sombrero.

87. Prepositional Pronouns

These pronouns are used as objects of any preposition. *Para*, the preposition used, is merely a sample.

Singular			Plural		
(para) **mí**	(for)	me	(para) **nosotros**	(for)	us
(para) **ti**	(for)	thee	(para) **vosotros**	(for)	you
(para) { **Vd.** / **él** (for) / **ella**		{ you / him, it (*m.*) / her, it (*f.*)	(para) { **Vds.** / **ellos** (for) / **ellas**		{ you (*pol.*) / them (*m.*) / them (*f.*)

EJERCICIO III.   *Answer these questions:*

1. Which of these pronouns have we been using already with *de* to explain *su* or with *a* to explain *le* and *les?*
2. Which two are not exactly like the subject pronouns?
3. Can you guess why *mí* has an accent and *ti* does not?   (Remember *mi libro?*)
4. Can these pronouns be used with any preposition?   (Look out for *con*.   With *con* the first two forms are *conmigo* and *contigo*; after that the pronouns are the same as with any preposition.   What would be the plural of *conmigo?*)
5. Name six short prepositions; then give the list of prepositional pronouns with one of them.
6. Prepositional pronouns have exactly the same meanings as the direct object pronouns *me, te, le, la, lo,* etc.   When must they be used instead of the direct object forms?

Prepositional pronouns are used for emphasis as well as for explanations.

EJERCICIO IV.   *In the following sentences which prepositions are used for explanation and which for emphasis?   Why?*

1. Tráigame Vd. a mí las figurillas.   2. A mí no me gusta estudiar.   3. Déle Vd. a él los animalitos.   4. Díganos Vd. a nosotros.   5. ¿A Vd. qué le importa?

88. Gustar, Faltar, Importar

Gustar (*to be pleasing*), *faltar* (*to be lacking*), and *importar* (*to be important, to matter*) are used mostly in the third person, singular or plural. With these verbs, the English object becomes the Spanish subject. Instead of saying *I like a train,* Spanish says *a train is pleasing to me.* (**Me gusta un tren.**)

me gusta	un tren	**nos gusta**	un tren
te gusta	un tren	**os gusta**	un tren
le gusta a Vd.	un tren	**les gusta a Vds.**	un tren
le gusta a él	un tren	**les gusta a ellos**	un tren
le gusta a ella	un tren	**les gusta a ellas**	un tren

EJERCICIO V.   *Answer these questions:*

1. Which pronouns are used with *gustar, faltar,* and *importar?*
2. Where does the subject of *gustar* stand?
3. If the subject of *gustar* is plural, what is the verb form?
4. In the story, why does Felipe add *a mí* to *me gusta un tren?*
5. What is the difference between *no me importa* and *a mí no me importa?*
6. What is the difference between these three ways of saying *I don't like?* Which is the most emphatic? *No me gusta. No me gusta a mí. A mí no me gusta.*

EJERCICIO VI.   *Continue as with* **gustar:** me falta dinero, no me importa.

EJERCICIO VII.   *Translate word for word; then change into smooth English:*

1. Me gusta comer.
2. Nos faltaba dinero.
3. A ellos les gusta dormir.
4. ¿Le gusta a Vd. bailar?
5. Al gato le gustaba beber leche.
6. Le faltan camellos para el portal.
7. ¿Les gusta a Vds. pasearse?
8. ¿Le gustaban a Vd. las flores?

EJERCICIO VIII.   *Substitute an indirect object pronoun for each noun or pronoun in italics:*

1. Doy el perro *a Felipe.*   2. Quería dar el gato *a Adelita.*   3. Tinita no quería traer los animalitos *a Domingo* y *a Felipe.*   4. Dé Vd. la caja *a Domingo.*   5. Dé Vd. el aeroplano *a la señora de Cervantes.*   6. ¿Quiere Vd. contar (*to tell*) la historia (*to me*)?   7. Traigan Vds. los pollos (*to us*).

PREGUNTITAS

I. 1. ¿Sobre qué han construido los niños su portal?
    2. ¿Qué hay en el paisaje (*landscape*)?
    3. ¿Quién está sacando las figurillas de la caja?
    4. ¿Qué ha dado la tía Catalina a los niños para su portal?
    5. ¿Va a ser más precioso el portal este año que antes?
    6. ¿Qué le gusta a Felipe?
    7. ¿Vuela el ángel por el aire?
    8. ¿Quién llamaba a la puerta?
    9. ¿Ha visto el señor Smith un portal antes?
   10. ¿Qué había en la montaña cubierta de nieve?
   11. ¿Por qué creía el señor Smith que había muchos errores en el portal?
   12. ¿Quién creía que el señor Smith era de un país muy curioso?
   13. ¿Quién tenía razón?

II. 1. ¿Le gusta a Vd. la Navidad?
    2. ¿Hacen Vds. un portal en su casa?
    3. ¿Quieren Vds. hacer un portal para la clase?
    4. ¿Ha visto Vd. jamás (*ever*) un perro en un árbol?
    5. ¿Le importa a Vd. no haber preparado la lección?
    6. ¿Le gustaba a Vd. jugar con un ferrocarril pequeño?
    7. ¿Le gusta a Vd. molestar a sus amigos?
    8. ¿Podían nadar los pollos en el río?
    9. ¿Dormían los gatos cerca de los ratones?
   10. ¿Hablaba Vd. por teléfono todos los días?
   11. ¿Ha estado Vd. trabajando en el ferrocarril?

REPASITO

I. Complete in Spanish and learn:

1. Me llamo ——. 2. Tengo —— años de edad (*age*). 3. Vivo en la calle de ——, número ——. 4. Asisto a la Escuela Superior (" *High* ") de ——. 5. Cada día me levanto a las —— de la mañana. 6. Me lavo las manos y la cara. 7. Me visto en seguida. 8. Voy al comedor (*dining room*). 9. Encuentro allí a mis padres. 10. Les digo, — Buenos días.

II. Change the subject of each verb in the preceding exercise to **ella** *and change the verb to the imperfect.* Example: Ella se llamaba ——.

III. Replace the English words with proper forms of the prepositional pronouns and translate:

1. Estaban cerca de *me.* 2. Voy al lado de *her.* 3. Estamos detrás de *them.* 4. Van sin *me;* no van con *me.* 5. Iban lejos de *us.* 6. Felipe está cerca de *him.* 7. Las figurillas están dentro de *it* (la caja). 8. Las palmeras están encima de *them* (las montañas). 9. El gato está debajo de *it* (el árbol). 10. No queríamos ir con *them.*

IV. Translate the English into Spanish. You will have to read the Spanish part of each exercise carefully to know which pronoun to use.

1. Juan ve a María; *he sees her.*
2. Juan va con María; *he goes with her.*
3. Tengo los caballos; *I have them.*
4. Iba con los caballos; *I was going with them.*
5. Vivo en la calle de Hidalgo; *I live in it.*
6. Comía los dulces; *I was eating them.*
7. No tengo dinero para dulces; *I haven't money for them.*
8. Entramos en la iglesia; *we enter it.*
9. Salíamos del edificio; *we were leaving it.*
10. No sé el día; *I don't know it.*

V. Make plural all the words you can in each sentence. (¡Cuidado!)

1. Me gusta el país. 2. El perro va conmigo. 3. Me río de ella. 4. Le faltaba dinero. 5. Me acostaba a la una. 6. Se ha comido la sopa. 7. No me importa el trabajo. 8. Traigo un criado para él. 9. Ponga Vd. la mano detrás de la cabeza. 10. ¿Le gustaba a Vd. el pájaro?

VI. Algo que leer para divertirse

Le gusta bailar

Ella — ¿Sabe Vd. que hay solamente dos cosas que le impiden (*keep from*) ser un buen bailarín (*dancer*)?

Él — ¿Sí? ¿Cuáles son?

Ella — Los pies.

288 EL CAMINO REAL

Un hueso grande

El profesor — Ahora, Juan, díganos Vd., ¿cuál es el hueso (*bone*) menos usado del cuerpo (*body*) humano?

Juan — La cabeza.

Dolor de cabeza

Ella — Cuando un hombre no me gusta, le digo que me duele (*hurts*) la cabeza.

Él — ¿Y ahora?

Ella — Me duele la cabeza.

Una canción vieja

Me gusta la leche,
me gusta el café;
pero más me gusta
bailar con usté (*d*).

Una canción ranchera

Me gustan el pan y el queso
que se venden en el rancho.
Pero me gusta más un beso (*kiss*)
debajo de un sombrero ancho.

PALABRAS PARA HOY

3	**arreglar**	to arrange	1	**llamar**	to knock, ring (new meaning)
3	**la caja**	box			
	Catalina	Catherine	4	**molestar**	to bother, to annoy
4	**construir**	to construct		**la Navidad**	Christmas
	Domingo	Dominick	2	**ocupado, -a**	busy (*occupied*)
3	**el extranjero**	stranger, foreigner	2	**la paz**	peace
	Felipe	Philip	4	**precioso, -a**	delightful, "precious"
2	**gustar**	to be pleasing			
2	**hacia**	toward	2	**el río**	river
1	**hasta**	as far as (new meaning)	1	**señorito**	young fellow
			1	**sobre**	on, upon
2	**importar**	to be important	1	**tal**	such
1	**les**	(to) you, (to) them	2	**la tierra**	earth (*territory*)

Tinita	nickname for Er-nestina	3 volar (ue)	to fly (*volplane*)
2 verdadero, -a	real	2 la voluntad	will (*voluntary*)

ANIMALES

el caballo	horse (*cavalry*)	la oveja	sheep
el camello	camel	el pollo	chicken
el gato	cat	la vaca	cow
el oso	bear	la ratón	mouse

EXPRESIONES

*a ver, let's see (vamos a ver could also be used)
buenas tardes, good afternoon
dar las gracias a, to thank
*de veras, really (usually an exclamation)

*faltar (nos faltan), to lack (we lack)
*hay que, one must, it is necessary to
*me importa, it is important (it matters) to me
por favor, please   (Remember favor de?)

CAPÍTULO 26

El día de los reyes [1]

Para los niños de habla española el seis de enero es tan importante como el veinte y cinco de diciembre.   Tal vez es más importante, porque es el día cuando reciben sus regalos. En nuestro país los niños los reciben en la Nochebuena o en el día de Navidad.   Pero en los países de habla española tienen que esperar hasta el seis de enero.   Nos parece una costumbre curiosa, ¿verdad?   Allí no tienen arbolitos de Navidad, ni

[1] *El día de los reyes* is the sixth of January.   In our church calendars it is called the Day of Epiphany or Twelfth Night.

cuelgan las medias delante de la chimenea,[1] ni saben nada de *Santa Claus.* ¿Por qué celebran el seis de enero?

10 Vds. saben la historia (*story*) del nacimiento (*birth*) del Niño Jesús. Tres hombres sabios ven la estrella y la siguen a Belén. Llevan regalos para el Niño y cuando le encuentran, se los dan. Los tres hombres son los Reyes Magos.

Los niños de habla española creen que los Reyes Magos van 15 a traerles regalos también si han sido buenos. Creen que los Reyes pasan por las calles durante la noche. Por eso los chicos ponen sus zapatos en el balcón. Algunas veces también dejan un poco de paja para los camellos, porque todo el mundo sabe que los Reyes no usan ni burros, ni caballos, ni 20 automóviles, sino camellos, porque tienen que pasar por el desierto.

Muy temprano por la mañana se despiertan los chicos y corren al balcón para ver lo que hay en los zapatos. ¡Qué alegría! ¡Qué contentos están!

25 — ¡Mire, mire! — grita Luisito. — Tengo una escopeta (*gun*).

— Yo tengo una muñeca, — dice Rosario, la hermanita.

— ¡Démela![2] — grita su hermano Arturo. — Voy a probar este cuchillo (*knife*). Me lo han traído los Reyes.

30 — No, no. ¡Es mía! Voy a cuidarla. ¡Cuidado! La palomita va a ponerle a **Vd.** en su lista negra, y los Reyes no le traen nada el año que viene.

Entonces el chico Arturo recuerda que los Reyes no traen nada a los muchachos malos y busca otra cosa con que probar 35 su cuchillo.

Los niños mayores ya saben que los Reyes son sus padres, y como buenos muchachos les dan las gracias.

Luisito ha recibido muchos juguetes. Uno de ellos es un tren mecánico.

---

[1] Typical Spanish-style houses rarely have chimneys. Heating and cooking is done by the use of **braseros** (*braziers*, little dish-like contraptions) in which charcoal (*carbón*) is burned. A large straw fan is kept handy to fan the glowing coals when the heat diminishes.

[2] You need all the practice you can get in the use of the polite forms. Therefore they will be used throughout this story although in real life the family would use the familiar forms.

Church bells ring often during the Christmas celebration from December sixteenth to January sixth. Small boys like to pull the ropes tied to the clappers in the church towers.

40 — Tráigamelo, Luisito, — dice su papá. — Voy a enseñarle a manejarlo (*run it*).

Luisito se lo trae a su papá, el cual (*who*) se sienta en el suelo y empieza a jugar con él. Se divierte mucho pero el [1] pobre Luisito se pone impaciente. Pero como es muy cortés
45 y sabe que si no es bueno los Reyes no le traen nada el año que viene, no dice nada.

Al fin la madre dice al padre, — Eduardo, ¿de quién es ese tren? ¡Déselo al niño! Recuerde que Vd. ya es hombre.

El padre se avergüenza (*feels ashamed*), y dándoselo a
50 Luisito, empieza a leer su periódico.

— Mire, Luisito, lo que me ha dado papá, — dice Arturo, el hermano mayor.

— No se lo ha dado papá. Los Reyes se lo han dado, — dice el chico.

55 — ¡Qué tonto es Vd.! Los Reyes no nos dan nuestros regalos; nuestros padres nos los dan.

— Es mentira. ¡Mire Vd.! He dejado un poco de paja en los zapatos y los camellos se lo han comido.[2]

— Pregunte Vd. a mamá.

60 Luisito corre a donde está su madre. — Mamacita, Arturo me ha dicho que Vd. y papacito nos dan los regalos y que los Reyes no nos los dan. Es mentira, ¿verdad?

Entonces la madre le explica que los padres tienen que ayudar a los Reyes. Más tarde Luisito entenderá (*will*
65 *understand*) que los Reyes representan el espíritu de la bondad (*kindness*) y del amor, y que los padres les dan regalos a sus hijos en nombre de este espíritu.

Al saber la verdad Luisito se pone un poco triste. Quiere decírsela a su hermanita, pero su madre le dice, — No se la
70 diga, hijito. Rosario es muy joven. No puede entender estas cosas. El año que viene, Vd. va a ayudar a los Reyes también.

Entonces Luisito cree que él es muy importante, porque sabe algo que no sabe su hermana. Y ahora está contento otra vez.

---

[1] Omit *el* in translating. Later you will learn the reason for its use.
[2] *se lo han comido = comerse + lo*.

Find These Expressions in the Story

1. when they find him, they give them to him
2. Give it to me.
3. The Wise Men have brought it to me.
4. It is mine.
5. next year (the year that is coming)
6. they don't bring anything to bad boys
7. they thank them
8. Bring it to me.
9. Louis brings it to his papa.
10. Give it to the child.
11. How silly you are!
12. our parents give them to us
13. he wants to tell it to his little sister
14. Don't tell it to her
15. Papa hasn't given it to you.

COSAS DE INTERÉS

89. Direct and Indirect Object Pronouns Combined

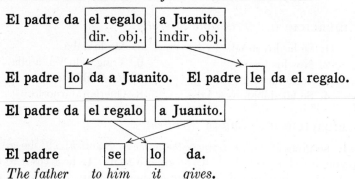

El padre da | el regalo | a Juanito.
             | dir. obj. | indir. obj.

El padre |lo| da a Juanito.   El padre |le| da el regalo.

El padre da | el regalo | a Juanito.

El padre |se| |lo| da.
The father   *to him* *it*   *gives.*

EJERCICIO I.   *Can you answer these questions?*

1. Where do the object pronouns stand?

2. When there are both direct and indirect object pronouns in a sentence, which comes first?

3. Can you think of any reason why the *le* is changed to *se* in the last sentence?

4. Where will the pronouns be placed if the verb is an infinitive, gerund, or affirmative command?

When both direct and indirect object pronouns are used, the indirect object pronoun always comes first.

Any combination of object pronouns when both begin with *l*, sounds awkward to a Spanish-speaking person. Therefore, *le* and *les* are changed to *se* when followed by the direct object forms *lo, la, los,* or *las.*

REMEMBER: $\frac{le}{les}$ + *lo, la, los, las* > *se*

When two object pronouns are attached to the verb, a written accent is always necessary. The accent is placed where the stress naturally falls when the verb form is given alone.

Infinitive: **traer** **traérmelas**
Gerund: **dando** **dándoselos**
Pol. Com.: **diga Vd.** **dígamelo Vd.**

EJERCICIO II. *Translate carefully:*

1. Se la doy a Vd.
2. Nos los traen.
3. Se lo dicen a ella.
4. Se las dábamos a Vds.
5. Me lo daba.
6. Tráigaselo Vd. a ella.
7. Están dándoselo.
8. Querían dárnoslo.

EJERCICIO III. *Say in Spanish:*

1. he gives it to me (*reverse the order in Spanish*) 2. he gives it to you, it to him, it to her 3. he gives it to us 4. he gives it to them 5. he gives them to me 6. he gives them to you 7. he gives them to him 8. he gives them to her 9. he gives them to us 10. he gives them to them

EJERCICIO IV. *Use pronouns in place of the words in italics.* (These are tricky! Think carefully. Is the pronoun the direct or indirect object of the verb? And remember your rule for the position of pronouns!)

1. El muchacho nos trae *las frutas.*
2. Los Reyes no les han dado *los regalos.*
3. La señora de Cervantes pone *los animalitos* en la mesa.
4. El hombre me vende *un billete.*
5. El niño no dice *la verdad a su padre.*

6. Arturo trae *el periódico a la mujer.*
7. La profesora habla *español a los alumnos.*
8. Mi amigo me ha escrito *la carta* a mí.
9. No le ha dicho *la verdad.*
10. Queríamos dar *el regalo a Felipe.*
11. No queríamos darlo *a Rosita.*
12. Rosario no quería dar *la muñeca a su hermano.*
13. Yo no iba a decirlo *a Enrique.*
14. Dé Vd. *la caja a Tinita.*
15. El campesino estaba vendiendo *los pollos al hombre.*

90. Prepositional Forms for Clearness

Juan se lo da. What are all the possible meanings for this sentence? What words of explanation can you add in Spanish to make the meaning clearer? (See section 86.)

EJERCICIO V. *Translate:*

1. nos lo da   2. me la da   3. se la da (*6 possible meanings*)   4. se las da (*6 meanings*)   5. me los da   6. nos las da

EJERCICIO VI. *In these sentences, add words to make the meaning clear:*

1. María se lo da (meaning *to Rosario*).   2. Yo se lo paso (*to you*).
3. Se la venden (*to Carlos*).   4. Están vendiéndosela (*to the boys*).
5. Él se los ha traído (*to the girls*).

91. Redundant Use of Pronouns

Carlos se lo da a Roberto. *Charles gives it to Robert.*

Spanish-speaking people frequently use a pronoun where it is not necessary. In the model sentence given above, *se* (replacing *le*) is not necessary because the meaning is given by *a Roberto.* In translating the sentence into English this unnecessary pronoun is omitted. This use of both the pronoun and the noun is called a redundant construction.

EJERCICIO VII. *Find six examples in the story of redundancy (six places where the pronoun and the noun are both used as the indirect object), and translate.*

PREGUNTITAS

I. 1. ¿Cuándo reciben sus regalos los niños españoles?
2. ¿Quiénes son los Reyes Magos?
3. ¿Por qué tienen camellos?
4. ¿Qué comen los camellos?
5. ¿Dónde dejan los niños los zapatos?
6. ¿Reciben regalos de los Reyes los muchachos malos?
7. ¿Qué juguete ha recibido Luisito?
8. ¿Por qué se ponía impaciente?
9. ¿Quiénes ayudan a los Reyes?
10. ¿Qué le ha dicho a Luisito su hermano mayor?

II. 1. ¿Es Vd. tonto (-a)?
2. ¿Tiene Vd. un camello? ¿un caballo? ¿una vaca?
3. ¿Ha visto Vd. un camello?
4. ¿Quién le da a Vd. sus regalos de Navidad?
5. ¿Cuándo los recibe Vd.?
6. ¿Quiere Vd. una escopeta, un cuchillo, un tren mecánico, o una muñeca?
7. ¿Cuál les gusta más a las niñas, una escopeta o una muñeca?
8. ¿Se pone Vd. impaciente algunas veces?

REPASITO

I. Define in Spanish. Example: una casa: Una casa es una clase de edificio donde vive una familia.

1. una viuda
2. un vecino
3. un escribiente público
4. un vendedor
5. un abuelo
6. un tío

7. un americano
8. un norteamericano
9. un rico (*a rich man*)
10. un pobre (*a poor man*)
11. una mantilla
12. un niño

II. Tell the difference in meaning (or use) between the two words in each pair:

1. piso, suelo
2. haber, tener
3. estar, ser
4. sino, pero

5. hace calor, tiene calor
6. salir, ir
7. por qué, porque
8. tocar, jugar

9. saber, conocer   12. aquí, acá
10. pues, bien   13. letra, carta
11. ese, aquel   14. poco, pequeño

III. What are the usual meanings of these endings?

1. -iendo   5. -aba   9. -er   13. -emos
2. -oso   6. -ando   10. -ísimo   14. -abas
3. -mente   7. -imos   11. -ad   15. -an
4. -amos   8. -en   12. -ito   16. -íamos

IV. For each word give another Spanish word which is related to it. Example: ahora (*now*), hora (*hour*); cortés (*courteous*), cortesía (*courtesy*).

1. sabio   7. vendedor   13. comida   19. español
2. juego   8. vestido   14. compañero   20. estudio
3. juguete   9. vivo   15. cuidado   21. estudioso
4. sombrero   10. baile   16. querido   22. lluvia
5. trabajo   11. bebida   17. entrada   23. necesario
6. cansado   12. canción   18. escribiente 24. en seguida

V. Translate:

1. We used to have a cat whose name was (*who was called*) Chico. 2. We thought (*creer*) that he was the prettiest cat in the world.   3. He liked meat and I used to give it to him every day.   4. We had a dog, too.   He didn't like (*los*) cats.   5. He liked bones (*los huesos*). 6. I used to say, "Bring me the bone."   7. My little sister would say, "No, bring it to me."   8. Then the poor[1] dog would not know what to do.   9. Generally he would take it into the (*al*) garden.

VI. Dos refranes

Marzo ventoso (*windy*) y abril lluvioso (*rainy*) hacen a mayo hermoso.   (*From what do ventoso and lluvioso come?*)

Más vale pájaro en mano que ciento (*one hundred*) volando.

VII. Algunos chistes para leer

El primer cliente

Un hombre llama apresuradamente (*hurriedly*) a la puerta de un doctor recién establecido.   La mujer del doctor sale a recibirle.

---

[1] Keep this word order because we wish to show pity, not poverty.

— ¿Desea Vd. ver al doctor? — le dice. — ¿No puede Vd. venir mañana por la mañana?

— ¿Por qué? ¿No está el doctor en casa?

— Sí, pero usted es el primer cliente que tiene, y quiero darle una sorpresa. Mañana es su santo.

Entre esposos

Ella — ¿No te parece que nuestra hija María hace muy bien en el canto?

Él — ¡Ya lo creo! Al principio solo se quejaban (*used to complain*) los vecinos de la casa. Ahora se queja (*complains*) todo el distrito.

PALABRAS PARA HOY

3 **la alegría**	happiness	**la paja**	straw
2 **el amor**	love	1 **ponerse**	to become (new
2 **buscar**	to look for		meaning)
2 **correr**	to run	3 **probar (ue)**	to test, try (*probe*)
1 **dejar**	to leave (new	2 **recordar (ue)**	to remember
	meaning)	2 **el rey**	king
Eduardo	Edward	**los Reyes**	the Wise Men,
3 **enseñar**	to show, teach	**Magos**	Magi Kings
1 **esperar**	to wait (for)	**Rosario**	girl's name
3 **gritar**	to call, shout	**sabio, -a**	wise
el juguete	toy, plaything	4 **tonto, -a**	foolish, stupid
Nochebuena	Christmas Eve		

EXPRESIONES

el año que viene, next year (the year that is coming)

*por eso, therefore

*tal vez, perhaps

Los gitanos del Albaicín[1]

Quizás ha visto Vd. a un grupo de gitanos, hablando su lengua curiosa, viajando por el país, pasando una noche aquí y otra lejos de aquí, sin casa en que vivir. Si no, al menos ha leído Vd. de la vida gitana, y quizás ha deseado ser gitanito, sin tener que asistir a la escuela, ni tener que quedarse en la 5 misma ciudad toda la vida.

Los gitanos más famosos del mundo son los (*those*) de España, del Albaicín de Granada,[2] donde han hecho cuevas en la ladera (*side*) de la montaña, entre los nopales (*cactus*) y los olivos (*olive trees*). Han pintado de blanco la tierra al- 10 rededor de la puerta de cada cueva, y viven dentro de ellas sin ventilación, ¡pero con luz eléctrica!

¿Cómo ganan la vida estos gitanos? Pues, son carniceros, herreros (*blacksmiths*),[3] pordioseros (*beggars*),[3] o ladrones; pero su manera favorita de ganar dinero es decir la buenaventura y 15 bailar para los turistas. Miles de viajeros iban a Granada para ver la Alhambra, el «Castillo Rojo» (*Red Castle*) de los

---

[1] *El Albaicín* (from an Arabic word meaning *cliff dwelling*) is the famous gypsy quarter of Granada, across the ravine from the Alhambra. Hundreds of gypsies live there under government supervision, forming a sort of home base for the wanderers who were born never to linger long in one place.

They secretly despised the gullible tourists who used to visit them in droves but were outwardly polite as long as their victims did not object to paying the ridiculous prices they demanded for "fortunes" and demonstrations of gypsy dancing.

[2] Granada is a beautiful old city of southeastern Spain, until Spain's Civil War a shrine for tourists. It was the last stronghold of the Moors, who were driven from it in 1492, and is famous for its Alhambra. (See footnote on page 300.)

[3] When tourists were scarce, the men of the Albaicín spent their time making little copper pans and kettles to sell to them when they did come.

The beggar asks alms «*por Dios*,» *for God's sake*, and so people call him a *pordiosero.*

The Albaicín is the famous gypsy quarter of Granada, across the ravine from the Alhambra. There the gypsies have dug caves back into the cactus-studded hillside and whitewashed each entrance.

moros, construido hace más de setecientos años;¹ y después iban sin falta a visitar a los gitanos.

20   ¿Le gustaría a Vd. visitarlos? Pues, vamos a fingir que somos invisibles, y que podemos ver y oír todo lo que pasa en una de las cuevas gitanas.

Mire Vd. Allá van hacia ellas unos viajeros — un joven extranjero y dos señoritas. Todos los gitanos los esperan con
25   una sonrisa (la sonrisa del gato cuando ve al ratón); pensando, sin duda, que allá va dinero. No saben si los extranjeros son franceses, ingleses, o norteamericanos; porque a ellos todos les parecen iguales.

¹ *hace más de setecientos años, more than seven hundred years ago.*

The Alhambra is a group of beautiful buildings on a wooded hill overlooking Granada. It was the residence of Moorish sultans, and later, of Spanish kings, for hundreds of years. Then it was abandoned for fifty years, while gypsies, beggars, and bandits camped in it and destroyed much of the carved stone lace of its stucco, and shattered its gaily colored tiles. Then, about 1865, the Spanish government, noticing how travelers from Europe and America always wanted to see it, took it over and started its restoration.

Before the War, professional guides lay in wait for strangers in its paths and patios, and collected four *pesetas* for entering the various buildings.

Una gitana vieja y fea, con vestido de los colores vivos que llevan todas las gitanas, los invita a entrar en su cueva; todos los demás entran también, para ver lo que pasa. 30

— ¿Le digo la buenaventura, niña?[1] — dice la anciana a la señorita más joven.

— Quizás, — contesta la señorita. — ¿Cuánto costará?

— Un duro,[2] — responde la anciana. — Digo la buena- 35 ventura muy bien, porque yo lo sé todo. Lo leo en la mano.

— Bueno, — dice la señorita.

En España un duro es mucho dinero, pero ella sabe que los turistas siempre tienen que pagar demasiado, y se lo da a la gitana sin decir más. 40

La anciana besa la moneda (*coin*) de plata, hace una cruz con ella en la mano de la señorita, y dice, — Vd. será muy afortunada. Es de buena familia, y vivirá muchos años, porque le gusta a Vd. dar limosna (*alms*). Nunca estará Vd. muy mala, y siempre ganará mucho dinero. Viajará Vd. por 45 muchos países, porque le gusta viajar.

— Vd. tiene una amiga, — sigue la gitana, — y le dice a ella todos los pensamientos del corazón. Pero, ¡tenga Vd. cuidado! Esta amiga tiene dos caras, y tratará de hacerle daño a Vd. Vd. perderá algo de valor dentro de poco, pero 50 pronto lo hallará otra vez. Vd. se casará dentro de un año con un señor muy simpático, y vivirá feliz con él muchos años. Él será un buen compañero y fiel, y Vd. le amará con todo el corazón. Eso es todo.

La señorita se pone como un chile, y sus amigos se ríen de 55 ella, mientras todos los gitanos la miran.

— Su señorita es muy bonita, — dice uno de los gitanitos al señor. — Déme Vd. un regalito.

---

[1] The name by which a person addresses a strange lady shows his own station in life, not the lady's. If he says *niña*, he is of the lowest class; if he says *señorita*, he shows more culture; and if he says *señora*, he is of the highest class or wishes to flatter the lady.

[2] A *duro* is a Spanish dollar, worth at par nearly as much as ours, but now worth much less.

Poor people in Spain usually count their money in *pesetas* (five to a *duro*), for *duros* do not often come their way. But the gypsies know how to get them!

Black Star

Gypsy dancer of Granada, characteristically pert, wears typical fringed shawl, spit curls, flower on top of her head, and uses castanets.

El señor finge no entender, y otra vez el gitanito trata de
60 hablarle. — Votre mademoiselle est très jolie,[1] — dice en francés, pensando que quizás el señor es francés. — Donnez-moi un cadeau.[1]

Pero nuestros turistas han visto bastante. Sin esperar el baile de los gitanos, que costaría (*would cost*) cincuenta pe-
65 setas[2] la hora, los tres empiezan a irse. Al salir de la cueva, la anciana les pregunta, — ¿Son Vds. franceses o ingleses?

— Somos norteamericanos, — responde la señorita bonita.
— ¿No sabía Vd. leerlo en mi mano?

Y se van los turistas, riéndose de la famosa buenaventura
70 que dicen las gitanas del Albaicín.

[1] This has exactly the same meaning in French as «*Su señorita es muy bonita.*» ... «— *Déme Vd. un regalito.*»

[2] Fifty *pesetas* an hour was about $6.50 in American money during the tourist days of Granada, but many tourists paid it! The gypsies would change their compliments to insults when their offer was refused, and slyly roll stones down upon the visitors from the paths above, or "accidentally" splash dirty water upon them as they passed.

Find These Expressions in the Story

1. they all seem the same to them
2. the most famous gypsies in the world
3. they have painted the earth white
4. more than seven hundred years ago
5. there go some strangers toward them
6. the smile of the cat when it sees the mouse
7. she gives it to the gypsy without saying any more
8. she will try to harm you
9. The lady turns "as red as a beet"
10. Give me a little gift.
11. You will marry within a year
12. laughing about the famous fortune
13. You will soon lose something of value
14. You will never be very ill
15. because I know all
16. Should you like to visit them?
17. it would cost fifty pesetas an hour
18. to see and hear all that happens

COSAS DE INTERÉS

92. Future Tense of Regular Verbs

The stem for the future tense of regular verbs of all three conjugations is the whole infinitive.

The endings for the future are like the present tense of the helping verb *haber* (remember *he, has, ha,* etc.?), except that they drop the **h** all the way through, and the **hab-** in the second person plural.

FUTURE TENSE MODEL FOR REGULAR VERBS		
	vivir, *to live*	
vivir é	*I shall* or *will live,* etc.	vivir emos
vivir ás		vivir éis
vivir á		vivir án

EJERCICIO I. *Answer these questions:*

1. What is the meaning of the future tense in English?
2. What is the stem of the future tense of regular verbs in Spanish?
3. What are the endings for the future tense in Spanish?
4. Where did they come from?
5. How many accents has the future tense?
6. What letter just preceding the ending is the sign of the future in Spanish? (*r*)

EJERCICIO II. *Continue:* compraré, pintaré, beberé, me divertiré.

EJERCICIO III. *Translate:*

1. nos pasearemos
2. «No pasarán»[1]
3. lo esperará
4. Vd. las hallará
5. me responderás
6. la besaré
7. costará mucho
8. nunca viajaremos
9. trataré de ir
10. me reiré de él

EJERCICIO IV. *Put in Spanish, using the verbs* **servir, llegar, escribir, perder, ir,** *and* **ser:**

1. we shall go
2. he will be
3. they will arrive
4. I shall write
5. she will serve
6. thou wilt go
7. you (*pol. pl.*) will lose
8. we shall be
9. she will arrive
10. I shall lose

PREGUNTITAS

I. 1. ¿Qué hablan los gitanos?
2. ¿Cuáles son los gitanos más famosos del mundo?
3. ¿Viven en casas? (*Use* sino *in your answer.*)
4. ¿Cómo ganan la vida?
5. ¿Qué les gusta más?
6. ¿Iban muchos viajeros a visitar a los gitanos? ¿Por qué?
7. ¿Cómo esperaban los gitanos a los turistas?
8. ¿Les parecían iguales todos los turistas?

[1] The watchword of the Loyalists in Madrid in 1936–39. Why?

9. ¿Sabían las gitanas decir la buenaventura?
10. ¿Era verdad todo lo que decían?
11. ¿Cuánto valía un duro?
12. ¿Viajará mucho la joven señorita?
13. ¿Por qué vivirá muchos años la señorita?
14. ¿Qué dice el gitanito al señor?

II. 1. ¿Sabe Vd. decir la buenaventura?
    2. ¿Besa Vd. una moneda al recibirla?
    3. ¿Le gustaría a Vd. visitar a los gitanos?
    4. ¿Viajará Vd. mucho en España?
    5. ¿Le gustaría a Vd. vivir en una cueva?
    6. ¿Tenía Vd. una amiga de dos caras?
    7. ¿Se pone Vd. como un chile algunas veces?
    8. ¿Es Vd. francés (francesa), inglés (inglesa), o norteamericano (-a)?
    9. ¿Se ríe Vd. de las gitanas?
   10. ¿Está Vd. muy malo (-a) hoy?
   11. ¿Quiere Vd. ser ladrón?
   12. ¿Ha perdido Vd. muchas cosas de valor?

REPASITO

I. In these pairs of words, which ones are opposites and which have the same meaning?

1. viejo, anciano
2. hallar, perder
3. responder, contestar
4. malo, enfermo
5. preguntar, contestar
6. algo, nada
7. alto, bajo
8. caliente, frío
9. sobre, encima de
10. salir de, entrar en
11. temprano, tarde
12. al fin, al principio
13. ir, volver
14. sino, pero
15. chico, pequeño
16. no —— más que, solamente
17. traje, vestido
18. corto, largo

II. What Spanish word or expression do you associate with each of these?

1. el gato (example: perro)
2. el caballo -
3. la Navidad -
4. llamar -
5. gracias
6. joven
7. hace frío
8. triste
9. el pie
10. los dientes
11. cara
12. carnicero

III. Here are the expressions we have had with **por**.　*Select one to complete each sentence, using each expression only once.*

por favor, please
por ejemplo, for example
por todas partes, everywhere

por la noche, at night
por la mañana, in the morning
por supuesto, of course

1. En el portal había caminos y casas por ——.
2. Tráigame Vd. una taza de chocolate, por ——.
3. Los vendedores venden muchas frutas, por ——, manzanas, plátanos (bananas), mangos, y piña (pineapple).
4. Me acuesto temprano por ——.
5. Los sábados me levanto más tarde por ——.
6. — ¿Sabe Vd. su lección?　— Por ——.

IV. Here are some expressions we have had with **a** or **al**. *Choose one to complete each sentence, using each one only once.*

al fin, at last, finally
al principio, at the beginning, at first
a ver, let's see
al menos, at least
a casa, home

al sol, in the sun
a la sombra, in the shade
al contrario, on the contrary
a pie, on foot
¿a qué hora?, at what time?

1. ——; ¿cuántos años tiene Vd.?
2. Voy —— después de asistir a la fiesta.
3. Me sentaba —— debajo del árbol.
4. Juanito estaba ocupado; ——, María no hacía nada.
5. Hace mucho calor —— en el verano.
6. —— hemos llegado al Albaicín.
7. Cuando no tenía mi caballo, iba ——.
8. —— se levanta Vd. los domingos?
9. El baile de las gitanas cuesta —— cincuenta pesetas.
10. Hay cohetes (*sky rockets*) —— de una fiesta mexicana.

V. Translate carefully:

1. Me lo daba.
2. Nos los daba.
3. Tráigamela Vd.
4. Se lo doy a ella.
5. Se los dará a Vd.
6. Dígamelos Vd.
7. A mí no me gustaba.
8. A ella no le gustan las casas.
9. ¡Dénoslos Vd. a nosotros!
10. Venga Vd. conmigo.

Voy decirle la buenaventura 2 - Vivirá muchos años,
3 - Ud. recibirá una carta dentro de poco; 4 Le traerá a Vd. las
noticias buenas. 5 - Le gusta viajar y viajará por muchas
a Vd.
paises. 6 -

LOS GITANOS DEL ALBAICÍN   307

VI. *Translate:*

1. I am going to tell your fortune.   2. You will live many years.
3. You will receive a letter in a short time.   4. (It) will bring you
good news.   5. You like to travel and you will travel in (*por*) many
countries.   6. You will meet a tall man who (*que*) will ask you for your
hand.   7. Be careful.   Do not believe him when he says that he loves
you.   8. You will marry a very nice man who (*que*) will be a faithful
companion.   9. You (*pl.*) will be very happy.   10. How can I know
these things?   11. A little bird tells them to me.

VII. *Algo que leer para divertirse*

La cabeza de la casa

Él — Si nos casamos, tú tendrás que obedecerme (*obey*), porque yo
seré la cabeza de la casa.

Ella — Bien.   Tú serás la cabeza, pero yo seré el cuello (*neck*), que
la hace dar vueltas (*turn*).

Tiene hambre

El médico (*doctor*) — Ahora va Vd. a tener una dieta especial.   Vd.
tomará legumbres, carne blanca y sopa.

El enfermo — Y eso ¿antes o después de comer, doctor?

La geografía

El profesor — ¿Quiere Vd. decirme qué es una isla (*island*)?

El alumno — Con mucho gusto.   Una isla es una porción de tierra
rodeada (*surrounded*) de agua por todas partes menos por una.

El profesor — ¿Cómo?

El alumno — Sí, señor; ¡menos por encima!

PALABRAS PARA HOY

2 **amar**	to love (*amiable*)	3 **feo, -a**	ugly
4 **anciano, -a**	old (person)	3 **fiel**	faithful
	(*ancient*)	4 **fingir**	to pretend (*feign*)
3 **besar**	to kiss	2 **francés**	French; *fem.*, **fran-**
el carnicero	butcher		**cesa**
3 **costar (ue)**	to cost	4 **el gitano**	gypsy (also used as
4 **la cruz**	cross		an adjective)
la cueva	cave	2 **hallar**	to find
2 **los demás**	rest	2 **igual**	alike (*equal*)

4 **el ladrón** thief
1 **malo, -a** ill (new meaning, used with **estar**)
1 **mismo, -a** same
3 **la montaña** mountain
2 **el pensamiento** thought (*pensive*)
3 **pintar (de)** to paint

3 **la plata** silver
1 **quizás** perhaps
2 **responder** to answer (*respond*)
1 **unos, -as** some
2 **el valor** value
  viajar to travel
  el viajero traveler

EXPRESIONES

decirle la buenaventura, to tell one's fortune
ganar la vida, to earn a living
hacerle daño (a uno), to harm
¿le gustaría a Vd.?, would you like (to)?

ponerse como un chile, to turn as "red as a beet" (red pepper)
sin duda, without doubt, doubtless
sin falta, without fail
tener dos caras, to be "two-faced"

CAPÍTULO 28

I. Así son los sueños

The irregular verb forms are explained in section 93.

Anita iba al mercado con una cesta de huevos. La llevaba a la cabeza como era costumbre en muchos países.[1] Iba a vender los huevos en el mercado. Estaba pensando en todas las cosas que quería hacer.

5 Mientras andaba, pensaba, — Venderé estos huevos en el mercado. Ganaré tres pesos. Con los tres pesos compraré otra gallina. Entonces tendré más huevos. Iré al mercado

---

[1] Next to using the burro, the most popular way of transporting goods in many countries is to carry them on the head or back. Everything from a jug to furniture, even livestock, is carried in this manner. You may see a man carrying a dozen chickens tied by the legs to either end of a pole which is slung across his shoulders, or a small goat draped around his neck like a fox fur.

Black Star

Anita went to market, carrying her basket on her head, as this girl does the wooden tray. Often a girl walks briskly along without lifting a hand to steady the carefully balanced load.

y los venderé también.   Compraré muchas gallinas y ganaré mucho dinero.   Ganaré más de doscientos pesos.   Entonces compraré una vaca.   La vaca dará leche y la venderé.   Me   10 haré rica.   Tal vez tendré mil pesos.

— Me casaré con un hombre elegante y viviremos en una casa grande.   Tendremos muchos hijos.   El hijo mayor será médico.[1]   Otro hijo será profesor[1] y sabrá mucho.   Mis hijas se casarán con hombres ricos también.   Tal vez una se casará   15 con un conde.   Entonces ella será condesa.[1]   Vendrá a visitarme en un automóvil muy grande y todas las vecinas la mirarán con envidia (*envy*).   Yo les diré, «Sí, ésta es mi hija, la condesa de Fulano.»   Me pondré un vestido nuevo y saldré a recibirla.   20

Anita estaba pensando así y no miraba las piedras que estaban en el camino.   Tropezó (*she tripped*) y dejó caer

---

[1] **será médico,** *will be a doctor.*   After the verb *ser* the article is usually omitted with an unmodified predicate noun.

(*dropped*) la cesta. Se rompieron (*broke*) los huevos. ¡Qué
lástima! Ya no podrá ganar mucho dinero. Ya no podrá
25 casarse con el hombre rico. ¿Qué hará? Tendrá que volver
a casa sin huevos y sin dinero. ¿Qué pasará? Su madre la
castigará y su padre se enfadará. Tal vez tendrá que acostarse sin cenar.

¡Pobre chica! Pero así salen los sueños algunas veces.[1]

II. Otra carta de Alfredo

México, D.F.,
10 de abril de 19——.

Querido amigo mío:

Acabo de volver del teatro. Esta noche he visto una come-
5 dia moderna escrita por Martínez Sierra.[2] ¿Recuerda Vd. las
comedias de Martínez Sierra que leíamos en la clase de
español? Son muy divertidas (*amusing*) y me da mucho gusto
verlas presentadas en la escena. Pero esta noche había una
cosa en el teatro mexicano que me parecía muy curiosa. En la
10 escena, delante de los actores, estaba lo que se llamaba la concha del apuntador.[3] El apuntador estaba debajo del suelo
con solamente la cabeza asomada (*showing*). Así podía ver a
los actores y ellos podían oírle. Pero lo más curioso de todo
era que el apuntador leía todos los papeles. Hasta era posible
15 oírle algunas veces. Si el actor olvidaba lo que iba a decir,
escuchaba al apuntador y seguía con la acción.

Al salir del teatro siempre voy al café donde encuentro a
mis amigos, para tomar café con ellos. Después vuelvo a

[1] What English proverb is illustrated by this story?

[2] Martínez Sierra is one of the best-known modern Spanish playwrights. He
has been in Hollywood assisting in the translation and filming of some of his
plays.

[3] *Concha del apuntador*, the *prompter's box*, is called *concha* (*shell*) because the
part visible to the audience is often shaped like a shell. It is placed near the foot-
lights.

Charles D. Jarrett

Old Spanish keys, still in use in Spain and in Mexico, weigh almost a pound; so the custom developed of leaving them with the *sereno.* Compare the modern door key with the others.

casa, pero no puedo entrar en seguida.   Primero tengo que llamar al portero,[1] y al fin se despierta y me abre la puerta.   20 Siempre le doy una propina (*tip*) por la molestia.

En tiempos antiguos, el sereno llevaba todas las llaves de las casas de una manzana entera, y era necesario llamarle para entrar en la casa.   Durante toda la noche gritaba el sereno la hora, por ejemplo, — ¡La una en punto y se-re-no (*all's well*)!   25 Pero hoy día ya no grita.   Lleva un pequeño pito (*whistle*), y pita (*he whistles*) cada quince minutos durante la noche, para decir a todo el mundo que todo está sereno y que él no se ha dormido.

Puedo oír el pito del sereno en la calle ahora, y sé que es   30 muy tarde y debo acostarme.

Sin más por hoy, quedo su afmo. amigo y S.S.,

Alfredo

---

[1] The **portero,** *janitor,* of a house still opens the door for people who come in late, because the keys used to be so large they were inconvenient to carry.   The **sereno,** *night watchman,* used to carry the keys of all the houses in a block, and it was necessary to call him in order to get in at night.

Find These Expressions in the Story

1. on her head
2. I shall have more eggs
3. he will know a lot (much)
4. he will be (a) doctor
5. she will come to visit me
6. I shall tell them
7. I shall put on a new dress

8. I shall become rich.
9. I shall go out to receive her
10. The eggs broke.
11. It was even possible to hear him
12. she will not be able to marry the rich man

COSAS DE INTERÉS

93. Future Tense of Irregular Verbs

tener *to have*	saber *to know*	hacer *to do, make*
STEM: tendr-	STEM: sabr-	STEM: har-
tendré	sabré	haré
tendrás	sabrás	harás
tendrá	sabrá	hará
tendremos	sabremos	haremos
tendréis	sabréis	haréis
tendrán	sabrán	harán
Like tener	Like saber	Like hacer
venir (vendr-)	querer (querr-)	decir (dir-)
salir (saldr-)	poder (podr-)	
poner (pondr-)	haber (habr-)	

Ten common verbs have irregular stems in the future tense. Those like *tener* have a *d* in place of the *e* or *i* of the infinitive ending; those like *saber* drop the *e* of the infinitive ending; *decir* and *hacer* drop the *c* and *e* of the infinitive. Notice that the endings for the future tense are always regular.

EJERCICIO I. *Conjugate in the future tense:*

ponerse	mantener	salir
decir	poder	querer

EJERCICIO II. *For each verb in italics give the first person singular, future tense, and translate.*

1. Mañana *levantarse* a las siete.
2. *Ponerse* el vestido (traje).
3. *Desayunarse* (eat breakfast) a las siete y media. *Tener* hambre y *comer* mucho.
4. *Salir* de la casa.
5. *Encontrar* a mi amigo cerca de la casa.
6. Le *decir*, — Buenos días.
7. *Ir* a la escuela con mi amigo.
8. *Entrar* en la primera clase a las ocho.
9. *Tener* un examen de álgebra.
10. *Salir* bien en el examen porque *haber* estudiado.
11. *Volver* a casa a las tres.
12. No *querer* estudiar en seguida y *jugar* con mis vecinos.
13. Después de comer *estudiar* mis lecciones.
14. *Acostarse* a las nueve.

EJERCICIO III. *Put each italicized verb in Ejercicio II in the future tense, using the following subjects:* (1) you; (2) we; (3) they.

EJERCICIO IV. *Change these verb forms to the future tense.* (Remember to start with the infinitive in forming the future.)

1. sé	5. es	9. hace	13. están
2. vienen	6. dan	10. quiero	14. veo
3. oye	7. tengo	11. sirve	15. traen
4. vamos	8. dice	12. duerme	16. me despido

EJERCICIO V. *Give the meanings:*

1. querrá 3. pondré 5. podré 7. vendrá 9. Vds. sabrán
2. pondrá 4. ¿saldrá Vd? 6. diremos 8. harán 10. habré visto

EJERCICIO VI. *Give in Spanish:*

1. I shall not want to do that (*eso*). 2. I shall leave early. 3. He will come at eleven o'clock. 4. What shall you do? 5. Who will be able to do it? 6. They were leaving. 7. We used to be. 8. She was giving. 9. I used to see. 10. We were going.

94. Cardinal Numbers

Review the numbers from 10 to 1000 on pages 234–35, and study these ways in which to use them.

The hundreds agree in gender with the noun they describe.

doscientos hombres   **doscientas mujeres**

In reading numbers, **y,** *and,* is never used between the hundreds and the tens, but only between the tens and the units.

142   **ciento cuarenta y dos**

In comparisons of numbers *more than* is translated **más de;** *less than* is translated **menos de.** In the negative, **que** is used instead of **de.**

He ganado más de diez dólares.
I have earned more than ten dollars.

No quiero más que dos.
I don't want more than two.

EJERCICIO VII.   *Count in Spanish:*
1. By tens to one hundred.   2. By hundreds to one thousand.

EJERCICIO VIII.   *Practice reading these for speed:*

138	5,223	14,827	3,820	5,555
987	2,306	15,008	38,200	7,777
878	1,884	15,080	9,999	125,735

EJERCICIO IX.   *Write figures for the numbers which the teacher dictates to you in Spanish.*

EJERCICIO X.   *Say in Spanish:*

1. more than ten times   2. less than five hours   3. after ten minutes   4. within five months   5. more than two hundred pesos

95. Dates

May 1, 1948: **1° de mayo de 1948** (**el primero de mayo de mil novecientos cuarenta y ocho**)

May 2, 1948: **2 de mayo de 1948** (el dos de mayo de mil novecientos cuarenta y ocho)

Primero, first, is used for the first day of the month.   After that the cardinal numbers (two, three, four, etc.) are used.

The year is read like any large number: 1.948; 1.492, etc. (The comma is a period in Spanish, and decimal points are commas.)

Notice that the order for a date is: (*day*) *de* (*month*) *de* (*year*).

EJERCICIO XI.   *Read these dates in Spanish:*

Jan. 1, 1889	Dec. 31, 1614	April 3, 1916
June 13, 1901	July 4, 1776	Sept. 15, 1582
May 12, 1900	Oct. 12, 1492	Feb. 1, 1943

PREGUNTITAS

I.   1. ¿A dónde iba Anita?
    2. ¿Qué llevaba a la cabeza?
    3. ¿Qué hacía mientras andaba?
    4. En sus sueños, ¿dónde venderá los huevos?
    5. ¿Cuánto ganará?
    6. ¿Con quién se casará?
    7. ¿Qué será el hijo mayor?
    8. ¿Con quién se casará una hija?
    9. ¿Qué había en el camino?
   10. ¿Por qué no las miraba Anita?
   11. ¿Qué le pasó (*happened*)?
   12. ¿Podrá vender los huevos?   ¿Por qué no?
   13. ¿Qué tendrá que hacer?
   14. ¿Tienen los actores que saber bien sus papeles?
   15. ¿Qué hacía el sereno durante la noche?

II.   1. ¿Nos da leche una gallina?
    2. ¿Qué nos da una vaca?
    3. ¿Grita Vd. durante toda la noche?
    4. ¿Acaba Vd. de volver del teatro?
    5. ¿Quiere Vd. ser conde?
    6. ¿Lleva Vd. la llave de su casa?

7. ¿Le gusta a Vd. romper los huevos?
8. ¿Ha tropezado Vd. en el camino muchas veces?
9. ¿Le ha castigado su madre de Vd.?
10. ¿Ha tenido Vd. que acostarse sin cenar?

REPASITO

I. Give verb synopses, following this model, of caer, querer, hacer, ver, volver, poner, decir (III RC), dormir (III RC).

Infinitive	salir
Gerund	saliendo
Past Participle	salido
Present	salgo
Command	¡salga Vd.!
Present Progressive	estoy saliendo
Imperfect	salía
Future	saldré
Present Perfect	he salido

II. Give the English meanings for the forms you wrote in Ejercicio I.

III. Answer in Spanish, using pronouns in place of the nouns. Example: ¿Tiene Vd. su libro? — Sí, señorita, lo tengo.

1. ¿Ha visto Vd. a Juan? 2. ¿Daba Vd. su papel a la profesora?
3. ¿Ha vendido Anita los huevos? 4. ¿Lleva Vd. la cesta a la cabeza?
5. ¿Han hecho los Cervantes un portal? 6. ¿Dónde han puesto los animalitos? 7. ¿Dónde pondrán los niños españoles los zapatos?
8. ¿Dirá Vd. la palabra a los otros alumnos?

IV. Write in Spanish:

1. I have done nothing. 2. I have seen no one. 3. I want nothing.
4. I don't understand anything. 5. He has no money. 6. Yes, indeed! 7. I like candy. (*Sweets please me.*) 8. We lack money. (*Money is lacking to us.*) 9. She likes flowers. 10. It doesn't matter to me. 11. It isn't for me; it's for you.

V. *Algunos chistes para leer*

En el juzgado (*court*)

— ¿Es verdad que ha llamado Vd. tonto al señor?

— No recuerdo bien; pero ahora al mirar bien la cara, lo creo posible.

En una reunión (*party*)

— ¡Qué tonto parece ese señor! — exclama una señora.

— Pues su aspecto engaña (*deceives*).

— ¿Por qué?

— Porque es mucho más tonto de lo que parece a primera vista.

Adivinanza (*riddle*)

— ¿En qué se parecen los médicos a la planta de la papa (*potato*)?

— En que tienen sus productos bajo tierra.

PALABRAS PARA HOY

4	castigar	to punish (*chastise*)	4 la llave	key
	cenar	to eat supper	4 el médico	doctor (*medical*)
4	el conde	count	2 olvidar	to forget
	la condesa	countess	1 papel	play part (new meaning)
	enfadarse	to become angry		
2	escuchar	to listen	2 romper	to break
2	la escena	stage	el sereno	night watchman
	Fulano	"So-and-So"	2 el sueño	dream
	la gallina	hen	4 el teatro	theater
	el huevo	egg	4 tropezar (ie)	to trip
	la leche	milk		

EXPRESIONES

a la cabeza, on his (her, etc.) head

¡Qué lástima!, What a pity!

esta noche, tonight

*dejar caer, to let fall, drop

*tal vez, perhaps

South of the Río Grande

Mexico City, seen from the hill above the Church of Guadalupe, is full of colonial buildings erected on top of Indian ruins, and lately overlaid with a Hollywood veneer.

THERE ARE MORE CONTRASTS in Mexico than in Spain. South of the Pyrenees, when you meet a donkey plodding along a country road, his driver will probably be a pretty girl like one of your own friends, with a bright print dress and smartly bobbed hair; but south of the Río Grande, the donkey's master is a white-pajama-clad Indian in a broad straw hat and sandals, with a hand-woven blanket slung over his shoulder. Of course, in the upper classes, you will find the people more alike, for at the top in each country there are stunning *señoritas* whose frocks come from Hollywood or Paris, and cultured gentlemen who speak many languages and have seen the world.

It is not strange that Mexico's people on the whole are still unlike Europeans. Remember that the Mexican melting pot of Indians and their conquerors has been simmering for only four hundred years, instead of the three thousand it took to melt many races into one and produce the Spaniard. When you think that even now three out of each four of Mexico's people are pure-blooded Indians, still using many of the ways of their ancient civilization, you realize that our neighbor's melting pot will have to simmer a long time to create a race of people with congenial, harmonious ideas. How to hasten the process is Mexico's big problem, and today there is many a little schoolhouse in the *sierras* (mountains) among Indians who are finally learning Spanish and beginning to hear all about the wonders of a civilization they had not known existed.

Meanwhile, this Indian element makes Mexico picturesque, a country more foreign than anything we can find in England or France or Spain. In addition to Nature's contrast of snow-capped volcanoes and tropical foliage, of cactus-dotted desert sands and forests of precious woods, there is the three-sided contrast of Indian, Spanish, and modern ways of life, of a primitive agricultural civilization overlaid first with the grandeur of sixteenth-century Spain, then lately with what might be called a Hollywood veneer.

The modern layer of chromium and plate glass and neon lights cannot hide the noble carved stone and wood of the colonial days, any more than the Spanish destruction of temples and frantic building of cathedrals and palaces could obliterate the original Indian civilization. Houses and pyramids built of stone do not burn down nor decay in a few years. A convent with walls three feet thick smiles patiently at a mere four centuries, for time only softens its carved ornamentation, mellows the colors of its tinted stucco, and grows fine moss upon its shady side.

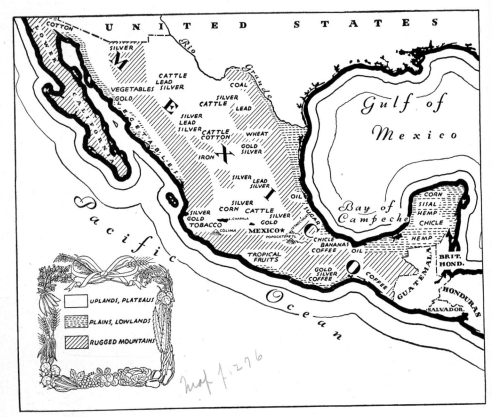

Mexico is rich in natural resources.

Buildings like these color nearly every Mexican town. Perhaps one that was once a convent is now a red-leather and chromium-fitted hotel;[1] perhaps the colonial mansion with the stone escutcheon over its great doorway is now a grain warehouse,[2] or the Bishop's Palace a beer garden,[3] but in their thick walls the Spain of the olden days lives on.

To see Mexico as a whole, you must visualize it first as a country rising geographically toward the capital from all directions. Whether you start at the American border or at sea level on either coast, you find yourself climbing as you approach the old Aztec capital, climbing to the top of some ten-thousand-foot mountain pass that opens into the vast oval bowl of the Valley of Mexico. At sea level you sweltered in tropical heat, but you shiver as you cross the mountains, perhaps between snow-capped Popocatépetl and Ixtaccíhuatl; and, when you

[1] Mexico City   [2] Acámbaro   [3] Monterrey

have dropped to the valley floor, you are still cool, for the bottom of the great bowl is seventy-five hundred feet above the sea.

There the wandering Aztecs found their eagle and serpent in the shallow lake that then nearly covered the valley; there the Spaniards tore down Aztec buildings to fill in canals after the conquest.   Now Mexico City is a modern capital of over a million people, as Parisian as Mexican, and as American as Parisian, better policed and safer after dark than some of our cities, and where you will often hear as much English as Spanish on the main streets.

More than any of the little towns, the capital shows the typical contrasts of Mexico.   There you can see, for instance, an open-air Aztec

South of the Río Grande one finds more contrasts than in Spain.   Narrow cobblestoned streets, colonial buildings, Indians and donkeys make Mexican small towns picturesque.

Sawders

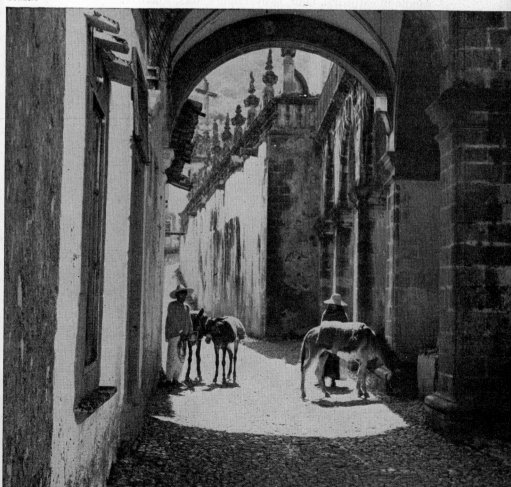

market with vegetables and fruits arranged on the ground in symmetrical little leaf-trimmed groups as they were five hundred years ago; but a few streets away you will find a haughty shop, labelled " *Ultramarinos Finos,*" where only luxurious imported foods are sold, such as French cheeses, Russian caviar, American tinned meats, Spanish olives, Italian anchovies, English cookies.

Not far from the city are thatched adobe huts with no windows and doorless doorways; in the metropolis stands a black and silver skyscraper, with sparkling plate glass show windows displaying Hollywood styles.

The roaring traffic of sleek motor cars on Carlotta's Paseo de la Reforma glides to a halt at the raised hand of a smartly uniformed officer, and a blanket-wrapped Aztec Indian on his lop-eared donkey has the right of way.

The swell of organ music and the perfume of incense fill the great, candle-lit cathedral, built, as everyone knows, where once there stood a templed pyramid with smoking human hearts upon its altars.

Modern apartment houses and office buildings have recently sprung up all over Mexico City in contrast with the ornate carved stone of colonial architecture, making the capital look as Parisian as Mexican.

Galloway

Blanket-wrapped Indians from the country stare at the sights of the busy city, little realizing that the great cathedral is built upon a foundation of Indian idols worshiped by their ancestors.

There are oxen pulling wooden plows, and gasoline taxes; there are bloody bullfights on Sunday afternoons, and world-famous operas in the evenings; there is the afternoon siesta, and daily plane service; and trucks and taxicabs travel the old Aztec causeways that have been in use for hundreds of years.

Although capitals, with their business and commerce, their tourists and traffic, are much alike the world over, the smaller towns keep their old-time charm, "unspoiled" by such things as paved streets, modernistic hotels, and the boom of big business. A sleepy tropical seaport, a state capital that has just acquired its first through railroad, another that is a museum piece from railroad station to marketplace, a mountain mining town — these are the places to go if you would know the heart of old Mexico.

The tropical seaport is Mazatlán, almost surrounded by a warm blue bay, crowned with vivid sunsets, and trimmed with leaning coco palms, scarlet hibiscus, and fiery flame trees.   It is as colorful today as when Spanish galleons from the Philippines four hundred years ago brought in their cargoes of Chinese treasures for the aristocrats of New Spain.   Nowadays silver passenger planes swoop down from the sky and luxury liners bring crowds of sightseers, while freighters and trains carry away Mazatlán's fresh fish and the fruits and tomatoes that grow in the interior.

Overnight from Mazatlán on the train, but three thousand feet above it in the wooded lap of scowling Sangangüey, is Tepic, perfect example of a colonial city.   For four hundred years Time stood still in that pastel town of Spanish-Moorish houses and cobbled streets, its only connection with the outside world the stagecoaches that creaked along the cobbled road through the *barrancas* from Guadalajara.   The Cora and Huichol Indians, who looked as distrustfully at the Spaniards then as they do at all strangers today, wanted no civilization, and retreated to the *sierra* to live on as they always had.   Only in recent years have they begun to stalk into town to market on Sundays, bringing their garden produce and beautiful weaving to sell to the Mexicans whose language they speak little better than the tourists do.

In 1912 the railroad reached Tepic from the north, and with it came more big business than the town had ever known before.   Fifteen years later the track was completed to Guadalajara, and now Tepic's medieval wandering minstrels, *mariachis*, have Hollywood engagements, and tourists sometimes come to sit in the plaza and feast their eyes on the beauty of those stone lace cathedral towers standing out against the bright blue sky.   Sugar plantations on the hillsides, tobacco fields down below at sea level, mines out in the mountains, a couple of cotton mills, and some tiny hat factories provide the *tepiqueños* with the same employment they have known for a hundred years.

Four hours from Tepic across the *barrancas* that blocked the railroad for such a long time is smart Guadalajara, cultured, sophisticated, cosmopolitan.   Colonized by the better classes of Spaniards, it became a base for exploration and conquest north along the West Coast and into California.   There the national dance, the *jarabe tapatío*, originated; there today aristocratic *charros* (horsemen) come out on Sundays, wearing gold-braided jackets and hats and tight trousers, to ride their prancing horses, while on Mondays the same gentlemen appear in business suits and inform you in perfect English that their Alma Mater was Notre Dame or Stanford or Massachusetts Tech! Aristocratic Guadalajara is more like the capital than Mexico's other towns are — a modern city, yet one which still keeps its old-world charm.

Oranges and grain grow outside of Guadalajara on the Jalisco plains at five thousand feet altitude, and in the bottom of the thousand-foot gashes in the earth that they call *barrancas* grow vanilla and coffee, tobacco, rice, and tropical fruits.   There are little pottery towns where all day long whole families make pottery in traditional designs; and bubble glass factories that turn out sets of hand-blown blue glass with no two pieces identical.

The town that should be in a museum is Querétaro, six hours north of Mexico City by rail, where history haunts you at every turn.   The long-legged colonial aqueduct sprawling across the valley still carries the town water; the city hall is the very one where on a night in 1810 the patriotic mayor's wife tapped on the floor with her foot to send a fellow conspirator galloping to warn Father Hidalgo that all was dis-

This mossy aqueduct, built by order of Cortés, still carries water to Cuernavaca, where the conqueror had a palace.

covered.   The abandoned convent where Maximilian spent his last days still crumbles in the sun, and a lonely chapel on the Hill of the Bells marks the place of his execution.   Over carved doorways still stand weather-beaten stone escutcheons of the noble families that once lived there; the cobblestones of the streets and the flagstones of the sidewalks have been worn into hollows for four hundred years by the shuffle of sandaled feet.

No chromium and neon have yet reached Querétaro; tourists come but for a day to visit its historical spots; but the opal vendors who meet every train, and the colorful markets, where *puestos* are piled high with local fruits and vegetables, tell the story of Querétaro's placid prosperity and the occupations of the people in its rolling countryside.

One more little town, still different from the rest, gives a last picture of real Mexico.   Overnight on the train, north of the capital on the way to El Paso, is Guanajuato.   Seven thousand feet up in the hills the sleepy old mining town lies wedged into a ravine, its stone houses climbing the steep hillsides like steps.   Gold and silver mines have made Guanajuato's living for centuries; its great red plush and gilt theater and glorious churches — one mortared with powdered silver

Oxen pull a primitive wooden plow, followed by a patient Indian farmer. According to superstition, the corn must be planted by a small boy in order to insure a good crop.

Gendreau

Crumbling stone and rusting iron of the old well curb still tell of colonial grandeur in a deserted convent patio near Guanajuato.

and Spanish wine, they say — dream of the days when wealth and aristocracy ruled the town, while descendants of its early Spanish settlers, Basques and Andalusians, still tend their grocery stores and drygoods shops.

Guanajuato is the town in which they say there is always a guitar to be heard somewhere at every hour of the day or night, the town of the "Lane of the Kiss," of the historical Granaditas where Father Hidalgo's head hung for ten years, of a popular state university, and of the yearly *Fiesta de la Cueva*.

In all these little towns and many more like them are people, mostly of the poorer class, it is true, but whether rich or poor, people of charming courtesy and leisurely ways. So fiercely patriotic they are that to fight for their "*tierra*" is a privilege; at the same time such a love of beauty lives within them that the most commonplace thing must have its adornment.

These are our neighbors south of the Río Grande.

Rodeo on a Mexican hacienda, where horsemen show their skill in riding and roping, attracts city and country people alike. Rodeos are also common in the South and West of the United States.

Some Interesting Books about Mexico

GARNER, BESS: NOTES IN THE MARGIN.

CARR, HARRY: OLD MOTHER MEXICO.

SQUIER, EMMA LINDSAY: GRINGA.

KING, ROSA E.: TEMPEST OVER MEXICO.

BARRETTO, LARRY: BRIGHT MEXICO.

O'BRIEN, HOWARD: NOTES FOR A BOOK ABOUT MEXICO.

JACKSON, JOSEPH: MEXICAN INTERLUDE.

RAMSEY, LEONIDAS: TIME OUT FOR ADVENTURE.

RICHARDS *and* LANDÁZURI: CHILDREN OF MEXICO.

MOATS, LEONE: THUNDER IN THEIR VEINS.

RUSSELL, PHILLIPS: RED TIGER.

La casa de los Navarro[1]

La casa de los Navarro es muy vieja,[2] y siempre ha sido de ellos. Está en una calle antigua en las afueras (*outskirts*) de la ciudad y tiene quince cuartos en un solo piso. Desde la calle no se ve más que la pared, y en ella la puerta grande del zaguán[3] y cuatro ventanas altas, cada una con su reja[4] y balcón. No hay *"front yard,"* porque dentro de la casa está el patio, con sus árboles, flores, fuente y jaulas (*cages*) de pájaros. En él juegan los chicos y platican los grandes.

Para entrar en esta casa, hay que llamar a la puerta, usando el llamador[5] antiguo. Al abrir la criada la puerta, se pasa por el zaguán y se llega al patio. Casi todos los cuartos de la casa dan al patio, así se puede entrar en cualquier cuarto sin pasar por los demás.

Los cuartos que dan a la calle son la sala y unos dormitorios. Las ventanas con sus rejas son tan grandes que desde la calle

[1] This typical old house is the kind most often found in Spain, Mexico, and many parts of South America. Of course nowadays one may see Spanish imitations of Hollywood copies of artists' ideas of Spanish houses, but these are not characteristic of Spanish-speaking countries.

[2] Do you realize that "old" buildings in Mexico or South America were built as much as three or four hundred years ago? "Old" in Spain means even more than that. A visitor to Ávila, a medieval walled Spanish town, asked an inhabitant, "Is that building old?" "Oh, my, no!" was the shocked answer. "Why, that's modern! That's sixteenth century!"
What would "old" mean in this country?

[3] See Note 2, page 208, if you have forgotten about the *zaguán*.

[4] **con su reja,** *with its grating* (bars). The **reja** is often of hand-wrought iron in such lacy patterns that one forgets its cold-blooded purpose, which is to keep outsiders out and the children in. The windows are really French doors opening onto little balconies, which are from a foot to five feet above the sidewalk, according to the lay of the land.

[5] A popular old knocker design is a cast-iron hand with a ring on its middle finger and a frilly cuff. Another one often seen is a lion's head with the knocker in its mouth. Of course many houses boast of doorbells now, but on the old houses the antique knockers still remain for those who care to use them.

An old, old doorway in Querétaro. The knockers are lions' heads; there is an escutcheon over the door; and under it the sill has been cut to let the family car pass. Compare the women with the height of the doorway.

se puede ver casi todo el cuarto, si las puertaventanas[1] están abiertas.

En la familia de Navarro hay catorce personas: la abuelita, viuda de Navarro; sus dos hijos, Pablo y Luis, con sus esposas; y nueve nietos, hijos de Pablo y de Luis. Pablo tiene cuatro hijos, sobrinos de Luis; y Luis tiene cinco hijos, sobrinos de Pablo. Juntos, los dos grupos de primos se divierten muchísimo. La abuelita también tiene tres hijas, pero ellas se han casado y han ido a vivir con sus esposos.

Para cuidar la casa y preparar las comidas, hay cuatro criados: una cocinera, dos criadas que limpian los cuartos, y el chófer, que maneja el automóvil y también cuida las flores y los árboles del patio.

Con todos estos criados, las tres señoras de Navarro nunca tienen que trabajar. Pero tampoco saben manejar el automóvil, así es que no salen más que los domingos con sus esposos y sus hijos para pasearse en la avenida principal de la ciudad.

[1] Analyze the word *puertaventanas*. They are wooden shutters inside the glass ones, and are used instead of blinds to shut out the light or to permit privacy.

Pasan la vida muy tranquilamente, con poco que hacer. Van a misa, cosen y bordan mucho, tocan el piano, leen y platican; pero rara vez asisten a los partidos (*games*) de "*bridge*" como las señoras ricas de nuestro país. 35

En cuanto a los niños de la familia de Navarro, les gusta mucho tener tantos primos y hermanos en su casa con quienes jugar. Así es que los hallamos en el patio, jugando a la «Casa Loca.» Vamos a ver como la juegan. Lupita es la «líder,» [1] 40 y cada uno de los otros niños ha escogido el nombre de una parte de la casa.

LUPITA — ¿Dónde estarás,[2] Juanito?

JUANITO — Estaré en la sala.

LUPITA — ¿Dónde estarás tú, Mariquita? 45

MARIQUITA — Estaré en el comedor.

(*Siga Vd. con el juego en español, como los niños lo juegan.*

[1] *líder*, a Spanish-American adaptation of our word *leader*.
[2] Do you notice that the children are using the familiar form today?

Old colonial knocker is a hand with a frilly cuff and a ring on its finger. It is probably several hundred years old.

Charles D. Jarrett

Dolores ha escogido la cocina; Alfonso, su dormitorio; Enrique, la galería; Miguel, el zaguán; Inés, la azotea.[1])

50 LUPITA (*empezando por segunda vez*) — ¿Qué tendrás en tu cuarto, Juanito?

JUANITO — Tendré un sofá en mi sala.

LUPITA — ¿Qué tendrás en tu cuarto, Mariquita?

MARIQUITA — Tendré un sofá en mi comedor.

55 (*Cada niño tiene que contestar de la misma manera con el nombre de su cuarto, y si alguien ríe, tiene que dar una prenda. Siga Vd. con el juego.*)

LUPITA (*empezando por tercera vez*) — ¿Qué tendrás en tu cuarto, Mariquita?

60 MARIQUITA — Tendré una mesa grande y catorce sillas en mi comedor.

(*Cada niño contesta de la misma manera. Siga Vd. con el juego.*)

LUPITA — ¿Qué tendrás en tu cuarto, Dolores?

65 DOLORES — Tendré una estufa [2] en mi cocina. (*Siga Vd. con el juego.*)

LUPITA — ¿Qué tendrás en tu cuarto, Alfonso?

ALFONSO — Tendré dos camas en mi dormitorio. (*Siga Vd. con el juego.*)

70 LUPITA — ¿Qué tendrás en tu cuarto, Enrique?

ENRIQUE — Tendré muchas macetas (*flowerpots*) de flores en mi galería. (*Siga Vd. con el juego.*)

LUPITA — ¿Qué tendrás en tu cuarto, Miguel?

MIGUEL — Tendré una tienda en mi zaguán. (*Siga Vd.*
75 *con el juego.*)

LUPITA — ¿Qué tendrás en tu cuarto, Inés?

INÉS — Tendré el perro y las gallinas en la azotea. (*Siga Vd. con el juego.*)

LUPITA (*empezando otra vez*) — ¿Qué harás en tu cuarto,
80 Juanito?

[1] The flat roof of the house often serves as the back yard. There the family dog and cat sun themselves, a few chickens wait in coops for their unfortunate end, and the maids hang the laundry to dry.

[2] *Estufa* is usually a heating stove. A modern cook stove is a *cocina económica*; and an old-fashioned built-in stone stove which burns charcoal is a *fogón*.

JUANITO — Tocaré el piano en mi sala.

(*Todos dicen que tocarán el piano en su cuarto. Lupita pregunta a todos lo mismo, y como contesta cada uno, así tienen que contestar los demás.*)

MARIQUITA — Pondré la mesa en mi comedor.   85

DOLORES — Lavaré los platos en mi cocina.

ALFONSO — Dormiré en mi dormitorio.

ENRIQUE — Cogeré flores en mi galería.

MIGUEL — Pondré el automóvil en mi zaguán.

INÉS — Colgaré la ropa limpia en mi azotea.   90

(*Durante el juego, todos han reído, uno después de otro; y todos han tenido que dar una prenda.*

¿Habría tenido Vd. que (would you have had) *dar una prenda, también?*)

Find These Expressions in the Story

1. the two groups of cousins enjoy themselves together
2. without passing through the rest
3. only the wall is seen
4. The rooms which face the street
5. neither do they know how to drive the automobile
6. As for the children
7. I shall be in the dining room.
8. one can enter any room
9. if anyone laughs
10. one passes through the *zaguán*
11. Continue with the game.
12. I will set the table in my dining room.
13. beginning for the third time
14. In it the little ones play
15. it has always been theirs

COSAS DE INTERÉS

96. Present Tense of Coger

coger, *to take hold of, pick*

cojo	cogemos
coges	cogéis
coge	cogen

POLITE COMMANDS

coja **Vd.**   cojan **Vds.**

Why does *cojo* have a *j* instead of a *g*?

EJERCICIO I.   *Conjugate* **escoger** *like* **coger.**

EJERCICIO II. *Review the sounds of* **g, ge, güe, gue, gi, güi, gui** *and* **j** *(Chapter 5, also section 80), then pronounce these old and new words:*

castigo	agregar	ejecutar	siguiente
consejo	guía	energía	oreja
afligir	conjunto	vergüenza	amiguito
agitar	elegir	espejo	género
distinguir	Miguel	averigüe	Jijona

EJERCICIO III.   *Now think twice and pronounce these:*

alhaja   hoja   almohada

PREGUNTITAS

I.   1. ¿De quiénes ha sido siempre la casa de los Navarro?
2. ¿Parece muy interesante la casa desde la calle?
3. ¿Qué tiene cada ventana?
4. ¿Para qué sirve el patio?
5. ¿Quién abrirá la puerta si alguien llama?
6. ¿Qué cuartos dan a la calle?
7. ¿Se divierten juntos los primos?
8. ¿Quiénes no saben manejar el automóvil?
9. ¿Están muy ocupadas las señoras para pasearse?
10. ¿Cuándo salen las señoras para pasearse?
11. ¿Qué vive en la azotea?
12. ¿Hay garage para el automóvil?

II.   1. ¿Le gusta a Vd. lavar los platos en la cocina?
2. ¿Le gusta a Vd. poner la mesa?
3. ¿Le gusta a Vd. hacer las camas?
4. ¿Le gusta a Vd. colgar la ropa limpia?
5. ¿Sabe Vd. tocar muy bien el piano?
6. ¿Tiene Vd. algunas gallinas en la azotea de su casa?

7. ¿Tendrá Vd. una tienda en su casa?
8. ¿Le gusta a Vd. un juego de prendas?
9. ¿Ha jugado Vd. jamás a la «Casa Loca»?
10. ¿Pasa Vd. muy tranquilamente la vida, sin nada que hacer?

EJERCICIOS DE PALABRAS

I. Haga Vd. una lista de los cuartos y las partes de la casa; de los muebles (furniture) *de la casa.*

II. Haga Vd. una lista de las partes de una casa española que rara vez tenemos aquí.

III. Haga Vd. una lista de al menos diez parientes (madre, padre, etc.).

IV. Siga Vd. estas frases (sentences), *usando su lista de parientes:*

1. La madre de mi madre se llama mi ——.
2. El hermano de mi madre se llama mi ——.
3. La hermana de mi padre se llama mi ——.
4. El hijo de mi tío se llama mi ——. .
5. La hija de mi abuelo se llama mi —— o mi ——.
6. El nieto de mi abuelo se llama mi —— o mi ——.
7. El sobrino de mi tía se llama mi —— o mi ——.
8. El padre de mi prima se llama mi ——.
9. La hija de mi hermano se llama mi ——.
10. La hija de mi padre se llama mi ——.
11. El hermano de mi hermana se llama mi ——.

V. Find one or more Spanish nouns which resemble each of these verbs in form and meaning:

1. comer	7. acostumbrarse	13. cenar
2. jugar	8. amar	14. pensar
3. viajar	9. bailar	15. faltar
4. responder	10. dormir	16. gustar
5. valer	11. casarse	17. llamar
6. acompañar	12. cuidar	18. entrar

VI. From what infinitives do these verb forms come?   If

you can't remember whether some are **-er** or **-ir** verbs, look in the general vocabulary.   Remember: *o>ue* or *u; e>ie* or *i*.

1. cuesta	6. se divierte	11. mueren
2. entienden	7. durmiendo	12. llueve
3. recuerdo	8. pruebas	13. vendré
4. harán	9. te despides	14. venderé
5. siga Vd.	10. sabré	15. duerman Vds.

VII. Complete in Spanish:

1. El cuarto en que comemos se llama el ——.
2. Los cuartos en que dormimos se llaman los ——.
3. Recibimos a nuestros amigos en la ——.
4. La cocinera prepara las comidas en la ——.
5. Los españoles dejan su automóvil en el ——.
6. El gato y el perro tienen que quedarse en la ——.
7. Las criadas tienen que —— los cuartos y —— la casa.
8. Los niños españoles no tienen que —— los platos ni —— la mesa para su mamá.

VIII. Which word does not belong with each group?

tío	peor	huevo	cocina
primo	mayor	leche	abuelo
nieto	mejor	carne	sala
nuevo	menor	paja	dormitorio
sobrino	amor	sopa	comedor
duro	montaña	caja	médico
peseta	rey	oso	carnicero
peso	valle	oveja	gallina
perro grande	llano	vaca	criado
salud	río	caballo	profesor

REPASITO

I. Go back to Chapters 7 and 11 and sing the little songs «Buenos Propósitos» *and* «Primavera.»   How much of them can you read now that you couldn't before?

II. Dos refranes

Más vale pan con amor que gallina con dolor (*sorrow*).
Donde hay amor hay dolor.   (*Compare:* "*Every rose has its thorn.*")

III. Complete in Spanish: (This one will make you think!
Watch out for *le>se,* and the position of object pronouns.)

1. Yo deseaba la paz; *I wanted it.*
2. Venderé los caballos; *I shall sell them.*
3. Jorge dirá las letras; *he will say them.*
4. Anita rompe los huevos; *she breaks them.*
5. Adelita está mirando a Alberto; *she is looking at him.*
6. Lupita está cubriendo la cabeza; *she is covering it.*
7. Estamos perdiendo nuestros amigos; *we are losing them.*
8. Ella deseaba venderme la leche; *she wanted to sell it to me.*
9. Enséñeme Vd. su regalo; *show it to me.*
10. Enséñele Vd. su regalo a Enrique; *show it to him.*
11. Tráigale Vd. la leche a Alfonso; *bring it to him.*
12. Sus parientes le han dado tres duros; *they have given them to him.*

IV. Make plural everything possible:

1. La señora de Navarro ha estado muy ocupada.
2. Siempre me despierto temprano por la mañana.
3. Ayer había un extranjero cerca del río.
4. En el verano siempre llueve por la tarde.
5. Hacía mucho frío cuando yo le esperaba.
6. Romperé el huevo si no tengo cuidado.
7. Le veo a Vd., señor.
8. La luz no es para mí, sino para ella.

V. Write a description in Spanish of your house. It may
help you to re-read the description of the Navarro's house.
There is an old Spanish proverb that says, "If you can't go
over the mountain, go around it." Applied to your composi-
tion this means that if you can't say a thing in one way, there
is always another way to say it.

VI. Tres chistes para leer

Cualquier cosa es posible

— Su mujer es rubia (*blonde*), ¿verdad?
— ¿Quién sabe? Ella acaba de ir al Salón de Belleza (*beauty shop*).

Anécdota curiosa

— Mamá, quiero contarle (*tell*) a Vd. una anécdota. ¿Le gustará?
— Sí, hija. Contada por ti, mucho.
— Es muy corta.
--- No importa. Me gustará.
— ¿Y no va Vd. a enfadarse?
— Por supuesto que no.
— Bueno. Pues, había una vez una maceta, muy bonita, llena de flores.... Y yo acabo de romperla....

Su nombre

— Cómo te llamas, chico?
— Como papá.
— Y ¿cómo se llama tu papá?
— Como yo.
— Pero, al llamarte para la comida, ¿cómo te llaman?
— No tienen que llamarme. Siempre estoy en el comedor mucho antes de que sirvan (*new form of* **servir**) la sopa.

PALABRAS PARA HOY

Alfonso	Alphonse	**limpiar**	to clean
bordar	to embroider	2 **limpio, -a**	clean
2 **la cama**	bed	2 **loco, -a**	crazy
la cocinera	cook	**manejar**	to drive (a car)
2 **coger**	take hold of; to pick (flowers)	**Mariquita**	nickname for **María**
		Miguel	Michael
coser	to sew	3 **la misa**	mass
el chófer	chauffeur (Spanish-American word)	**el nieto**	grandson
		platicar	to chat
2 **escoger**	to choose	4 **la prenda**	forfeit
la estufa	stove	4 **el primo**	cousin
Inés	Inez	3 **el sobrino**	nephew
1 **jamás**	never, ever	2 **solo, -a**	single (new meaning)
2 **juntos** (*adj.*)	together		

LA CASA Y LOS CUARTOS [1]

la azotea	flat roof	**el comedor**	dining room
el balcón		**el cuarto de baño**	bathroom
la cocina	kitchen	**el dormitorio**	bedroom

[1] The words without English meanings have been given before. Do you know them?

la galería	porch	las puertaventanas	shutters
el llamador	knocker	la reja	grating
el patio		la sala	
el piso		la ventana	
la puerta		el zaguán	

EXPRESIONES

de la misma manera, in the same way
en cuanto a, as for, concerning
lo mismo (*neuter*), the same thing

poner la mesa, to set the table
por segunda (tercera) vez, for the second (third) time
rara vez, rarely

CAPÍTULO **30**

¿Cuánto sabe usted?

*Read these descriptions of places and guess the name of each.
Then you might try to write some descriptions of your own for the
class to guess.*

All new words except cognates are translated.

TENOCHTITLÁN

Ésta es una ciudad muy antigua, mucho más antigua que
las ciudades de los Estados Unidos del Norte. Estaba en un
lago (*lake*) y antiguamente las calles eran canales. Los
habitantes de esta ciudad tenían jardines flotantes (*floating*),
porque había demasiado agua en que plantar sus legumbres 5
y sus flores. La ciudad tenía un emperador (*emperor*) que
llevaba una capa (*cape*) hecha de plumas de pajaritos. Había
palacios y templos, y un gran mercado central con muchos
vendedores. Cada casa tenía una azotea, en la cual (*which*)
había flores. Los aztecas la llamaban «Tenochtitlán.» 10
¿Cómo se llama esta ciudad hoy día?[1]

[1] See "Spain Comes to America," page 176.

Streets were canals before the Spaniards took Tenochtitlán from the Aztecs. Not far from Mexico City today, at Xochimilco, there still exists an Aztec village of "floating gardens" that no longer float.

Una ciudad de California

Es una ciudad muy moderna. Se dice que es la ciudad más famosa del mundo. Verdaderamente no es una ciudad en sí misma (*itself*) sino parte de otra ciudad más grande.

En las calles se ve gente muy curiosa. Allá va un vaquero
5 (*cowboy*) hablando a un hombre vestido muy de moda. Después pasan dos señoritas. Pero ¡qué cosa! Tienen la cara pintada de un color muy raro; casi es rojo o amarillo. Ahora pasa una señora muy bonita. La conocemos porque la hemos visto muchas veces en el cine.

10 Aquí está un teatro. Delante de él hay mucha gente. Parece que todos están esperando a alguien. Hay un niño entre ellos con un librito lleno de nombres famosos. Tiene un lápiz y es evidente que espera poner otro nombre en su librito.

Por las calles pasan muchos automóviles. Muchos de ellos
tienen placas (*license plates*) de otros estados. Son turistas   15
que están visitando esta ciudad para ver a las estrellas del
cine. ¿Cómo se llama la ciudad?

LA AMÉRICA DEL SUR

Los españoles fundaron (*founded*) esta hermosa ciudad en
1535. Está cerca de un río importante en la América del Sur,
y es la capital de un país grande e (y) importante. Tiene
calles grandes, edificios y tiendas modernas, y parques bonitos.
Hay muchos teatros y muchas escuelas. También hay una   5
universidad.

Cuando tenemos invierno aquí, allí tienen verano. Por
eso los niños de aquella ciudad tienen sus vacaciones de
verano en los meses de noviembre, diciembre, y enero.

Se habla español aunque se oyen otras lenguas también,   10
porque a todo el mundo les gusta visitar esta famosa ciudad.
Alguien la ha llamado la «París de la América del Sur.» Es la
ciudad más grande de aquel continente. ¿Cómo se llama?

"Paris of South America" is the name often given to Buenos Aires. It
boasts of the widest street in the world, and its plazas and monuments
are unsurpassed.

Sawders

REPASO DE VOCABULARIO

EJERCICIO I.   *What Spanish word is the opposite of each of these:*

1. joven	8. despertarse	15. dar	22. alguien
2. comprar	9. antes	16. difícil	23. algo
3. levantarse	10. pequeño	17. tonto	24. mentira
4. feliz	11. izquierda	18. con	25. morir
5. bueno	12. perder	19. menor	26. siempre
6. corto	13. preguntar	20. abrir	27. verano
7. despacio	14. cielo	21. algún	28. más

EJERCICIO II.   *See how long a list of words you can make under each classification:*

Los animales   La ropa   Las comidas   El cuerpo

EJERCICIO III.   *Give a synonym for:*

pensar, favor de, tal vez, hay que, no —— más que, andar, unos

EJERCICIO IV.   *Give in Spanish eight expressions using* **tener,** *nine using* **hacer,** *and three using* **dar.**

EJERCICIO V.   *Say in English:*

1. varias veces	5. algunas veces	9. de vez en cuando
2. tal vez	6. unas veces	10. otra vez
3. esta vez	7. muchas veces	11. una vez
4. en vez de	8. por tercera vez	12. rara vez

EJERCICIO VI.   *Complete in Spanish:*

1. El veinte y cinco de diciembre es el día de ——. 2. El seis de enero es el día de ——. 3. Un portal es una representación del ——. 4. Para los españoles un portal es como nuestro ——. 5. Tratan de tener toda clase de —— en un portal. 6. Granada es ——. Está en ——. 7. Los —— viven en el Albaicín. No tienen casas sino ——. Su manera favorita de ganar dinero es ——. 8. La Alhambra es ——. 9. Los moros vivían en España hace ——. 10. Si no tiene burro, el hombre pobre lleva las cosas ——.

EJERCICIO VII.   *Give eight Spanish proverbs.   Can you write them, with no errors, from memory?*

REPASO DE COSAS DE INTERÉS

EJERCICIO I. *Complete each sentence or give the correct answer:*

1. The future stem is the —— ——. (§ 92)
2. The sign of the future tense is therefore ——. (§ 92)
3. The future endings are ——. (§ 92)
4. Give the first person singular future tense of *venir, hacer, saber.* (§ 93)
5. Give the first person singular future tense of verbs resembling *venir, hacer, saber.* (§ 93)
6. Instead of *I like a train,* Spaniards say ——. (§ 88)
7. Name the direct object pronouns. (§ 44)
8. Name the indirect object pronouns. (§ 86)
9. *Le* or *les* followed by *lo, la, los,* or *las* changes to ——. (§ 89)
10. Name the prepositional forms of pronouns. (§ 87)
11. The explanatory forms for *le* are ——; the explanatory forms for *les* are ——. (§ 90)
12. Can you use the explanatory forms without the pronouns? Why? (§ 86)
13. All object pronouns stand —— a conjugated verb. (§ 45)
14. When do object pronouns follow a verb? (§ 79)
15. What is often needed when pronouns are attached to a verb? (§ 46, § 89)
16. Three verbs that are used mostly in the third person are ——. (§ 88)
17. Give lists of long and short forms of possessive adjectives (§ 66, § 17); of demonstratives (§ 26).
18. *Ser* is always used to tell —— or ——. Example: —— ——. (§ 40)
19. *Estar* is always used to tell ——. Example: ——. (§ 40)
20. *Ser* is used with a predicate adjective when it expresses a —— condition. Example: ——. (§ 40)
21. *Estar* is used with a predicate adjective when it expresses a —— condition. Example ——. (§ 40)
22. What are both sets of endings for the imperfect? (§ 82)
23. What does the imperfect tense mean? (§ 82)
24. What three verbs are irregular in the imperfect, and how is each conjugated? (§ 83)

MUCHOS POCOS HACEN UN MUCHO

EJERCICIO I. *Answer in complete sentences.* (¡Mucho cuidado!)

1. ¿Qué hará Vd. mañana? ¿el sábado? ¿el domingo? ¿esta noche?
   (*Warning: don't try to use a form of* hacer *in your answer!*)
2. ¿A qué hora come Vd.?
3. ¿A qué hora comerá Vd.?
4. ¿A qué hora saldrá Vd. de la escuela?
5. ¿Cuándo asistirá Vd. a la iglesia?
6. ¿Cuándo asistía Vd. al cine el año pasado?
7. Si hace frío ¿qué se pondrá Vd.?
8. Si Vd. tiene sed ¿qué hará?
9. ¿Le gustaba a Vd. el baile?
10. ¿Le gustan a Vd. los dulces?
11. ¿Le falta a Vd. dinero?
12. ¿Le molestan a Vd. los exámenes?

EJERCICIO II. *Give the meaning of each expression:*

1. duérmase Vd.	8. he esperado	15. ha colgado
2. oiga Vd.	9. nos interesaba	16. Vd. ha construido
3. me gustará	10. ¿necesita Vd.?	17. gritábamos
4. han caído	11. me quedaré	18. corra Vd.
5. está durmiendo	12. salían	19. corriendo
6. esperaban	13. he visto	20. dando
7. esperaré	14. se casarán	21. estoy leyendo

EJERCICIO III. *Give a synopsis of each verb (see model in Chapter 28,* REPASITO*) in third person singular:*

morir (III RC)	estar	leer
contar	saber	tener

EJERCICIO IV. *Conjugate in the imperfect:*

quedarse	oír	ir

EJERCICIO V. *Replace the nouns in italics with pronouns. Use explanatory forms with the first four.*

---

¹ Omit present progressive and command.

1. Lleve Vd. *la manzana a Carlos.*   2. No quiero dar *los huevos a su hermano.*   3. Ha vendido *la cesta a la mujer.*   4. Felipe da *los papeles a Anita.*   5. Ponga Vd. *el sombrero* aquí.   6. Busco *mi pluma* (*mine*) (section 66).   7. Carlos está usando *el libro.*   8. Ha leído *la lección* en voz baja.

EJERCICIO VI.   *Complete in Spanish:*

1. La mesa está cerca de *me.*   2. La mesa está lejos de *him.*   3. La mesa estaba entre *him* y *her.*   4. Los niños vivían lejos de *us.*   5. Pablo está delante de *you* pero detrás de *me.*   6. ¿Quién estaba al lado de *them?*

EJERCICIO VII.   *Complete in Spanish:*

1. *It seems to me* que va a llover.   2. *I liked* tener dinero que gastar.
3. *I lack* dinero que gastar.   4. *It doesn't matter to me* lo que dice.
5. *It bothers me* hablar a la gente.

Make the preceding sentences emphatic.
Change the preceding sentences, first using you (*polite*), *then using the first person plural.*

EJERCICIO VIII.   *Study the following passage for dictation. You should make a perfect score.*   (There are 100 words.)

Son las doce de la noche.   Todo el mundo se ha dormido.   La luz de la luna ilumina la tierra.   En el cielo se pueden ver las estrellas.   No cantan los pájaros porque se han dormido también.

Los animalitos de la noche salen.   Un ratón corre por el jardín. Tiene hambre y busca algo que comer.   Pero el gato, Félix, también está buscando algo que comer.   A él le gusta la carne fresca.   ¡Pobre ratoncito![1]   No ve al gato.   En un momento ya no hay ratón.

¡Qué lástima!   Así es la vida.   Los grandes se comen a los chicos.

EJERCICIO IX.   *Put into Spanish:*

1. It is mine; it is his.   2. Where are you?   Here I am.   3. I never go; no one comes.   4. I know Mr. García.   5. Do you know where he is?   6. books to read; nothing to study   7. It is hot (*weather*); I am hot.   8. It isn't red, but blue.   9. They have gone away.   10. I have put on my shoes.   11. Bring me the book; bring it to me.   12.

[1] «*Miguelito Ratoncito*» is *Mickey Mouse* in Spanish, and «*Pato Pascual*» is *Donald Duck.*

What time is it? It is one o'clock. 13. I am working (*prog.*); he is reading. 14. She is very beautiful! 15. He used to go early. 16. It isn't for me; it is for you. 17. I don't like to study. 18. He gives it to me; I give it to you. 19. Give it to her! 20. They will tell me.

EJERCICIO X. *Algo para leer*

Conoce a su papá

El profesor, en la lección de aritmética, pregunta a uno de los alumnos:

— Supongamos (*let's suppose*) que es el día de Navidad y su mamá ha comprado una torta (*cake*). A la mesa están su padre, su madre, sus dos hermanas, y Vd. Su padre va a dividir la torta. ¿En cuántas partes la dividirá?

— En cinco, señor profesor.

— Muy bien, chico. Pero supongamos que en el momento de ir a dividir la torta llegan su tío y su tía. ¿En cuántas partes dividirá su padre la torta?

El niño piensa un momento y contesta:

— Entonces no dividirá la torta. La esconderá (*hide*) rápidamente.

De mal en peor

(El artista y su amigo estaban delante de un retrato [*portrait*].)

El artista. — ¿Qué le parece a Vd. (*How do you like it*)?

El amigo. — ¡Terrible!

El artista. — Pues lo he pintado yo.

El amigo. — No, yo hablaba del modelo.

El artista. — Es mi esposa.

Dos refranes

Cortesía de boca, mucho vale y poco cuesta.

Mientras en casa estoy, rey soy.

La higuera encantada[1]

This story has past tense verb forms which are not in the vocabulary, but in the COSAS DE INTERÉS section.

El tío Manuel era el jardinero de los Gutiérrez, quienes vivían en Tepic. Era un viejecito muy simpático, que trabajaba casi todo el día cuidando las flores y las plantas que crecían en su patio. Muchas tardes, durante la hora de la siesta, contaba historias a los hijos de la familia, Felipe, 5 Susita, y Miguel. Los niños creían que sus cuentos eran maravillosos, porque el tío Manuel sabía de memoria todas las leyendas (*legends*) del país; o si no las sabía de memoria, al menos sabía inventarlas al gusto. Parecía que el viejecito tenía una imaginación muy buena. 10

Por supuesto, el tío Manuel no trabajaba más que de día, pero una noche volvió a casa de los Gutiérrez después de la cena para pedir dinero a su patrón (*employer*). El señor se lo pagó, y el jardinero trató de irse. Pero los niños le vieron; y Miguel, el menor, gritó, — ¡Cuéntenos Vd. una historia, tío 15 Manuel! No puede salir sin contarnos un cuento.

Al fin el jardinero se sentó para contárselo a ellos, diciendo, — Les diré uno que los asustará mucho, ¿eh?

— ¡Qué cosa! — respondió Felipe. — ¡No puede Vd. asustarnos a nosotros! 20

— Pues, una noche de luna del año pasado, — empezó el viejecito, — salí de casa en mi mula para ir a Santa María del Oro,[2] que está muy lejos de aquí. Solito, viajaba por un

---

[1] The "haunted fig tree" really grows outside of Tepic, and several people there will swear that they have had the experience described in this story.

[2] Santa María del Oro is a village some seven hours' horseback ride from Tepic through the beautiful wooded *sierra*, as the people call their mountain country. There are tribes of Indians living in the *sierra* whose customs are still the same as they were before the Spaniards came to Tepic in 1524, and who are only now learning to speak Spanish.

camino poco usado, pero yo, siendo un hombre muy valiente,
25 no tenía miedo. Canté para divertirme, miré la luna y las
estrellas, y al fin me dormí, y mi mula fiel escogió su propio
camino. Cuando, casi a medianoche, me desperté lejos de
Tepic, reconocí delante de mí la higuera grandísima que crece
al lado del camino, una higuera silvestre (*wild*), tan grande
30 que casi cubre el camino en aquel lugar. Muchas veces he
visto aquella higuera de día, y cerca de ella la cruz de madera
y el montón de piedras que marcan la tumba (*tomb*) del
bandido a quien mataron allí hace muchos años.[1] Pero yo,
siendo un hombre muy valiente, no tenía miedo; y mi mula
35 y yo seguimos por el camino hasta entrar en la sombra de la
higuera.

— En ese momento oí un susurro (*rustling*) violento de las
hojas del árbol, y como era una noche sin viento, esto me
parecía algo curioso. El susurro continuó con mucho más
40 ruido, y de repente me dí cuenta de (*I realized*) que el árbol
estaba cayendo sobre nosotros.

Mi mula, oyéndolo también, y entendiéndolo más pronto
que yo, empezó a correr lo más rápidamente posible para
escapar de las ramas inmensas del árbol. Al momento en que
45 salimos de su sombra a la luz de la luna, lo oí caer con un
ruido terrible; y mi mula, estando tan asustada, corrió tan de
prisa que no me fué (*was*) posible mirar hacia atrás para verlo.

Así seguimos hasta Santa María del Oro, mi mula todavía
temblando del susto (*fright*), y yo dando gracias a Dios por
50 haber escapado. Al día siguiente, volví a Tepic por el mismo
camino, y, llegando al lugar de la higuera, se puede imaginar
mi sorpresa al ver creciendo allí, — alta, verde, y bonita como
siempre a la luz del sol, — ¡aquella higuera inmensa que yo
había oído caer la noche anterior!

---

[1] Anywhere along country roads or trails in Spain, Mexico, or South America
may be found rude crosses of wood, stone, or even pipe, set up to mark the spot
where someone died "with his boots on."

Each cross becomes a sort of wayside shrine, and near it is usually a pile of
stones, each one representing a prayer said by a passer-by for the soul of the de-
ceased. Superstitious people dread passing these places after dark, no doubt
fully expecting to meet the uneasy soul in its wanderings.

Along country roads, crosses mark the graves of those who died "with their boots on." Each stone represents a prayer said at the shrine by a passer-by.

— ¡Ay, caray! — interrumpió Felipe, con los ojos grandes 55 como platillos. — ¿No tenía Vd. miedo, tío Manuel?

— No, — respondió el viejecito. — Siendo un hombre tan valiente, pasé por debajo del árbol como antes, y esta vez mi mula y yo no oímos nada. Pero ahora sé que aquel árbol está encantado, sin duda porque mataron allí a aquel bandido. 60 Y cualquier persona que pase[1] por allí a medianoche oirá el

[1] *pase*, a subjunctive form of *pasar* which you will not learn how to use for a long time. Translate it as it sounds best.

mismo ruido terrible, y creerá que la higuera está cayendo
sobre él.

65 El tío Manuel se levantó, y despidiéndose de todos, pronto
salió con el criado que le acompañó al zaguán para abrirle la
puerta.

— ¡Qué hombre tan valiente es ese tío Manuel! — exclamó Susita, temblando todavía del susto. — ¡En cuanto a
mí, nunca quiero yo ver aquel árbol encantado!

70 — Ni yo tampoco, — respondió Miguel. — Su cuento me
asustó a mí también.

En este momento volvió el criado solo y preguntó al señor
Gutiérrez, — ¿Me permite Vd. acompañar al tío Manuel a
casa? Parece que tiene miedo de ir solo esta noche.

75 Todos los Gutiérrez empezaron a reír.

— ¡Qué hombre tan valiente es ese tío Manuel! — exclamó Felipe. — ¡Asustándonos a nosotros con su cuento, se
ha asustado a sí mismo también!

Find These Expressions in the Story

1. Uncle Manuel worked only in the daytime
2. I'll tell you one that will frighten you much, shall I?
3. near it the wooden cross
4. this seemed somewhat curious to me
5. I heard it fall with a terrible noise
6. you can imagine my surprise to see growing there
7. at least he could invent them to suit
8. to ask his employer for some money
9. he sat down to tell it to them
10. the tomb of the bandit whom they killed there
11. understanding it more quickly than I
12. this time my mule and I heard nothing
13. we came out of its shadow into the moonlight
14. saying goodnight to (taking leave of) everyone
15. What a brave man is that Uncle Manuel!
16. he has frightened himself too

COSAS DE INTERÉS

97. Definite Article with Expressions of Time

el año pasado	*last year*
el lunes próximo	*next Monday*
el año que viene	*next year*

It is necessary to use the definite article with words expressing time (*mes, semana, año*, the seasons, and days of the week) when they are modified.

EJERCICIO I. *Put into Spanish:*

next year, last week, next Friday, last month, last summer, next spring.

98. The Preterite Tense (*"Past Definite"*)

Here is our second simple past tense. Its stem in regular verbs (including first and second conjugation radical-changing verbs) is the infinitive minus the last two letters.

Its endings are new; there is one set for *-ar* verbs, and another for *-er* or *-ir* verbs.

The preterite tense is used for verbs which express *action* in the past:

volvió a casa	se sentaron	abrimos la puerta
he returned home	*they sat down*	*we opened the door*

PRETERITE TENSE OF REGULAR VERBS		
cantar, *to sing*	responder, *to answer*	salir, *to leave*
canté, *I sang, did sing*	respondí, *I answered, did answer*	salí, *I left, did leave*
cantaste	respondiste	saliste
cantó	respondió	salió
cantamos	respondimos	salimos
cantasteis [1]	respondisteis	salisteis
cantaron	respondieron	salieron

[1] A trick way to check your spelling of the second person plural is to cover the last two letters (*-is*) and compare with the second person singular.

EJERCICIO II. *Answer these questions:*

1. What is the regular preterite stem? 2. What are the first conjugation endings? 3. What are the second and third conjugation endings? 4. How many accents has the regular preterite? Where? 5. What is the difference between *canto* and *cantó*? 6. What two tenses can *cantamos* be? 7. What two tenses can *salimos* be? 8. Can *respondimos* be either present or preterite? Why? 9. What is the difference between *canté* and *cantaré*? 10. How do you say "did" with another verb (*did he sing*)?

EJERCICIO III. *Conjugate in the preterite:*

mirar, abrir, parecer, levantarse, ver

EJERCICIO IV. *Give the meanings.* (¡Cuidado!)

1. volvió temprano	6. esperamos (*2 tenses*)	11. halla la calle
2. la miré	7. corrieron de prisa	12. costó mucho
3. la miraré	8. acompañó a Juan	13. no lo haré
4. lo oí caer	9. acompaño a Juan	14. lo sabremos
5. lo rompemos	10. hallará la calle	15. corrió a casa

EJERCICIO V. *Put into Spanish, using the verbs* **volver, salir, exclamar, ver:**

1. I saw	5. she left	9. we shall see
2. we returned	6. you saw	10. we saw
3. they exclaimed	7. they returned	11. you (*pl.*) left
4. they will exclaim	8. I exclaimed	12. he will see

99. The Imperfect Versus the Preterite Tense

The imperfect is used for:

1. Past description ("*was —— ing*"):
   el sol brillaba   *the sun was shining*

2. Repeated or habitual past action ("*used to*"):
   cantaba todos los días   *he used to sing every day*

The preterite is used for: [1]

1. Definitely past action:
   cerró la puerta   *he closed the door*

---

[1] To the teacher: The use of the preterite with the "perspective of time" is left for second year.

If we could draw pictures of these two tenses, they might look like this:

IMPERFECT
$\left\{\begin{array}{l}\rule{3cm}{0.4pt}\left\{\begin{array}{l}\text{descriptive or continued}\\\text{happening: }\textit{"was ——— ing"}\end{array}\right.\\\textbf{+ + +}\quad\text{happened over and over: }\textit{"used to"}\end{array}\right.$

PRETERITE $\quad\quad\textbf{+}\quad\quad\left\{\begin{array}{l}\textit{"}\textbf{+}\text{ marks the spot" where some-}\\\text{thing happened}\end{array}\right.$

Here is another way to remember how to use these tenses:

The imperfect is used for the *"stage setting"* or the scene of events: *The sun was shining; the sky was blue; the birds were singing.*

The preterite is used for the *actions* that happened in this setting: *A man came out of the house; he slammed the door; he looked at his watch; he said, "Dear me!"*

EJERCICIO VI. *Answer these questions:*

1. What does **+** stand for?   What does **+ + +** stand for?
2. What do *"was ——— ing"* and *"used to"* always show?
3. Which tense is used for a *single* past action?
4. Which tense is used for a *repeated* past action?
5. Which tense will such expressions as *de vez en cuando* and *todos los días* take?   Why?
6. Which tense is used for description in the past?
7. Which tense is used for telling time in the past?   Why?

EJERCICIO VII.   *Read these English sentences and tell whether the imperfect or preterite should be used for each verb.* (Do not try to translate the sentences into Spanish.)

1. I used to take my music lesson every Monday.   2. Every time I saw you (Monday, Tuesday, Wednesday, *etc.*), you were in a hurry. 3. He sold the cow for fifty dollars and went home.   4. Mr. Gutiérrez paid Uncle Manuel his money.   5. He was finding much to paint every day.   6. The clock struck twelve.   The clock was striking twelve when I arrived.   7. She said that he was going from house to house.   8. The vendor sat down on a bench to rest.   9. He saw his friend, who was coming out on the balcony.   10. Didn't you tell me that you used to buy flowers?

EJERCICIO VIII. *Translate these sentences, name the tense of each verb, and explain why it is used:*

1. No trabajaba más que de día. 2. Vine (*pret. of* **venir**) a México con mi esposa a la edad de veinte y dos años. 3. Díganos Vd. algo que hacía cuando niño. 4. Una noche me acosté muy temprano. 5. Siempre me acostaba muy temprano. 6. Miré la luna y las estrellas, y canté para divertirme. 7. La luna y las estrellas brillaban en el cielo. 8. Eran las ocho y media cuando me levanté. 9. — Sí, ¿cómo no? — respondió con una sonrisa. 10. Al fin vendí todo y volví a casa. 11. ¿Qué hacía el gato en la cocina?

PREGUNTITAS

I.
1. ¿Qué hacía el tío Manuel?
2. ¿Trabajaba el tío Manuel de día o de noche?
3. ¿Por qué eran buenos los cuentos del tío Manuel?
4. ¿Por qué volvió una noche a casa de los Gutiérrez?
5. ¿Se lo pagó el patrón?
6. ¿Era una noche obscura cuando el tío Manuel salió para Santa María del Oro?
7. ¿Cuándo se despertó el tío Manuel?
8. ¿Qué vió al lado del camino?
9. ¿Qué vió cerca de la higuera?
10. ¿Qué oyó (*pret. of* oír, *third sing.*) el tío Manuel?
11. ¿Lo oyó también la mula?
12. ¿Cómo escapó la mula?
13. Al día siguiente, ¿cómo encontró el árbol?
14. ¿Se asustó el tío Manuel contando el cuento?

II.
1. ¿Tiene Vd. miedo de ir solito (-a) a casa?
2. ¿Están encantados muchos árboles?
3. ¿Se asustó Vd. el año pasado?
4. ¿Mató Vd. a un bandido la semana pasada?
5. ¿Se despertó Vd. en la clase hoy?
6. ¿Trató Vd. de tener muchas plantas el verano pasado?
7. ¿Tembló Vd. al leer este cuento?
8. ¿Rompió Vd. muchos platos cuando los lavó?
9. ¿Le gustan a Vd. más (*best*) las noches de luna?
10. ¿Asistió Vd. al cine el sábado pasado?

11. ¿Comió Vd. carne ayer?

12. ¿Tomó Vd. café, chocolate o leche esta mañana?

REPASITO

I. In the story, why is **el tío Manuel** *used in some places, and just* **tío Manuel** *in others?* (See section 36.)

II. Change any words necessary to make these statements true:

1. Muchos árboles están encantados. 2. Siempre había luna en una noche obscura. 3. El tío Manuel no trabajaba más que de noche. 4. El tío Pepe decía que era un hombre muy valiente. 5. El tío Manuel se despertó cerca de Tepic. 6. Nadie oyó caer la higuera. 7. La cocinera se despidió de todos después de contar el cuento. 8. Una cruz y un montón de periódicos marcaban la tumba (*tomb*) del bandido. 9. El criado tenía miedo de ir a casa solo. 10. Las manzanas crecen en las higueras. 11. Las criadas cuelgan la ropa limpia en el zaguán. 12. Había una estufa grande en la sala. 13. Anita llevaba la cesta de huevos en la mano izquierda. 14. Los gitanos han pintado de verde la tierra alrededor de cada puerta.

III. Translate:

1. He used to return home at seven o'clock. 2. One night he returned at eight o'clock. 3. It was a moonlight night. 4. He was walking along (**por**) the road when he met a friend. 5. "Where have you been?" his friend asked him. 6. "I have been in the market," he answered. 7. I saw Uncle Manuel there. He was frightened. 8. At midnight he has to go to Santa María. 9. He is afraid to go all alone. 10. Will you go with him? 11. Of course. With pleasure.

IV. Chistes para leer

Mucha carne

— ¿Cómo encontró Vd. la carne?

— Con mucha dificultad.... ¡buscando entre las patatas!

Es mejor no reír

— ¡Mamá! ¡Papá se ha dado un martillazo (*blow with a hammer*) en un dedo (*finger*)!

— Pero, ¿por qué lloras (*cry*) tú?

— ¡Es que yo empecé (*1st pers. sing. pret. of* empezar) a reír!

EL QUELITE* (*The Watercress*)

As in the seagull song, there is only one stanza which mentions the title.   After that, any subject will do.   Here are three of its ten stanzas.

Canción Sinaloense
Arr. by E. M. JARRETT

¡Qué bo - ni - to es el que - li - te! . . . ¡Bien ha - ya quien lo for - mó! . . . Por-que en es - ta ca - lle vi - ve, . . la jo - ven que a-do - ro yo . . . .

*The alto is often sung an octave higher

1. ¡Qué bonito es el quelite!   How pretty is the watercress!
¡Bien haya quien lo formó!   Bless him who made it!
Porque en esta calle vive   Because on this street lives
la joven que adoro yo.   The girl that I adore.

2. Debajo de un limón verde,   Beneath a green lemon tree,
   me dió sueño y me dormí;   I felt sleepy and went to sleep;
   y me despertó un gallito   And a little rooster awoke me
   cantando, — Quiquiriquí.   Singing, «quiquiriquí» (*Cock-a-doodle-doo*).

3. Mañana me voy, mañana;   Tomorrow I am going away, tomorrow;
   me voy por el Nacional;   I am going on the National (Railway);
   adiós, muchachas bonitas,   Good-by, pretty girls,
   de esta hermosa capital.   Of this beautiful capital.

Algo que leer para divertirse

— Papá, ¿quiere Vd. ayudarme a hacer mi traducción latina?
— No me es posible, hijo mío.   Yo no aprendí el latín.
— ¡Qué padres tan buenos tuvo Vd.!

PALABRAS PARA HOY

1	algo	somewhat (new meaning)		la madera	wood
				Manuel	Emmanuel
3	anterior	before	4	marcar	to mark
	asustado, -a	frightened	2	matar	to kill
	asustar (se)	to frighten *or* to be frightened	1	pasado, -a	last (most recent)
			1	pedir, (i)	to ask for
	el bandido	bandit		el platillo	saucer
2	coger	to pick up, to take up (new meaning)		(plat(o) + illo)	
2	contar, (ue)	to tell, relate (new meaning)	4	próximo	next (*approximate*)
			4	la rama	branch
3	crecer	to grow (increase)	3	reconocer	to recognize
4	el cuento	story (account)	3	el ruido	noise
1	Dios	God	1	solito, -a	all alone
	¿eh?	used like ¿verdad?		(sol(o) + ito)	
3	encantado, -a	haunted (*enchanted*)	3	temblar, (ie)	to tremble
	la higuera	fig tree	1	viejecito	little old man
3	la hoja	leaf		(viej(o) + ecito)	
	el jardinero	gardener			

EXPRESIONES

*al día siguiente, on the following day
al gusto, to taste, to suit
a medianoche, at midnight
a quien, whom
a sí mismo, himself (emphatic)
¡Ay, caray! My goodness! (or some expression of sympathetic concern)

*de día, by day, in the daytime
de luna, moonlight
*de noche, by night
*de prisa, fast
*de repente, suddenly
mirar hacia atrás, to look back
*tener miedo (de), to be afraid (of)

CAPÍTULO **32**

Las aventuras del albañil[1]

PRIMERA PARTE

En otros tiempos vivía en Granada un albañil muy pobre. Una noche se acostó sin cenar. Algunos momentos después, oyendo un golpe en la puerta, se levantó y la abrió. Vió a un hombre muy viejo y muy flaco (*thin*) a quien no conocía.

5 — ¿Qué quiere Vd.? — le preguntó.

— Amigo, se dice que Vd. es un hombre honrado. ¿Quiere Vd. ganar algunas pesetas?

— ¡Ya lo creo! Haré cualquier cosa para ganar dinero.

[1] While the Moors and Spaniards were fighting for the possession of Spain, people often hid their valuables and never went back to get them, so it is not strange that hidden hoards of money and jewels are still being found. Every old Moorish castle has legends of treasure connected with it.

Washington Irving, an American writer who was connected with the American embassy in Spain from 1826 to 1829, became so interested in the legends concerning the Alhambra that he wrote a book about them. Since then the Spaniards have set a plaque in a wall of the room in the Alhambra where he worked, for his book made the whole world interested in Spain.

— Bueno. Le pagaré a Vd. bien, pero tendrá que acompañarme con los ojos vendados. 10

El albañil consintió y se vistió rápidamente. El viejo le vendó los ojos, y salieron los dos. Pasaron por varias calles y dieron muchas vueltas. Al fin entraron en una casa antigua, y al entrar, el viejo cerró la puerta con llave. Pasaron por un corredor muy largo y al fin llegaron a un patio. Allí el viejo 15
le quitó la venda, y el albañil vió que estaban en un patio obscuro. En el centro había una fuente morisca de piedra.

El viejo le mandó construir una cueva subterránea en aquel lugar, y el albañil trabajó toda la noche. Un poco antes del amanecer (*dawn*) el viejo le dió una moneda de oro, le vendó 20
los ojos otra vez y le llevó a su casa.

— ¿Quiere Vd. volver mañana por la noche para concluir el trabajo? — le preguntó el viejo.

— ¡Ya lo creo! Siempre quiero ganar dinero.

— Bueno. Volveré a la misma hora. 25

The summer palace of the Alhambra looks down from its hill upon the town of Granada. Ferdinand and Isabella lived in it after the Moors were driven out in 1492.

Galloway

Al día siguiente el albañil compró varias cosas y él y su familia comieron bien.

A las once de la noche siguiente volvió el anciano. Llevó al albañil otra vez a la misma casa. Aquella noche terminó 30 el albañil la cueva. Entonces el viejo le dijo (said), — Ayúdeme Vd., por favor. Tenemos que poner los cuerpos en la cueva.

El pobre albañil casi murió de miedo. Pero siguió al viejo a una sala en donde había cuatro jarras muy grandes. Al 35 levantarlas vió que estaban llenas de monedas de oro. Los dos llevaron las jarras a la cueva y las enterraron (buried) allí. Después cerró el albañil la cueva y borró todo rastro (trace) del trabajo. El viejo le llevó a casa como antes y le dió dos monedas de oro.

40 Al despedirse de él, le dijo (said), — No diga Vd. nada de esto a nadie. Tendrá mala suerte toda la vida si dice una palabra de este asunto.

El albañil le prometió no decir nada.

SEGUNDA PARTE

Pasaron los años y el albañil olvidó el asunto. Como tenía 45 una familia muy grande, cada día era más pobre que el anterior. Un día cuando estaba sentado a la puerta de su casa miserable, se acercó un hombre bien conocido en Granada como dueño de varias casas.

— Me han dicho que Vd. es muy pobre.

50 — Sí. Es verdad.

— Entonces supongo que Vd. trabajará por muy poco dinero. No puedo pagar mucho pero tengo una casa antigua que necesita reparaciones (repairs).

— La compondré lo mejor posible por muy poco dinero.

55 — Bueno. Sígame Vd.

Le llevó a una casa desierta. Entraron en el patio. En el centro del patio había una fuente morisca de piedra. El albañil recordó otra fuente semejante, la fuente del patio de la cueva.

60 — ¿Quién ha vivido aquí? — preguntó.

— Un viejo avaro. ¡Maldita sea su alma! Dejó encantada la casa. Se dice que era muy rico, pero cuando murió no encontré nada de valor. Nadie quiere vivir aquí porque todo el mundo dice que la casa está encantada y que el espíritu del avaro vuelve por la noche para contar su dinero. Se dice que 65 por la noche se puede ver la luz de su vela y se puede oír el ruido que hace el viejo con las monedas. Pero no puedo hallar nada. ¿Qué haré con esta casa?

— Se lo diré, — contestó el albañil. — Déjeme vivir aquí sin pagar nada y compondré la casa y trataré de romper el 70 encanto.

El hombre aceptó la propuesta (*proposition*) y el albañil y su familia fueron (*went*) a vivir en la casa encantada. Cumplió con su promesa y dejó la casa como nueva. Y ¡qué curioso! Pasando los días, ya no se oía el ruido del avaro contando su 75 dinero. Pero sí se oía ahora el ruido de monedas en el bolsillo del albañil.

Dentro de poco el albañil era uno de los hombres más ricos de Granada. Pero no reveló el secreto de la cueva hasta la hora de su muerte. Antes de morir, se lo reveló a su hijo. Y 80 así es como lo sabemos nosotros.

Find These Expressions in the Story

1. hearing a knock
2. I will do anything
3. You will have to accompany me with your eyes blindfolded.
4. he dressed (himself) rapidly
5. he took off his blindfold
6. he took him home
7. At eleven o'clock the following night
8. he almost died of fright
9. he followed the old man
10. As the days passed
11. he gave him two gold coins
12. Don't say anything about this to anyone.
13. What shall I do

100. The Preterite of Third Conjugation Radical-Changing Verbs

Do you remember the gerunds of III RC verbs? What

stem changes occur in the gerund? (Section 77.) Now look
at these models of the preterite of III RC verbs:

pedir (i, i)
to ask for

ped	í
ped	iste
pid	ió
ped	imos
ped	isteis
pid	ieron

consentir (ie, i)
to consent

consent	í
consent	iste
consint	ió
consent	imos
consent	isteis
consint	ieron

dormir (ue, u)
to sleep

dorm	í
dorm	iste
durm	ió
dorm	imos
dorm	isteis
durm	ieron

Only third conjugation radical-changing verbs change in
the preterite. III RC verbs have the same change in the
preterite as in the gerund ($e > i$; $o > u$), which comes in the
third persons singular and plural. The endings are regular.
The first change indicated after a verb in the dictionary or
vocabulary refers to the present tense, the second change to
the preterite and gerund.

> REMEMBER: III RC Verbs change
> $o > u$; $e > i$
> in the gerund and the
> third persons of the
> preterite.

EJERCICIO I. *Conjugate in the preterite and give the gerund
to match:*

morir (ue, u) [1]   seguir (i, i)   despedirse (i, i)
servir (i, i)   preferir (ie, i)   vestirse (i, i)

EJERCICIO II. *What do these verbs mean?*

1. murieron 2. me vestí 3. no consintió 4. Vds. refirieron
5. Vd. pidió 6. se durmieron 7. me sirvió 8. se despidió 9. siguió 10. prefirieron

[1] The first change, **ue**, is for the present tense; the second change, **u**, is for the
preterite and gerund.

EJERCICIO III.   *Give the infinitive of each form in Ejercicio II.*

EJERCICIO IV.   *Change each form in Ejercicio II to the same person of the present tense.*

EJERCICIO V.   *Change each form in Ejercicio II to the imperfect tense.*

101. Verbs with an i>y Change in the Preterite

PRETERITE TENSE, **oír,** *to hear*

oí	oímos
oíste	oísteis
oyó	oyeron

What happens to an unaccented *i* between two vowels? (*Remember the gerunds?*)

Did you notice the number of accents? Any verb of the second or third conjugation with a stem ending in *a, o,* or *e* has accents on five of the preterite endings.

REMEMBER:	Unaccented *i>y* between vowels in the preterite and gerund

EJERCICIO VI.   *Conjugate in the preterite the following verbs, which have the same changes as* **oír.**

leer   caer   creer

EJERCICIO VII.   *Give the gerunds of the verbs in Ejercicio II.*

EJERCICIO VIII.   *Read these sentences aloud first in Spanish and then in English:*

1. Oyó un ruido en la cocina. 2. El árbol estaba cayendo. 3. El tío Manuel está leyendo el periódico. 4. Construyeron un edificio grande en aquel lugar. 5. La cesta se cayó. 6. No lo creyeron. 7. ¿Qué estás construyendo con las piedras, chico? 8. ¿Leyó Vd. la carta? Sí, la leí ayer. 9. Se durmió en seguida. 10. Juan se despidió de su amigo.

102. *The Preterite Tense of* **Dar**

dí	dimos
diste	disteis
dió	dieron

Does *dar* use *-ar* endings?   Can you guess why?

EJERCICIO IX.   *How do you translate these verbs?*

doy,   estoy dando,   he dado,   daré,   dí,   daba

EJERCICIO X.   *With the same tenses of* **dar** *as in Ejercicio IX,* use (1) **usted** *as the subject,* (2) **nosotros** *as the subject,* (3) **ellos** *as the subject.*

EJERCICIO XI.   *Say in Spanish:*

1. I gave it to him; I used to give it to him.   2. Did you give it to him? [1]   3. He gave him a gold coin.   4. We gave them money; we were giving them money.   5. Did they give you a present? [1]

PREGUNTITAS

I.   1. ¿Dónde vivía el albañil?
2. ¿Quién llamó a su puerta?
3. ¿Consintió el albañil a la propuesta del anciano?
4. ¿Dónde construyó la cueva?
5. ¿Qué le dió el anciano?
6. ¿Por cuántas noches trabajó el albañil en la casa antigua?
7. ¿Qué enterraron en la cueva?
8. ¿Qué prometió el albañil?
9. ¿Cumplió con su promesa?
10. ¿Cuándo reveló su secreto?
11. ¿Reconoció el albañil la casa después de muchos años?
12. ¿Rompió el encanto?

II.   1. ¿Ha visto Vd. jamás una casa encantada?
2. ¿Ha vivido Vd. jamás en una casa encantada?
3. ¿Tiene Vd. monedas de oro en el bolsillo?

[1] Remember that *did* is in the verb.

4. ¿Ha hecho Vd. una cueva alguna vez?
5. ¿Es Vd. honrado (-a)?
6. ¿Está cerrada su puerta? ¿Está cerrada con llave?
7. ¿Es posible morir de miedo?
8. ¿Usamos monedas de oro en los E. U. A.? ¿Las hemos usado?
9. ¿Se vistió Vd. rápidamente esta mañana?
10. ¿Se quita Vd. el sombrero al entrar en una casa?

REPASITO

I. Have you noticed that the ending *-ero* often indicates occupation? **Carta** is *letter*; **cartero** is the *letter carrier* or *postman*. *Tell what each of these words means and give the noun or adjective from which it is derived.*

1. cocinero	4. enfermera	7. zapatero
2. viajero	5. lechero	8. herrero (hierro, *iron*)
3. carnicero	6. jardinero	9. pordiosero [1]

II. Give the person and tense of these verb endings:

1. -(r)é	5. -ó	9. -iendo	13. -ió, -yó	17. -í
2. -ando	6. -iste	10. -(r)emos	14. -ieron	18. -ado
3. -an	7. -aron	11. -é	15. -yeron	19. -ábamos
4. -aban	8. -ía	12. -e	16. -asteis	20. -yendo

III. Translate the words in italics:

1. Yo tengo mis libros; Vd. tiene *los suyos*. 2. *Esas* manzanas son de Juan; *éstas* son *de Lola*. 3. Sí, son *de ella*, pero Carlos ha comido *las de Juan*. 4. *La voz de Tinita* es muy buena; *la mía* no es buena.

IV. Turn each statement into a question. Ask your question of some other pupil and let him answer with his book closed.

1. Arturo ha comido la fruta. 2. Los niños se levantaron a las ocho. 3. El albañil era un hombre honrado. 4. El albañil recibió tres monedas de oro. 5. Entraron en la casa. 6. El albañil recordó otra fuente semejante. 7. Juan se lo dió. 8. El hombre no le preguntó nada.

[1] See page 299, note 3.

V. Write ten sentences in Spanish telling what you did yesterday. Use these verbs:

1. despertarse　2. levantarse　3. vestirse　4. comer　5. leer
6. estudiar　7. jugar　8. volver　9. acostarse　10. dormirse

VI. Chistes del día

Un dialoguito

— ¿Y no llevas zapatos, cuando tu padre es zapatero?
— También el tuyo es dentista, y tu hermanito no tiene dientes.

Ocupación imposible

Hablaba el director de la prisión a un prisionero:
— Ya sabe Vd. que aquí el trabajo es obligatorio para todos, y supongo que Vd. preferirá hacer lo que sabe hacer.
— Sí, señor. Muchas gracias.
— ¿Qué profesión es la suya?
— Aviador, para servirle a Vd.

PALABRAS PARA HOY

2 acercarse (a)	to approach
el albañil	mason
3 el asunto	matter, affair
el avaro	miser (*avaricious*)
el bolsillo	pocket
borrar	to erase
3 componer	to repair (conj. like **poner**)
2 el cuerpo	body (*corpse*)
2 cumplir (con)	to fulfill, keep
2 el dueño	owner
3 el encanto	charm
3 el golpe	blow
honrado, -a	honest

2 mandar	to order, command
3 el miedo	fear
la moneda	coin, money
morisco, -a	adj., Moorish
la muerte	death
2 el oro	gold
2 quitarse	to take off
2 semejante	similar
2 suponer	to suppose (conj. like **poner**)
2 terminar	to finish
2 varios, -as	several (*various*)
la venda	blindfold
vendar	to blindfold

EXPRESIONES

cerrar con llave, to lock (to close with a key)
*dar vueltas, to turn
lo mejor, the best

¡maldita sea su alma! cursed be his soul!
pasando los días, as the days passed

Great Days in Mexico

Mexico's Liberty Bell, which came from Father Hidalgo's little church at Dolores, now hangs over the main entrance of the National Palace, and is rung only on the night of September fifteenth, Mexico's "Fourth of July."

Emilio Amero

W<small>HAT</small> <small>FUN</small> it would be to go to Mexico City's main plaza on the night of September 15! No Mexican would think of missing that celebration if he were within reach of it, for he loves his country fiercely and patriotic holidays mean a great deal to him.

The *Zócalo*, as everyone calls the thirteen-acre plot of flower beds and paths once covered by a huge Aztec pyramid built of mud bricks, is packed with thousands of people in festive mood. There has been no vehicular traffic allowed in the great square since seven o'clock, and as the hour nears midnight, there is practically standing room only. Every building around the *Zócalo* is dotted with red, white and green lights and every balcony is crowded with waiting people.

The great old cathedral with its twin bell-shaped towers looks down at the noisy crowd and waits, too, for it has witnessed this same ceremony each year for nearly a century and a quarter. The long, low National Palace facing the cathedral across those historic thirteen acres is flood-lit tonight, for it is the stage for the drama to come — the greatest patriotic ceremony of Mexico.

Aristocrats dressed in the national fiesta costumes of *china*[1] and *charro*[2] mingle with blanketed Indians from the back country who have brought baskets or pottery or toys to sell. Vendors elbow their way through the milling crowd, selling ice cream, *tacos*, popcorn, bright pink Mexican candies and confetti, for what is a fiesta without goodies to eat and confetti in your hair!

Boys carry horns and drums and noise-makers, and bands stationed here and there are tuning up in the general confusion.

The hour nears midnight. People turn their backs on the cathedral to face the main entrance of the National Palace; the vendors are still, then suddenly a great roar bursts from the tightly packed crowd. The President has come out upon the balcony over the great door, and all eyes look up at the "Liberty Bell" hanging above him as it begins to ring madly, for this is the one and only time in all the year it is ever heard.

Its din dies down, and the President steps to the edge of the balcony and lifts his hand. — *¡Viva la independencia!* — he shouts.

— *¡Viva!* — roars the great crowd.

— *¡Muera el mal gobierno!* — shouts the President.

— *¡Muera!* — repeat the people madly.

[1] An embroidered white blouse and a red and green skirt almost covered with colored spangles is the *china* costume. See page 263.

[2] See "South of the Río Grande," page 324; also page 262.

Twin bell-shaped towers of the old cathedral look down upon the Zócalo with its crowd of merry people on the night of September fifteenth. The Zócalo is a thirteen-acre square once covered by an Aztec pyramid, built where the symbolic eagle and serpent appeared.

— *¡Viva México!*

And every voice in the great throng roars a *¡Viva!* that makes the very cathedral towers tremble, and from the top of the National Palace a scarlet fan of skyrockets flares triumphantly into the darkness above.

Once again the old ceremony of the *Grito de Dolores* has honored Father Hidalgo, the George Washington of his country, who on the sixteenth of September in 1810 rang that same old bell in his little church of Dolores to call the people to him and start them off on the ten-year revolution that was to end in Mexico's freedom from Spain.

All the next day is a holiday, and there is no thought of anything but celebration. There is a great parade of decorated floats, and a *combate de flores* with everyone throwing flowers at everyone else, and at every monument to Father Hidalgo a crowd gathers to listen patiently to long "Fourth of July" speeches praising the kindly priest who gave his life for his country. Military bands play over and over the National Anthem, which may not be performed in public except on the two national holidays, and all day and all night skyrockets whizz into the air.

The lottery puts on a special drawing for a million *pesos* and many lucky people suddenly become wealthy; there is a special bullfight with the very best bulls and bullfighters, and wherever a group of people gathers to celebrate, the festivities are not complete until some pretty *china* and some handsome *charro* have performed the *jarabe tapatío*, Mexico's national dance.

How would you like to celebrate the Fourth of July like that twice each year?   That is what it amounts to in Mexico, for as well as this sixteenth of September holiday, commemorating their freedom from Spain, Mexicans celebrate almost as enthusiastically the fifth of May, commemorating a battle won in 1862 from the French invaders who were determined to put Maximilian and Carlotta on a Mexican throne.

The battle took place at Puebla, some ninety miles south of Mexico City, and is famous mainly because four thousand furious Mexicans routed ten thousand well-armed Frenchmen.

The French were trying to take a fort on a hill, and the Mexicans, led by General Zaragoza, raised the battle cry of «*¡No subirán!*»   It

Mexico's national folk dance, the *jarabe tapatío*, is performed by *china* and *charro* to celebrate every fiesta.   The place may be theater, plaza, street, home, or even — as here — a bull ring.

Black Star

was a tight spot where regular military tactics were not enough, and the story goes that each of a pair of reckless Mexican cowboys tied one end of a lariat to his saddle horn and with the long rope taut between their horses, galloped down the hill tripping rank after rank of oncoming French soldiers, followed by Mexican fighters with swords who dispatched their enemies before they could pick themselves up.

Nowadays the *cinco de mayo* is the second "Fourth of July" of Mexico, and in almost every town you will find a Fifth of May Street as well as a Sixteenth of September Street.

Statues of General Zaragoza, Father Hidalgo and Benito Juárez are found in plazas all over the country, and on July 18 everyone gathers at the monument to Benito Juárez to hear long speeches about "Mexico's Lincoln," for that day is the anniversary of his death. There are towns named after him, and the best street in most cities is named Avenida Juárez in honor of the full-blooded Indian who was twice president of his country.

Patriotism, as you see, is something really serious to a Mexican, and he is never too busy to drop his personal affairs and help to celebrate one of his country's great days.

Benito Juárez is honored by a great white-and-gold monument on the avenue that bears his name.

Galloway

Otro cuento del tío Manuel

Uncle Manuel, who lives in Mexico, tells a story of Spain this time.

Un día durante la hora de la siesta, los niños de la familia Gutiérrez querían otro cuento por el viejo jardinero.

— Díganos Vd. algo que hizo¹ cuando niño, — le pidió Susita, la hermanita.

5 — ¿Siempre ha vivido Vd. en Tepic, tío Manuel? — quiso saber Felipe.

— No, hijos míos,² — respondió el viejecito. — Nací en Jijona,³ pueblecito de España, y vine a México con mi esposa a la edad de veinte y dos años. ¡Cuánto sentí salir de Jijona!

10 — ¿Por qué, tío Manuel? — preguntó Miguel.

— Pues, tal vez porque vivía en una fábrica de dulces, — dijo el jardinero con una sonrisa.

— ¡De veras! — exclamó Miguel. — ¡Qué suerte tan buena! A mí me gustaría vivir en una fábrica de dulces.

15 Me gustaría poder comerlos de día y de noche.

— Pues, un año yo no pude comer nuestro turrón.⁴ Siendo tan pobres, aquel año tuvimos que venderlo en vez de comerlo; y solamente después de volver del mercado podíamos comer

---

¹ You will find the new irregular verb forms in this story in the COSAS DE INTERÉS section.

² *hijos míos,* my children. *Hijos* is used this way in speaking to anyone's children, just as *tío* is often used when the person addressed isn't really one's uncle.

³ Jijona is a little mountain town too small to be on most maps, about halfway (by airline) between Valencia and Murcia, and not far from the east coast. It is the original candy town of Spain, and clings to the steep hillsides, its narrow streets turning into stairways.

⁴ *turrón,* almond nougat. What would a *turronero* be?
Almost every home in Jijona is a *turrón* factory, and in the fall the whole town sociably shells almonds in the streets, while from every kitchen comes the sweet aroma of boiling sugar and honey.

More popular than turrón in Mexico are candied fruits and slices of solid fruit jam. Young vendors sell them everywhere, usually carrying the trays upon their heads.

lo que no habíamos podido vender. Recuerdo una vez cuando no quería venderlo todo, aunque teníamos poco dinero.   20

— ¿Cuándo fué eso? — quiso saber Felipe. — ¿Por qué no quería Vd. venderlo todo?

— Pues, es un cuento largo, — dijo el tío Manuel. — ¿Quieren Vds. oírlo?

— ¡Sí, sí! ¡Díganoslo! — gritaron los tres niños.   25

— Pues, — empezó el tío Manuel, — Jijona, mi pueblo natal (*native*), es el lugar más famoso de España por su turrón, dulce muy popular que se come siempre en Navidad por todo el país. El turrón se hace con almendras, y mi padre tenía unos almendros en las montañas [1] cerca de Jijona. Aquel   30 año le ayudé a recoger (*gather*) las almendras, y las trajimos a casa, donde mi madre y mis hermanas las descascararon

---

[1] The mountains around Jijona are dry, rocky, and metallic-looking; but every little ravine has been check-dammed; and on each little terrace perches a lone almond tree, the only thing besides cactus that will grow there.

(*shelled*). Todavía puedo verlas. Se sentaban en la calle
con las otras mujeres del pueblo, cada una con un montón de
35 almendras, y allí trabajaban juntas, platicando y riendo
felizmente.

— ¿No trabajaban ellas en la fábrica de dulces? — preguntó Felipe.

— Sí, hijo; porque la fábrica era nuestra casa. En nuestra
40 cocina mi madre preparaba la miel (*honey*) y el azúcar y hacía
las barras de turrón. En nuestro patio mi padre y yo las
metíamos en cajas para llevarlas a la ciudad. ¿Saben que
los turroneros nunca pueden pasar la Navidad con su familia?
Todo el mundo quiere comprar turrón durante los días de
45 fiesta, y así los vendedores van a las ciudades para venderlo,
y tienen su Navidad un mes más tarde que los demás.

— ¡Ay, qué lástima! — murmuró Susita. — Pero, ¿qué
le pasó aquel año?

— Pues, yo era joven, — continuó el tío Manuel. — De
50 camino a Albacete,[1] ciudad a que íbamos, mi padre y yo
pasamos la noche en una posada pequeña. En esta posada
conocí yo a una joven, llamada Chavela; era la joven más
bonita que había visto en mi vida. Hablé con ella, y supe[2]
que ella nunca había comido el dulce famoso de mi pueblo.
55 Pedí permiso a mi padre para darle unas barras de nuestro
turrón como regalo, pero él me dijo, «Hijo mío, somos pobres,
y este año tuvimos una cosecha (*crop*) pequeña. Tendremos
que vender todo el turrón si podemos. Pero te prometo que
si todavía nos quedan unas barras al fin de la fiesta, al volver
60 puedes dárselas a Chavela.» Esto me puso muy triste, pero
tuve que contentarme (*be satisfied*) con su promesa.[3]

En Albacete yo puse mi puesto en la plaza principal,

---

[1] Albacete is about halfway between Madrid and the Mediterranean, and the
turroneros travel about a hundred and fifty kilometers in their two-wheeled donkey
carts to take their *turrón* to the Albacete fair or the Christmas market.

[2] **supe** (preterite of **saber**), *I found out* (new meaning).

[3] We might think it strange that a young fellow would ask his father's permission to give the girl some candy, but parental authority lasts much longer among
Spanish-speaking people than with us. Even when a young man is of age, if his
father gives a command, the argument is over. «*Es costumbre.*»

Do you notice that a quotation inside a quotation has a different marking?

mientras que mi padre puso el suyo en un portal.[1] Allí vendimos turrón de día y de noche, y poco a poco ví desaparecer (*disappear*) mis barras de dulce, siempre pensando tristemente, «No me va a quedar nada para mi Chavela.» 65

— ¿Por qué no escondió Vd. unas barras para ella? — preguntó Miguel.

— ¡Qué cosa! — exclamó el tío Manuel. — Ya sabes, Miguelito, que hay que obedecer al padre, ¿verdad? 70

— Sí, por supuesto, — murmuró Miguel con mucha vergüenza. — Siga Vd.

— Pues,[2] se puede imaginar mi tristeza cuando al fin vendí la última barra. Fuí a buscar a mi padre, y le encontré muy contento. «¡Qué suerte tan buena!» exclamó. «¡Acabo de 75 vender todo mi turrón también, y ahora podemos volver a casa!»

Al llegar a la posada en que vivía la bonita Chavela, estaba yo más triste que nunca, y no quería hablar con ella. Mi padre, viendo mi tristeza, me llamó y dijo, «Oye,[3] Manuelito. 80 ¿No vas a dar a la bonita Chavela un regalo de turrón?»

«Pues, padre,» contesté yo, «ya sabe Vd. que lo vendí todo.»

«Ah, sí,» rió mi padre, «es verdad. Pero mira.[3] Aquí tienes dos barras grandes que yo he guardado para ti y tu amiguita. Dáselas[3] a ella, si quieres.» 85

— ¡Ay, qué bueno era su padre! — exclamó Susita. — ¿Se las dió Vd. a ella?

— Por supuesto, hija. Y ella me dió las gracias tan bonitamente que nunca olvidaré aquella cara linda.

— Pero nunca la vió Vd. después, ¿verdad? — preguntó 90 Miguel.

— Sí, ¿cómo no?[4] — respondió el tío Manuel con una sonrisa. — ¿No sabes que mi esposa se llama Chavela?

---

[1] This *portal* isn't part of a Christmas celebration, but is the arcade usually found bordering the shops which face the plaza. Under the *portales* the vendors set up their *puestos*, protected from the sun and rain.

[2] Uncle Manuel uses *pues* a great deal, just as many people do.

[3] This is a familiar singular command.

[4] *¿Cómo no? Why not? (Of course!)* An everyday expression implying that the question it answers was a little foolish.

Find These Expressions in the Story

1. I remember one time when I didn't want to sell it all
2. something that you did when a boy
3. the most famous place in Spain
4. if we still have some bars left
5. I am not going to have any left
6. I was sadder than ever (never)
7. Did you give them to her?
8. what we had not been able to sell
9. we brought them home
10. What good luck!
11. a month later than the rest
12. Tell it to us!
13. Give them to her
14. they can never spend Christmas with their family
15. and made the bars of nougat
16. Why didn't you hide some bars for her?

COSAS DE INTERÉS

103. Preterite Tense of Irregular Verbs

Some commonly used verbs have irregular preterite stems, as well as slightly different endings which have no accents.

MODEL PRETERITE TENSE, IRREGULAR VERBS

tener, *to have*

PRETERITE STEM, **tuv-**

tuv e	tuv imos
tuv iste	tuv isteis
tuv o	tuv ieron

The following verbs are conjugated like *tener*, using throughout the stem given in the first person singular. Note that the preterite of *poner* has an **s** like *puesto* (past participle), and that *poder* has a **d** like the infinitive.

andar:	anduve	poder:	pude
estar:	estuve	venir:	vine
saber:	supe	querer:	quise
poner:	puse		

EJERCICIO I. *Complete the conjugation of each of the verbs given above.*

EJERCICIO II. *Answer these questions:*

1. What do the forms you gave in *Ejercicio I* mean?
2. Is there any danger of confusing the irregular preterite in the third person singular with the first person singular of the present tense?
3. Can you check the spelling of the second person plural as you did with regular preterite?

EJERCICIO III. *Learn these preterite forms:*

Decir, *traer*, and *traducir* (to translate) have irregular preterites which drop the *i* after the *j* in the third person plural:

decir: dije, dijiste, dijo; dijimos, dijisteis, dijeron
traer: traje, trajiste, trajo; trajimos, trajisteis, trajeron
traducir: traduje, tradujiste, tradujo; tradujimos, tradujisteis, tradujeron

Hacer has a change in spelling like none of the others. Why?

hacer: hice, hiciste, hizo;[1] hicimos, hicisteis, hicieron

Ser, *ir*, and *dar* are so irregular in the preterite that they even have accents. *Ser* and *ir* have the same preterite.[2] You learned the preterite of *dar* in Chapter 32.

ser or **ir:** fuí, fuiste, fué; fuimos, fuisteis, fueron

EJERCICIO IV. *Give the first person singular preterite of each of these infinitives and tell what it means:*

1. decir	5. poder	9. ir	13. dar
2. morir	6. venir	10. querer	14. tener
3. oír	7. leer	11. saber	15. poner
4. caer	8. ser	12. hacer	16. nacer (*reg.*)

EJERCICIO V. *Now give the third person plural of the preterite and the gerund of the first seven verbs in Ejercicio IV.*[3]

---

[1] «*¿Qué hizo el oso?*» *"What did the bear do?"* will help you remember this form.

[2] They say *ser* borrowed the preterite of *ir* and never returned it!

[3] The gerund of *poder* is *pudiendo*, even though *poder* is not a III RC verb.

EJERCICIO VI.   *Translate these short sentences:*

1. Vino a casa.	6. No oyó nada.	11. Me puse el traje.
2. Le dije a ella.	7. Me lo dió.	12. ¿Qué dijo Vd.?
3. Lo leyó.	8. Se fueron.	13. ¿Quién lo trajo?
4. No lo supe.	9. Lo traduje.	14. No quise hacerlo.
5. ¿Qué hizo el oso?	10. Estuvieron allí.	15. Nació en Jijona.

104. Nouns in Apposition

Jijona, pueblecito de España; *Jijona, a little town of Spain*
su turrón, dulce que se come
its nougat, a candy which is eaten

What English word does Spanish omit?

> **REMEMBER:** With nouns in apposition usually omit the article.

EJERCICIO VII.   *Complete in Spanish and read aloud several times:*

1. El señor Ramos, *the nougat vendor* de Jijona   2. Albacete, *a beautiful city* de España   3. El tío Manuel, *the gardener* de los Gutiérrez   4. Alfonso, *the grandson* de la señora Navarro   5. Antonio, *the chauffeur* de los Herrera   6. Madrid, *the capital* de España

PREGUNTITAS

I.   1. ¿Dónde nació el tío Manuel?
2. ¿Por qué sintió salir de Jijona?
3. ¿Tuvieron que comer el turrón?
4. ¿Siempre querían venderlo todo?
5. ¿De qué se hace el turrón?
6. ¿Dónde crecían los almendros?
7. ¿Dónde se sentaban las mujeres para prepararlas?
8. ¿Quién hacía el turrón?
9. ¿Quiénes no pueden pasar nunca la Navidad con su familia?
10. ¿Dónde pasaron la noche Manuel y su padre?
11. ¿Qué quiso hacer Manuel antes de salir de la posada?

12. ¿Por qué no escondió Manuel unas barras de turrón en vez de venderlas?
13. Al fin, ¿con quién se casó el joven Manuel?

II.   1. ¿Le gustaría a Vd. vivir en una fábrica de dulces?
      2. ¿Pudo Vd. pasar la Navidad con su familia el año pasado?
      3. ¿Ha comido Vd. turrón jamás?
      4. ¿Le dió Vd. dulces a su amiguita la semana pasada?
      5. ¿Cuándo quiere todo el mundo comprar turrón?
      6. ¿Tradujo Vd. este cuento sin ninguna dificultad?
      7. ¿Pudo Vd. coger almendras?
      8. ¿Tuvo Vd. miedo alguna vez de un lugar encantado?
      9. ¿Puso Vd. la mesa para su madre esta mañana?

REPASITO

I. Answer briefly in Spanish, using pronouns in your answer instead of the words in italics. (If you can do this correctly, you are good!)

1. ¿Supo Vd. *la lección* hoy?   2. ¿Trajo Vd. *su libro* a la clase?
3. ¿Puso Vd. *su papel* en *la mesa* ayer?   4. ¿Hizo Vd. *muchos errores* en *la lección*?   5. ¿Tradujo Vd. bien *las palabras*?   6. ¿Tuvo Vd. que vender *la casa* ayer?   7. ¿Estuvo Vd. debajo del *automóvil* esta mañana?   8. ¿Quiso Vd. dormir en *la sala*?   9. ¿Dió Vd. los dulces a *su amiguita*?   10. ¿Vino Vd. a ver a *Teresa*?

II. Use these short conversations with different objects or with different names, over and over again in class until everyone has memorized them.

1. — Buenos días, Chavela.
   — Buenos días, Pedro.   ¿Cómo está Vd.?
   — Muy bien, gracias.   ¿Y Vd.?
   — Bien, gracias, como siempre.
   — Y tan bonita como siempre.
   — Favor que Vd. me hace.
   — Dé Vd. mis recuerdos a sus padres.
   — Con mucho gusto.   Hasta luego.
   — Adiós.
2. — Hágame Vd. el favor de darme su libro.
   — Con mucho gusto.   Aquí lo tiene Vd.

— Muchas gracias, amigo (-a).

— De nada.

(*Now the person who gave up the book must get it back in the same way.*)

3. — Teresa, ¿de quién es ese lápiz?

— Éste no es de Vd.   Éste es mío.

— ¿Dónde está el mío?

— Aquel niño tiene el de Vd.

(*Go to* «aquel niño» *and start over again.   This may be played like* «Déme pan y queso.»)

III. Rearrange these word groups to form complete sentences:

1. dulces, en, gustaría, fábrica, a mí, me, vivir, de, una
2. jardinero, caer, la, el, higuera, vió, no, viejo, grandísima
3. mesa, comedor, el, que, poner, tiene, en, la, la, criada
4. cabeza, Anita, huevos, a, de, la, la, deja, cesta, que, caer, lleva
5. buenaventura, gitanos, la, los, dicen, Albaicín, del, decir, saben, que

IV. Translate:

1. Uncle Manuel is a little old man who lives in Tepic, a small town of Mexico.   2. He was not born in Tepic but in Jijona, a small town of Spain.   3. He and his wife came to Mexico in order to earn more money.   4. Uncle Manuel told me this story.   5. I like this story. Do you like it?   6. Chavela, Uncle Manuel's wife, was born in Spain, too.   7. She was the prettiest girl in the town.   8. She came to Mexico with her husband.   9. Her son died when a child.   10. Uncle Manuel gave me a present.

V. Los chistes del día

¿Qué debe esperar?

— ¡Mozo (*waiter*)!   ¿Dónde está esa sopa?   ¡La pedí hace media hora!

— Recuerde Vd., señor, que pidió sopa de tortuga (*turtle*).

Entre novios

La novia — Estas cucharas (*spoons*), regalo de la tía Emilia, no son de plata, sino de níquel.

El novio — Pero, ¿conoces tú los metales?

La novia — No, pero conozco a la tía Emilia.

¿A dónde irán?

— Mi esposo quiere hacer un viaje alrededor del mundo, pero yo no quiero.

— ¿De veras? ¿Y por qué no?

— Me gustaría más ir a otra parte.

VI. Learn one of the jokes you have had in preceding chapters to tell for roll call.

PALABRAS PARA HOY

la almendra	almond	3 obedecer	to obey (*obedient*)
el almendro	almond tree	1 por	(new meaning),
la barra	bar		throughout
1 conocer	(new meaning), to meet (when used in preterite)	la posada	inn
		3 prometer	to promise
		1 quedar	to remain (have left) (new meaning)
3 continuar	to continue		
Chavela	Betty (nickname for Isabel)	3 recuerdos	regards (new meaning)
2 la edad	age	rió	third person singular preterite of **reír**
3 esconder	to hide		
la fábrica	factory	1 sentir, (ie, i)	to regret
2 guardar	to keep	traducir	to translate
4 lindo, -a	pretty	3 la tristeza	sadness
2 meter	to put (in)	el turrón	almond nougat
2 nacer	to be born		

Expresiones

*a mí me gustaría, *I* should like (to) (emphatic)

con mucha vergüenza, very much ashamed (with much shame)

cuando niño, when a boy (child)

días de fiesta, holidays

*hasta luego, until later

en Navidad, at Christmas time

¡Qué suerte tan buena! What good luck!

*si todavía nos quedan, if we still have left (new meaning for quedar)

Desde el balcón

Una mañana de domingo, Paco se sentó en su balcón para pintar un cuadro. Su cuarto estaba en el primer piso, y daba a la calle y al «Jardín de la Unión.»[1] Como cualquier artista sabio, Paco pasaba otro verano en México, pintando allí
5 muchos cuadros de la vida mexicana. En Guanajuato, donde las casas suben la montaña como los escalones (*steps*) de una escalera,[2] hallaba mucho que pintar en las calles estrechas y tortuosas (*winding*).

Era una mañana hermosísima. El sol brillaba, y el cielo
10 estaba tan azul que las nubes parecían más blancas que la nieve (*snow*). En los árboles de la plaza cantaban los pájaros; y por las calles estrechas pasaba la gente, platicando y riendo. Contra la montaña, Paco podía ver la antigua catedral de piedra, y de vez en cuando oía el reloj grande, dando la hora.
15 — Voy a pintar la catedral, — decidió el artista.

Pero había tanto que ver en la calle que era muy difícil no mirarla, y muchas veces Paco dejaba de pintar y miraba desde arriba la escena alegre. Primero (*first*) llegó el mozo de la Canastita de Flores,[3] gritando, — ¡Panaderoooooo! —
20 Llevaba a la cabeza una cesta grande de pan dulce,[4] e iba de casa en casa, vendiéndolo.

---

[1] The «*Jardín de la Unión*» is Guanajuato's most popular plaza, not square as plazas should be, but triangular to fit in the only little flat space there is in the mountain town.

[2] Guanajuato was settled about four hundred years ago by Basques and Andalusians (from what parts of Spain?), and in form resembles the ancient town of Jijona, with its winding streets and stairstepped houses. One little street is so narrow that it is officially named «*El Callejón del Beso*» (" *Kiss Lane*"), because they say two people standing on opposite balconies can kiss each other!

[3] There is a Basque grocery store in Guanajuato called "The Little Basket of Flowers."

[4] **pan dulce,** *sweet bread,* consists of fat, sugared buns of all shapes and sizes; and brittle, glazed pieces of what we would call pie crust.

Paco could see the stone cathedral of Guanajuato and hear the big clock strike the hour.

Un viejecito con una cesta de flores blancas entró en la plaza y se sentó en un banco para arreglarlas mejor.   Eran flores pequeñas, pero evidentemente muy fragantes, porque el vendedor las olía (*smelled*) con gusto, gritando cada vez 25 que pasaba alguien, — ¡Flores de San Juan![1]   ¡Diez centavos el ramito!

Su primera compradora (*purchaser*) fué una señorita bonita que pasaba con su madre.   Paco vió que llevaba la cara muy triste, y que apretaba (*pressed*) las flores contra el corazón sin 30 decir palabra.   — Las pintaré a aquellas dos en mi pintura, — pensó el artista, mirándolas entrar en la iglesia, mientras que el viejecito con sus flores pasaba calle arriba.

[1] St. John's flowers are small waxy-white blossoms with a very sweet perfume. They are supposed to encourage true love, and when dried are made into a tea which is believed to cure certain ailments.

Mariachis wander through winding streets in picturesque Guanajuato, playing and singing to earn a few *centavos*. They say there is always a guitar to be heard somewhere in Guanajuato, night or day.

Un ranchero[1] pasó a caballo. Llevaba vestido de domingo
35 ricamente bordado, sombrero de ala ancha y espuelas (*spurs*) plateadas (*silver-mounted*). — Debo pintarle a él también, — pensó Paco, — pero no puedo poner a todo el mundo en el cuadro.

[1] A **ranchero,** *rancher,* is a country gentleman, not quite so important as an *hacendado,* for a *rancho* has only ten thousand acres or less, while an *hacienda* has more. City people call anyone from the country «*ranchero,*» sometimes with a "hillbilly" significance.

En la esquina (*corner*) había un verdadero mariachi,[1] que tocaba y cantaba canciones populares. Era evidente que los músicos no eran de Guanajuato, porque el traje y sus canciones eran de la Costa Oeste.[2] En las piedras de la calle tenían su puesto, el cual consistía en varios montones de papelitos de colores vivos con la letra[3] de las canciones que cantaban.

Entonces pasó otro mozo, que llevaba a la cabeza una bandeja (*tray*) de tamales y gritaba, — ¡Tamaaaaaales! ¡Tamales calientitos!

— Un cinco por lo que piensa Vd.,[4] — dijo una voz detrás de Paco, y volviéndose, vió a su amigo Lorenzo, que salía al balcón.

— ¡Hola, amigo! — gritó Paco, muy contento de verle. — ¿Qué tal?

— Regular (*so-so*), — contestó Lorenzo. — O quizás debo decir «compuesto y sin novia.»[5] Y dió un suspiro (*sigh*).

— ¿Por qué dice Vd. eso? — preguntó Paco. — Todavía tiene su Carmencita de quien habla Vd. tanto. ¿No me dijo hace poco que iba a hacer el oso[6] a su reja?

— Sí, fuí a su reja, pero tuvimos una riña (*quarrel*), y nunca le hablaré más.

— ¡Ay, qué lástima! — dijo Paco. — Me parecía que llevaba Vd. la cara muy triste. — Y Paco seguía con su pintura, mientras Lorenzo miraba tristemente la calle.

— ¡Flores de San Juan! ¡Diez centavos el ramito! — Era el viejo vendedor que volvía a la plaza.

[1] A *mariachi* is a typical West Coast orchestra, a group of wandering troubadors almost like those of the Middle Ages. They travel all over the country, playing in the streets, plazas, and **cantinas** (*saloons*) to earn a living.

[2] Their hats always tell from what region these troubadors come, for there is no mistaking those shallow-crowned, braid-trimmed *sombreros* from Tepic or Guadalajara.

[3] Only the words (*letra*) are sold, for, as those untutored musicians will tell you unconcernedly, "Anyone can remember the tune!"

[4] **Un cinco por lo que piensa Vd.,** "*a penny for your thoughts.*"

[5] **Compuesto y sin novia,** *all dressed up and no sweetheart;* or as we should say, "no place to go."

[6] **Hacer el oso** (*to play the bear*), to make love at the barred window or below the balcony. Few girls are free to go out with their "boy friends" in Spanish-speaking countries, and most of the love-making is done at the *reja* after dark.

El callejón del beso — "Kiss Lane" — is the official name of one of Guanajuato's streets, because two people standing on opposite balconies can kiss each other.

65   — ¿Por qué compran aquellas flores? — preguntó Paco.
— Son pequeñas y no me parecen muy bonitas.
    — ¿No sabe Vd.?   Pues, se dice que las flores de San Juan son milagrosas.   Dándoselas a la Virgen o a un santo favorito, una señorita puede hacer que su novio la quiera.[1] Muchas
70 jóvenes por aquí se las dan a Nuestra Señora de Guanajuato[2] para pedir un novio, — explicó Lorenzo.
    — Pues, — dijo Paco, — eso explica la tristeza de la joven

---

[1] *una señorita puede hacer que su novio la quiera, a girl can make her sweet-heart love her.*

[2] *Nuestra Señora de Guanajuato* is a beautiful little wooden madonna sent to the town from Granada, in 1557, by Felipe II, because he was so pleased with the quantity of gold and silver shipped from there. (See page 171.)   In the entryway of the cathedral are always found grateful little notes thanking her for her miracles and favors, for Guanajuato is a very religious town.

bonita a quien ví hace poco. Compró un ramo de aquellas
flores y las llevó a la iglesia. Mire, ¡allá va ahora! Acaba
de salir. 75

Lorenzo la miró, y exclamó, — ¿De veras? ¿Fué ella?[1]
¡Pues es mi Carmencita!— Se levantó de repente, con la
cara llena de alegría. — ¡Mire! ¡Ya no tiene las flores!
¡Las ha dejado en la iglesia! ¡Me quiere! Con su permiso,
Paquito. ¡Ahora voy yo a decirle flores a ella! 80

— Vd. lo tiene, Lencho, — [2] dijo Paco con una sonrisa.
— Me parece que aquellas flores de San Juan son verdaderamente milagrosas. Ya no está Vd. «compuesto y sin novia.»

Pero Lorenzo no le oyó. Bajaba la escalera, de tres en
tres escalones (*three steps at a time*).[3] 85

Find These Expressions in the Story

1. through the narrow streets the people were passing
2. Frank often stopped painting
3. Ten cents a bunch!
4. A penny for your thoughts
5. he was finding much to paint
6. of whom you talk so much
7. I shall put those two in my painting
8. there was so much to see in the street
9. I'll never speak to her again
10. the pretty young girl whom I saw a while ago
11. three steps at a time
12. and he was going from house to house
13. the musicians weren't from Guanajuato
14. turning around, he saw his friend Lorenzo
15. calling every time anyone passed by

[1] *¿Fué ella? Was it she?*

[2] *Vd. lo tiene* (*go ahead,* or, *you are excused*) is the answer to *con su permiso* when the person who says it is leaving one's presence.
Lencho is a familiar nickname for *Lorenzo.*

[3] Lorenzo cannot go to call on Carmen right now, but he can follow her home at a safe distance, knowing that she will be conscious of his presence and realize that the quarrel is over. Then after dark he will show up at her *reja* as usual, probably with his guitar.

COSAS DE INTERÉS

105. Orthographical-Changing Verbs

Orthography means *spelling*.   In Spanish some verb forms must change their spelling in order to keep the original sound as it is in the infinitive.   Here are some verbs that have orthographical changes in the preterite and in the polite commands.

PRETERITE TENSE

pagar, *to pay*	sacar, *to take out*	empezar, *to begin*
pagué	saqué	empecé [1]
pagaste	sacaste	empezaste
pagó	sacó	empezó
pagamos	sacamos	empezamos
pagasteis	sacasteis	empezasteis
pagaron	sacaron	empezaron

POLITE COMMANDS

pague Vd.	saque Vd.	empiece Vd.[1]
paguen Vds.	saquen Vds.	empiecen Vds.

EJERCICIO I.   *Answer these questions:*

1. What orthographical change does *coger* have in the present tense?   (Section 96)   2. What orthographical change does *hacer* have in the preterite tense?   (Section 103)   3. What consonants have two sounds, depending on the letters following them?   (Chapters 2 and 10)   4. Why is *poco + ito* written *poquito*?   5. Why is the absolute superlative of *feliz* spelled *felicísimo*?   6. Why are two dots (diaeresis) placed over *u* in *vergüenza*?   7. When does *z* change to *c*?   Why?   8. How is the plural of nouns and adjectives ending in *z* formed?   9. Will the imperfect of verbs ending in *-car, -gar,* or *-zar* be irregular?

---

[1] With a very few exceptions, *e* or *i* is not written after *z*.

EJERCICIO II. *Conjugate in the preterite:*

1. llegar   2. tocar   3. jugar   4. comenzar (*to commence*)   5. colgar   6. tropezar   7. atacar (*to attack*)

EJERCICIO III. *Write the polite commands for the verbs in Ejercicio II.* (Some of them are radical-changing!)

PREGUNTITAS

I.   1. ¿Cuándo se sentó Paco en su balcón?
    2. ¿Hacía buen tiempo?
    3. ¿Qué oía de vez en cuando mientras pintaba?
    4. ¿Qué vió en la calle?
    5. ¿Qué llevaba el viejecito en la cesta?
    6. ¿Eran bonitas las flores de San Juan?
    7. ¿Quién compró unas flores?
    8. ¿Por qué estaba muy triste Lorenzo?
    9. ¿Por qué compran las señoritas flores de San Juan?
   10. ¿Está Lorenzo todavía «compuesto y sin novia»?

II.   1. ¿Sabe Vd. llevar cestas grandes a la cabeza?
    2. ¿Le gustaría a Vd. comer pan dulce?
    3. ¿Está Vd. «compuesto y sin novia»?
    4. ¿Fué Vd. a hacer el oso hace poco?
    5. ¿Decía Vd. flores a una señorita esta mañana?
    6. ¿Baja Vd. la escalera de tres en tres escalones?   ¿Por qué no?
    7. ¿Cuándo se dice «un cinco por lo que piensa Vd.»?
    8. ¿Iba Vd. de casa en casa la semana pasada?

REPASITO

I. Review the sounds of c (ce, ci), *and also* que *and* qui (Chapters 2, 9), *and then pronounce these strange words:*

1. jaqueca	6. requiebro	11. quiquiriquí	16. poquito
2. queche	7. caracoles	12. delinquen	17. blanquillo
3. cercillo	8. Quiroga	13. Cuzco	18. Metepec
4. cerquita	9. cárcel	14. Cuicuilco	19. Siqueiros
5. juicio	10. triquitraque	15. Palenque	20. tequila

II. Use one of the following adverbial expressions to complete each sentence, using each expression only once:

1. —— saldré de la ciudad.
2. El tío Manuel volvió a Tepic ——.
3 — Ven acá, hijito. — —— voy.
4. —— lo vendía todo.
5. Llegábamos temprano ——.
6. —— oí un ruido.
7. —¿Dónde está Carlos? — —— está.
8. Me quedaré en casa ——.
9. Fuí a Europa ——.
10. El jardinero no trabaja ——.
11. Me levantaré a las seis ——.
12. —— me faltaba dinero.

de la mañana
el año pasado
muchas veces
de noche
la semana próxima
allá
allí
al día siguiente
de repente
esta noche
rara vez
de vez en cuando

III. Say these short conversations over and over in class until everyone has memorized them:

1. — ¿Tiene Vd. mi pluma?
— No, yo tengo la mía.   Aquel niño tiene la de Vd.
— ¿Dónde está la de él?
— Teresa tiene la de él.
(*Now* «aquel niño» *must ask the same of* «Teresa.»)
2. (*An introduction.*)
— Antonio, quiero presentarle a un amigo mío.
— Antonio Reyes, servidor de Vd.
— Francisco Ramírez.   Tengo mucho gusto en conocerle a Vd.
— Muchas gracias.
3. — ¿Cómo se llama Vd., niño?
— Me llamo ——, servidor de Vd.
— ¿Cuántos años tiene Vd.?
— Tengo —— años.
— ¿Dónde vive Vd.?
— En la Calle de Córdoba, número doscientos veinte y seis, tiene Vd. su casa.
— Muchas gracias.   Con su permiso.   Adiós.
— Vd. lo tiene.   Vaya Vd. con Dios.

IV. Give a word or expression that is either the opposite or a synonym of each of these words (give both for the ones starred):

1. bajar de	7. volver	13. olvidar
2. principio	8. amar	14. último
3. estrecho	9. continuar *	15. componer *
4. oír	10. guardar	16. concluir
5. alegre *	11. lindo *	17. quitarse
6. caliente	12. meter	18. de noche

V. Translate these sentences freely:

1. En cuanto a mí, yo no iré.	6. El año que viene nos iremos.
2. Replicó de la misma manera.	7. Me divertí muchísimo.
3. Se despertó de repente.	8. Trataba de hacer un viaje.
4. La cerraremos con llave.	9. Nos paseábamos por la calle.
5. — Hasta luego, — dijo.	10. Acaban de salir.

VI. Change the infinitives to the proper tense and person. (Use a past tense for all except the first four.)

1. Mañana yo *salir* tarde.   2. El mes próximo ella *ir* a Córdoba.
3. El miércoles próximo Susita *poder* coser.   4. El verano próximo ellos *venir* a verme.   5. Ayer yo *despertarse* temprano.   6. El año pasado nosotros *viajar* por España.   7. La semana pasada Miguel *matar* un pájaro.   8. El viernes pasado nosotros *coger* muchas flores. 9. De vez en cuando el vendedor *pasar*.   10. Lorenzo *estar* «compuesto y sin novia.»   11. El ranchero siempre *llevar* un sombrero de ala ancha.   12. Todos los días el panadero *vender* pan.   13. Nosotros nunca *ir* a la iglesia los lunes.   14. Paco *sentarse* en su balcón por la mañana.

VII. Change these verbs to the preterite of the same person and number:

1. volveré	4. me despertaré	7. se levantará
2. mirarán	5. viajarás	8. saldremos
3. correrá	6. empezaremos	9. verá

VIII. Give the singular and plural polite commands for these verbs, and add an object pronoun (lo, la, los, las) unless they are starred.   Where must the pronoun stand?

1. coger	5. dejar	9. traer
2. bordar	6. volar (ue) *	10. salir *
3. escoger	7. seguir (i)	11. hacer
4. poner	8. oír	12. volver (ue) *

IX. Say in Spanish:

1. *I like:* la leche, poner la mesa, los dulces, manejar el automóvil, los cuentos.
2. *Do you like:* viajar, el río, los gatos, estar contento, las canciones?
3. *We like:* volar, los árboles, el baile, llamar a la puerta, los viajes.

X. Change these present tenses to the present progressive of the same person and number:

1. sirvo 2. trae 3. oímos 4. da 5. ella se sienta 6. ponen
7. leemos 8. cojo 9. traduzco 10. me duermo 11. ríe 12. dicen

XI. Here is a speed test. *Say these problems in Spanish in class three days in succession, the teacher calling on pupils as fast as possible and timing the exercise with a stop watch.* How much faster can your class say them the third day than the first?

28 − 15 = 13	30 − 12 = 18	59 − 32 = 27
42 + 37 = 79	100 − 100 = 0	61 − 12 = 49
2 × 45 = 90	53 + 47 = 100	3 × 33 = 99
11 + 16 = 27	29 + 31 = 60	20 + 39 = 59
74 − 31 = 43	100 − 25 = 75	10 + 15 = 25

XII. Give a synopsis of each of the following verbs in the third person singular, including the Infinitive, Gerund, Past Participle, Present, Command, Present Progressive, Imperfect, Preterite, Future, *and* Present Perfect:

decir, comprar, oír, ir (*omit pres. prog.*), hacer

XIII. Tres chistes para leer

¡Qué lástima!

— ¿Cómo? ¿No es Vd. Pérez? Me dijeron que Vd. murió el año pasado.
— No, es mi hermano el que murió.
— ¡Oh, cuánto lo siento!

Un pueblo sano

— Este pueblo es tan sano (*healthful*) que en diez años no ha muerto más que un hombre.

— ¿Y quién fué?

— El médico. Murió de hambre.

Cuento andaluz

El primer andaluz — Mi abuelo paterno murió a los noventa y ocho años.

El segundo andaluz — Eso no es nada, hombre. Yo tuve un tío que llegó a la edad de ciento diez y siete años.

El tercer andaluz — No sé como viven tan poco tiempo los parientes de Vds. Ninguno de los míos ha muerto hasta la fecha.

PALABRAS PARA HOY

3	**alegre**	happy, merry	1	**mirar**	to watch (new meaning)
3	**arriba**	above			
2	**bajar**	to go down	3	**el mozo**	boy (servant)
4	**brillar**	to shine (*brilliant*)	3	**la nube**	cloud
	calientito, -a	warm	2	**el pan**	bread
	(calient(e)		2	**el panadero**	baker
	+ ito)			**la pintura**	painting
1	**dejar de**	to leave off, to stop	1	**querer (a)**	to love (new meaning)
3	**el cuadro**	picture			
1	**e**	and (used in place of **y** before words beginning with *i* or *hi*)		**el ramito (ram(o) + ito)**	little bunch, bouquet
	la escalera	stairs (*escalator*)		**el reloj**	clock *or* watch
2	**la escena**	scene	1	**tanto**	so much
3	**estrecho, -a**	narrow	1	**volverse**	to turn around (new meaning)
3	**explicar**	to explain	2	**la voz**	voice (*vocal*)
	milagroso, -a	miraculous			

EXPRESIONES

*a caballo, on horseback

*a la vez, at a time, at the same time

calle arriba, up the street

dar la hora, to strike the hour

*de casa en casa, from house to house

decir flores a, to compliment, to make love to

hacer el oso, to make love to ("play the bear")

*hace poco, not long ago, a little while ago

llevar la cara muy triste, to have a very sad face

*por aquí, around here

*¡Qué tal! How goes it? (informal greeting)

LA CUCARACHA

When a Mexican folk song has a chorus, it is usually sung first, as well as between the stanzas. This song about the cockroach (and other things) was Pancho Villa's marching song in 1916, when that bold, bad bandit was making history by trying to be President of Mexico when there already was one. Ever since, people have been making up new words for it, and the four stanzas given here are only a few samples.

Arr. by E. M. JARRETT

Coro: (fast)

La cu - ca - ra - cha, la cu - ca - ra - cha,

ya no quie - re ca - mi - nar, por - que no

tie - ne, por-que le fal - ta di - ne - ro pa - ra gas - tar. - tar.

Verso (slowly)

U - na cu - ca - ra - cha pin - ta le di - jo a u - na co - lo -

ra - da —Vá - mo - nos pa - ra mi tie - rra

a pa - sar la tem - po - ra - da. - da.

Coro:

La cucaracha, la cucaracha
ya no quiere caminar,
porque no tiene,
porque le falta
dinero para gastar.

Chorus:

The cockroach, the cockroach,
No longer wants to travel,
Because it hasn't,
Because it lacks
Any money to spend.

1. Una cucaracha pinta
le dijo a una colorada,
— Vámonos para mi tierra
a pasar le temporada.   (Coro)

A spotted cockroach
Said to a red one,
"Let's go to my country
To spend the summer."   (Chorus)

2. Todas las muchachas tienen
en los ojos dos estrellas;
pero las mexicanitas
de seguro son más bellas.

All girls have
Two stars in their eyes;
But the little Mexican girls
Surely are the most beautiful.

3. Para sarapes, Saltillo,
Chihuahua para soldados;
para mujeres, Jalisco,
para amar, toditos lados.

For sarapes,[1] Saltillo,[2]
For soldiers, Chihuahua;[3]
For women, Jalisco;[4]
For love, just anywhere.

4. Una cosa me da risa
Pancho Villa sin camisa.
Ya se van los Carrancistas,
porque vienen los Villistas.

One thing makes me laugh
Pancho Villa without a shirt.
Now the Carrancistas are leaving,[5]
Because the Villistas are coming.

---

[1] *Sarapes* are the colorful hand-woven wool blankets of Mexico; the poor Indian's overcoat by day and his bed-clothing by night. Each tribe has its own different color scheme and general pattern, so that it is easy to tell by his *sarape* where an Indian lives.

[2] Saltillo is the town where Mexico's most famous *sarapes* have been made for over a century. They are of fine wool and linen, and their modern pattern of bright stripes shading from one vivid color to another represents conventionalized sunsets.

[3] Chihuahua is a desert mining town of the north central part of Mexico, and has been featured in history as the scene of much fighting.

[4] Jalisco is the aristocratic state of Mexico, where the national dance, the *Jarabe Tapatío*, originated. The women of Guadalajara, Jalisco's capital, are supposed to be the most beautiful of Mexico.

[5] Carranza was a revolutionary leader during Villa's time, when both were trying to be president at once. Carranza won, in spite of the song.

Las comidas españolas

A todo el mundo le gusta comer, pero todo el mundo no come las mismas cosas. Cada país tiene sus platos[1] favoritos. En los E. U. A. tenemos el *pie*, los *hot-cakes*, el *hot dog*. En otros países no se conocen estos platos. ¿Les parece a
5   Vds. curioso? Hay que recordar que a los españoles les parece curioso no comer garbanzos, puchero, membrillate, o beber horchata.[2]

Vamos a acompañar al señor Romero durante un día para ver lo que come. El señor Romero es bastante rico y no tiene
10 que comer garbanzos o puchero. Se levanta a las ocho o a las ocho y media. Un poco después, la criada le trae el desayuno y él lo toma en su cuarto. Toma chocolate o café[3] y un panecillo. Éste es el desayuno típico de Europa y por eso se llama un desayuno europeo. No sirven huevos, ni frutas, ni
15 cereal. El café es muy diferente del nuestro. La criada echa media taza de café y después llena la taza de leche caliente. Se llama café con leche.

Después de desayunarse, el señor Romero va a la oficina. Vuelve a casa a eso de la una. A las dos toma la comida.

[1] **Plato** has several meanings: *plate, dish* (used as we use it when we say "baked beans is a favorite American dish"), or *course*. It is used with all three of these meanings in this chapter. The rest of the sentence will usually tell you which one it means.

[2] **Garbanzos,** *chick-peas,* constitute one of the main items of food for the poorer people because they are cheap and nourishing.
Puchero is a stew made of vegetables, *garbanzos,* and a little meat. This dish derived its name from the pot in which it is cooked.
Membrillate is a very stiff jelly made of quinces, served in slices and eaten with a spoon.
Horchata is a cool drink, rather milky in appearance, made from roots. In Spain it is also made from almonds or truffles.

[3] **Café** has two meanings — *coffee* and *café.* The rest of each sentence will show you which meaning it has.
Spanish chocolate is very different from ours, being highly seasoned with cinnamon, nutmeg, and other spices.

Galloway

Spain's daily bread is made in crusty, round loaves and delivered from house to house by the baker's boy, who carries the basket on his head.

Toda la familia se reúne para esta comida. No hay prisa, y todos pasan una hora o una hora y media en la mesa comiendo y platicando. 20

En la comida generalmente sirven al menos seis platos. Si es una ocasión especial, sirven más. En la mesa hay pan,[1] que se come con los diferentes platos. Pero no hay mantequilla.[2] Primero, la criada sirve los huevos. Muchas veces los sirve en tortilla con una salsa hecha de tomate, ajo, y cebollas. Lleva los platos a la cocina y trae el segundo plato, que es la sopa. Tal vez es una sopa de legumbres con garbanzos y pedacitos de chorizo que se llaman albóndigas.[3] 30 Tal vez es una sopa de pollo.

Después de la sopa viene el pescado, que es el cuarto plato.

[1] The bread eaten in Spain and other European countries is like our French bread.

[2] Butter is a luxury, and is usually made from goat's milk.

[3] *Albóndigas* are well-seasoned meat balls served in the soup.

Sidewalk cafés, another heritage from Spain, are found in most Spanish-American countries. Here in Buenos Aires the custom of afternoon "tea" — any light refreshment — is carefully observed.

Hay varias maneras de prepararlo. Generalmente se pone una salsa, porque los españoles tienen salsas muy sabrosas.

35 Para prepararlas y para preparar todos los platos usan aceite de oliva[1] y ajo.

La carne sigue al[2] pescado. Será carne asada, biftec, o pollo. Si es una comida especial, habrá carne y pollo también. Con la carne hay patatas. El quinto plato será de legumbres.

40 No se comen las legumbres con la carne, sino después.

El sexto plato es el postre, que generalmente consiste en frutas y queso. Las frutas que se comen más son los higos, las manzanas, y los duraznos. Las manzanas y los duraznos son más pequeños que los nuestros pero también son más

45 sabrosos.

Si hay convidados, habrá tres o cuatro platos más. En-

[1] Olives, you know, are one of the important crops of Spain; consequently the great use of olive oil in cooking is quite natural.

[2] This "personal *a*" is used only to show which word is the object.

tonces habrá huevos, sopa, pescado, carne, pollo, legumbres, ensalada, postre (frutas cocidas, membrillate, o un helado [1]) y frutas frescas y queso.

Los españoles no comen tantas legumbres como nosotros.   50 Tampoco comen tantas ensaladas como nosotros.   Su ensalada ordinaria consiste en lechuga con aceite.

Es una comida muy grande, ¿verdad?   Ahora Vds. pueden entender la necesidad de una siesta.   Después de la siesta el señor Romero vuelve a la oficina.   A eso de las cuatro y media   55 o las cinco va a un café para tomar café; o, si hace calor, una limonada, o una horchata.   La señora Romero tal vez irá a casa de una amiga, donde tendrán refrescos.   O si va de compras, irá con sus amigas a una pastelería para tomar te o un helado con pasteles (*pastry*).   No irá al café porque no es cos-   60 tumbre.   Los cafés son para los hombres.

El café es un lugar muy interesante.   Da a la calle y hay

[1] An *helado* is a frozen dessert resembling sherbet, since it does not have the custard base of our ice cream.   *Nieve* (*snow*) is ice cream in Mexico.

Mexico's popular daily bread is the *tortilla*.   Here an Indian woman makes one from corn crushed on a stone *metate*, baking it on a hot clay *comal* as her people have done for centuries.

Galloway

mesitas en la banqueta. Así todo el mundo puede ver y ser visto, platicar con los amigos y oír las noticias (*news*) del día.

65 La costumbre de tomar algo durante la tarde es muy necesaria en España, porque no tienen la última comida del día antes de las nueve de la noche. Esta costumbre es semejante a la costumbre inglesa de tomar *afternoon tea*. Pero en España se llama la merienda y generalmente no beben te, sino

70 chocolate.

La cena se sirve entre las nueve y las diez de la noche, y es muy semejante a la comida. Todos se divierten muchísimo en la mesa, y después pasan un rato en el patio o en la sala. Algunas veces salen para visitar a sus amigos, o quizás van al

75 cine. Se acuestan muy tarde.

Las comidas mexicanas

Lo que se llama una comida española en los E. U. A. es generalmente una comida mexicana. Los españoles no conocen los frijoles refritos, los tacos, los tamales, las enchiladas, ni el chile con carne.[1] Y, como han visto Vds., en España una

5 tortilla es un plato hecho de huevos. Tampoco tienen los españoles salsas muy picantes (*hot*) hechas con chiles.[2]

En México los pobres comen frijoles y tortillas.[3] Algunas

[1] *Frijoles* are red beans, first boiled, then mashed and fried. They are often served with every meal, including breakfast!

Tacos are made with *tortillas* folded and fried crisp, then stuffed with various things — highly seasoned *chorizo*, *frijoles*, lettuce, cheese. They are eaten in the fingers.

Enchiladas are *tortillas* rolled around a stuffing of meat, chicken, or rice, and covered with *chile* sauce, chopped onion, and cheese.

You learned about *tamales* in footnote 1, page 139.

Chile con carne is meat served with *chile* sauce.

[2] *Chiles* are peppers, usually kept hanging in long strings in every Mexican household.

[3] You learned about *tortillas* in footnote 1, page 140. They take the place of bread in the poor man's diet.

Tamales made of corn meal, meat, and chili pepper are wrapped in corn husks and steamed in a great copper kettle. Small ones like these are called "Texas tamales" in this country.

Argentina's favorite drink is *mate*, a kind of tea. It is sipped from a decorated gourd with a silver tube called a *bombilla*. The men are wearing *alpargatas* like those used in Spain.

veces los comen tres veces al día.   Pero hasta los ricos los comen a veces.

10   Un desayuno típico para los ricos consiste en frutas, huevos, frijoles refritos, panecillos o pan dulce,[1] y chocolate o café. Una comida típica consiste en blanquillos (*huevos* en España), sopa, arroz,[2] carne, frijoles refritos, pollo, y un postre.   Hay pan o tortillas para comer con los varios platos.   Una cena

15   típica consiste en sopa, carne, tamales o enchiladas, frijoles refritos y chocolate o café con pan dulce.   Como ya hemos dicho, los pobres generalmente no comen más que frijoles y tortillas.

¿Cuál les gustaría más a Vds. — una comida española o una

20   mexicana?

Find These Expressions in the Story

1. Spanish meals; Mexican meals
2. Supper is served (one serves supper) between nine and ten
3. the poor (people) eat beans
4. at about one o'clock
5. There is no hurry
6. Cafés are for men.
7. everyone can see and be seen
8. It faces the street
9. there will be meat and chicken
10. Neither do they eat as many salads as we (do).
11. After eating breakfast
12. One must remember

COSAS DE INTERÉS

106. Nouns in a General Sense

El dinero es muy necesario.   *Money is very necessary.*
Las comidas españolas son buenas.   *Spanish meals are good.*
Los cafés son para los hombres.   *Cafés are for men.*

What is omitted in translating these sentences?   In the Spanish stories you have had many more examples of this usage.   In the examples given above, *dinero* means *money*

[1] You read about *pan dulce* in footnote 4, page 382.

[2] Rice is seasoned with peppers, garlic, and a little tomato.   It is first fried in oil, then steamed until very dry.   In Spain it is called «*arroz a la valenciana.*»

in general, **cafés** means *cafés in general,* **hombres** means *men in general.* Spanish rarely starts a sentence with a common noun.

> **REMEMBER:** Nouns used in a general sense take the definite article.

EJERCICIO I. *Say in Spanish:*

1. Donkeys are good. 2. Flowers are pretty. 3. Fruit is necessary. 4. Girls are nice. 5. Friends are agreeable. 6. American meals are good. 7. Pastry shops are for women. 8. Gold is important.

107. Words for Shops or Stores

What is a common ending denoting occupation?

Look at this list of words and tell what the ending is for shops or stores:

la pastelería	la carnicería	la zapatería	la librería
la dulcería	la panadería	la relojería	la papelería

EJERCICIO II. *Translate the words in the list given above.*

EJERCICIO III. *Answer:*

1. **Sastre** means *tailor;* what is **una sastrería?** 2. **Joya** means *jewel;* what is **una joyería?** 3. **Muebles** means *furniture;* what is **una mueblería?** 4. What is **una perfumería?** 5. **Barba** means *beard;* what is **una barbería?**

108. Ordinal Numbers

primer(o), -a	first	**sexto, -a**	sixth
segundo, -a	second	**séptimo, -a**	seventh
tercer(o), -a	third	**octavo, -a**	eighth
cuarto, -a	fourth	**noveno, -a**	ninth
quinto, -a	fifth	**décimo, -a**	tenth

Ordinal numbers are not used as much in Spanish as in English. Beyond *tenth* they are almost never used. They agree with their nouns in gender and in number like any other adjective.

In dates the only ordinal number that is used is **primero.** (See section 95.)

When do *primero* and *tercero* drop the *o?*   (See section 42.)

EJERCICIO IV.   *Read in Spanish:*

1. Alfonso II   2. Alfonso XIII   3. Fernando VII   4. Pedro II
5. 1° de agosto

PREGUNTITAS

I.   1. ¿En qué país comen "*hot dogs*"?
   2. ¿En qué país comen enchiladas?
   3. ¿En qué país beben horchata?
   4. ¿Dónde se sirve el desayuno en España?
   5. ¿Para qué comidas se reúne la familia?
   6. ¿A qué hora se sirve el desayuno?
   7. ¿A qué hora se sirve el almuerzo?
   8. ¿A qué hora se sirve la cena?
   9. Generalmente ¿en qué consiste un almuerzo en España?
  10. ¿Qué se sirve en ocasiones especiales?
  11. ¿Qué usan los mexicanos en sus salsas?   ¿Son picantes?
  12. ¿En qué consiste la comida de los pobres en México?

II.   1. ¿Qué come Vd. cuando se desayuna?   ¿cuando almuerza? ¿cuando cena?
   2. ¿A qué hora se desayuna Vd.?
   3. ¿A qué hora toma Vd. el almuerzo?   ¿la cena?
   4. Si hace calor, ¿qué bebida (*drink*) nos gusta?
   5. ¿Ha comido Vd. jamás una comida española?   ¿mexicana?
   6. ¿Come Vd. pan y mantequilla o pan solo?
   7. ¿Cuándo puede Vd. tomar el desayuno en su cuarto?
   8. ¿Quién sirve la comida en su casa de Vd.?
   9. ¿Cómo se dice en español: *fruit salad, potato salad, vegetable salad, fish salad, meat salad, lettuce salad?*
  10. ¿Qué clase de ensalada le gusta a Vd. más?
  11. ¿Le gustaría a Vd. comer tortillas?
  12. ¿Ha comido Vd. jamás un tamal?
  13. ¿Le gusta a Vd. una salsa picante?

REPASITO·

I. Give the correct forms of the Spanish verbs:

1. Hoy *is* lunes. 2. Mañana *will be* martes. 3. Ayer *was* domingo.
4. El año pasado *I went* a México. 5. El año· que viene *I shall go* a
México. 6. Todas las noches *I used to go to bed* a las diez. 7. Cuando
vivía en el campo, *I used to eat* muchos huevos. 8. Arturo no contestó
porque *he didn't know* las palabras. 9. Arturo no contesta porque *he
doesn't know how to read* la lección. 10. La semana pasada *I didn't see*
a mi amigo.

II. Supply suitable numbers:

1. Tengo —— años. El año pasado tuve —— años. El año que
viene tendré —— años.
2. Mi padre tiene —— años. El año pasado tuvo —— años. El
año que viene tendrá —— años.

III. Translate:

1. he sat down 2. he was going 3. she entered 4. he will come
5. have they worked? 6. we shall see 7. I don't know 8. they are
using (*two ways*) 9. they were using (*two ways*) 10. they will use

*IV. Say the multiplication tables up to the eights, in Span-
ish.* You may do it in chorus or individually as a speed
contest.

Example: tres por uno son tres; tres por dos son seis, *etc.*

V. Chistes para leer

Cosas de niños

— ¿Está en casa tu mamá?
— No, señor; ha salido.
— ¿Y sabes cuándo volverá?
— Espere Vd. un momento. Voy a preguntárselo.

Respuesta sabia

— ¿Cuándo empezó la guerra (*war*) de los siete años?
— Eso. . . . no lo recuerdo.
— Diga Vd. lo que sepa (*may know*) de esa guerra.
— Que terminó después de siete años de lucha (*fighting*).

Cuestión de matemáticas

— ¿Cuántos años tienes, chica?
— Ocho.
— Y ¿cuántos años tuviste el año pasado?
— Siete.
— Entonces debes tener quince años.
— No. Tengo ocho años no más.
— Pues ocho y siete son quince, ¿verdad?

PALABRAS PARA HOY

la banqueta	sidewalk	desayunarse	to eat breakfast
la comida	food (new meaning)	llenar de	to fill with
		la pastelería	pastry shop
el convidado	guest	4 la prisa	hurry, speed
2 echar	to pour	3 el rato	short time

LAS COMIDAS

4 el aceite	oil	el panecillo	roll
el ajo	garlic	3 el pedacito	little piece
el arroz	rice	(pedazo	
asado, -a	roasted	+ ito)	
la cebolla	onion	el pescado	fish
cocido, -a	boiled, cooked	el postre	dessert, pudding
el chorizo	sausage	el queso	cheese
el desayuno	breakfast	el refresco	refreshment (soft
el durazno	peach		drinks in Mexico)
los frijoles	beans (Mexican)	sabroso, -a	tasty, savory
el helado	frozen dessert, ice cream	la salsa	sauce
		el te	tea
el higo	fig	la torta	cake, pie
la lechuga	lettuce	la tortilla	omelet (Spain)
la mantequilla	butter	la tostada	toast
la merienda	lunch, "tea"		

ORDINAL NUMBERS

primer(o), -a	first	sexto, -a	sixth
segundo, -a	second	séptimo, -a	seventh
tercer(o), -a	third	octavo, -a	eighth
cuarto, -a	fourth	noveno, -a	ninth
quinto, -a	fifth	décimo, -a	tenth

EXPRESIONES

a eso de, at about (used only in telling time)

ir de compras, to go shopping
tres veces al día, three times a day

CAPÍTULO 36

¿Cuánto sabe usted?

*You should be able to remember or guess most of the words in this
story. Answer the questions, pointing out the sentences that prove
your answer is right.*

EL ZAPATERO LISTO (*The Clever Shoemaker*)

Había un zapatero que vivía en una pequeña ciudad de
México donde tenía su zapatería, llamada «La Sin Rival,» en
una de las calles principales. Allí ganaba la vida haciendo
zapatos para los ricos y los pobres.

Un día llegó a la ciudad otro zapatero, el cual (*who*) es- 5
tableció otra zapatería cerca de la tienda de nuestro amigo.
La nueva zapatería era más grande y más espléndida que la
primera, y el pobre zapatero estaba muy inquieto (*worried*),
especialmente cuando el recién llegado (*newcomer*) puso sobre
la tienda nueva el letrero (*sign*), «La Mejor Zapatería de Esta 10
Ciudad.»

Después de unas semanas llegó a la ciudad un tercer zapatero, el cual (*who*) se estableció en la misma calle, también con
una tienda espléndida con zapatos de moda. Este zapatero
miró los letreros de las otras dos zapaterías, y puso sobre la 15
puerta de su tienda, «La Mejor Zapatería de Este País.»

El zapatero que había vivido muchos años en la ciudad

miró los dos letreros nuevos, y pensó día y noche.   Al fin tuvo
una idea magnífica, y sobre la puerta de su establecimiento
20   puso un nuevo letrero que decía,«La Mejor Zapatería de Esta
Calle.»

1. How many shoemakers had stores on the same street?   2. Why
was the first shoemaker worried when he saw the signs on the new
shoeshops?   3. Why did the third shoemaker call his shop the best
one in the country?   4. After the original shoemaker had changed his
sign, who had the cleverest one?

REPASO DE VOCABULARIO

EJERCICIO I.   Here are some "spelling demons."   *Listen
to them, pronounce them to yourself, and then spell them according to the sound.*   Your teacher will dictate them to you.

1. higuera	9. hijo	17. próximo
2. viejecito	10. continuar	18. panecillo
3. semejante	11. milagroso	19. llenar
4. bolsillo	12. bajar	20. pastelería
5. siguiente	13. brillar	21. desayuno
6. recuerdo	14. mantequilla	22. cebolla
7. fábrica	15. aceite	23. higo
8. obedecer	16. banqueta	24. cualquier

EJERCICIO II.   *Give the English meanings of the preceding
words.*

EJERCICIO III.   *Choose an appropriate noun for each of these
adjectives.*   Don't forget to make them agree.   (Incidentally,
where will the adjectives be placed?)

1. próximo	5. cocido	9. estrecho	13. honrado
2. pasado	6. sabroso	10. último	14. asustado
3. solito	7. milagroso	11. lindo	15. encantado
4. asado	8. calientito	12. cansado	16. primero

EJERCICIO IV.   *¿Verdad o mentira?*

1. Los bandidos roban a la gente pero no la matan.
2. Se sirve la carne en un plato.

3. Se sirve el café en un platillo.
4. Un artista no puede encontrar mucho que pintar en México.
5. Los ruidos asustan a los niñitos.
6. La higuera nos da duraznos.
7. Los pordioseros piden dinero a todo el mundo.
8. Todo lo que brilla no es de oro.
9. No debemos obedecer a nuestros padres.
10. Todas las calles de Guanajuato son anchas.
11. En España la cena se sirve a las dos.
12. El tío Manuel era dueño de una fábrica.
13. A los niños les gustaban los cuentos del tío Manuel.
14. Hemos leído de una casa encantada y una higuera encantada.
15. Los pobres llevan mucho dinero en los bolsillos.
16. Todo el mundo va al café para tomar la merienda.
17. En España un joven puede seguir a su novia y hablarle por la reja.
18. Los moros construyeron la Alhambra hace muchos años.
19. Los moros vivieron en España por doscientos años.
20. El tío Manuel nunca tuvo miedo.

EJERCICIO V. *Change the false statements in Ejercicio IV to make them true.*

EJERCICIO VI. *Define in Spanish:*

Examples: higuera: La higuera es un árbol que nos da higos.
reloj: Un reloj sirve para decirnos la hora.

1. avaro 2. jardinero 3. panadero 4. mozo 5. almuerzo 6. cena 7. desayuno 8. merienda 9. turrón 10. panadería

EJERCICIO VII. *Name in Spanish:*

1. diez cosas que comer 2. seis tiendas 3. cinco cosas que vió el artista en la plaza (*Remember to say* vió a *if you name a definite person.*) 4. seis bebidas 5. cinco platos puramente mexicanos 6. tres platos puramente españoles

EJERCICIO VIII. *Choose an appropriate word to complete these sentences:*

1. El —— se sirve entre las ocho y las nueve de la mañana. 2. La —— se sirve entre las nueve y las diez de la noche. 3. En el cielo hay

——. 4. Paco era ——. 5. El albañil era ——. 6. El mariachi —— y —— canciones populares. 7. El tío Manuel —— en Jijona. 8. Lorenzo bajó la ——. 9. La joven y su madre entraron en la ——. 10. Las flores de San Juan son ——. 11. La cruz de —— y el montón de —— marcan la tumba del ——.

REPASO DE COSAS DE INTERÉS

EJERCICIO I. *Complete these statements:*

1. Expressions of time must have the ——— when modified. (§ 97)
2. The preterite endings for *-ar* verbs are ——, ——, ——, ——, ——, ——. (§ 98)
3. The preterite endings for *-er* and *-ir* verbs are ——, ——, ——, ——, ——, ——. (§ 98)
4. The preterite is used for past ——. (§ 99)
5. The imperfect is used for past ——. (§ 99)
6. III RC verbs change the stem in the —— persons of the preterite; *o>* ——, *e>* ——. The same change occurs in the ——. (§ 100)
7. The endings of the preterite of III RC verbs are ——. (§ 100)
8. Unaccented *i> y* between —— ——. (§ 101)
9. The preterite of *dar* has —— endings. (§ 102)
10. The endings for most irregular preterites are ——, —— —— ——, ——, ——. (§ 103)
11. —— and —— have the same preterite. (§ 103)
12. Nouns in apposition do not have an —— in Spanish. (§ 104)
13. Every verb except ——, ——, —— is regular in the imperfect. (§ 83)
14. The imperfect is also called the —— ——. (§ 82)
15. The imperfect endings for *-ar* verbs are ——, ——, ——, ——, ——, ——. (§ 82)
16. The imperfect endings for *-er* and *-ir* verbs are ——, ——, ——, ——, ——, ——. (§ 82)
17. Repeated or habitual past action is shown by the ——. (§ 82)
18. A picture of the imperfect tense would be ——. (§ 99)
19. A picture of the preterite tense would be ——. (§ 99)
20. Nouns used in a general sense must have the ——. (§ 106)

REPASO DE VERBOS

EJERCICIO I. *Give the imperfect of the following verbs:*
coger, ir, matar, ser, pedir, ver

EJERCICIO II. *Give the preterite and gerund of these verbs:*
caer, hacer, ser, ir, dar, pedir, morir, concluir

EJERCICIO III. *Give the first person preterite for:*

poner	poder	estar	decir
componer	saber	tener	traer
suponer	querer	venir	traducir

EJERCICIO IV. *Using the model on page 316, give verb synopses for:*

prometer (*he* or *she*)	suponer (*we*)	temblar (*I*)
sentir (*they*)	bajar (*they*)	reconocer (*we*)
echar (*he* or *she*)	cumplir (*you*)	abrir (*we*)

EJERCICIO V. *Change this series of sentences (1) to the past, using* **ayer;** *(2) to the past, using* **todos los días;** *(3) to the future, using* **mañana:**

1. Me levanto a las siete.
2. Me lavo la cara.
3. Me visto.
4. Bajo al comedor.
5. Como.
6. Me pongo el sombrero.
7. Salgo a la calle.
8. Voy a la escuela.
9. Asisto a mis clases.
10. Vuelvo a casa.
11. Estudio mis lecciones.
12. Me acuesto a las diez.

EJERCICIO VI. *Change the series in Ejercicio V to* **we;** *to* **they;** *to* **he.**

QUIEN HABLA DOS LENGUAS VALE DOS HOMBRES

EJERCICIO I. *Read this story aloud, putting the italicized verb forms into Spanish as you read:*

Yo nunca *have had* buena suerte. Por eso no *buy* billetes de lotería. Sin embargo ayer *I bought* uno.

It was un día hermosísimo. *I was going* al mercado. En la calle *I met* a mi amigo, Paco. Él me *told* que *he had* (*just*) de comprar un billete de lotería y que *was hoping* ganar mil pesos porque había muchos premios. Me *asked*, — ¿Por qué no *buy* Vd. un billete, Lorenzo? Así Vd. *will be able* ganar mil pesos también.

En aquel momento *passed* un vendedor de billetes. Él me *sold* uno. Mi amigo me *helped* a *to choose* un número afortunado. *It was* el número 13531. *I took* el billete y lo *put* en el bolsillo de la camisa (*shirt*). *I went* al mercado y *forgot* el asunto.

Esta mañana *I was dressing* cuando *entered* mi amigo, Paco.

— *I came* para darle mis felicitaciones (*congratulations*) — me *said*.

— ¿Qué *do you mean?* — yo le *asked*.

— ¡Hombre! No *have heard* Vd. la noticia? El número 13531 *won* el premio gordo. *I have* (*just*) de leerlo en el periódico. *¡Look!* — y me *showed* el periódico. — *Bring* el billete y *let's go* a la oficina del cajero (*cashier*). El dinero le *awaits*. ¿Dónde *is* el billete?

¡Qué alegría! Mientras *I was dressing*, Paco y yo *were making* planes para gastar el dinero. Al fin *I put* la mano en el bolsillo para *to take out* el billete. No lo *find*. Entonces *I remembered* que el mozo de la lavandería (*laundry*) se había llevado la ropa antes de *getting up* yo.

Paco y yo *went* con toda prisa a la casa de la lavandera. Pero ¡ay de mí (*woe is me*)! La lavandera ya había lavado la camisa. No *there was* más que una manchita (*little spot, stain*) azul en el bolsillo.

¡Ay! ¡Caray!

EJERCICIO II. *Write ten questions in Spanish, based on the story given above, to ask of the other members of the class.*

EJERCICIO III. *Make a play out of the story, and put it on for the class.* (Suggestion: Act I. In the Street. Act II. In Lorenzo's Room. Act III. At the House of the Laundress. Write in parts for the lottery vendor and the laundress to say.)

JUEGOS DE REPASO

I. Vocabulary Review Game

The leader stands in front of the class, points to a member of the class, and calls out «*comida*,» or «*color*,» or «*cuerpo*.» The person designated must name something from that group of words before the leader can count to eight in Spanish. If he fails, he takes the leader's place, and tries to catch someone else. Of course, the same word cannot be repeated by another pupil.

Variations: Use «*Ropa, Tienda, o Casa*»; «*Escuela, Plaza o Mercado*»; «*Verbo, Nombre* (noun), *o Adjetivo.*»

II. Memory Training Game

The leader or teacher asks «*¿Qué ve Vd.?*» The first person called on answers, for example, «*Veo la mesa.*» The next person answers «*Veo la mesa y la ventana.*» Each person called on must name all the preceding articles and add one to the list. The names of those making mistakes are written on the board. They may be asked to do a stunt at the end of the game.

Suggestions for stunts: 1. Count by tens to a hundred in Spanish. 2. Name the months in Spanish. 3. Name the days of the week in Spanish. 4. Imitate three animals. 5. Show sorrow, rage, joy. 6. Give three Spanish proverbs. 7. Pay someone a compliment in Spanish. 8. Answer five questions in Spanish asked by the class. 9. Tell a joke in Spanish.

III. Game for Quick Thinking

The leader addresses a pupil, points to something and calls it something else. The person addressed must point to the thing named and call it the thing pointed to by the leader before the leader can count to twelve. For example, the leader says «*Ésta es la cabeza*» and points to his foot. The person addressed must point to his head and say «*Éste es el pie.*»

IV. Algo para leer

Después de la batalla

Ella — Todo lo que hay en la casa es mío; dinero, muebles (*furniture*), ropa. ¿Qué tenías tú antes de casarte conmigo?
Él — Paz.

V. Tres refranes nuevos

Después de la lluvia sale el sol.
Del dicho al hecho hay gran trecho (*distance*).
Todo lo que brilla no es de oro.

Along El camino real

"El camino real" in California refers especially to the portion of the Old Spanish Trail made by the mission fathers between San Diego and Sonoma. Bell markers now show the route of the patient Spanish friars.

R. C. McManus

I. St. Augustine

IF YOU WERE to be asked where history began in your country, you would say, "At Plymouth Rock."

Our English heritage did spread from there, but fifty-five years before the Pilgrim Fathers landed on that famous spot, this country's first white settlement was started at St. Augustine in northern Florida. And those settlers were not even the first white men to set foot there, for Ponce de León, searching for the Fountain of Youth, had passed that way over a hundred years before the Pilgrims' arrival. So perhaps we may say that America's real "Plymouth Rock" is St. Augustine.

Cities have personality, just as people do. Perhaps you live in a part of the country that has much French culture, or Dutch, or Irish. Then the customs that you take for granted might seem strange to boys and girls from the Southwest, while you would be puzzled at their Spanish inheritance, with its fiestas and rodeos and barbecues. Since we have been studying Spanish, suppose we take a look at what Spain brought into our country, for all along the thousands of miles of *El camino real* lie cities with a Spanish atmosphere so definite that we could almost trace the route of the old trail by looking for the things we know came from Spain.

St. Augustine was founded by the Spaniards in 1565. There they laid out the customary plaza, constructed a rugged city wall of coquina — crushed seashells and lime — and built flat-roofed houses along narrow Moorish streets as they had in Spain so the buildings would shade the passers-by from the hot sun. One of the houses still standing is known to have been there in 1571, and the one-time residence of the Spanish Governor is now a customs house and post office. For defense the Spaniards spent a hundred years building the "Castle of San Marcos" and surrounding it with a thick wall and medieval moat. Now we call it Fort Marion, and it is kept up by the government as one of the historical spots of our country.

For two hundred and forty years altogether St. Augustine was under Spanish rule before the United States bought Florida from Spain in 1819, and during all those years it was the eastern end of the *camino real* that led north from Mexico City and spread, fan-wise, to the eastern and western and central parts of our country. A modern coquina stone globe with a bronze tablet now rests in the plaza, marking the zero milestone of the Old Spanish Trail to San Diego, California, for this is the end of the road.

Twenty-foot coquina stone globe in St. Augustine commemorates Spanish days with its bronze plaque. Inscription: Old/Spanish Trail/Zero mile-stone/St. Augustine, Fla./to/San Diego, Calif.

Now the little town with its Spanish past sits peacefully in the sun, carefully tending its priceless remnant of city wall, waiting on the northerners who come down to get away from the winter cold, and watching the sightseeing buses full of tourists roll in to see "the Mother City of the Nation."

II. Santa Fe

Forty years after St. Augustine was founded, Santa Fe, the capital of New Mexico, became what we might call even another Plymouth Rock, for fifteen years were still to pass before the Pilgrims would set sail in the Mayflower.

From Spain by way of Mexico City in 1598 came the New World's first millionaire promoter, Juan de Oñate, financing an expedition from his own pocket and bringing with him two hundred young Spanish aristocrats with adventure in their blood. On the old *camino real*, in about 1609, they founded the city of «La Villa Real de Santa Fe de San Francisco de Asisi,» although "Holy Faith" is all that remains of the name now.

Unless you happen to be Spanish, Mexican, or Indian, when you go to Santa Fe you are casually classed as an "Anglo," whether you are Greek, Chinese or British. The aristocrats of the tradition-minded town are the descendants of those old Spanish families who came from Spain with Juan de Oñate, and no one is surprised to hear a lady remark over the bridge table, "Grandfather has a good deal of trouble with his adobe house. The walls are so thick they sink into the earth a little each rainy season, and he's always having a door fixed. His house is over three hundred years old, you know."

And only a newcomer is surprised when the same lady turns to another and starts a discussion in fluent Spanish, for even the State Legislature conducts its business in both languages.

Santa Fe-ans seriously observe a whole calendarful of fiestas, one of which they have put on each September for over two hundred years in succession, when everyone turns out dressed in the authentic costumes of the days of the grandees to dance the old Spanish folk dances and sing the old Spanish songs.

Christmas in Santa Fe is a Spanish-Mexican-Indian affair, with every flat-roofed adobe house outlined with *luminarias* — lighted can-

Santa Fe, New Mexico, at the northern end of *El camino real*, combines Pueblo Indian and old Spanish architecture in its interesting buildings made of adobe and heavy beams.

dles set in paper bags partly filled with sand — and there is a nativity scene in every home.   A Christmas eve procession representing Mary and Joseph on their way to Bethlehem marches to music around the old plaza and ends up at the cathedral, where bonfires burn in the churchyard to light the way for the Christ Child.   Children — Spanish, Mexican and Anglo — sing carols in Spanish and English beside the old Governor's Palace, and at midnight the people go, just as their ancestors did in Spain, to the *Misa del gallo* which lasts till daylight.

So the old city that once marked the northern end of the *camino real* from Mexico City lives proudly on, keeping alive memories of the dignified past it inherited directly from Spain.

III. SAN ANTONIO

There lay the Old Spanish Trail, stretching across North America from St. Augustine to Santa Fe.   Since such a great territory was too much to develop all at once, when travel was by oxcart and on horseback, the mother country found herself neglecting a great deal of the central section of New Spain.

But when some Spanish soldiers found St. Denis, a French trader from Louisiana, marching over their *camino real* in the Province of Tejas, they promptly took him to Mexico City to inquire into his intentions.   What he told them must have been alarming, for orders went out to establish missions along the *camino real* to prevent a general French invasion.

In 1718, therefore, Mission San Antonio de Valero was founded in order to establish the Spanish ownership of Texas, and there priest and soldier tamed a wilderness.   The King of Spain sent fifteen Spanish families from the Canary Islands to settle around the mission, and today their names live on in street and story.

Modern San Antonio is not a sleepy little town with a past, but a bustling city with a past, present and future.   Here the traveler finds sharper contrasts than almost anywhere else along the Old Spanish Trail.   Ancient landmarks doze beside smart new skyscrapers; over the Governor's Palace, where Spanish viceroys ruled almost two centuries ago, zoom hundreds of planes from the "West Point of the Air." And when the visitor drives up to make his pilgrimage to the historic Alamo mission, he must put a nickel in a parking meter!

Boys and girls of San Antonio are conscious of their city's rich heritage.   Since there are many Spanish-speaking residents nearby, they also find much use for their study of Spanish.   In the Mexican quarter they can bargain for the native handicrafts of Mexico, eat typical spicy foods, and hear the tinkle of guitars while they practice their Spanish lessons.

Christmas in the Mexican quarter is celebrated with religious processions, *piñatas,* and nativity scenes in the homes; churches present medieval mystery plays that have been given for two hundred years, and on Christmas eve everyone goes to the *Misa del gallo.*

In April comes the Fiesta San Jacinto, celebrated for fifty years by the whole city, beginning officially with a dignified and silent pilgrimage to the Alamo, that sacred shrine of Texas history. Many dress in Spanish costume, and wandering musicians stroll in the shadow of the skyscrapers. The traditional *Combate de flores* has turned into an evening program at the Municipal Auditorium, but *La noche de fiesta* recreates the atmosphere of Mexico and Spain to climax a week of celebration.

Big and busy as San Antonio is now, the old *conquistadores* could still find familiar things there, for cities once built upon Spanish culture seldom lose it entirely.

Governor's Palace in San Antonio still bears the Hapsburg coat-of-arms and the date 1749. Here Spanish viceroys once lived and ruled sternly in their little frontier town.

Sawders

Santa Barbara's Mission sets the architectural style for the town, and is one of the few missions along *El camino real* continuously occupied since its founding in 1786.

IV. SANTA BARBARA

Santa Barbara, a pretty little seaport of California, was visited by Sebastián Vizcaíno two years before Juan de Oñate founded Santa Fe, but no Spanish town was built there until 1782. Now it is a wealthy little city of proud old Spanish family names, its beautiful old Mission, founded by Father Junípero Serra, still occupied by brown-robed Franciscan padres. In the Spanish-Moorish courthouse are filed building restrictions that forbid any construction that does not harmonize with the town's Spanish architecture, for Santa Barbara, like all California, is tradition-minded and conscious of its romantic past.

Years ago there was revived the old Spanish custom of visiting neighboring ranches each May, and a cavalcade of hundreds of men on horseback or in antiquated stagecoaches and wagons, goes to the Mission for a blessing on the trip, then sets out for nearly a week's ride from *rancho* to *rancho* in the back country of Santa Barbara County. Each night the «*Rancheros visitadores*» are guests at a different estate, where they are told, "My ranch is yours," and at each stop they are entertained with rodeos and dances and barbecues.

Traditional bride and groom ride at each Old Spanish Days Fiesta in Santa Barbara, as they did when California was young. The archway is part of the famous Spanish-Moorish Courthouse.

An Easterner passing through Santa Barbara during the full moon in August of any year is likely to think he has stepped into an early California history book, for almost every citizen of the town, even before the fiesta begins, is going calmly about his business dressed in a costume of old Spanish days. A soda clerk wears a gold-braided jacket, flaring trousers with a bright sash and a Cordovan hat, to go with his Spanish mustache, while the salesgirl in the ten-cent store is as likely as not to have on a long ruffled skirt, a Spanish shawl, and great dangling earrings. Old ladies dress like the *dueñas* of olden times; hitching racks and watering troughs appear on State Street for the horses of the *rancheros*, and when the old Mission bells ring out at twilight and skyrockets flare from its towers, the fiesta is on for three merry days. Pageants and parades tell the story of the town since the time when it was an Indian village, and all over the festive little city go strolling serenaders and dancing merrymakers. Spanish-style *puestos* spring up in the streets, and the old families hold open house for all their friends. The movie theaters even feature pictures with a Spanish theme, for everyone tries to create again the spirit of Santa Barbara's past.

So you see how old Spain lives on even in our modern United States, for St. Augustine, Santa Fe, San Antonio and Santa Barbara are but four of the many cities located on the old *camino real* which brought Spanish culture into our great southwest and gave us traditions far older than that first Thanksgiving of the Pilgrim Fathers.

Interesting Books to Read

JACKSON, HELEN HUNT: RAMONA.
BARTLETT, LANIER *and* VIRGINIA: ADIÓS.
FITCH, A. H.: JUNÍPERO SERRA.
OTERO, NINA: OLD SPAIN IN OUR SOUTHWEST.

CAPÍTULO 37

La cajita del moro[1]

This will be the longest story you have read in Spanish.   Take a look at the new verb forms in COSAS DE INTERÉS *and then see how easily you can read it.*

PRIMERA PARTE

Vivía una vez en Granada un aguador que se llamaba Peregil.   Era un hombre bueno y honrado.   Tenía una familia grande y tenía que trabajar mucho para ganar la vida.

5   Como no había agua corriente en las casas de Granada, los aguadores iban a una fuente cerca de la Alhambra donde había agua muy fría.   La llevaban en jarras[2] hasta la ciudad,

---

[1] This is another story of hidden treasure and Moorish enchantment.   (See footnote on page 358.)

[2] *Jarras* are large earthen jars.   In Mexico they are called *ollas*.

donde la vendían.   Al principio Peregil llevaba el agua a cuestas (*on his back*).   Pero era industrioso y pronto ganó bastante dinero para comprar un burro.   Entonces Peregil llenaba las jarras y las ponía en las alforjas (*saddle-bags*) de su   10 burro.

Una noche decidió hacer otro viaje a la Alhambra, aunque era muy tarde, para ganar unos reales[1] más.   Así podría comprar unos dulces para sus hijitos.   Los otros aguadores ya estaban en casa y él fué solo a la Alhambra.   Al acercarse a la   15 fuente vió a un hombre sentado en un banco.   Era un moro muy viejo.

El moro llamó a Peregil.   Le dijo que estaba enfermo y no podía bajar la cuesta[2] solo.   Peregil ofreció ayudarle y el

[1] *Real* is an old Spanish coin of silver equal to about twenty-five *céntimos* (a quarter of a *peseta*).

[2] You will remember that the Alhambra is on a hill (*cuesta*) overlooking the city of Granada and the plain (*vega*) beyond.   (See footnote on page 300.)

Water-carriers are common in Spanish America as well as in Spain.   A spring on the outskirts of Tepic, Mexico, supplies good water which the *aguadores* deliver for five *centavos* a jar.

Keystone

20 moro prometió que le pagaría bien. Pero el aguador, hombre
muy bondadoso, no quería nada.

Con mucha dificultad le ayudó a montar al burro y le llevó
a la ciudad. Al llegar, el moro le dijo que no tenía amigos en
la ciudad y no sabía a donde ir. Pidió a Peregil permiso para
25 pasar la noche en su casa. Viendo que el moro estaba muy
enfermo, el buen hombre no pudo decirle que no.

La esposa de Peregil era una mujer perezosa. Pasaba los
días platicando con las vecinas, y las noches quejándose a
Peregil de la mala suerte que tenía ella, siendo esposa de un
30 hombre pobre. Cuando entraron Peregil y el moro, la mujer
empezó a quejarse. — ¿Por qué has traído a un huésped? —
dijo ella. — No tenemos bastante que comer y ¿cómo vamos
a dar de comer a otro? Además no hay cama para otra
persona.

35 Generalmente Peregil trataba de complacer a su esposa,
pero esta vez no la escuchó y el moro se quedó con ellos. Le
dieron de comer y le prepararon una cama en el suelo.

Durante la noche el moro llamó a Peregil. Le dijo que
estaba muriéndose y que quería pagarle. — Lo único que
40 tengo es esta cajita. Tómela y guárdela bien. — Diciendo
esto, murió.

Pues, amigos, ¡cuántas cosas dijo aquella mujer! — ¡Todo
el mundo creerá que hemos muerto (*killed*) a este hombre! —
dijo ella. — El alguacil nos llevará a la cárcel. Y tú tienes
45 la culpa. ¿Por qué trajiste a ese hombre a nuestra casa?
¡Maldita sea su alma!

Para calmarla, Peregil dijo que llevaría el cuerpo del moro
al campo y allí lo enterraría y que nadie sabría lo que había
pasado (*had happened*). La mujer le ayudó, y cubrieron al
50 moro con una manta grande y le pusieron en el burro. Un
poco antes del amanecer salió Peregil y enterró al moro.

SEGUNDA PARTE

Cerca del aguador vivía un barbero. Era un hombre muy
preguntón. Quería saberlo todo y repetía todo lo que sabía.
Lo que no sabía, lo inventaba. El barbero vió al moro entrar

en la casa de Peregil. Lleno de curiosidad, pasó las horas 55
mirando la casa. Así fué que cuando salió Peregil, el barbero
le vió. Le siguió y le vió enterrar al moro.

Por la mañana fué el barbero a la casa del juez para cortarle
el pelo. Mientras trabajaba, hablaba. Y por supuesto, lo
primero que le dijo fué el asunto del moro muerto. — Es 60
evidente, — dijo el barbero, — que nuestro vecino Peregil ha
muerto al hombre y ha guardado el dinero que éste tenía.

El juez, hombre muy avaro y muy cruel, creyó todo lo que
le dijo el barbero. Llamó a Peregil y le dió un susto (*fright*)
terrible. Peregil le contó la historia del moro muerto, y le 65
enseñó la cajita, que no contenía más que un papel y una vela.
La esposa de Peregil contó la misma historia, y al fin el juez
tuvo que dejar libre a Peregil.

Ahora Peregil tenía que trabajar más que antes. Otra vez
tenía que llevar el agua a cuestas, porque el juez tenía su 70
burro. Al volver a casa tenía que escuchar los lamentos de su
esposa.

Una noche, desesperado, arrojó la cajita al suelo, excla-
mando, — ¡Maldita sea la hora en que dejé entrar a aquel
hombre en mi casa! — Cuando cayó la caja, el papel saltó 75
(*came out*) de ella. Peregil lo cogió y vió que contenía algunas
palabras árabes. No sabía leerlas, pero al día siguiente llevó
el papel a un moro, amigo suyo. Éste lo leyó con cuidado, y
al fin le dijo que el papel contenía el secreto de una cueva
encantada donde había un tesoro escondido. 80

— Pero, — añadió el moro, — este papel no vale nada sin
una vela de cierta clase. Y no sé donde se puede obtener una
vela semejante.

Pues, como saben Vds., Peregil tenía la vela. Los dos
decidieron ir a la Alhambra para buscar el tesoro. A media- 85
noche salieron de la ciudad, subieron a la Alhambra y en-
contraron la entrada de la cueva. Peregil encendió la vela y
el moro leyó en voz alta las palabras árabes que contenía el
papel. Al concluir, se oyó un ruido terrible, y se abrió[1] la

---

[1] *Se abrió, se cerró* — *opened, closed.* No one opened or closed the earth; it
opened and closed itself; that is, of its own accord.

90   tierra. Vieron una escalera subterránea. Temblando de miedo, bajaron la escalera a la luz de la vela y entraron en una sala grande. La sala estaba llena de jarras, y en el centro había una caja grandísima. ¿Qué había en las jarras? Había monedas de oro, joyas de todas clases, y piedras pre-

95   ciosas. El aguador y el moro se llenaron los bolsillos y salieron con mucha prisa porque tenían miedo. Al salir apagaron la vela, se oyó otra vez el ruido, y la tierra se cerró. Dividieron en dos partes iguales el dinero y las joyas que se habían llevado (*they had taken*) de la cueva. Volvieron a la

100   ciudad y prometieron no decir nada a nadie.

TERCERA PARTE

Es muy difícil no decir nada a una esposa. La esposa de Peregil quiso saber por qué salió de la casa a medianoche. Peregil tuvo que darle algunas monedas para calmarla. Después tuvo que explicarle como obtuvo el dinero. ¡Ya no

105   había secreto! La mujer prometió no decir nada. Y es verdad que cumplió con su promesa... por unos días. Pero un día se puso algunas joyas, y estaba admirándose en el espejo cuando pasó el barbero. Él miró por la ventana y la vió con las joyas. Casi no podía creer lo que le decían los ojos.

110   Se fué con toda prisa a la casa del juez para contárselo. Y en pocos minutos el alguacil prendió a Peregil. Lo único que podía hacer éste era decir la verdad. Entonces prendieron al moro.

El juez escuchó la historia de los dos hombres. Pensó que

115   sería una buena idea obtener el tesoro, y por eso dijo, — Hay que ver la evidencia. No lo creo, pero lo creeré si veo este tesoro. Vds. tendrán que enseñármelo. — Para sí pensaba que, al obtener el tesoro, mataría al aguador y al moro, y así podría tener todo el tesoro.

120   No había otra cosa que hacer, y los dos consintieron en volver a la cueva con el juez, el barbero, y el alguacil.

A medianoche salieron los cinco hombres. Llegaron a la cueva, encendieron la vela, y el moro leyó las palabras árabes. Se abrió la tierra y bajaron los hombres. Se llevaron todas

las jarras.   Pero todavía quedaba la caja grande.   El juez y   125
sus dos compañeros avaros bajaron para llevarse la caja.
Entonces el moro, sin decir nada a Peregil, apagó la vela.
Se cerró la tierra y el moro arrojó la vela. — Son hombres
malos, — dijo a Peregil. — Déjelos que se queden [1] ente-
rrados. —   Peregil y el moro dividieron el tesoro y bajaron a   130
la ciudad.

Al día siguiente el moro volvió a África y Peregil llevó a su
familia a Portugal.   Allí, siendo un hombre rico, era un
hombre importante.   Se llamaba don Pedro Gil.   Su esposa
estaba muy contenta, porque tenía muchos vestidos y muchas   135
joyas y ya no tenía que trabajar.

¿Y los otros hombres?   Se dice que todavía están en la
cueva encantada, esperando la hora de salir.

Find These Expressions in the Story

1. The barber saw the Moor enter
2. that they had taken away from the cave
3. how he obtained the money
4. she put on some jewels
5. the constable arrested Peregil
6. Thus he would be able to buy
7. he would pay him well
8. he said that he would take the body
9. he would bury it there
10. he told him that he was dying
11. Take it and guard it well.
12. how are we going to feed another?
13. this paper is worth nothing
14. no one would know
15. he thought (that) it would be a good idea
16. he would kill the water carrier
17. he would be able to have all
18. she was admiring herself
19. by the light of the candle
20. They fed him
21. the only (thing) that I have
22. they went down to carry away the box
23. it contained only a paper
24. a certain kind of candle
25. He followed him and saw him bury the Moor.
26. At midnight the five men went out.
27. being a rich man

[1] *Déjelos que se queden,* let them remain.

COSAS DE INTERÉS

109. The Conditional Tense

Did you notice this new tense in the story?

CONDITIONAL TENSE OF REGULAR VERBS		
pagar	**leer**	**vivir**
pagar ía	leer ía	vivir ia
pagar ías	leer ías	vivir ías
pagar ía	leer ía	vivir ía
pagar íamos	leer íamos	vivir íamos
pagar íais	leer íais	vivir íais
pagar ían	leer ían	vivir ían
I should pay,	*I should read,*	*I should live,* I
I would pay, etc.	*I would read,* etc.	*would live,* etc.

The conditional tense is used in Spanish as it is in English.

Dice que irá.   *He says he will go.*
Dijo que iría.   *He said he would go.*
Pensó que volvería.   *He thought he would return.*

EJERCICIO I.   *Answer these questions:*

1. What is the stem for the conditional tense?
2. Do all conjugations form the conditional in the same way?
3. What other tense has the same endings?
4. How will you be able to tell the difference?
5. What is the sign of the future tense?
6. What is the sign of the conditional tense?
7. How is the future tense indicated in English?
8. How is the conditional tense expressed in English?

EJERCICIO II.   *Complete in Spanish:*

1. Dijo que *he would go.*   2. Dijo que *he would be* aquí a las diez.
3. Dijeron que *would see* a su amigo.   4. No dijimos que lo *would translate.*   5. ¿Dijo Carlos que lo *would look for?*   6. ¿Le *would please* a Vd. ser rico?

110. Conditional Tense of Irregular Verbs

The conditional tense uses the future stem. In Chapter 28 you learned the future stems for irregular verbs. Use the conditional tense endings with those same stems and you will have the conditional tense for the irregular verbs.

REMEMBER:	Future tense ⎫ ⎬ use same stem. Conditional tense ⎭

EJERCICIO III. *Give the future stem of:*

saber, querer, poder, haber, venir, tener, salir, poner, decir, hacer

EJERCICIO IV. *Conjugate the verbs in Ejercicio III in the conditional tense.*

PREGUNTITAS

I. 1. ¿Qué clase de hombre era Peregil?
    2. ¿Cuál era su ocupación?
    3. ¿Dónde encontró al moro?
    4. ¿Por qué se enfadó la esposa del aguador?
    5. ¿Cómo pagó el moro a Peregil?
    6. ¿Qué hizo Peregil con el cuerpo?
    7. ¿Decía el barbero la verdad siempre?
    8. ¿A quién contó lo que había visto?
    9. Describa Vd. al barbero. Al juez. A la mujer.
    10. ¿Qué contenía la cajita?
    11. ¿Quién acompañó a Peregil a la cueva?
    12. ¿Qué encontraron en la cueva?
    13. ¿Cómo supo el juez que Peregil tenía un tesoro?
    14. ¿Por qué le prendió?
    15. ¿Qué pensaba hacer el juez, después de encontrar el tesoro?
    16. ¿Quiénes fueron a la cueva por segunda vez?
    17. ¿Por qué no podía Peregil leer el papel?
    18. ¿Quiénes se quedaron en la cueva?
    19. ¿A dónde fué Peregil? ¿Cómo se llamaba allí?
    20. ¿A dónde fué el moro?

II. 1. ¿Le gustaría a Vd. encontrar un tesoro?
2. ¿Qué hacen los aguadores?
3. ¿Se queja Vd. mucho?
4. ¿Hay tesoros en muchas cuevas?
5. ¿Qué quiere decir preguntón?   (¡En español!)
6. ¿Sabe Vd. leer el árabe?   ¿Es fácil o difícil el árabe?
7. ¿Es Vd. bondadoso (-a)?
8. ¿Qué hora es a medianoche?
9. ¿Tendría Vd. miedo en una cueva encantada?
10. ¿Cree Vd. que hay muchos tesoros escondidos?
11. ¿Tiene Vd. espejo?   ¿Se (yourself) mira Vd. mucho en él?

REPASITO

I. Give these verbs in the tenses or forms indicated. (Be careful. Some are radical-changing verbs and some are irregular.)

1. enterrar — *future*
2. esconder — *imperfect*
3. dar — *conditional*
4. añadir — *imperfect*
5. encender — *present*
6. pedir — *preterite*
7. prender — *gerund* and *commands*
8. arrojar — *preterite*
9. apagar — *present*
10. volverse — *present perfect*
11. querer — *preterite*

II. Translate into Spanish:

1. I shall not go.
2. Did you see him?
3. Have you seen him?
4. Has he studied them?
5. He would know it.
6. Dress (yourself)!
7. Come here!
8. He has gone away.
9. She was singing.
10. He spoke to me.

III. What do these endings on regular verbs tell you about their person and tense?

1. -(r)é	4. -o	7. -ábamos	10. -an	13. -(r)emos
2. -e	5. -ó	8. -ía	11. -ieron	14. -(r)án
3. -é	6. -aron	9. -(r)ían	12. -á	15. -imos [1]

[1] What two tenses could this be?

IV. Arrange these words in pairs of opposites. There will
be some left over.

bajar	subir	recordar	mejor
apagar	olvidar	cesar de	buscar
jamás	encender	encima de	tierra
cruel	empezar	morir	luna
siempre	vivir	encontrar	peor
bondadoso	debajo de	cielo	sol

*V. Choose carefully the correct tense for the verbs in italics;
then translate the entire sentence into Spanish.*

1. Where *were* you when I *called?*   2. What *has he done?*   3. *Did
you see* my friend?   4. *Have you seen* my friend?   5. He *was looking
for* you.   6. I *used to paint* in Mexico every summer.   7. After *eating*
he *fell asleep.*   8. *Did you understand* what he *was saying?*   9. The
barber *told* the judge what he *saw.*

PALABRAS PARA HOY

2 **además**	moreover, besides	3 **contener**	to contain
el aguador	water carrier	3 **encender**	to light (*incendi-*
el alguacil	constable	**(ie)**	*ary*)
el amanecer	dawn	**enterrar (ie)**	to bury (**en tierra**)
2 **añadir**	to add (in talking)	3 **la entrada**	entrance
4 **apagar**	to extinguish, put	2 **escuchar**	to listen
	out	4 **el espejo**	mirror
3 **arrojar**	to throw, throw	**el huésped**	(paying) guest
	away	**la joya**	jewel
3 **bondadoso,**	kind	4 **el juez**	judge
-a		2 **libre**	free (*liberate*)
2 **el campo**	country	1 **llevarse**	to carry away
4 **la cárcel**	prison (*incarcerate*)	**la manta**	blanket
1 **cierto, -a**	certain, a certain	**preguntón**	inquisitive
4 **complacer**	to please (*compla-*	**prender**	to arrest
	cent)	4 **quejarse**	to complain
2 **el cuidado**	care	4 **el tesoro**	treasure

EXPRESIONES

a la luz de, by the light of
dar de comer, to feed
lo único, the only thing

*tener la culpa, to be to blame, **to**
be the fault of (*culprit*)
para sí, to himself

El arte del indito[1]

Hay mucho en la vida española que es exactamente igual a la mexicana. Hay costumbres sociales, hay fiestas, y por supuesto, España y México tienen la misma lengua, con sus dichos (*sayings*) y refranes, su poesía y su literatura. Pero
5 cuando estudiamos el arte de los dos países, hallamos que hay algo en México que no existe en España. Los dos (*both*) tienen sus bellas artes[2] como las (*those*) de cualquier otro país moderno, pero en México hay todavía más.

Cuando llegó Cortés a México, hace más de cuatrocientos
10 años, encontró allí a los indios, que ya tenían sus artes indígenas (*native*). Y hasta hoy los indios todavía conservan estas artes antiguas, tan bien como su afición a (*fondness for*) hacer cosas con las manos. Siempre les gusta trabajar cuidadosamente, sin tener prisa, y con un orgullo en su trabajo
15 que no se encuentra entre gente más moderna. Para un español práctico, como para nosotros, un artículo útil no tiene que ser bonito a la vez; pero para un indio mexicano, cualquier cosita de uso diario necesita su adorno (*decoration*) y siempre lo tiene.

20 Hay familias enteras de indios que pasan sus días haciendo loza, sarapes,[3] deshilados,[4] cestas, molinillos,[5] petates,[6] muebles

[1] «*indito*» (*ind(io)* + *ito*) is what the upper class Mexican often calls the Indian, with a slightly affectionate or tolerant meaning.

[2] *bellas artes, fine arts.* The "fine arts" include painting, architecture, sculpture, and sometimes music and drama; that is, the beautiful things of life.

[3] See Note 1 to *La Cucaracha*, on page 395.

[4] *deshilados, drawnwork.* This famous Mexican spiderweb lace resembles that made in Paraguay.

[5] *molinillos* (*little mills*), *chocolate whirlers.* These everyday kitchen utensils are of hand-turned and hand-carved wood, often inset with mother-of-pearl dots. Many are so beautiful that they really should be kept in the living room instead of the kitchen!

[6] A *petate* is a hand-woven straw mat which serves the Indian for bed, rug, or *puesto*, and for a coffin when he dies.

Kitchen utensils are often made of wood or clay. The carved wooden chocolate beater (*molinillo*) is used in the taller jug. The wooden tray (*batea*) is lacquered in bright colors.

o juguetes. Los niños trabajan como sus padres, y en su casa humilde (*humble*) hay una fábrica sin maquinaria (*machinery*), sin huelgas (*strikes*), y con empleados contentos que trabajan con cuidado y con cariño porque les gusta, y que 25 aman cada artículo que hacen.

El indio, cuando hace de barro los jarros más corrientes,[1] no está satisfecho sin adornarlos al menos un poquito. Y rara vez hace iguales sus jarros, aunque puede hacer docenas a la vez. Adorna cada uno, hasta el más barato, con el dibujo 30 de una flor, un animal, un pájaro, o un nombre, para hacerlo más bonito. Por ejemplo, en un jarro puede pintar «Julia,» «Lola,» o «Susita»; en una cazuela (*bowl*) puede pintar «Un regalo a mi amiguita Lupita,» o «María, María, dame tu amor.» En un botellón[2] escribe «Recuerdo de Juanita,» 35 «Viva Teresita,» o «Pedro Ramírez me hizo.»

[1] Anything of ordinary quality, for everyday use, is called *corriente*.

[2] A *botellón* is a fat, red clay water bottle with a cup to match turned upside down over its long neck. Its porous clay always leaks a little, keeping the water cool inside.

There is one in every small town hotel bedroom, and on every dining room table.

Cuando el indio ha hecho unos jarros y cazuelas, los mete
en un huacal[1] y los lleva al mercado. Quizás vive lejos de
una población, y tiene que llevar su loza a cuestas (*on his back*)
40 una gran distancia. Pero eso no importa; para él el tiempo
no vale nada, tampoco el viaje; y hasta menos le importa el
trabajo de hacer su loza. Así es que vende muy baratos sus
jarros y cazuelas. Si gana unos pocos centavos por cada uno,
está satisfecho.

45 Los indios tienen sus costumbres antiguas, y cada familia
usa su propio dibujo en los artículos que hace. Nunca imitan
el dibujo de otra familia, aunque sea (*it may be*) más popular
y más fácil que vender. — No es costumbre, — dicen.

A los indios les gusta su trabajo, porque son verdaderos
50 artistas. Un señor rico una vez pidió media docena de sarapes
como uno que un indio le había hecho. El primero había
costado cuatro pesos, pero por media docena, el indio pidió
veinte y seis pesos.

[1] A *huacal* is a handmade crate of willow sticks built up like a log cabin, its
corners laced together with rawhide.

Ropes and petates (straw mats), like other handiwork, are sold in one section of the market. A traveling Indian carries for his bed his *petate* and
sarape, and lies down to sleep anywhere.

R. C. McManus

Potter's wheel, turned by the workman's foot, is the only piece of machinery in the factory. The soft clay jar is painted in an original design, then baked in a crude kiln.

— ¡Qué cosa! — exclamó el comprador. — Si compro media docena, Vd. debe darme una rebaja.

55

— No, señor, — contestó el indio. — Me gustó hacer el primero, pero si tengo que hacer seis igualitos, estaré muy aburrido (*bored*), y será un trabajo muy desagradable. Así tendré que cobrarle a Vd. veinte y seis pesos la media docena.

Pottery factories in Mexico are a simple matter of working in your own patio. The large vase has an authentic old-fashioned floral design, but the bowl being decorated shows modern tourist influence.

60   Había otro indio que había hecho cuidadosamente unas cajitas hermosísimas de madera tallada (*carved*). Un turista las vió y quería hacer un pedido (*order*) de ciento para vender en su país. Al pedírselas al indio, el pobre hombre casi murió de sorpresa y consternación.

65   — ¡Cien cajitas! — exclamó. — Pues, señor, ¡nunca podría yo hacer tantas! — Y el pensamiento de tal cosa le dió un susto (*shock*) tan grande que desde aquel día nunca hizo otra cajita.

     Los indios hacen unas cosas que nosotros creemos muy

70 curiosas. Por ejemplo, hacen cerdos pequeños de barro que sirven de bancos (*banks*) a los niños. Estos cerditos están pintados de muchos colores, con flores vivas en el lomo (*back*), ojos azules, y una cinta color de rosa pintada en el cuello. Estos bancos son muy populares con los niños, porque entre los

75 indios pobres el cerdo es el emblema de la prosperidad. (Se cree que una familia que tiene un cerdo nunca morirá de hambre.)

Charles D. Jarrett

Hat, charro, and basket are good examples of handicrafts in straw, clay, and split bamboo. The hat is for everyday wear in Tepic; the *charro* and basket are toys from Guadalajara.

Por supuesto, los cerdos pintados así no se parecen a ningún cerdo del mundo. Un indito adornó uno, y un viajero lo vió.

— ¡Ay, caray! — dijo el viajero. — ¡Los cerdos no tienen flores en el lomo ni cintas en el cuello! 80

El indio le miró seriamente. — Pues, señor, — contestó, — al fin, el cerdo es mío.

Una vez un artista indio había hecho un cántaro (*pitcher*) grande de barro, y había pintado sobre él un venado pequeño al lado de una mariposa enorme. Un turista, viéndolo, dijo, 85 — Es la primera vez que he visto una mariposa tan grande como un venado. ¿No sabe Vd. que las mariposas son pequeñas y los venados grandes?

El indio se mostró muy paciente con el turista ignorante. — ¿No ve Vd., señor, — explicó, — que es solamente un dibujo? 90

No cabe duda de que el indio mexicano tiene el alma verdaderamente artística.

Find These Expressions in the Story

1. which an Indian had made for him
2. There was another Indian who had made
3. without decorating them a little, at least
4. for him time is worth nothing
5. One hundred little boxes!
6. easier to sell
7. butterflies are small and deer large
8. if I have to make six just alike
9. from that day he never made another little box
10. Pigs don't have flowers on their backs
11. although he may make dozens at a time
12. even less does the work matter to him
13. they resemble no pig in the world
14. The first one had cost two pesos
15. I could never make so many!
16. because they like to

COSAS DE INTERÉS

111. Compound Tenses

You learned the present perfect tense long ago.   Here are the other compound tenses.

PAST PERFECT [1]	FUTURE PERFECT	CONDITIONAL PERFECT
había comprado	habré comprado	habría comprado
habías comprado	habrás comprado	habrías comprado
había comprado	habrá comprado	habría comprado
habíamos comprado	habremos comprado	habríamos comprado
habíais comprado	habréis comprado	habríais comprado
habían comprado	habrán comprado	habrían comprado
I had bought, etc.	*I shall have bought*	*I should have bought*

[1] This is also called the Pluperfect Tense.

Any tense of the verb *haber* may be used with the past participle to form a compound tense. The use of the compound tenses is generally the same in English and Spanish. The future perfect and the conditional perfect are not used a great deal in either language. However, you must be able to recognize these tenses when you meet them.

	he vivido	I have lived
REMEMBER:	**había vivido**	I had lived
	habré vivido	I shall have lived
	habría vivido	I should have lived

EJERCICIO I. *Answer these questions:*

1. What is the helping verb used in compound tenses?
2. Does the past participle change when used with the helping verb?
3. Are all conjugations alike in the past perfect tense?
4. What is the other name for the past perfect tense?
5. Is the future perfect used much in English? In Spanish?
6. What letter tells you that *habría* is the conditional and not the imperfect of *haber?*
7. Knowing the tenses of *haber* and the past participles of other verbs, can you give the compound tenses of all the verbs we have studied?
8. Will there be such an awkward combination as *had had* in Spanish? Why not? How do you say *he had had?*

EJERCICIO II. There are four compound tenses in this exercise. *Translate, watching the tense of each helping verb carefully:*

1. he vivido
2. han salido
3. habíamos dado
4. habrán ido
5. yo había ido
6. Vd. había venido
7. hemos visto
8. habremos oído
9. se había sentado
10. ha traído
11. habrían servido
12. habían servido

112. Gran; cien

Do you remember the seven adjectives which sometimes drop the *o?* (Section 42) Name them and tell when they are shortened.

Here are two more: *grande* and *ciento.*

Grande becomes *gran* when it stands before any singular noun, masculine or feminine. Its meaning then changes from *large* to *great*:

un hombre grande	un gran hombre
a large man	*a great man*

Ciento becomes *cien* when it stands, an exact hundred, before any noun or *mil* (*thousand*):

cien hombres	cien mil hombres
100 men	*100,000 men*

Before any other number, *ciento* does not change:

ciento diez hombres   *110 men*

EJERCICIO III.   *Complete in Spanish:*

1. *100* sillas
2. *100* caballos
3. *109* sillas
4. *109* caballos
5. *100,000* libros
6. un *great* artista
7. una *great* mujer
8. un *large* artista
9. una *large* mujer
10. el *great* médico

113. Neuter Pronouns Esto and Eso

Esto and *eso* are neuter, and do not agree with any noun in gender nor in number. They always refer to a *whole idea* or situation, instead of to a single word:

eso no importa, *that doesn't matter*
esto es muy difícil de hacer, *this is very hard to do*

114. Adjectives Used as Nouns

Almost any adjective may be used alone as a noun, which often requires the addition of the English word *one* in the translation:

el primero, *the first one*   **el viejo,** *the old man*

EJERCICIO IV.   *Say in Spanish* (Watch the gender!):

1. the red one (*rosa*) 2. an old one (*perro*) 3. the last one (*casa*)
4. a big one (*árbol*) 5. the third one (*lección*) 6. the black ones
(*caballos*) 7. a young man 8. a Spanish woman

PREGUNTITAS

I. 1. ¿Existen indios hoy en México?   ¿En España?
2. ¿Qué le gusta a un indio hacer?
3. Describa Vd. una fábrica de loza de un indio.
4. ¿Les gusta a los indios adornar todo?
5. ¿Qué pone un indio en un jarro para adornarlo?
6. ¿Valen mucho para un indio el tiempo y el trabajo?
7. ¿Le gusta a un alma artística hacer media docena de cosas igualitas?
8. ¿Cuál es el emblema de la prosperidad entre los indios?
9. ¿Por qué había pintado el indio flores en el cerdo?
10. ¿Por qué no hizo el indio nunca otra cajita de madera?

II. 1. ¿Tiene Vd. un alma artística?
2. ¿Están adornados todos los artículos útiles que usamos?
3. ¿Ha visto Vd. jamás un cerdito pintado de flores?
4. ¿Adornamos nosotros los utensilios de cocina?
5. ¿Podría Vd. hacer un huacal?
6. ¿Mete Vd. mucho dinero en su banco?
7. ¿Cuál es el emblema de la prosperidad en este país?
8. Comprando media docena de artículos en este país, ¿generalmente recibimos una rebaja?
9. ¿Tiene Vd. orgullo en todo lo que hace?
10. ¿Ha visto Vd. una mariposa más grande que un venado?

REPASITO

I. Aquí tiene Vd. un chiste que leer.

Entierro (*funeral*) agradable

Un norteamericano, viajando por México, siempre encontraba dos expresiones típicas de los mexicanos que le molestaban muchísimo. Por ejemplo, cada vez que pedía algo, le decían, — Mañana, mañana, — y como sabe Vd., mañana nunca llega.

También, cada vez que hacía una pregunta, alguien le contestaba sin falta, — ¿Quién sabe?

Un día el norteamericano andaba por la calle cuando vió pasar un funeral. — ¿Quién murió? — preguntó a un señor.

— ¿Quién sabe? — contestó el mexicano.

— ¿«Quién sabe» murió? ¡Bueno! — dijo el norteamericano. — Y ahora si entierran (*bury*) a ese «mañana» también, ¡tanto mejor!

What did the American hope would happen to the two expressions that annoyed him?

II. Tell the tense of each verb in the last eighteen lines of the story «El arte del indito,» explaining the use of each imperfect and preterite.

III. Use these expressions in original sentences, changing the verbs to any form or tense you wish:

1. tener prisa	5. había	9. a eso de
2. color de rosa	6. a la vez	10. esta noche
3. viva	7. a caballo	11. a medianoche
4. dar la hora	8. hace poco	12. hay que

IV. Translate word for word, then change to everyday English:

1. A mí me gustaría comprarlo. 2. ¿Le gustan a Vd. los cerdos? 3. Me gustó hacer el primero. 4. A los indios les gusta su trabajo. 5. A Lupita le gustan las mariposas. 6. ¿Le gustaría a Vd. vender su perro?

Where is the subject of *gustar* always found, if it is expressed? Is the *a* in sentences 4 and 5 personal?

V. Complete in Spanish:

1. *Indians* hacen muchas cosas bonitas. (*Indians in general!*) 2. *Spaniards* tienen costumbres antiguas. 3. *Pigs* son el emblema de la prosperidad. 4. *Beans* son un plato importante en México. 5. *Bread* es necesario en una comida norteamericana. 6. *Gold* vale más que *silver*. 7. *Milk* es más útil que *eggs*.

What rule governs all these sentences? (Section 106)

VI. In these sentences use the proper forms of the adjectives:

1. El gato y la vaca son *black*. 2. El caballo y el oso son *white*.
3. Mi tía y mi abuela son *old*. 4. La estufa y la cama son *new*. 5. La
mesa y el suelo están *clean*.

VII. Aquí tienen Vds. un juego que usar en la clase.

Play «Fruta, Flor, o Animal» *as you played* «Comida, Color,
o Cuerpo» *in* Chapter 36.

You have had these names of fruits: durazno, piña, plátano,
manzana, higo, mango; *these flowers:* violeta, rosa, flores de
San Juan; *these animals:* oso, perro, gato, vaca, oveja, cerdo,
caballo, mula, burro, camello, ratón, venado.

Here are some new words you may want for the game:

FRUTAS	FLORES	ANIMALES
la **naranja**, orange	el **clavel**, carnation	el **mono**, monkey
el **limón**, lemon	el **pensamiento**, pansy	la **cabra**, goat
la **sandía**, watermelon		el **coyote**, coyote
el **melón**, cantaloupe	el **lirio**, lily	el **elefante**, elephant
la **fresa**, strawberry	el **geráneo**, geranium	la **zorra**, fox
la **pera**, pear	la **gardenia**, gardenia	el **conejo**, rabbit
la **cereza**, cherry	la **margarita**, daisy	la **jirafa**, giraffe
las **uvas**, grapes	la **amapola**, poppy	la **rata**, the rat
la **granada**, pomegranate	el **dompedro**, morning glory	la **llama**, llama
		Miguelito Ratoncito, Mickey Mouse
		Pato Pascual, Donald Duck

VIII. Algo para leer.

¡Qué cosa!

El ilusionista (*magician*) — Como Vds. ven, la señora López ha
desaparecido y se ha convertido en un ramito de flores. ¡Vamos a
ver si la encontramos!

El señor López — ¡Nada, hombre, nada! ¡Ya está bien! Me
llevaré las flores.

PALABRAS PARA HOY

1 el alma (*f.*) — soul
2 el arte (*m.* or *f.*) — art
barato, -a — cheap
el barro — clay
el cerdo — pig
la cinta — ribbon
3 cobrar — to charge
2 conservar — to conserve
dame — give me (fam. command)
3 diario, -a — daily (*diary*)
el dibujo — drawing, design
2 igualito (igual + ito), -a — just alike

la docena — dozen
2 el empleado — employee
el jarro — jug
la loza — pottery
la mariposa — butterfly
los muebles — furniture
4 el orgullo — pride
4 la población — town (*population*)
poquito (poco + ito) — a little
3 satisfecho, -a — satisfied
4 útil — useful (*utility*)
el venado — deer
viva (pol. com. of vivir) — hurrah for, long live

EXPRESIONES

color de rosa, pink
con cariño, lovingly
*en cambio, on the other hand, to the contrary
hacer una pregunta, to ask a question

no cabe duda, there is no doubt
*tener prisa, to be in a hurry
*hace más de cuatrocientos años, more than four hundred years ago

Una vieja costumbre mexicana

Here is a simple but colorful little play to put on for your assembly (12 to 15 minutes) or for any audience that does not necessarily understand Spanish. In it you use five of the songs you learned in this book.

The only new words are translated or can be guessed.

PERSONAS

PANCHO
JUANITO
LUIS
ALBERTO, *who plays the violin*
LORENZO, *who plays the guitar*[2] } «Gallos» *who are out serenading their sweethearts.*[1]
ENRIQUE
MANUEL

EL SERENO, *the Night Watchman*[3]

Before the curtain rises, ALBERTO *steps out in front and addresses the audience in English.*

ALBERTO — We are going to show you an old Mexican custom. Often in Mexico groups of young men start out after midnight with their guitars and violins to serenade their girl friends, going from house to house singing beneath the balconies. To do this in some towns, they must first obtain an official permit from the city hall, for whenever a night watchman finds a group of serenaders, he asks to see this permit.

5

[1] The boys' parts may be taken by girls in appropriate costumes. Although the serenaders would really be dressed like any college boys, it is colorful to use short, fitted, gold-braided jackets, red sashes, flowing neckties and big hats. To complete the *charro* effect, trouser legs should be folded over down the outside and pinned with black safety pins to make them fit tightly.

[2] The guitar player may fake his playing, although a real guitar accompaniment for these simple songs is easy for anyone who does "hillbilly" music. Or a pianist offstage, with sheets of paper laid across the strings of a grand piano, can effectively produce tinkling chords played like a guitar.

[3] The Sereno wears a big hat and long dark cape, and carries an old-fashioned lantern. He is a leisurely, jovial person, and his cry of "Serenooooooo" should run down at the end like a phonograph that needs more winding.

Nowadays *serenos* walk quietly about with their lanterns, not calling out the hour as they used to do; but for the sake of the play we shall follow the old custom.

After the boys have serenaded all their girl friends, they often play and sing in the plaza until dawn, which explains why they are called **gallos,** — *roosters.*

SCENE:

> *The curtain rises on a street scene or bare stage dimly lit by "moonlight." At left, offstage, are heard voices, all talking at once;* [1] *then all seven boys stroll into view.*

PANCHO — Esperen Vds. Aquí está la casa.

JUANITO — Sí, aquí vive Carmen.

LUIS — Es el día de su santo, ¿no?

ALBERTO — Sí, hoy es el día de Carmen.

PANCHO — Vamos a cantarle «Las mañanitas.»

ENRIQUE — Sí, cantémosle [2] «Las mañanitas.» (*All sing.*)

PANCHO — ¡Miren Vds.! Carmen encendió su luz. [3] Nos oyó. ¡Felicidades (*congratulations*), Carmen!

LORENZO — ¡Sí, seguro! ¿Quién no nos ha oído? ¡Con tanto ruido nos han oído todos los vecinos!

ALBERTO — ¿Qué importa?

PANCHO — Todos saben que somos gallos. Todo señor de la población hacía esto cuando joven.

ENRIQUE — ¡Sí, señor!

LUIS — ¡Es costumbre!

ALBERTO — ¿A dónde vamos ahora?

MANUEL — Vamos a casa de Adelita.

PANCHO — Adelita es la novia de Manuel, ¿verdad? (*They move on.*)

JUANITO — Sí. Y vive aquí cerca.

LORENZO — Aquí estamos. ¿Qué vamos a cantar?

---

[1] The whole play should be done quickly as far as the conversation is concerned. If everyone talks at once all the time except when singing, using everyone else's lines as well as his own, so much the better. The players should stroll along in an informal group, even turning their backs on the audience as they chatter, for they are not supposed to be understood.

As they sing, they move around a little, looking up at the imaginary balcony out over the audience which they are serenading.

[2] *cantémosle* (notice *-emos* instead of *-amos*), *let's sing.* The opposite vowel in a first person plural verb often means *let's.*

[3] *Carmen encendió su luz, Carmen turned on her light.* A girl who is awakened by a serenade at 4 A.M. doesn't go out on her balcony, but merely turns on her light for a moment to let the serenaders know that she hears and appreciates the music.

MANUEL — A Adelita le gusta «El quelite.»

LUIS — Sí, cantémosle «El quelite» a Adelita.

LORENZO — Esperen Vds. un momentito. Esta maldita (*confounded*) guitarra no está afinada (*in tune*). (*Tries it* 35 *with violin.*) ¡Ah! ¡Ya está! ¿Listos (*ready*)?

ALL — Sí. (*They sing.*)

MANUEL — Creo que Adelita oyó nuestra canción. Encendió su luz.

ENRIQUE — Sí, ¿cómo no? 40

PANCHO — ¿Le cantamos otra?

ENRIQUE — Sí, por supuesto.

ALL —
{ Sí, ¿cómo no?
{ ¡Otra canción para Adelita!
{ ¿Qué cantamos? 45

ALBERTO — Cantemos «Pajarillo barranqueño.»

LORENZO — No, es muy difícil esa canción. No quiero tocarla. No sé tocarla bien.

PANCHO — Sí, la sabe bastante bien. Dos versos solamente. Vamos. 50

LORENZO — Bueno, dos versos, no más, ¿eh? (*All sing.*)

MANUEL — (*Lingering*) ¡Buenas noches, Adelita! ¡Hasta la vista! ¡Qué sueñe[1] Vd. color de rosa!

ALL — ¡Vámonos!

PANCHO — Venga, Manuel. Su Adelita no saldrá. Vámo- 55 nos. (*All move on.*)

LORENZO — ¿A dónde?

PANCHO — A casa de Ramona, por supuesto.

ALL — ¡Sí, a casa de Ramona! ¡Aquí vive! ¡Aquí estamos!

PANCHO — Parece que todos duermen. No hay luz. 60

ENRIQUE — Por supuesto que no.

ALBERTO — ¿Qué cantamos?

LUIS — Cantemos «La rogona.»

PANCHO — No, a Ramona no le gustaría[2] esa canción. Ni a mí tampoco. 65

---

[1] *¡Qué sueñe Vd. color de rosa!* (literally *may you dream rose-colored*), "sweet dreams."

[2] *a Ramona no le gustaría,* *Ramona wouldn't like.*

LORENZO — Bueno, si no les gusta «La rogona,» ¿cantamos «Las gaviotas»?

PANCHO — Sí, le gusta «Las gaviotas.»

ENRIQUE — Bueno.

70 LUIS — ¿Cómo empieza la letra?

JUANITO — «Ya las gaviotas tienden su vuelo —» ¿Recuerda?

LUIS — Sí. Ya recuerdo perfectamente.

ALL — Vamos. (*All start to sing, when* SERENO *enters* 75 *right.*)

SERENO — (*Calling loudly*) ¡Las cuatro en punto y serenooooo!

ALL — ¡Chis! (*Sh!*) ¡El sereno!

SERENO — (*Approaching*) ¡Oigan Vds., señoritos!

80 ALL — ¿Mande Vd.?[1]

SERENO — ¿Tienen Vds. permiso para dar esta serenata?

ALL — Sí, hombre, ¿cómo no?

SERENO — Pues, favor de enseñármelo, ¿eh?

LORENZO — Con todo gusto. Oiga, Pancho, Vd. lo tiene. 85 Déselo al sereno.

PANCHO — Pero yo no lo tengo. Es Vd. que lo tiene.

LORENZO — Yo no.

ALBERTO — ¿No recuerda Vd. que Luis se lo dió?

PANCHO — A mí no.

90 ALBERTO — Sí, a Vd. se lo dió.

JUANITO — Busque[2] Vd. en los bolsillos. (PANCHO *searches in pockets, while everyone looks anxious.*)

LUIS — ¡Busque Vd. en el chaleco (*vest*)!

ENRIQUE — ¡Busque Vd. en el cinto (*belt*)!

95 ALBERTO — ¿No lo tiene Vd. en el bolsillo de la camisa?

PANCHO — (*Taking paper from belt with a sigh of relief*) ¡Ah! ¡Miren Vds.! (*Hands it to* SERENO *with a flourish.*) Aquí lo tiene Vd., señor sereno.

---

[1] *¿Mande Vd.? Command (me)* or *at your service.* This is the polite way to reply when called, especially by an elder or superior.

[2] *Busque Vd.*, polite command from *buscar.* Why must it be spelled with a *qu* instead of a *c*?

SERENO — Ah, sí. Gracias. (*Inspects it carefully by light of lantern.*) Sí, está bien. (*Hands it back with a flourish.*) 100 Dispensen Vds. la molestia (*excuse the annoyance*), pero es necesario. Con permiso. Buenas noches, señores.

PANCHO — Espere Vd. un momentito, señor sereno. ¿No quiere Vd. cantar con nosotros unos versos de «Las gaviotas»?

SERENO — ¿«Las gaviotas»? ¿Saben Vds. «Las gaviotas»? 105 Sí, con mucho gusto. (*All begin over and sing* «Las gaviotas.»)

SERENO — (*As they finish*) ¡Ay, qué rebonita (*very pretty*)!

PANCHO — Buena, ¿eh? Pues hemos dado una serenata a todas nuestras novias. ¿Qué hacemos ahora? 110

JUANITO — ¡Pues no vamos a casa tan temprano! Son solamente las cuatro y media.

LORENZO — ¿Por qué no vamos a la plaza a cantar?

ALL — ¡Sí, vamos a la plaza!

ALBERTO — ¿Qué cantamos por el camino? 115

SERENO — ¿Saben Vds. «La cucaracha»?

ALL — Sí, ¿cómo no?

JUANITO — Todavía no la hemos cantado esta noche.

LORENZO — Ah, sí. Es mi canción favorita. ¡Vámonos!

All start singing «La cucaracha,» *walking slowly offstage, song dying away in distance.* As they finish, SERENO, *following them, cries loudly,* — ¡Las cinco en punto y serenooooo!

CURTAIN

Appendix

Some Interesting Books to Read[1]

I. SPAIN

BAEDEKER, KARL: GUIDE TO SPAIN AND PORTUGAL.   Scribner.

Travel.

Baedeker's guide is the traveler's bible.   This is a reference book which contains information and maps about every nook and corner of Spain.

CALLCOTT, FRANK: WHEN SPAIN WAS YOUNG.   McBride.

Folk legends.

Rodrigo, Bernardo del Carpio, Fernán González, Pelayo, the Seven Lords of Lara are legendary heroes of Spain.   The stories of their lives and exploits are "tall tales" that you will enjoy.

CANFIELD, DOROTHY: BASQUE PEOPLE.   Harcourt, Brace.

Fiction.

The Basques and their customs are described in a series of short stories.

CLARK, SYDNEY A.: SPAIN ON FIFTY DOLLARS.   McBride.

Travel.

Written in an informal way, this is a combination guide and travel book which you will find entertaining.

ELLIS, HAVELOCK: THE SOUL OF SPAIN.   Houghton Mifflin.

Description.

This, one of the best-known books on Spain, is a serious, philosophical study of the Spanish people.

FRANCK, HARRY A.: FOUR MONTHS AFOOT IN SPAIN.   Appleton-Century.

Travel and description.

Mr. Franck tired of teaching school.   He had $172, so he decided to go to Spain.   Naturally he didn't travel in luxury.   That's probably why he saw so much and had so many interesting experiences.   Though Spain has had her terrible Civil War since then, the people have not changed fundamentally and this book will help you to understand them.

GALLOP, RODNEY: A BOOK OF THE BASQUES.   Macmillan.

Description.

Here is a description of the history, language, songs, daily life of those people whose origin still mystifies scholars.

---

[1] You will probably not be able to find all of these books in your library.   A generous list has been provided here so that you may select the titles which you can find conveniently at hand.

GORDON, JAN *and* CORA: TWO VAGABONDS IN SPAIN. McBride.
Travel.

Daily life in little towns, the bull fight, the customs, the people, as well as many other things, are described in an amusing style.

LAUGHLIN, CLARA E.: SO YOU'RE GOING TO SPAIN. Houghton Mifflin.
Travel.

This is a good descriptive guidebook for Spain.

MCBRIDE, ROBERT M.: SPANISH TOWNS AND PEOPLE. McBride.
Travel.

Of course this is Spain before the Civil War. Nevertheless, it is worth reading.

MCNEILL-MOSS, GEOFFREY: SIEGE OF THE ALCÁZAR. Knopf.
Recent history.

Here is a thrilling blow-by-blow account of the siege of the Alcázar (an old Moorish palace) in Toledo, Spain. It happened during the Civil War in 1936.

MERCEIN, ELEANOR: BASQUERIE. Harper.
Fiction.

This is a book about those interesting Basques who live in the Pyrenees, half on the French side, half on the Spanish side.

DE LA MORA, CONSTANCIA: IN PLACE OF SPLENDOR. Harcourt, Brace.
Autobiography and recent history.

Read the exciting story of Spain's Civil War (1936–1939) as told by a woman who worked with the Loyalists.

NEWMAN, EDWARD: SEEING SPAIN AND MOROCCO. Funk and Wagnalls.
Description and travel.

If you want information on historic places and cities of Spain, you will find this book helpful.

NEXÖ, MARTIN ANDERSON: DAYS IN THE SUN. Coward-McCann.
Description.

Written before Spain's Civil War and translated from Danish, this is a good description of Spanish towns, people, and customs by an understanding traveler.

PAUL, ELLIOT: THE LIFE AND DEATH OF A SPANISH TOWN. Random House.
Description and recent history.

Santa Eulalia is a small town on an island off the coast of Cataluña in the Mediterranean. The town and its people are described by a man who lived there and became a part of the town. Then comes the war of 1936–1939 and you see what happens to the town and to the people.

PECK, ANNE M., *and* MÉRAS, E. A.: SPAIN IN EUROPE AND AMERICA. Harper.
History and travel.

Written for young people, this book of description and history is good reading.

PHILLIPS, HENRY ALBERT: MEET THE SPANIARDS. Lippincott.
Travel.

Mr. Phillips describes the people and their everyday life so that you really "meet the people."

SEDGWICK, HENRY: SPAIN, A SHORT HISTORY. Little, Brown.
History.

Here history is given as the story of people, not as a series of dates and battles. Art and literature are woven into the story because they are an expression of the people. This is intended to be popular rather than erudite, if you know what that means!

TANNER, LAWLER, *and* RILEY: ADVENTURES IN LANGUAGE. Prentice-Hall.
History of languages.

All language students will enjoy this interesting story of how language in general, and individual languages, developed. It is written in simple, non-technical English, and is easy to read. Chapter 15 tells about the language of Spain.

TAPPAN, EVA: THE STORY OF THE ROMAN PEOPLE. Houghton Mifflin.
History.

The history of the Romans is told in a simple way.

VAN LOON, HENDRIK: VAN LOON'S GEOGRAPHY. Garden City.
Geography and description.

If all geographies were as interesting as this, everyone would read them. Read Chapter 10 on Spain and then you will probably be so interested that you will want to read the rest of the book. Chapters 46 and 47 tell about the New World.

WILBERFORCE, ARCHIBALD: SPAIN AND HER COLONIES (Nations of the World Series). Collier and Son.
History.

This is an old book, but it is brief, accurate, and easy to read. It tells the story of Spain up to the Spanish-American War (1898).

II. SPANISH AMERICA

EMBREE, EDWIN: INDIANS OF THE AMERICAS. Houghton Mifflin.
Indian civilizations.

Here is the story of the Mayas of Central America, the Aztecs of Mexico, and the Inca Empire of Peru. If you are interested in our North American Indians, you will want to read the last part of the book, too, in order to compare their cultures.

FRANCK, HARRY A., *and* LANKS, HERBERT C.: THE PAN-AMERICAN HIGHWAY. Appleton-Century.
Description.

Put this on your "must read" list. Everyone talks about the Pan-American Highway. Here is a book that describes it, with many excellent pictures, from the Río Grande to the Canal Zone. That means you see Mexico and the five Central American countries.

HALLIBURTON, RICHARD: NEW WORLDS TO CONQUER. Bobbs-Merrill.
  Travel.
    Personal adventures and experiences in Mexico, Central America and
  South America are described in popular, fast-moving style.
MAGOFFIN, RALPH VAN DEMAN, *and* DAVIS, EMILY C.: MAGIC SPADES: THE
    ROMANCE OF ARCHEOLOGY. Henry Holt.
  Indian civilizations.
    There are interesting chapters on the Mayas of Mexico and Central
  America and on the Incas of Peru, written in a style anyone can enjoy.
PEART, BARBARA: TÍA BARBARITA. Houghton Mifflin.
  Autobiography and description.
    An English woman tells the story of her life in South America and in
  Mexico.
RICHMAN, IRVING B.: THE SPANISH CONQUERORS. Yale University Press.
  History.
    Here are given the stories of the great explorers: Columbus, Balboa,
  Cortés, Pizarro, Pedro de Alvarado, and others.
SPENCE, LEWIS: THE MYTHS OF MEXICO AND PERU. Crowell.
  Folk legends.

III. MEXICO

BANKS, HELEN WARD: THE STORY OF MEXICO. Stokes.
  History.
    This history of Mexico to the administration of President Calles is not a
  collection of dry facts and dates. Based on Prescott's great work, it is
  accurate and is written for young people to enjoy.
BARRETTO, LARRY: BRIGHT MEXICO. Farrar and Rhinehart.
  Travel.
    Stay at home and see Mexico! Mr. Barretto calls it "bright" Mexico
  because he believes a new Indian culture is coming back and the old
  Spanish culture is fading in the sun of its brilliance.
BIART, LUCIEN: THE AZTECS: THEIR HISTORY, MANNERS, CUSTOMS. McClurg.
  Indian civilization.
BLOM, FRANS: THE CONQUEST OF YUCATÁN. Houghton Mifflin.
  History and Indian civilizations.
    What we know of the ancient life, customs, religion of the Indians before
  the coming of the Spaniards as well as the story of the conquest in Yucatán
  (southeastern Mexico) is told in an interesting way.
BOWMAN, HEATH, *and* DICKINSON, STERLING: MEXICAN ODYSSEY. Willett,
    Clark and Co.
  Travel.
    If you like to be amused, take a trip to Mexico with these two young
  men and "Daisy." You will have to read the book to appreciate "Daisy."

BURBANK, ADDISON: MEXICAN FRIEZE. Coward-McCann.
Travel.

The author, an artist, takes trips by horse, mule, and foot into remote regions. He is particularly interested in the people and their customs and dress. He describes his experiences and what he saw in an entertaining way.

CARR, HARRY: OLD MOTHER MEXICO. Houghton Mifflin.
Travel.

A California newspaper man visits Mexico and its West Coast. He sees Mexico, New Spain as it was called in Spanish days, as the "mother" of California.

CHASE, STUART: MEXICO. Macmillan.
Description.

This is probably one of the best-known books on Mexico. History, customs, the people, problems of daily life — all these are included. Meet our neighbors and try to understand them with Mr. Chase.

DOBIE, J. FRANK: TONGUES OF THE MONTE. Doubleday, Doran.
Folklore.

Here is a book of Mexican folk stories and superstitions which you will enjoy reading.

FERGUSSON, ERNA: FIESTA IN MEXICO. Knopf.
Description.

Begin with Chapter II and see the fiestas and dances of Mexico. You will see the Dance of the Moors and the Christians, the Indian dance of *Los Voladores*, and all the other interesting events that many tourists never see.

FRANCK, HARRY A.: TRAILING CORTÉZ THROUGH MEXICO. Stokes.
Travel.

In the twentieth century the author sets out to trace and follow the route Cortés took in his conquest of Mexico in the sixteenth century.

GARNER, BESS ADAMS: MEXICO: NOTES IN THE MARGIN. Houghton Mifflin.
Travel.

In a charming and entertaining manner Mrs. Garner describes her experiences in Mexico.

HASBROUCK, LOUISE S.: MEXICO. Appleton-Century.
History.

The history of Mexico from Cortés to Carranza furnishes the subject matter for this book. Written especially for young people, it is easy to read.

HOLMES, BURTON, *ed.*: MEXICO. Wheeler Publishing Co.
Description.

Don't miss this picture-book. It really is almost a picture-book because over half the pages are filled with excellent pictures. Holidays, legends, historic places, food, dress, homes, farm life, and so forth are described and illustrated. The book lives up to its aim of helping to promote international understanding.

JACKSON, J. H.: MEXICAN INTERLUDE.   Macmillan.
Travel.
You will find this book easy to read and entertaining.

JANVIER, THOMAS A.: LEGENDS OF THE CITY OF MEXICO.   Harper.
Folklore.
This is a collection of popular Mexican folk legends such as the Obedient Dead Nun, La Llorona, Accursed Bell, Casa de la Cruz Verde.   All are well told.

KING, ROSA E.: TEMPEST OVER MEXICO.   Little, Brown.
Description and recent history.
As a young woman Mrs. King went to Mexico and settled in Cuernavaca where she established the Bella Vista Hotel.   She tells of her personal experiences during the Revolution which followed the overthrow of President Díaz.   Her story is vividly told.

MOATS, LEONE: THUNDER IN THEIR VEINS.   Century.
Recent history.
When she was a bride of nineteen, Mrs. Moats went to Mexico.   Her experiences form an interesting narrative of life in the days of President Díaz.

MORRIS, ANN AXTELL: DIGGING IN YUCATÁN.   Doubleday, Doran.
Description and Indian civilizations.
An archeologist tells the story of her work in Yucatán in Mexico.   You will find her story easy to read.

O'BRIEN, HOWARD VINCENT: NOTES FOR A BOOK ABOUT MEXICO.   Willett, Clark and Co.
Travel.
The notes from a newspaper column written by an American journalist during a trip to Mexico have been published in book form.

OGLESBY, CATHARINE: MODERN PRIMITIVE ARTS.   Whittlesey House.
Indian arts.
Pages 122–174 describe the arts and crafts of Mexico.   If you are interested in native arts, you will want to read the part describing the Indians of our American Southwest.

PECK, ANNE MERRIMAN: YOUNG MEXICO.   McBride.
Description.
This is not the usual type of description.   It describes Mexico entirely from the standpoint of boys and girls — their holidays, school life, daily life, surroundings, amusements.   You will enjoy it and find that you can read it very rapidly.

PHILLIPS, HENRY ALBERT: NEW DESIGNS FOR OLD MEXICO.   McBride.
Description.
History, economic conditions, handicrafts, picturesque sights, people are described in an interesting way.

PRESCOTT, WILLIAM H.: THE CONQUEST OF MEXICO.   Doubleday, Doran.
History.
Written long ago, this book is a classic and is consulted by modern writers and historians.   This edition is a short version telling the story of Cortés and his men.

QUINN, VERNON: BEAUTIFUL MEXICO.   Stokes.
Description and history.
This is a sugar-coated history of Mexico which is easy to read.

RAMSEY, LEONIDAS: TIME OUT FOR ADVENTURE.   Doubleday, Doran.
Description and travel.
Two American business men travel all over Mexico looking for adventure. They find many interesting stories to tell.   The book is well illustrated with photographs and sketches.

RICHARDS, IRMAGARDE, *and* LANDÁZURI, ELENA: CHILDREN OF MEXICO.   Harr Wagner Publishing Co.
History.
History, legends, and stories of pre-Conquest times are written in a very, very simple style.

RUSSEL, PHILLIPS: RED TIGER.   McBride.
Travel and description.
A trip through Yucatán and tropical Mexico is described.   Hunting and fishing trips and an unusual trip across wild country make this book different from the average travel book.

SPINDEN, HERBERT: ANCIENT CIVILIZATIONS OF MEXICO.   American Museum of Natural History.
Indian civilizations.
Dr. Spinden is a world-famous authority in this field.   If you are interested in archeology, don't fail to read this book.   This is a book to read for information, not for entertainment.

SQUIER, EMMA-LINDSAY: GRINGA.   Houghton Mifflin.
Travel and description.
A newspaper woman goes to Mexico.   Her experiences written in a gay, informal way make excellent reading.

TANNENBAUM, FRANK: PEACE BY REVOLUTION.   Columbia University Press.
Recent history and social conditions.
For a serious interpretation of Mexico dealing with religion, political conditions, labor, education, and other problems of daily life, read this book.

TERRY, T. PHILIP: TERRY'S GUIDE TO MEXICO.   T. Philip Terry, Hingham, Mass.
Travel.
All the information needed by the traveler is given in this book.

WALLACE, GENERAL LEW: THE FAIR GOD.   Houghton Mifflin.
Historical fiction.
In a dramatic way, Mr. Wallace, the author of *Ben Hur*, gives us the

story of the Aztecs and the coming of the Spaniards with Cortés, the
"Fair God."

IV. CENTRAL AMERICA AND CUBA

CLARK, SYDNEY A.: CUBAN TAPESTRY.   McBride.
  Travel.
  The central piece in the tapestry may be Havana, but it takes all parts
of the island to complete the design.   Too many tourists see only Havana.
Here is a complete reproduction of the whole cloth.
FERGUSSON, ERNA: GUATEMALA.   Knopf.
  Description and travel.
  Spanish-speaking people say that Miss Fergusson is *muy simpática.*
When you read her book, you will agree.   She studies people, places,
history and tells you about them in an interesting way.
HEWETT, EDGAR L.: ANCIENT LIFE IN MEXICO AND CENTRAL AMERICA.   Bobbs-
    Merrill.
  Indian civilizations.
  In a painless and non-technical way we learn about the Mayas of Central
America.
ROTHERY, AGNES: IMAGES OF EARTH: GUATEMALA.   The Viking Press.
  Description.
  The Tierra Caliente, Tierra Templada, Tierra Fría — the three zones of
Guatemala — are described in an entertaining way.   There is lots of
"human interest" in this book.
VERRILL, A. HYATT: CUBA OF TODAY.   Dodd, Mead.
  Description.
  Here is a successful attempt to give accurate and unbiased information
about the republic and its capital.   History, plant and animal life, sights
of interest to tourists, customs are described.   This is informative and
readable.
WELLS, CARVETH: PANAMEXICO.   McBride.
  Travel and history.
  Panama really receives more attention than does Mexico.   The history
of Panama from the days of the buccaneers to the present, and a description
of modern Panama are given.

V. SOUTH AMERICA

BEMELMANS, LUDWIG: THE DONKEY INSIDE.   The Viking Press.
  Ecuador: Description.
  The author says that this is really a portrait of the entire continent,
but that he has focused on Ecuador because the things peculiar to South
America are more noticeable there than anywhere else since tourists

haven't invaded Ecuador as yet. His observations and experiences make entertaining reading.

BOWMAN, HEATH, *and* DICKINSON, STERLING: WESTWARD FROM RÍO. Willett, Clark and Co.

Travel.

An unusual trip through Brazil, Bolivia, and Peru is described in popular style. Beautiful prints illustrate the journey.

FERGUSSON, ERNA: VENEZUELA. Knopf.

Description and travel.

You probably know very little about Venezuela. Here is a pleasant way to see the country with an excellent and understanding guide.

FLORES, AUGUSTO: MY HIKE: BUENOS AIRES TO NEW YORK. Putnam.

Travel.

A Peruvian Boy Scout who has been attending school in Buenos Aires starts with four companions and two dogs to make the trip on foot to New York. Only Flores succeeds in completing the 10,000-mile journey.

GILL, RICHARD D.: WHITE WATER AND BLACK MAGIC. Henry Holt.

Ecuador: Description.

In an absorbing personal narrative the author describes life on a ranch in Ecuador. An accident paralyzes him. Slowly he learns to use his body again and, after four years, returns to the ranch. From there he goes into the jungle to search for *curare*, a poison made by the Indians, which doctors think has scientific value.

NILES, BLAIR: PERUVIAN PAGEANT. Bobbs-Merrill.

Travel and description.

A novelist flies to Peru and describes for us what she sees and learns about that interesting land.

PECK, ANNE MERRIMAN: ROUNDABOUT SOUTH AMERICA. Harper.

Description.

PECK, ANNIE S.: FLYING OVER SOUTH AMERICA. Houghton Mifflin.

Travel.

A lady mountain climber, after several expeditions to South America, became so interested in the country that she began to write and lecture about it. In 1929 she made the first and longest tour of South America that had then been made in a commercial plane.

ROTHERY, AGNES: SOUTH AMERICA: THE WEST COAST AND THE EAST. Houghton Mifflin.

Description and travel.

ROTHERY, AGNES: SOUTH AMERICAN ROUNDABOUT. Dodd, Mead.

Description.

For an easy-to-read book, try this. Descriptions of various peoples, places, plants, and animals are given.

STRODE, HUDSON: SOUTH BY THUNDERBIRD.   Random House.
Travel and description.
The author tries to help us to understand our neighbors by reporting personal contacts with them.   To be accurate, he wrote down his conversations within twenty-four hours after they occurred.   The Thunderbird, as you can guess, is an airplane.

TSCHIFFELY, AIME FELIZ: TSCHIFFELY'S RIDE.   Grosset and Dunlap.
Travel.
The writer, with two Argentine horses, Mancha and Gato, made the trip from Buenos Aires to New York on horseback.   It took him almost three years to make that 10,000-mile journey.   Boys will be interested in this book.

VON HAGEN, VICTOR WOLFGANG: RICHES IN SOUTH AMERICA.   D. C. Heath.
Description.
Facts and stories are given about some of the products of South America. Coffee, chocolate, tin, Panama hats (that are made in Ecuador!) and balsa wood are described.

VI. SPANISH CULTURE IN THE UNITED STATES

BARTLETT, LANIER *and* VIRGINIA: ADIÓS.   Morrow.
California: Fiction.
Here is a novel with plenty of romance and excitement.   The scene is laid in Southern California; the time is in the 1850's when the Americans were moving in and Spanish and Mexican days were ending.

FERGUSSON, ERNA: OUR SOUTHWEST.   Knopf.
History and description.
Read Chapters 3, 4, 14, 15, 19.   Perhaps you will want to read all of the book, but these chapters concern things and places that have been mentioned in *El Camino Real.*

FITCH, A. H.: JUNÍPERO SERRA.   McClurg.
Biography.
This is the story of the life and work of Father Serra, the founder of the Franciscan missions in California.

JACKSON, HELEN HUNT: RAMONA.   Little, Brown.
California: Fiction.
This love story of the Indian, Alessandro, and the beautiful Spanish girl, Ramona, is well known.   Ramona's birthplace and marriage place are landmarks in Southern California.   An annual pageant is given by the townspeople of Hemet, California, dramatizing this story.

OTERO, NINA: OLD SPAIN IN OUR SOUTHWEST.   Harcourt, Brace.
Fiction and description.
Here are described the stories, songs, customs of New Mexico that have been handed down from Spanish days.   This is very easy to read.

More About Spanish-Speaking Countries

I. IF YOU LIKE MOVIES [1]

The following companies or agencies will sell, rent, or lend films and slides showing Spanish-speaking countries, which you can use in class, assembly, or for your Spanish Club.

De Vry Corporation. 1111 Armitage Ave., Chicago, Ill. Catalogue 25¢.

EDUCATIONAL FILM CATALOG. H. W. Wilson Co. 950 University Ave., New York City.

Metropolitan Motion Picture Council. Room 75, 100 Washington Square, New York City. List 50¢.

U. S. Film Service. Washington, D.C.

Pan-American Union. Division of Intellectual Cooperation. Washington, D.C.

Bell and Howell Co. 1801 Larchmont Ave., Chicago, Ill.; 30 Rockefeller Plaza, New York City; 716 N. La Brea Ave., Hollywood, Calif.

Erpi Classroom Films, Inc. Rochester, New York.

Burton Holmes, Inc. 7510 N. Ashland Ave., Chicago, Ill.

Slides and Strip Film

American Museum of Natural History. Educational Dept., 77th and Central Park West, New York City.

Cambosco Scientific Co. Chicago, Ill.

Will H. Dudley. 736 S. Wabash Ave., Chicago, Ill.

Keystone View Co. Educational Dept., Meadville, Pa.

Society for Visual Education. 100 E. Ohio St., Chicago, Ill.

II. IF YOU WANT PICTURES

Acme. 220 E. 42d St., New York City.

International News Service. 235 E. 45th St., New York City.

Wide World. 229 W. 43d St., New York City.

Banks Upshaw & Co. 707 Browder St., Dallas, Texas (post cards).

Sanborn's. Av. Francisco I. Madero, Mexico, D.F. (post cards).

[1] Write the Extension Division or Division of Visual Aids of your state university for catalogues or information regarding nearby sources of films and slides.

III. IF YOU LIKE MUSIC

R.C.A. Manufacturing Co., Camden, New Jersey. Catalogue of DISCOS VICTOR, Catálogo Internacional (phonograph records).

ÁLBUM DE MÚSICA POPULAR MEXICANA. Wagner & Levien, Mexico, D.F.

ÁLBUM POPULAR NO. 2. Repertorio de Música de Angela Peralta, V. Carranza 20, Mexico, D.F.

MOLINA, CARLOS: ALBUM OF SPANISH FAVORITES. Edward B. Marks Music Corporation, New York City.

TOOR, FRANCES: EL CANCIONERO MEXICANO. Manchester 8, Mexico, D.F.

CANTEMOS. Penny Press, 366 Greenwich St., New York City.

HAGUE, E.: FOLKSONGS FROM MEXICO AND SOUTH AMERICA. American Folklore Society, Augustin, Inc., 141 East 29th St., New York City.

IV. IF YOU LIKE TO DANCE

HARRISON, SALOMAY, and GILSTRAP, OPAL: CLAVELITO. Tardy Publishing Co., Dallas, Texas. *Cucaracha* and *Jarabe Tapatío.*

MEXICAN FOLK DANCES (colored folder, 25¢). Banks Upshaw, Dallas, Texas.

JARRETT, EDITH MOORE: SAL Y SABOR DE MÉXICO. Houghton Mifflin Co. *Jarabe Tapatío.*

SHAMBAUGH, MARY EFFIE: FOLK FESTIVALS. A. S. Barnes.

V. IF YOU LIKE TO COOK

SCOTT, NATALIE: YOUR MEXICAN KITCHEN. Putnam.

BUENAS RECETAS, BUENA HARINA, BUENA SALUD. Sperry Flour Co., Los Angeles, Calif. Free pamphlet.

RECETAS CULINARIAS ROYAL. Royal Baking Powder Co., New York City.

VI. IF YOU ARE REALLY GOING TO MEXICO

BRENNER, ANITA: YOUR MEXICAN HOLIDAY. Putnam. Guidebook.

TERRY, PHILIP: GUIDE TO MEXICO. Philip Terry, Hingham, Mass.

Pemex Travel Club, Bucareli 35, Mexico, D.F. Write for free folders.

GRISMER, R. L., and OLMSTED, R. H.: A MÉXICO POR AUTOMÓVIL. Macmillan.

FORRESTER, K. T., and LOLY, K. D.: VAMOS A MÉXICO. Heath.

CONSOLIDATED VISITOR'S GUIDE. Av. 5 de Mayo 11, Mexico, D.F. Free booklet.

VII. IF YOU LIKE TO READ SPANISH

LA LUZ. Banks Upshaw & Co., Dallas, Texas. Periodical for beginners.

EL ECO. The Odyssey Press, New York City. Periodical for beginners.

FORRESTER, K. T., and LOLY, K. D.: VAMOS A MÉXICO.　Heath.
GRISMER, R. L., and OLMSTED, R. H.: A MÉXICO POR AUTOMÓVIL.　Macmillan.
WATSON, J. C., and QUINAMOR, T. E.: SOUTH TO MEXICO.　Holt.

VIII.　IF YOU LIKE TO ACT

BROOMHALL, E.: SPOKEN SPANISH.　Allyn & Bacon.
HENRY, RUTH: PIECECITAS ESPAÑOLAS FÁCILES.　Allyn & Bacon.
HARRISON, SALOMAY, and GILSTRAP, OPAL: CLAVELITO.　Tardy Pub. Co.,
Dallas, Texas.

IX.　IF YOU LIKE TO MAKE THINGS

JARRETT, EDITH MOORE: SAL Y SABOR DE MÉXICO.　Houghton Mifflin.　Directions for making Mexican costumes, etc.

X.　IF YOU WANT CURIOS FROM SPANISH-AMERICAN COUNTRIES

Banks Upshaw & Co., 707 Browder St., Dallas, Tex.　Catalogue of favors,
post cards, maps, figurettes, etc., from Mexico.
Dextre Shop, 1401 Mason St., San Francisco, Calif.　Curios from all Spanish-
speaking countries.
Estrellita Shop, 527 Pacific Ave., San Francisco, Calif.　Curios.

XI.　OTHER THINGS YOU MAY LIKE

JONES, WILLIS KNAPP: CALENDAR OF SPANISH ANNIVERSARIES.　Tardy Pub.
Co., Dallas, Texas.
ESPINOSA, J. M.: ROMPECABEZAS ESPAÑOLES (Crossword Puzzles), Allyn &
Bacon.

Verb Appendix

Note: Only tenses and verbs used in the text are given.

115. Regular Verbs

	FIRST CONJUGATION	SECOND CONJUGATION	THIRD CONJUGATION
INFINITIVE	ganar *to earn*	responder *to answer*	vivir *to live*
GERUND	ganando *earning*	respondiendo *answering*	viviendo *living*
PAST PARTI-CIPLE	ganado *earned*	respondido *answered*	vivido *lived*
PRESENT INDICATIVE	*I earn, am earning, do earn* gano ganas gana ganamos ganáis ganan	*I answer, am answering, do answer* respondo respondes responde respondemos respondéis responden	*I live, am living, do live* vivo vives vive vivimos vivís viven
IMPERFECT INDICATIVE	*I was earning, used to earn, earned* ganaba ganabas ganaba ganábamos ganabais ganaban	*I was answering, used to answer, answered* respondía respondías respondía respondíamos respondíais respondían	*I was living, used to live, lived* vivía vivías vivía vivíamos vivíais vivían
PRETERITE INDICATIVE	*I earned, did earn* gané ganaste ganó ganamos ganasteis ganaron	*I answered, did answer* respondí respondiste respondió respondimos respondisteis respondieron	*I lived, did live* viví viviste vivió vivimos vivisteis vivieron

	FIRST CONJUGATION	SECOND CONJUGATION	THIRD CONJUGATION
FUTURE INDICATIVE	*I shall earn, I will earn* ganaré ganarás ganará ganaremos ganaréis ganarán	*I shall answer, I will answer* responderé responderás responderá responderemos responderéis responderán	*I shall live, I will live* viviré vivirás vivirá viviremos viviréis vivirán
CONDITIONAL INDICATIVE	*I should earn, I would earn* ganaría ganarías ganaría ganaríamos ganaríais ganarían	*I should answer, I would answer* respondería responderías respondería responderíamos responderíais responderían	*I should live, I would live* viviría vivirías viviría viviríamos viviríais vivirían
PRESENT PERFECT INDICATIVE	*I have earned* he ganado has ganado ha ganado hemos ganado habéis ganado han ganado	*I have answered* he respondido has respondido ha respondido hemos respondido habéis respondido han respondido	*I have lived* he vivido has vivido ha vivido hemos vivido habéis vivido han vivido
PLUPERFECT INDICATIVE	*I had earned* había ganado habías ganado había ganado habíamos ganado habíais ganado habían ganado	*I had answered* había respondido habías respondido había respondido habíamos respondido habíais respondido habían respondido	*I had lived* había vivido habías vivido había vivido habíamos vivido habíais vivido habían vivido
FUTURE PERFECT INDICATIVE	*I shall have earned* habré ganado habrás ganado habrá ganado habremos ganado habréis ganado habrán ganado	*I shall have answered* habré respondido habrás respondido habrá respondido habremos respondido habréis respondido habrán respondido	*I shall have lived* habré vivido habrás vivido habrá vivido habremos vivido habréis vivido habrán vivido

	FIRST CONJUGATION	SECOND CONJUGATION	THIRD CONJUGATION
CONDITIONAL PERFECT INDICATIVE	*I should have earned* habría ganado habrías ganado habría ganado habríamos ganado habríais ganado habrían ganado	*I should have answered* habría respondido habrías respondido habría respondido habríamos respondido habríais respondido habrían respondido	*I should have lived* habría vivido habrías vivido habría vivido habríamos vivido habríais vivido habrían vivido
POLITE COMMANDS	*earn!* gane Vd. ganen Vds.	*answer!* responda Vd. respondan Vds.	*live!* viva Vd. vivan Vds.

Irregular Verbs

Note: Only the irregular tenses are given here; tenses not given are regular.

116. andar *to walk*
    PRETERITE: anduve, anduviste, anduvo; anduvimos, anduvisteis, anduvieron

117. caer *to fall*
    GERUND: cayendo
    PAST PARTICIPLE: caído
    PRESENT: caigo, caes, cae; caemos, caéis, caen
    PRETERITE: caí, caíste, cayó; caímos, caísteis, cayeron
    POLITE COMMANDS: caiga Vd., caigan Vds.

118. dar *to give*
    PRESENT: doy, das, da; damos, dais, dan
    PRETERITE: dí, diste, dió; dimos, disteis, dieron
    POLITE COMMANDS: dé Vd., den Vds.

119. decir *to tell, to say*
    GERUND: diciendo
    PAST PARTICIPLE: dicho
    PRESENT: digo, dices, dice; decimos, decís, dicen
    PRETERITE: dije, dijiste, dijo; dijimos, dijisteis, dijeron
    FUTURE: diré, dirás, dirá; diremos, diréis, dirán
    CONDITIONAL: diría, dirías, diría; diríamos, diríais, dirían
    POLITE COMMANDS: diga Vd., digan Vds.

120. estar *to be*
    PRESENT: estoy, estás, está; estamos, estáis, están

PRETERITE: estuve, estuviste, estuvo; estuvimos, estuvisteis, estuvieron
POLITE COMMANDS: esté Vd., estén Vds.

121. haber   *to have* (auxiliary verb)
PRESENT: he, has, ha; hemos, habéis, han
PRETERITE: hube, hubiste, hubo; hubimos, hubisteis, hubieron
FUTURE: habré, habrás, habrá; habremos, habréis, habrán
CONDITIONAL: habría, habrías, habría; habríamos, habríais, habrían

122. hacer   *to do, to make*
PAST PARTICIPLE: hecho
PRESENT: hago, haces, hace; hacemos, hacéis, hacen
PRETERITE: hice, hiciste, hizo; hicimos, hicisteis, hicieron
FUTURE: haré, harás, hará; haremos, haréis, harán
CONDITIONAL: haría, harías, haría; haríamos, haríais, harían
POLITE COMMANDS: haga Vd., hagan Vds.

123. ir   *to go*
GERUND: yendo
PRESENT: voy, vas, va; vamos, vais, van
IMPERFECT: iba, ibas, iba; íbamos, ibais, iban
PRETERITE: fuí, fuiste, fué; fuimos, fuisteis, fueron
POLITE COMMANDS: vaya Vd., vayan Vds.

124. oír   *to hear*
GERUND: oyendo
PAST PARTICIPLE: oído
PRESENT: oigo, oyes, oye; oímos, oís, oyen
PRETERITE: oí, oíste, oyó; oímos, oísteis, oyeron
POLITE COMMANDS: oiga Vd., oigan Vds.

125. poder (ue, u)   *to be able, can*
GERUND: pudiendo
PRESENT: puedo, puedes, puede; podemos, podéis, pueden
PRETERITE: pude, pudiste, pudo; pudimos, pudisteis, pudieron
FUTURE: podré, podrás, podrá; podremos, podréis, podrán
CONDITIONAL: podría, podrías, podría; podríamos, podríais, podrían

126. poner   *to put, to place*
PAST PARTICIPLE: puesto
PRESENT: pongo, pones, pone; ponemos, ponéis, ponen
PRETERITE: puse, pusiste, puso; pusimos, pusisteis, pusieron
FUTURE: pondré, pondrás, pondrá; pondremos, pondréis, pondrán
CONDITIONAL: pondría, pondrías, pondría; pondríamos, pondríais, pondrían
POLITE COMMANDS: ponga Vd., pongan Vds.

127. querer (ie)   *to wish, to want; to love* (with **a**)
PRESENT: quiero, quieres, quiere; queremos, queréis, quieren

PRETERITE: quise, quisiste, quiso; quisimos, quisisteis, quisieron
FUTURE: querré, querrás, querrá; querremos, querréis, querrán
CONDITIONAL: querría, querrías, querría; querríamos, querríais, querrían
POLITE COMMANDS: quiera Vd., quieran Vds.

128. reír (i) *to laugh*
GERUND: riendo
PAST PARTICIPLE: reído
PRESENT: río, ríes, ríe; reímos, reís, ríen
PRETERITE: reí, reíste, rió; reímos, reísteis, rieron
POLITE COMMANDS: ría Vd., rían Vds.

129. saber *to know, to know how to*
PRESENT: sé, sabes, sabe; sabemos, sabéis, saben
PRETERITE: supe, supiste, supo; supimos, supisteis, supieron
FUTURE: sabré, sabras, sabrá; sabremos, sabréis, sabrán
CONDITIONAL: sabría, sabrías, sabría; sabríamos, sabríais, sabrían

130. salir *to leave, to go out*
PRESENT: salgo, sales, sale; salimos, salís, salen
FUTURE: saldré, saldrás, saldrá; saldremos, saldréis, saldrán
CONDITIONAL: saldría, saldrías, saldría; saldríamos, saldríais, saldrían
POLITE COMMANDS: salga Vd., salgan Vds.

131. seguir (i) *to follow, to continue*
GERUND: siguiendo
PRESENT: sigo, sigues, sigue; seguimos, seguís, siguen
PRETERITE: seguí, seguiste, siguió; seguimos, seguisteis, siguieron
POLITE COMMANDS: siga Vd., sigan Vds.

132. ser *to be*
PRESENT: soy, eres, es; somos, sois, son
IMPERFECT: era, eras, era; éramos, erais, eran
PRETERITE: fuí, fuiste, fué; fuimos, fuisteis, fueron
POLITE COMMANDS: sea Vd., sean Vds.

133. tener *to have*
PRESENT: tengo, tienes, tiene; tenemos, tenéis, tienen
PRETERITE: tuve, tuviste, tuvo; tuvimos, tuvisteis, tuvieron
FUTURE: tendré, tendrás, tendrá; tendremos, tendréis, tendrán
CONDITIONAL: tendría, tendrías, tendría; tendríamos, tendríais, tendrían
POLITE COMMANDS: tenga Vd., tengan Vds.

134. traducir *to translate*
PRESENT: traduzco, traduces, traduce; traducimos, traducís, traducen
PRETERITE: traduje, tradujiste, tradujo; tradujimos, tradujisteis, tradujeron
POLITE COMMANDS: traduzca Vd., traduzcan Vds.

135. traer *to bring, to carry*
GERUND: trayendo
PAST PARTICIPLE: traído
PRESENT: traigo, traes, trae; traemos, traéis, traen
PRETERITE: traje, trajiste, trajo; trajimos, trajisteis, trajeron
POLITE COMMANDS: traiga Vd., traigan Vds.

136. venir *to come*
GERUND: viniendo
PRESENT: vengo, vienes, viene; venimos, venís, vienen
PRETERITE: vine, viniste, vino; vinimos, vinisteis, vinieron
FUTURE: vendré, vendrás, vendrá; vendremos, vendréis, vendrán
CONDITIONAL: vendría, vendrías, vendría; vendríamos, vendríais, ven-
  drían
POLITE COMMANDS: venga Vd., vengan Vds.

137. ver *to see*
PAST PARTICIPLE: visto
PRESENT: veo, ves, ve; vemos, veis, ven
IMPERFECT: veía, veías, veía; veíamos, veíais, veían
POLITE COMMANDS: vea Vd., vean Vds.

**138. Radical-Changing Verbs of the First or Second Conjugation with
  o>ue Change**
contar (ue) *to count*
PRESENT: cuento, cuentas. cuenta; contamos, contáis, cuentan
POLITE COMMANDS: cuente Vd., cuenten Vds.

**139. Radical-Changing Verbs of the First or Second Conjugation with
  e>ie Change**
perder (ie) *to lose*
PRESENT: pierdo, pierdes, pierde; perdemos, perdéis, pierden
POLITE COMMANDS: pierda Vd., pierdan Vds.

140. Radical-Changing Verbs of the Third Conjugation with e>i Change
pedir (i) *to ask for*
GERUND: pidiendo
PRESENT: pido, pides, pide; pedimos, pedís, piden
PRETERITE: pedí, pediste, pidió; pedimos, pedisteis, pidieron
POLITE COMMANDS: pida Vd., pidan Vds.

**141. Radical-Changing Verbs of the Third Conjugation with o>ue and o>u
  Changes**
dormir (ue, u) *to sleep*
GERUND: durmiendo
PRESENT: duermo, duermes, duerme; dormimos, dormís, duermen
PRETERITE: dormí, dormiste, durmió; dormimos, dormisteis, durmieron
POLITE COMMANDS: duerma Vd., duerman Vds.

142. Radical-Changing Verbs of the Third Conjugation with e>ie and e>i Changes

sentir (ie, i)   *to feel*
GERUND: sintiendo
PRESENT: siento, sientes, siente; sentimos, sentís, sienten
PRETERITE: sentí, sentiste, sintió; sentimos, sentisteis, sintieron
POLITE COMMANDS: sienta Vd., sientan Vds.

143. Orthographical-Changing Verbs Ending in -gar

pagar   *to pay*
PRETERITE: pagué, pagaste, pagó; pagamos, pagasteis, pagaron
POLITE COMMANDS: pague Vd., paguen Vds.

144. Orthographical-Changing Verbs Ending in -car

tocar   *to play*
PRETERITE: toqué, tocaste, tocó; tocamos, tocasteis, tocaron
POLITE COMMANDS: toque Vd., toquen Vds.

145. Orthographical-Changing Verbs Ending in -ger or -gir

coger   *to take hold of, to pick up*
PRESENT: cojo, coges, coge; cogemos, cogéis, cogen
POLITE COMMANDS: coja Vd., cojan Vds.

146. Orthographical-Changing Verbs Ending in -zar

cruzar   *to cross*
PRETERITE: crucé, cruzaste, cruzó; cruzamos, cruzasteis, cruzaron
POLITE COMMANDS: cruce Vd., crucen Vds.

147. Verbs Ending in -cer or -cir (Inceptive)

conocer   *to know*
PRESENT: conozco, conoces, conoce; conocemos, conocéis, conocen
POLITE COMMANDS: conozca Vd., conozcan Vds.

148. Verbs with Irregular Past Participles

abrir	abierto	morir	muerto
cubrir	cubierto	poner	puesto
decir	dicho	romper	roto
escribir	escrito	ver	visto
hacer	hecho	volver	vuelto

149. Second and Third Conjugation Verbs with the Stem Ending in a Vowel

leer   *to read*
GERUND: leyendo
PAST PARTICIPLE: leído [1]
PRETERITE: leí, leíste,[1] leyó; leímos,[1] leísteis,[1] leyeron

[1] -uir verbs do not need the written accent on this form.

Pronunciation

150. Vowels

Spanish vowels are pronounced clearly and distinctly. They must not be prolonged as in English when we say *go-u* for *go* and *my-e* for *my*.

LETTER	NEAREST ENGLISH EQUIVALENT	SPANISH EXAMPLE	RULE
A	father, ah!	**casa**	Everywhere
E	1. they (but not *they-e*)	**ese**	In open syllables [1]
		cesta	In syllables closed by **m, n, s, x**
	2. let	**lección**	In closed syllables unless closed by **m, n, s, x**
		tierra	Next to trilled **r**
		mejor	Before **j, ge, gi**
		rey	In diphthongs **ei, ey**
I [2]	see	**piso**	
O	1. tone	**todo**	In open syllables [1]
	2. or	**contar**	In closed syllables [1]
		rosa	Next to trilled **r**
		ojo	Before **j, ge, gi**
		hoy	In diphthongs **oi, oy**
U [2]	rule	**puro**	
Y [3]	boy	**doy**	Alone or final

[1] An open syllable is one that ends in a vowel or diphthong; a closed syllable is one that ends in a consonant.

[2] *To the teacher:* The distinction between the two sounds of this letter is slight

151. Semi-Consonants

LETTER	NEAREST ENGLISH EQUIVALENT	SPANISH EXAMPLE	RULE
I	*you*	bien	Preceded by a consonant and followed by a vowel in the same syllable
U	*we*	bueno hueso	u or *hu* before a vowel in the same syllable

152. Diphthongs

I, y used as a vowel, and *u* are weak vowels; *a, e, o* are strong vowels. A diphthong is a combination of (1) a strong and a weak vowel or (2) two weak vowels. They form one syllable which is a combination of the individual sounds.

In a diphthong the strong vowel, regardless of position, or the second of two weak vowels gets the stress. A written accent breaks the diphthong.

Initial *i* and *u* in a diphthong are semi-consonants.

153. Consonants

LETTER	NEAREST ENGLISH EQUIVALENT	SPANISH EXAMPLE	RULE
B V	1. Weaker than in *boy*	¡basta! ¡vamos! un hombre un vaso	When initial or after *m* or *n* in a breath group [1]
	2. None (lips not completely closed)	Cuba uva	All other times
	3. Silent	obscuro substituir	In these and a very few other words

and difficult for English-speaking pupils to master. It is suggested that only the closed sound be taught and imitation of the teacher be relied upon for the acquisition of the open sound.

[3] Y is a semi-consonant, that is, sometimes it is used as a vowel and sometimes as a consonant.

[1] See footnote on page 474.

LETTER	NEAREST ENGLISH EQUIVALENT	SPANISH EXAMPLE	RULE
C, QU	*cat*	cama quema	Takes the place of English **k** **u** is never pronounced after **q**
C(E) C(I) Z	1. *thin* 2. *sin*	veces cinco vez	1. Castilian (*th*) 2. Span. Amer. (*s*)
CH	*church*	techo	Everywhere
D	1. *din* (made against the teeth)	dar	Initial in a breath group [1]
		el día mundo	After *l* or *n* within or between words
	2. None. **d + th** made against the teeth. Somewhat like English *this*	padre	All other times and especially between vowels
	3. None	estado usted	Weak when final or in endings *-ado*, *-ido* (Often omitted in careless speech)
F	*fall*	fama	Like English
G	1. *go*	gana grande	Usually
	2. None	agua hago	Between vowels is pronounced very weakly
G(E) G(I) J	*Hey!*	gente jarro	Like a strong English **h** (Similar to German **ch**)
H	None	hasta ahora	Always silent

[1] We do not talk with single words, but with groups of words between slight pauses. For example, we do not say: The | cow jumped | over | the | moon. We say: The-cow jumped-over the-moon. This grouping of words between slight pauses is called a breath group.

LETTER	NEAREST ENGLISH EQUIVALENT	SPANISH EXAMPLE	RULE
L	*let*	la alto	Tip of tongue to upper gums. Avoid raising back of tongue
LL	1. *William* 2. *you*	silla	1. Castilian (*ly*) 2. Span. Amer. (*y*)
M	*more*	más	Like English
N	1. *more*	invierno	Before *p, b, v, m*
	2. *no*	uno	All other times like Eng.
Ñ	*canyon, onion*	señor	Always
P	1. *push*	palo	Like English but without letting out as much air
	2. *pneumonia*	séptimo septiembre	Silent in a very few words
R	1. None	rosa	When initial it is trilled like *rr* with a rapid vibration of tongue against gums
	2. None	padre	Other times it has a slight trill
RR	None	perro	Trilled (two to five vibrations)
S	1. *rose*	mismo desde asno	Before some consonants such as *m, n, d, g, b, v, l*
	2. *sister*	sala, este	All other times
T	None	tinta patio	Tongue against inside of upper front teeth
X	1. *sir*	explicar	Before a consonant, pronounced *s*
	2. *examine*	examen	Before a vowel, pronounced like Eng. *gs*

LETTER	NEAREST ENGLISH EQUIVALENT	SPANISH EXAMPLE	RULE
Y	*you*	áyer	As a consonant, i.e., not alone or final
K W			Do not appear in Spanish words. Pronounce them as they should be pronounced in the foreign language from which they have been borrowed. Examples: Wáshington, Wágner, kilómetro.

154. Syllabication

The formal rules for syllabication do not always conform to the way Spanish-speaking people actually divide words when speaking. The following are the rules for orthographic syllabication, that is, for the division of words when writing.

1. There are as many syllables as there are vowels and diphthongs in a word.

a ma ri llo   au tor   pa gas teis   ca ca o
1 2   3 4   1 2   1 2 3   1 2 3

2. A single consonant, *ch, ll,* or *rr* between two vowels begins a syllable.

pe-re-zo-so   co-me-dor   si-lla   pi-za-rra   mu-cha-cho

3. Two consonants are divided, one remaining and one going with the following syllable.

en-ten-der

4. A consonant plus *l* or *r* is inseparable (except *rl, sl, tl, sr*).

de-trás   a-pli-ca-do   (at-le-ta)

5. When there are three or more consonants, only the last or an inseparable combination begins a syllable.

sem-brar

6. Prefixes are kept intact regardless of the usual rules.

des-a-pa-re-cer

7. A diphthong is broken by a written accent.

ca-í-do   re-ír

8. Weak vowels (*i*, *u*) followed by another vowel become semi-consonants and lose their syllabic value. To retain it they must have a written accent.

siem-pre   en-tien-de   ha-cia   ha-cí-a

Phonetic syllabication: Within a breath group the final consonant of a word goes with the initial vowel or diphthong of the following word and forms a syllable with it. Prefixes are not kept intact.

de español	*des-pa-ñol*
con alegría	*co-na-le-grí-a*
en un año	*e-nu-na-ño*
mis amigos	*mi-sa-mi-gos*

155. Accentuation

1. Words that end in a vowel or **n** or **s** accent the next to the last syllable.

americ*a*no   extran*j*ero   *j*oven   *co*sas

2. Words that end in a consonant except **n** or **s** accent the last syllable.

gene*ral*   ver*dad*   enten*der*

3. All exceptions have a written accent (').

ú*ltimo   in*glés*   lec*ción

4. The addition of a syllable sometimes causes the insertion or omission of a written accent to preserve the original stress.

lec*ción*, lec*ciones*   joven, jóvenes   dando, dándolo

5. A written accent is used to distinguish words with similar spelling.

el, él; si, sí; se, sé

156. The Alphabet (*El alfabeto*)

SYMBOL	NAME	SYMBOL	NAME
a	a	n	ene
b	be	ñ	eñe
c	ce	o	o
ch	che	p	pe
d	de	q	cu
e	e	r	ere
f	efe	rr	erre
g	ge	s	ese
h	hache	t	te
i	i	u	u
j	jota	v	ve
k	ka	w	ve doble, doble uve
l	ele	x	equis
ll	elle	y	i griega
m	eme	z	zeta

English-Spanish Dictionary

NOTE: The following dictionary contains only those English words used in the completion and translation exercises which do not appear in the vocabulary for the chapters containing the exercises. For numerals, months, and days, see Index.

Numbers following verbs refer to sections in the Appendix where they, or similar verbs, may be found conjugated. Third conjugation radical-changing verbs have their present, preterite, and gerund change indicated: *preferir (ie, i)*.

ABBREVIATIONS

abbr.	abbreviation	indir.	indirect
adj.	adjective	inf.	infinitive
adv.	adverb	m.	masculine
Amer.	American	obj.	object
com.	command	pers.	person
cond.	conditional	pl.	plural
dim.	diminutive	p.p.	past participle
dir.	direct	prep.	preposition
f.	feminine	pres.	present
fam.	familiar	pret.	preterite
fut.	future	pron.	pronoun
ger.	gerund	ref.	referring to
impf.	imperfect	sing.	singular

A

able, to be poder (ue, u) *125*
after después de
again otra vez
  to ... again volver a ...
ago hace
  two hundred years ago hace
    doscientos años
agreeable simpático, -a, agradable
all todo, -a
all right bueno
also también
always siempre

I am soy, estoy
American americano, -a
anachronism el anacronismo
and y, e (*before* i *or* hi)
animal el animal
answer, to contestar
anything (*after a negative*) nada
apple la manzana
are son, están
  you are Vd. es, Vd. está
around alrededor de
arrive, to llegar *143*
Arthur Arturo

artist   el artista

as . . . as   tan . . . como

ashamed, to be   tener vergüenza, avergonzarse (ue)

ask, to   preguntar; to ask for   pedir (i) *140*

   to ask a question   hacer una pregunta

at   a; en

   at home   en casa

   at school   en la escuela

aunt   la tía

await, to   esperar

B

back, in back of   detrás de

bandit   el bandido

basket   la cesta

be, to   ser *132*, estar *120*

   to be . . . years old   tener . . . años

   to be careful   tener cuidado

beans   los frijoles

beautiful   hermoso, -a

because   porque

bedroom   el dormitorio

before   (*prep.*) antes de; (*adv.*) antes

begin (to), to   empezar (ie) (a) *139, 146*

behind, in back of   detrás de

believe, to   creer *149*

beneath   debajo de

bench   el banco

best   el (la, lo) mejor

better   mejor

big   grande

bird   el pájaro

birth   el nacimiento

black   negro, -a

blackboard   la pizarra

blame, to be to   tener la culpa

blouse   la blusa

blue   azul

book   el libro

born, to be   nacer *147*

bother, to   molestar (*used with the pers. as the indir. obj.*)

boy   el muchacho

bread   el pan

breakfast   el desayuno

bring, to   traer *135*

brother   el hermano

but   pero, sino

buy, to   comprar

C

call, to   llamar

can (to be able)   poder (ue, u) *125*

candy   los dulces

capital   la capital

careful!   ¡cuidado!

careful, to be   tener cuidado

carry, to   llevar

cat   el gato

cave   la cueva

center   el centro

Charles   Carlos

chauffeur   el chófer (*Mex.*)

child   el niño

choose, to   escoger *145*

Christmas   la Navidad

church   la iglesia

city   la ciudad

class   la clase

clean   limpio, -a

clean, to   limpiar

climb, to   subir

close, to   cerrar (ie) *139*; **closed**   cerrado, -a

coin   la moneda

come, to   venir *136*

companion   el compañero

continue, to   seguir (i) *131*

country   el país (*nation*); el campo (*opposite of city*)

cousin   el primo, la prima

curious   curioso, -a

custom   la costumbre

   it is not the custom   no es costumbre

D

dance el baile
day el día
die, to morir (ue, u) *141, 148*
difficult difícil
dining room el comedor
dinner la comida
do, to hacer
dog el perro
done hecho (*p.p. of* hacer)
donkey el burro
door la puerta
dress el vestido
dress, to vestirse (i) *140*
drink, to beber

E

ear la oreja
early temprano
earn, to ganar *115*
easy fácil
eat, to comer
egg el huevo, el blanquillo
eight ocho
eleven once
English el inglés; (*adj.*) inglés, inglesa
enter, to entrar (en)
equals son
evening, in the por la noche
everybody, everyone todo el mundo
every day todos los días
exclaim, to exclamar
eye el ojo

F

fall el otoño
fall asleep, to dormirse (ue, u) *141*
family la familia
far from lejos de
fast rápido, -a
fat gordo, -a
father el padre
feed, to dar de comer

fifty cincuenta
five cinco
find, to hallar, encontrar (ue) *138*
first primer (o), -a
flower la flor
fly, to volar (ue) *138*
follow, to seguir (i) *131*
foot el pie
for para
forget, to olvidar
fortunately afortunadamente
friend el amigo
from de; **from . . . to** desde . . . hasta
front of, in delante de
fruit la fruta

G

gardener el jardinero
generally generalmente
get up, to levantarse
girl la muchacha, la niña
give, to dar *118*; (*com.*) dé Vd., den
  Vds.
go, to andar; **to go (in** *or* **to)** ir *123*;
  to go away irse
go to bed, to acostarse (ue) *138*
goes va (*from* ir)
gold el oro
good buen(o), -a
  good morning buenos días
grandmother la abuela
grandson el nieto
great gran, grande
green verde
gypsy el gitano

H

happy alegre; feliz (*used with* ser)
has tiene
hat el sombrero
have, to tener *133*; haber (*auxiliary
  verb*) *121*
have just, to acabar de
have to, to tener que

head   la cabeza
  on his (her) head   a la cabeza
hear, to   oír   *124*
heart   el corazón
hello   hola
help, to   ayudar
her   (*dir. obj. pron.*) la; (*indir. obj. pron.*) le; (*after a prep.*) ella; (*possession*) su, sus; (*possession following a noun*) suyo, -a, -os, -as
here   aquí; acá (*after a verb of motion*)
hers   el suyo, la suya, los suyos, las suyas (*article omitted after* ser)
herself   se
him   le; él (*after a prep.*)
himself   se
his   (*before a noun*) su, sus; (*after a noun or* ser) suyo, -a, -os, -as; (*alone*) el suyo, la suya, los suyos, las suyas
home   la casa
  to go home   ir a casa
  at home   en casa
hope, to   esperar
hot   caliente
  it is hot   (*weather*) hace calor
  to be hot   (*persons*) tener calor
hour   la hora
house   la casa
how?   ¿cómo?
hundred (a) (one)   cien, ciento
hungry, to be   tener hambre
  are hungry   tienen hambre
husband   el esposo

I

the idea! what an idea!   ¡qué cosa!
if   si
ill   enfermo, -a
important   importante
in   en; de (*with the superlative of an adjective*)
indeed; yes, indeed   ya lo creo
independent   independiente

Indian   el indio
industrious   aplicado, -a
inside of   dentro de
intelligent   inteligente
is, he is, she is, it is   es, está
  is it?   ¿es?
it   (*obj. of a verb*) lo, la; (*after a preposition*) él, ella

J

jacket   la chaqueta
Johnny   Juanito

K

kitchen   la cocina
know, to   saber   *129*;   conocer   *147*

L

lack, to   faltar (*used with the pers. as indir. obj.*)
large   grande
last   último, -a
lazy   perezoso, -a
learn (to), to   aprender (a)
leave, to; to go out   salir (de)   *130*
left   izquierdo, -a
  to the left   a la izquierda
less   menos
lesson   la lección
let's, let us   vamos a
  let's go   vamos, vámonos
letter   la carta
lie, falsehood   la mentira
light   la luz (*pl.* luces)
  by the light of   a la luz de
like, to (to please)   gustar (*used with pers. as the indir. obj.*)
little   pequeño, -a
live, to   vivir   *115*
living room   la sala
long   largo, -a
look (at), to   mirar
look for, to   buscar   *144*
lose, to   perder (ie)   *139*
Louise   Luisa

M

make, to hacer *122*
man el hombre
many muchos, -as
Marie María
market el mercado
marry, to casarse (con)
matter, to importar (*used with the pers. as the indir. obj.*)
me me; (*after a prep.*) mí; **with me** conmigo
meal la comida
meet, to encontrar (ue) *138*
Mexican mexicano (*spelled* mejicano *in Spain*)
Mexico México (*spelled* Méjico *in Spain*)
milk la leche
mine el mío, la mía, los míos, las mías (*article omitted after* ser)
minus menos
Miss señorita
mistake el error
money el dinero
month el mes
moon la luna
more más; **more than** más que, más de (*with numbers*)
morning la mañana
most el (la) más
mother la madre
Mrs. señora
much mucho, -a
  very much muchísimo, -a
music la música
must tener que
  I must go tengo que ir
my mi, mis; mío, -a, -os, -as (*after the noun*)

N

named, to be llamarse
  what is your name? ¿cómo se llama Vd.?

near cerca de
necessary necesario, -a
necktie la corbata
nest el nido
never nunca, jamás
new nuevo, -a
news las noticias
newspaper el periódico
nice simpático, -a
niece la sobrina
night la noche
noise el ruido
no one, nobody nadie
none ninguno (ningún), -a
nor ni; **neither ... nor** ni ... ni
not no
nothing nada
nougat el turrón
  nougat vendor el turronero
now ahora

O

o'clock es la —— ; son las ——
  At (two) o'clock a las (dos)
of de
of course por supuesto, ya lo creo
old viejo, -a; (*things*) antiguo, -a; (*people*) anciano, -a
  how old are you? ¿cuántos años tiene Vd.?
old man el viejo; **little old man** el viejecito
older mayor
on en, encima de, sobre
one (*numeral*) un(o), -a
one (*indef. pron.*) uno, se
  one sees se ve
open abierto, -a (*p.p. of* abrir)
open, to abrir
or o, u (*before* o *or* ho)
order to, in para
other, another otro, -a
our nuestro, -a, -os, -as

ours   el nuestro, la nuestra, los
   nuestros, las nuestras
ourselves   nos

P

page   la página
paint, to   pintar
palace   el palacio
parents   los padres
pass, to   pasar
pen   la pluma
pencil   el lápiz (*pl.* los lápices)
people   la gente
piano   el piano
pink   color de rosa
play, to   (*a game*) jugar (ue) a *143*;
   (*an instrument*) tocar *144*
pleasant   simpático, -a
pleasure   el gusto
  with (the greatest of) pleasure   con
   (mucho) gusto
plus   y
poor   pobre
  poor people   los pobres
prefer, to   preferir (ie, i)   *142*
prepare, to   preparar
present, gift   el regalo
pretty   bonito, -a; lindo, -a
pupil   el alumno
put, to   poner *126*; (*com.*) ponga(n)
   Vd(s).
  to put on   ponerse

R

rapidly   rápidamente
read, to   leer *149*
receive, to   recibir
red   rojo, -a
remain, to   quedarse
remember, to   recordar (ue)   *138*
return, to   volver (ue)   *138, 148*
rich   rico, -a
right   derecho, -a
  to the right   a la derecha

road   el camino
rock   la piedra
roof   (*flat*) la azotea
room   el cuarto

S

sad   triste; sadly   tristemente
Saturday   el sábado
say, to   decir (i)   *119, 148*
school   la escuela
  at school   en la escuela
  to go to school   ir a la escuela
second   segundo, -a; (*in dates*) dos
see, to   ver   *137, 148*
seem, to   parecer   *147*
  it seems to me   me parece
seen   visto (*p.p. of* ver)
sell, to   vender
sentence   la frase
serve, to   servir (i)   *140*
set (*table*), to   poner   *126*
seven   siete
she   ella
shoe   el zapato
show, to   enseñar
silver   la plata
sing, to   cantar
sister   la hermana
sit down, to   sentarse (ie)   *139*
sky   el cielo
sleep, to   dormir (ue, u)   *141*
small   pequeño, -a
some   alguno (algún), -a
something   algo
sometimes   algunas veces
son   el hijo
Spain   España
Spaniard   el español
Spanish   el español;   (*adj.*) español,
   española
speak, to   hablar
spring   la primavera
stairway   la escalera
stand up, to   levantarse

Spanish-English Dictionary

Numbers preceding words refer to their frequency in Buchanan's *Graded Spanish Word Book.* Those marked **1** are in the first 189; **2,** 190–500; **3,** 501–1000; **4,** 1000–1500.

Words translated in the reading text or explained in the footnotes are not included in this dictionary unless they are used subsequently.

The article *el* or *la* shows the gender of a noun unless it is an exception or does not take an article. Exceptions are marked *m.* or *f.*

Numbers following verbs refer to sections in the Appendix where they, or similar verbs, may be found conjugated. Third conjugation radical-changing verbs have their present, preterite, and gerund change indicated: *preferir (ie, i).*

A

1   **a**   to, at; (*sign of personal object*)

2   **abandonar**   to abandon, to leave

  el abanico   fan

2   **abierto** (*p.p. of* **abrir**) opened; **abierto, -a** open

  la abreviatura   abbreviation

  abril *m.*   April

2   **abrir** (*p.p.* **abierto**)   to open

3   **absoluto, -a**   absolute

  el abuelo   grandfather; **la abuela** grandmother; **los abuelos** grandparents

1   **acá**   here (*usually with a verb of motion*)

1   **acabar de**   to have just

2   **la acción** (*pl.* **acciones**)   action

4   **el aceite**   oil

3   **aceptar**   to accept

4   **acerca de**   about, concerning

2   **acercarse (a)**   to approach, to draw near (to) *144*

2   **acompañar**   to accompany

  acostarse (ue)   to go to bed, to lie down *138*

3   **acostumbrarse (a)**   to become accustomed to

  el actor   actor

2   **además**   moreover, besides

3   **adiós**   goodby

  el adobe   adobe (*mud brick used by Moors for building construction; now a popular building material in some parts of the U.S.*)

  adoptado, -a   adopted

  adoptar   to adopt

3   **admirarse**   to admire oneself

  adornado, -a   adorned, decorated

  adornar   to adorn, to decorate

  afortunado, -a   lucky, fortunate

  agosto *m.*   August

3   **agradable**   agreeable

2   **el agua** *f.*   water (*used with* **el** *for sound*)

  el aguador   water-carrier

  el aire   air

  el ajo   garlic

1   **al**   to the (**a** + **el**); **al** + *inf.* on, upon

el ala *f.* wing: **de ala ancha** wide-brimmed (*used with* **el** *for sound*)

el albañil mason

Alberto Albert

3 alegre happy, merry

3 la alegría happiness

el alfabeto alphabet

Alfonso Alphonse

Alfredo Alfred

1 algo (*pron.*) something; (*adv.*) somewhat

el alguacil constable

1 alguien someone, somebody

1 alguno (**algún**), -a some

1 el alma *f.* soul (*used with* **el** *for sound*)

la almendra almond

el almendro almond tree

4 alrededor de around

2 alto, -a high, tall

el alumno pupil; **la alumna** pupil *f.*; **los alumnos** pupils *m. and f.*

1 allá there (*usually with a verb of motion*)

1 allí there

4 amable kind

el amanecer dawn

2 amar to love

amarillo, -a yellow

la América del Sur South America

4 americano, -a American

1 el amigo friend; **la amiga** friend *f.*; **los amigos** friends *m. and f.*

1 el amiguito little friend, "pal"

2 el amor love

4 anciano, -a old (*ref. to a person*)

3 ancho, -a wide

el andaluz Andalusian

2 andar to go, to walk *116*

2 anduv- *pret. stem of* **andar**

la anécdota anecdote, story

3 el ángel angel

3 el animal animal

3 anterior before, preceding

1 antes (*adv.*) before, beforehand

1 antes de (*prep.*) before (*ref. to time*)

2 antiguo, -a old (*ref. to a thing*)

2 añadir to add

1 el año year; **el año que viene** next year

4 apagar to extinguish, to put out *143*

el apellido surname, last name

el apetito appetite

1 aplicado, -a industrious

3 aprender to learn; **aprender a** to learn to

1 aquel, aquella (*adj.*) that (*over there*)

1 aquél, aquélla (*pron.*) that (*one*)

1 aquellos, -as (*adj.*) those (*over there*)

1 aquéllos, -as (*pron.*) those

1 aquí here; **por aquí** around here

árabe Arabian; Arabic

3 el árbol tree; **arbolito** little tree; Christmas tree

la aritmética arithmetic

2 el arte (*m. and f.*) art

4 el artículo article

3 el artista artist

artístico, -a artistic

Arturo Arthur

¡arre! get up! (*said to animals*)

3 arreglar to arrange

3 arriba above

3 arrojar to throw; **arrojarse** to throw away

el arroz rice

asado, -a roasted

1 así so, thus

3 asistir (a) to attend

3 el asunto affair, matter

asustado, -a frightened

asustar (se) to frighten, to be frightened

1 aunque although

4 **la ausencia** absence
el automóvil automobile
el avaro miser
la avenida avenue
4 **la aventura** adventure
el aviador aviator
¡ay! oh!; **¡ay! ¡caray!** my goodness!
1 **ayer** yesterday
3 **ayudar** to help
la azotea flat roof
el azteca Aztec (*Indian of Mexico*)
3 **el azúcar** sugar
3 **azul** blue

B

4 **bailar** to dance
4 **el baile** dance
2 **bajar** to descend, to go down
2 **bajo** under, below
4 **el balcón** balcony
el banco bench, bank
4 **la banda** band
la bandera flag
el bandido bandit
la banqueta sidewalk
el baño bath; **cuarto de baño** bathroom
barato, -a cheap, inexpensive
la barbería barber shop
el barbero barber
la barra bar
la barranca ravine
el barro clay
2 **bastante** enough, fairly, quite
2 **beber** to drink
Belén Bethlehem
3 **besar** to kiss
1 **bien** well
el biftec beefsteak
el billete ticket, lottery ticket, bank-note
2 **blanco, -a** white
el blanquillo egg (*Mex.*)

la blusa blouse, shirt
2 **la boca** mouth
la boina beret (*cap worn by men in northern Spain*)
el bolsillo pocket
3 **bondadoso, -a** kind
1 **bonito, -a** pretty; **bonitamente** prettily
bordado, -a embroidered
bordar to embroider
borrar to erase
la botella bottle
4 **brillar** to shine
1 **bueno (buen), -a** good; all right
el burro donkey, burro
2 **buscar** to look for, to seek 144
2 **busqué** *pret. of* buscar

C

el caballo horse; **a caballo** on horseback
2 **la cabeza** head; **a la cabeza** on her (his, etc.) head
1 **cada** each
1 **caer (*p.p.* caído)** to fall 117
3 **el café** coffee; cafe
1 **caigo** *1st pers. sing. pres. of* caer
3 **la caja** box; **cajita** little box
el calendario calendar
caliente hot; **calientito** warm
calmar to calm
la calle street; **calle arriba** up the street
2 **la cama** bed
3 **el cambio** change; **en cambio** on the other hand, on the contrary
el camello camel
1 **el camino** road; **camino real** royal road, king's highway
la camisa shirt
el campesino farmer, country person
2 **el campo** country, field
el canal canal
la canción song

3 **cansado, -a** tired
   cansarse to grow weary
2 **cantar** to sing
4 **el canto** song; singing
   la caña sugarcane
3 **la capital** capital (*of a country*)
4 **el capítulo** chapter
2 **la cara** face
   caracoles snails; (*exclamation*)
     Dear me!
   caray: ¡ay! ¡caray! my goodness!
4 **la cárcel** prison
3 **el cariño** affection; **con cariño**
     lovingly, affectionately
   Carlos Charles, Carl
   carmín carmine
   la carne meat
   el carnicero butcher
2 **la carta** letter
   el cartero postman, mailman
4 **el carro** car
1 **la casa** house, home; **a casa** home
     (*used with verb of motion*); **de
     casa en casa** from house to
     house; **en casa** at home; **en
     casa de** at the home of
2 **casarse (con)** to marry
   el cascarón *decorated eggshell filled
     with confetti (Mex.)*
2 **casi** almost
4 **castigar** to punish *143*
4 **castigué** *1st pers. sing. pret. of*
     castigar
   Catalina Catherine
   la catedral cathedral
   católico, -a catholic
1 **cayendo** (*ger. of* caer) falling
1 **cayó** *3rd pers. sing. pret. of* **caer**
   la cebolla onion
   la celebración celebration
3 **celebrar** to celebrate
4 **célebre** celebrated, famous
   la cena supper
   cenar to eat supper

   el centavo cent; **ni un centavito**
     "not a red cent"
3 **el centro** center
2 **cerca de** near, near to
   el cerdo pig; **cerdito** little pig
   el cereal cereal
   la ceremonia ceremony
   cero zero
2 **cerrar (ie)** to close, shut; **cerrar
     con llave** to lock *139*
   la cesta basket
2 **el cielo** sky, heaven
1 **ciento (cien)** one hundred, a
     hundred
1 **cierto, -a** certain, a certain
1 **cinco** five
1 **cincuenta** fifty
   el cine "movies"
   la cinta ribbon
1 **la ciudad** city
2 **claro, -a** light
3 **la clase** class, kind; **a la clase** to
     class
   el cliente client
3 **cobrar** to charge
4 **cocido, -a** boiled, cooked
   la cocina kitchen
   la cocinera cook
2 **coger** to take hold of, to pick, to
     pick up *145*
2 **cojo** *1st pers. sing. pres. of* **coger**
3 **colgar (ue)** to hang *143*
3 **colgué** *1st pers. sing. pret. of*
     colgar
2 **el color** color
   color de rosa rose-colored, pink
   de colores colored
   ¿de qué color es? what color
     is it, what color is ——?
   el combate battle
4 **la comedia** comedy
   el comedor dining room
2 **comer** to eat; **comerse** to eat all
   la comida dinner, meal; food

1 **como** like, as

1 **¿cómo?** how?; **¿cómo no?** why not?

2 **el compañero** companion

4 **complacer** to please *147*

2 **completo, -a** complete, finished

3 **componer** (*p.p.* **compuesto**) to fix, to repair *126*

el **comprador** buyer

comprar to buy; **estar de compras** to be shopping; **ir de compras** to go shopping

3 **compuesto** (*p.p. of* **componer**) fixed, repaired

1 **con** with

3 **concluir** to finish *149*

3 **concluyendo** *ger. of* **concluir**

3 **concluyó** *3rd pers. sing. pret. of* **concluir**

4 el **conde** count; la **condesa** countess

condensado, -a condensed

confiscar to confiscate

1 **conmigo** with me

1 **conocer** to know, to be acquainted with; to meet (*when used in pret.*) *147*

1 **conozco** *1st pers. sing. pres. of* **conocer**

el **conquistador** conqueror

2 **conservar** to conserve

3 **consistir (en)** to consist (of)

la **consternación** consternation

4 **construir** to construct, build *149*

4 **construyendo** *ger. of* **construir**

4 **construyó** *3rd pers. sing. pret. of* **construir**

2 **contar (ue)** to count, to tell, to relate *138*

3 **contener** to contain *133*

3 **contento, -a** pleased, satisfied, contented; **estar muy contento (-a) de** to be very happy to

2 **contestar** to answer

1 **contigo** with thee, with you (*fam. sing.*)

el **continente** continent

3 **continuar** to continue

2 **contra** against

2 el **contrario: al contrario** on the contrary

el **contraste** contrast

el **convidado** guest

1 el **corazón** heart

la **corbata** necktie

cortés (*pl.* **corteses**) polite, courteous

la **cortesía** courtesy

cortésmente courteously

3 **corto, -a** short

correctamente correctly

el **corredor** corridor

2 **correr** to run

3 **corriente** running

1 la **cosa** thing; **¡qué cosa!** the idea!

coser to sew

1 la **cosita** little thing

3 **costar (ue)** to cost *138*

3 la **costumbre** custom; **no es costumbre** it isn't done

3 **crecer** to grow *147*

1 **creer** (*p.p.* **creído**) to believe *149*

1 **creyendo** *ger. of* **creer**

1 **creyó** *3rd pers. sing. pret. of* **creer**

2 el **criado** servant; la **criada** maid

3 el **cristiano, -a** Christian

4 la **cruz** (*pl.* **cruces**) cross

3 el **cuadro** picture

1 **¿cuál? ¿cuáles?** which (one)? what?

1 el **cual** which, who

1 **cualquier** any

1 **cuando** when; **¿cuándo?** when? **cuando niño** when a boy (child) **de vez en cuando** from time to time

1 ¿cuánto, -a? how much?

1 ¡cuánto! how! how much!; **en cuanto a** as for, concerning

1 ¿cuántos, -as? how many?

1 cuarenta forty

1 cuarto, -a fourth

2 el cuarto room, quarter

el cuate "pal" (*Mex. slang*)

1 cuatro four

1 cuatrocientos, -as four hundred

2 cubierto (*p.p. of* cubrir) covered

2 cubrir (*p.p.* **cubierto**) to cover *148*

el cuchillo knife

3 el cuello neck, collar

4 el cuento story, tale

2 el cuerpo body

3 la cuestión (*pl.* **cuestiones**) question

la cueva cave

2 el cuidado care; ¡cuidado! careful! Be careful!

cuidadosamente carefully

3 cuidar to take care of

el cumpleaños (*pl.* **los cumpleaños**) birthday

2 cumplir (con) to fulfill, keep

4 la curiosidad curiosity; curio

4 curioso, -a curious; curiosamente curiously

CH

la chaqueta jacket

el charro *name given to Mexican horsemen or to their elaborate gold-braided costume*

Chavela Betty (*nickname for Isabel*)

el chicle chewing gum

chico, -a little, little boy (girl), young fellow

la china Chinese girl; *name given to anyone wearing women's colonial fiesta costume (Mexico)*

el chiste joke

el chófer chauffeur (*word borrowed from French through English*)

el chorizo sausage

D

dame give me (*fam. com. of* **dar**)

la danza dance

1 dar to give *118*

dar a to face

dar de comer to feed

dar la hora to strike the hour

dar la lección to recite the lesson

dar las gracias a to thank

dar muchas vueltas to turn many times

1 de of, from, about

1 dé (*com. of* **dar**) give; **déme** give me; **déle** give him (her)

3 debajo de under, beneath, below

1 deber ought to, must

3 decidir to decide

1 décimo, -a tenth

1 decir (i) to say, to tell *119*

decir flores a to compliment, to make love to

decir la buenaventura to tell one's fortune

1 dejar to let, to allow, to leave; dejar caer to drop

dejar de to leave off, to stop

1 del (de + el) of the

2 delante de in front of, before (*place*)

2 los demás the rest

3 demasiado too much, too

el dentista dentist

1 dentro de in, within, inside (*of*); dentro de poco in a short time

derecho, -a right: a la derecha to the right

desagradable disagreeable

3 desaparecer to disappear *147*

desayunarse to eat breakfast

el **desayuno** breakfast

4 **describir** (*p.p.* **descrito**) to describe *148*

4 **descrito** (*p.p. of* **describir**) described

2 **descubierto** (*p.p. of* **descubrir**) discovered

2 **descubrir** (*p.p.* **descubierto**) to discover

1 **desde** from, since; **desde niño** since a child

2 **desear** to desire, to wish

4 **desesperado, -a** desperate

4 **desierto, -a** deserted

4 el **desierto** desert

despacio slowly

3 **despedirse (de) (i)** to say good-by (*to*), to take leave (*of*) *140*

2 **despertarse (ie)** to awake *139*

1 **después** then, afterwards, next

1 **después de** after

2 **detener** to stop *133*

3 **detrás de** in back of, behind

1 **dí** *1st pers. sing. pret. of* **dar**

1 el **día** *m.* day

al día siguiente the following day

buenos días good morning, good day

de día by day, in the daytime

días de fiesta holidays

todos los días every day

el **dialoguito** little dialogue

3 **diario, -a** daily

el **dibujo** drawing, design, picture

1 **dice** (*3rd pers. sing. pres. of* **decir**) he (she) says, tells

diciembre *m.* December

1 **diciendo** (*ger. of* **decir**) saying, telling

1 **dicho** (*p.p. of* **decir**) said, told

3 el **diente** tooth

la **dieta** diet

1 **diez** ten

1 **diez y nueve** nineteen

1 **diez y ocho** eighteen

1 **diez y seis** sixteen

1 **diez y siete** seventeen

3 **diferente** different, various

3 **difícil** difficult, hard

4 la **dificultad** difficulty

1 **diga** *com. of* **decir**; **dígame Vd.** tell me; **dígale Vd.** tell him

1 **digo** *1st pers. sing. pres. of* **decir**

1 **dij-** *pret. stem of* **decir**

2 el **dinero** money

1 el **dios** god; **la diosa** goddess; **Dios** God

1 **diré** *fut. of* **decir**

el **director** director

1 **diría** *cond. of* **decir**

3 la **distancia** distance

el **distrito** district

la **diversión** diversion

4 **divertirse (ie, i)** to enjoy oneself *142*

3 **dividir** to divide

3 **divinamente** divinely

4 **divirtiéndose** *ger. of* **divertirse**

1 **doce** twelve

la **docena** dozen

el **documento** document

el **dólar** dollar (*Amer.*)

2 el **dolor** sorrow, pain; **dolor de estómago** stomach ache

Dolores girl's name

el **domingo** Sunday, on Sunday

Domingo (*boy's name*) Dominick

don (*abbr.* **D.**) *title used before a gentleman's Christian name*

1 **donde** where

1 **¿dónde?** where?;

¿a dónde? where, to where

¿de dónde? where, from where

¿en dónde? where, in where

¿por dónde? where, through where

doña (*abbr.* **Da.**) *title used before a lady's Christian name*

dormir (ue, u) to sleep; dormirse
to fall asleep, to go to sleep *141*
el dormitorio bedroom
1 dos two; los dos both
1 doscientos, -as two hundred
2 la duda: no cabe duda there is no
doubt; sin duda doubtless,
without doubt
la dueña chaperone
2 el dueño owner, master
2 dulce sweet
2 los dulces candy, sweets
2 durante during
3 durar to last
el durazno peach
durmiendo *ger. of* dormir
2 el duro dollar (*Spanish*)

E

1 e and (*used instead of* y *before a
word beginning with* i *or* hi)
2 echar to pour; echarse to
throw oneself
2 la edad age
4 el edificio building
Eduardo Edward
¿eh? used like ¿verdad?
2 ejemplo: por ejemplo for example
1 el the (*m.*)
1 él he; him, it (*after a prep.*)
eléctrico, -a electric
elegante elegant
1 ella she; her, it (*after a prep.*)
1 ellos, ellas they; them (*after a
prep.*)
embargo: sin embargo
nevertheless, however
el emblema emblem
2 empecé *pret. of* empezar
2 empezar (ie) to begin *146*
el empleado employee
2 emplear to employ, to use
1 en in, into, on
3 encantado, -a haunted

3 el encanto charm, enchantment
3 encender (ie) to light *139*
3 encima de on, upon
2 encontrar (ue) to meet, encounter
138
enero *m.* January
enfadarse to become angry
3 enfermo, -a sick, ill
3 enorme enormous
Enrique Henry
la ensalada salad
3 enseñar to show, to teach
1 entender (ie) to understand *139*
2 entero, -a whole
enterrar (ie) to bury *139*
1 entonces then
3 la entrada entrance
1 entrar (en) to enter, come in, go
in
1 entre among, between
3 envuelto, -a wrapped
1 era *impf. of* ser
1 eres (*2nd pers. sing. pres. of* ser)
thou art, you are (*fam. sing.*)
3 el error error, mistake
1 es (*3rd pers. sing. pres. of* ser) he,
she, or it is; Vd. es you are; es
que the fact (idea) is that
la escalera stairway
3 escapar to escape
2 la escena stage, scene
3 escoger to choose *145*
3 escojo *1st pers. sing. pres. of*
escoger
3 esconder to hide
el escondite hide-and-seek
la escopeta gun
el escribiente scribe, clerk
escribir (*p.p.* escrito) to write
148
escrito (*p.p. of* escribir) written
2 escuchar to listen
3 la escuela school; a la escuela to
school

1 **ese, -a** (*adj.*) that (*near the person addressed*)

1 **ése, -a** (*pron.*) that (one) (*near the person addressed*)

1 **eso** that (*ref. to an idea or statement*)

   a eso de at about (*used only in telling time*)

   por eso therefore

España Spain

1 **español, -a** Spanish

   el español Spanish (*language*), Spaniard

   la española Spanish woman

   la clase de español Spanish class

3 **especial** special

3 **especialmente** especially

4 **el espejo** mirror

1 **esperar** to wait

2 **el espíritu** spirit

   espléndido, -a splendid

2 **el esposo** husband; **la esposa** wife

1 **está** *3rd pers. sing. pres. of* **estar**

3 **establecer** to establish *147*

   el establecimiento establishment

   la estación season; station

   los **Estados Unidos del Norte** (*abbr.* **E.U.A.** *or* **E.E.U.U.**) the United States

1 **estar** to be *120*

   la estatua statue

1 **este, -a** (*adj.*) this

1 **éste, -a** (*pron.*) this (one); the latter

1 **esto** this (*ref. to an idea or statement*)

1 **estos, -as** (*adj.*) these

1 **éstos, -as** (*pron.*) these

1 **estoy** *1st pers. sing. pres. of* **estar**

3 **estrecho, -a** narrow

2 **la estrella** star

3 **estudiar** to study

3 **el estudio** study

   la estufa stove

1 **estuv-** *pret. stem of* **estar**

   E.U.A. (*abbr.*) **Estados Unidos de América**

   europeo, -a European; **a la europea** European style

   la evidencia evidence

   evidente evident; **evidentemente** evidently

4 **exactamente** exactly

   el examen examination

3 **exclamar** to exclaim

2 **existir** to exist

3 **explicar** to explain *144*

3 **expliqué** *1st pers. sing. pret. of* **explicar**

3 **el extranjero** stranger, foreigner

   extravagante extravagant

F

   la fábrica factory

3 **fácil** (*pl.* **fáciles**) easy; **fácilmente** easily

4 **la falda** skirt

2 **la falta: sin falta** without fail

4 **faltar** to lack

2 **la familia** family

3 **famoso, -a** famous

2 **el favor** favor

   favor que Vd. me hace you flatter me

   favor de please (*followed by an inf.*)

   hágame el favor de please (*followed by an infinitive*)

   por favor please (*following a command*)

   favorito, -a favorite

   febrero *m.* February

   la fecha: ¿Cuál es la fecha? What is the date?

   Felipe Philip

2 **feliz** (*pl.* **felices**) happy; **felizmente** happily

3   feo, -a   ugly
3   fiel   faithful
3   la fiesta   celebration, holiday
2   la figura   figure; **figurillas** little
      figures
1   el fin   end;   **al fin**   finally, at last
4   fingir   to pretend   *145*
4   finjo   *1st pers. sing. pres. of* **fingir**
3   fino, -a   fine
2   la flor   flower
    el forastero   stranger
    Fordecito   Mexican popular name
      for a Ford
    fragante   fragrant
4   francamente   frankly
2   francés, -a   (*pl.* **franceses, -as**)
      French; **el francés**   French
      (*language*), Frenchman
3   fresco, -a   fresh
    los frijoles   beans
3   la fruta   fruit
1   fué   *3rd pers. sing. pret. of* ser *or* ir
3   la fuente   fountain
2   fuera de   outside of
1   fueron   *3rd pers. pl. pret. of* ser *or* ir
1   fuí   *1st pers. sing. pret. of* ser *or* ir
1   fuimos   *1st pers. pl. pret. of* ser *or*
      ir
    Fulano, -a: Fulano de Tal   So and
      So

G

    la galería   gallery, porch
    la gallina   hen
    el gallo   cock, rooster; **Misa del
      Gallo**   Christmas Eve Mass
2   ganar   to earn, win; **ganar la
      vida**   to earn a living
4   gastar   to spend
    el gato   cat
2   generalmente   generally
2   la gente   people
    la geografía   geography
4   el gitano, la gitana   gypsy

3   el golpe   blow, knock
    gordo, -a   fat, big (*prize*)
2   la gracia   grace
2   las gracias   thanks
    dar las gracias a   to thank
    gracias   thank you
    mil gracias   thanks a thousand
      times, a thousand thanks
    muchas gracias   thank you
      very much, many thanks
1   grande (gran)   big, large;
    grandísimo, -a   very big
    gratis   free, gratis
3   gritar   to shout, to cry out
    el Grito de Dolores   shout of Dolores
3   el grupo   group
2   guardar   to keep
    la guitarra   guitar
2   gustar   to be pleasing
    a mí me gustaría   I should like
      (*to*)
    ¿le gustaría a Vd.?   should you
      like to?
2   el gusto   taste, pleasure
    al gusto   to taste, to suit
    con mucho gusto   with the
      greatest of pleasure

H

1   haber   to have (*auxiliary verb*)
      121
1   había   (*inf.* **haber**)   there was,
      there were, there used to be
    el habitante   inhabitant
    hablar   to speak, to talk; **de habla
      española**   Spanish-speaking
1   hacer   to do, to make   *122*
    hace buen tiempo   it is a nice
      day, the weather is nice
    hace calor   it is hot (*ref. to
      weather*)
    hace fresco   it is cool
    hace frío   it is cold (*ref. to
      weather*)

hace mal tiempo   it is bad weather

hace más de setecientos años more than seven hundred years ago

hace (hacía) muchos años many years ago

hace poco a little while ago

hace viento it is windy

hacer el oso to make love to, "to play the bear"

hacer el (un) viaje to make the (a) trip, to take the trip

hacer una pregunta to ask a question

hacerle daño (a) to harm, to injure

hágame el favor de (*followed by an inf.*) please

2 **hacia** towards; **hacia atrás** backward

1 **haga(n) Vd(s).** *com. of* **hacer**

1 **hago** *1st pers. sing. pres. of* **hacer**

2 **hallar** to find

3 **el hambre** *f.* hunger (*used with* **el** *for sound*)

1 **haré** *fut. of* **hacer**

1 **haría** *cond. of* **hacer**

1 **hasta** to, until, even, as far as

hasta la vista until I see you again, good-by

hasta luego until later, good-by

1 **hay** (*inf.* **haber**) there is, there are

hay que one must, it is necessary to

hay sol it is sunny

1 **hecho** (*p.p. of* **hacer**) done, made

hecho a mano hand-made

el helado frozen dessert, ice cream

1 **el hermano** brother; **la hermana** sister; **los hermanos** brothers and sisters

1 **hermoso, -a** beautiful

el héroe hero

1 **hice** *1st pers. sing. pret. of* **hacer**

el higo fig

la higuera fig tree

1 **el hijo** son; **la hija** daughter; **los hijos** sons and daughters, children; **el hijito** little son, sonny

4 **el hilo** thread

2 **la historia** story, history

histórico, -a historic

1 **hizo** *3rd pers. sing. pret. of* **hacer**

3 **la hoja** leaf

1 **el hombre** man

honrado, -a honest

1 **la hora** hour

¿a qué hora? at what time?

es hora de it is time to

¿qué hora es? what time is it?

horrible horrible

el hotel hotel

1 **hoy** today

hoy día nowadays

hoy no not today

el huésped (*paying*) guest

3 **el huevo** egg

2 **humano, -a** human

3 **humilde** humble

¡huy! exclamation of surprise

I

1 **iba** *impf. of* **ir**

2 **la idea** idea

identificarse, to identify oneself

el, la idiota idiot

3 **la iglesia** church

ignorante ignorant

1 **igual** same, equal; **igualitos** just alike

3 **la imaginación** imagination

3 **imaginar** to imagine

4 **imitar** to imitate

impaciente impatient

2 **importa: me importa** it is important to me, it matters to me

3   **importante** important
2   **importar** to matter, be of
       importance
2   **imposible** impossible
     independiente independent
     indicar to indicate
     el indio Indian
4   **el individuo** individual
     industrioso, -a industrious
     Inés Inez
3   **el inglés** (*pl.* **ingleses**) English,
       Englishman; **la inglesa**
       Englishwoman
3   **inglés, inglesa** (*adj.*) English
3   **inmenso, -a** immense
     inteligente intelligent
4   **interesante** interesting
4   **interesar** to interest
3   **interrumpir** to interrupt
     inventar to invent
3   **el invierno** winter
     invisible invisible
     invitar to invite
1   **ir** to go; **irse** to go away, to go
       off *123*
     ir de compras to go shopping
3   **izquierdo, -a** left; **a la izquierda**
       to the left

J

     ¡ja! ¡ja! ha! ha!
1   **jamás** never, ever
     el jarabe tapatío national folk
       dance of Mexico
3   **el jardín** garden
     el jardinero gardener
     la jarra earthen jar
     el jarro jug, jar
     la jaula cage
     Jorge George
1   **el joven** young man; **la joven** young
       woman
1   **joven** (*pl.* **jóvenes**) young
     la joya jewel

     Juan John; **Juanito** Johnny
4   **el juego** game
     el jueves Thursday, on Thursday
       (*pl.* **los jueves**)
4   **el juez** (*pl.* **jueces**) judge
3   **jugar (ue) (al, a la)** to play (*a
       game*) *138, 143*
3   **jugué** *1st pers. sing. pret. of* **jugar**
     el juguete toy, plaything
     julio *m.* July
     junio *m.* June
2   **juntos, -as** together

K

     el kilogramo 2⅕ lb.; *usually called*
       «**kilo**»

L

1   **la, las** the (*f.*)
1   **la** her, you, it (*f.*) (*dir. obj.*)
2   **el lado: al lado de** beside, at the
       side of
4   **el ladrón** thief, robber
     el lamento complaint, lament
     el lápiz (*pl.* **lápices**) pencil
2   **largo, -a** long
1   **las** them, you (*pl.*) (*dir. obj.*)
4   **lástima: ¡qué lástima!** what a
       pity! that's too bad!
4   **lavar** to wash
1   **le** him, you (*dir. obj.*); him, her,
       you; to him, to her, to you
       (*indir. obj.*)
     la lección (*pl.* **lecciones**) lesson
     la leche milk
     la lechuga lettuce
2   **leer** (*p.p.* **leído**) to read *149*
     la legumbre vegetable
2   **lejos** far
     lejos de far from
2   **la lengua** language, tongue
     el león (*pl.* **leones**) lion
1   **les** them, you; to them, to you
       (*indir. obj.*)

2 **la letra** letter (*of the alphabet*)
el letrero sign
1 **levantarse** to rise, to stand up
2 **leyendo** *ger. of* **leer**
2 **libre** free
1 **el libro** book
la limonada lemonade
limpiar to clean
2 **limpio, -a** clean
4 **lindo, -a** pretty
3 **la línea** line
la linterna lantern
la lista list
la literatura literature
1 **lo** it (*m.*) (*dir. obj.*); **lo que** that which, what
2 **loco, -a** crazy
Lola, Lolita *nicknames for Dolores*
1 **los** the (*m. pl.*)
1 **los** them, you (*dir. obj.*)
la lotería lottery
la loza pottery
2 **el lugar** place
Luis Louis
4 **la luna** moon; **de luna** moonlight
el lunes Monday, on Monday (*pl.* **los lunes**)
Lupita *nickname for Guadalupe*
2 **la luz** (*pl.* **luces**) light; **a la luz de** by the light of

LL

1 **llamar** to call, to knock
llamarse to be called, named
¿Cómo se llama usted? What is your name?
me llamo my name is
se llama his (her) name is
4 **la llave** key
1 **llegar** (a) to reach, to arrive (*at*) *143*
1 **llegué** *1st pers. sing. pret. of* **llegar**
llenar (de) to fill (*with*)

2 **lleno de** filled with, full of
1 **llevar** to take, to carry, to wear
llevarse to take away
llevar la cara muy triste to have a very sad face
2 **llorar** to cry, to weep
llover (ue) to rain *138*
la lluvia rain

M

la madera wood
1 **la madre** mother
4 **magnífico, -a** magnificent
majestuoso, -a majestic
¡maldita sea! cursed be!
1 **malo (mal), -a** bad, ill
mamá mama; **mamacita** dear mother
2 **mandar** to command, order
manejar to drive
2 **la manera** manner, way; **de la misma manera** in the same way
1 **la mano** hand
la manta blanket
mantener to maintain
la mantequilla butter
la mantilla *lace scarf worn over the head by women of Andalusia*
Manuel boy's name
la manzana apple; city block
1 **la mañana** morning
de la mañana in the morning, A.M.
por la mañana in the morning (*when no definite hour is stated*)
1 **mañana** (*adv.*) tomorrow
4 **la máquina** machine
escribir a máquina to typewrite
la máquina de escribir typewriter
la maquinaria machinery
2 **el mar** *or* **la mar** sea

4 la maravilla marvel
maravilloso, -a marvelous;
maravillosamente marvelously
4 marcar to mark *144*
Margarita Margaret, Marguerite
María, Mariquita Mary, Marie
la mariposa butterfly
el martes Tuesday, on Tuesday (*pl.*
los martes)
marzo *m.* March
1 más more, any more
el (la) más most
más —— que more than
no —— más que only
2 matar to kill
las matemáticas mathematics
mayo *m.* May
1 mayor older; el (la) mayor oldest;
el hijo mayor oldest son
1 me me, to me, myself
mecánico, -a mechanical
la media stocking
4 el médico doctor
2 medio, -a half; a medianoche at
midnight
1 mejor (*adj. or adv.*) better; lo
mejor the best
2 la memoria memory; de memoria
by heart
menor younger; el (la) menor
youngest
1 menos less, minus; al menos at
least
3 la mentira lie
el mercado market
la merienda lunch, "tea"
1 el mes month
2 la mesa table
el metal metal
2 meter (en) to put in
el metro meter
el mexicano (*spelled* mejicano *in
Spain and other Spanish-speaking
countries*) Mexican

México (*spelled* Méjico *in Spain*)
Mexico
1 mi, mis my
1 mí me (*after a prep.*)
3 el miedo fear: tener miedo de to
be afraid of
2 mientras while
el miércoles Wednesday, on
Wednesday (*pl.* los miércoles)
Miguel Michael
1 mil thousand, a thousand, one
thousand
milagroso, -a miraculous
4 el minuto minute
1 mío, -a, -os, -as (*adj.*) mine, my,
of mine
1 el mío, la mía, los míos, las mías
(*pron.*) mine
1 mirar to look, look at, to watch
3 la misa mass (*church service*)
1 mismo, -a same
lo mismo the same
a sí mismo, -a to himself
(herself)
la moda style; de moda stylish
3 moderno, -a modern
4 molestar to bother, annoy
la molestia bother, annoyance
2 el momentito short time
2 el momento moment
la moneda coin
3 la montaña mountain
4 montar to mount
el montón (*pl.* montones) pile
1 morir (ue, u) to die *141*
morisco, -a Moorish
el moro Moor
2 mostrar (ue) to show; mostrarse
to appear
3 el mozo boy (*servant*), waiter
1 el muchacho boy; la muchacha girl;
los muchachos boys and girls
1 mucho, -a much; muchísimo
very much

1   **muchos, -as** many
   los muebles furniture
2   **la muerte** death
1   **muerto** (*p.p. of* **morir**) died; *used with* **haber** *and person as object,* killed
1   **la mujer** woman
   la mula mule
1   **el mundo** world; **todo el mundo** everyone
   la muñeca doll
1   **muriendo** (*ger. of* **morir**) dying
4   **murmurar** to murmur
3   **la música** music
   el músico musician
1   **muy** very

N

2   **nacer** to be born *147*
   el nacimiento birth
1   **nada** nothing; **de nada** you're welcome, don't mention it
1   **nadie** no one, nobody
   la naranja orange
2   **naturalmente** naturally
   la navidad Christmas; **en Navidad** at Christmas
2   **necesario, -a** necessary
2   **necesitar** to need
3   **el negocio** business
   Negrito Blackie
2   **negro, -a** black
1   **ni** nor, not even; **ni ... ni** neither ... nor (*used with* **no** *before the verb*)
   el nieto grandson; **la nieta** granddaughter
1   **ninguno** (**ningún**), **-a** no, none, not any
1   **el niño** child, little boy; **la niña** little girl; **los niños** little children
1   **no** no, not
1   **la noche** night

   de la noche in the evening, at night, P.M.
   de noche at night
   esta noche tonight
   por la noche in the evening (*when no definite time is stated*)
   la Nochebuena Christmas Eve
2   **el nombre** name, noun
4   **norteamericano** North American (*applied to citizens of the U.S.*)
1   **nos** us, to us, ourselves
1   **nosotros, -as** we; us (*obj. of prep.*)
   la nota grade (*school*)
3   **la noticia** news, notice, information
1   **novecientos, -as** nine hundred
1   **noveno, -a** ninth
1   **noventa** ninety
   noviembre *m.* November
4   **el novio, la novia** sweetheart
3   **la nube** cloud
1   **nuestro, -a, -os, -as** (*adj.*) our, ours
1   **el nuestro, la nuestra, los nuestros, las nuestras** (*pron.*) ours
1   **nueve** nine
1   **nuevo, -a** new; **nuevecito** brand-new
2   **el número** number
1   **nunca** never

O

1   **o** or
3   **obedecer** to obey *147*
   obligatorio, -a obligatory
2   **obscuro, -a** dark
4   **obtener** to obtain, to get *133*
4   **obtuv-** *pret. stem of* **obtener**
2   **la ocasión** occasion
1   **octavo, -a** eighth
   octubre *m.* October
4   **la ocupación** occupation
2   **ocupado, -a** busy
2   **ocupar** to occupy

1   ochenta eighty
1   ocho eight
1   ochocientos, -as eight hundred
    la oficina office
2   ofrecer to offer *147*
1   oigo *1st pers. sing. pres. of* oír
1   oír to hear *124*
1   el ojo eye
    la oliva olive
2   olvidar to forget
1   once eleven
    la oportunidad opportunity
4   ordinario, -a ordinary; ordinariamente ordinarily
4   la oreja ear
4   el orgullo pride
2   el oro gold
1   os you, to you, yourselves (*fam. pl.*)
    el oso bear
    hacer el oso to make love to, "play the bear"
    el otoño autumn, fall
1   otro, -a other, another
    la oveja sheep
    los «overoles» overalls (*borrowed from Amer.*)
1   oye *3rd pers. sing. pres. of* oír
1   oyendo *ger. of* oír
1   oyó *3rd pers. sing. pret. of* oír

P

    Pablo Paul; Pablito little Paul
    paciente patient
1   el padre father
1   los padres parents
2   pagar to pay (for) *143*
    la página page
2   pagué *1st pers. sing. pret. of* pagar
2   el país country
    la paja straw
4   el pájaro bird
1   la palabra word
3   el palacio palace

    la paloma, la palomita dove
2   el pan bread
    el panadero baker
    el panecillo roll
    el pantalón trousers
    el pañuelo handkerchief
1   el papel paper; play part; papelito little paper
1   para in order to, for; para sí to himself
1   parecer to seem, to appear; parecerse a to resemble *147*
3   la pared wall
    el pariente relative
    el parque park
1   la parte part; por todas partes everywhere
1   pasado, -a last, past
1   pasar to pass, to happen, to occur
    pase Vd. come in
4   pasearse to take a walk, ride or drive
    el pastel pastry, cake
    la pastelería pastry shop
    la patata potato
    paterno, -a paternal
    el patio patio, courtyard
2   la paz peace
    P.D. *abbr. for* posdata postscript (*like our P.S.*)
3   el pedacito little piece
1   pedir (i) to ask for, order *140*
    la película film
3   el pelo hair
2   el pensamiento thought
1   pensar (en) (ie) to think (about), to intend to *139*
1   peor worse; el (la) peor worst
    Pepe (*nickname for* José) Joe
1   pequeño, -a little, small
1   perder (ie) to lose *139*
    perezoso, -a lazy
3   perfectamente perfectly
4   el periódico newspaper

503 SPANISH-ENGLISH DICTIONARY

la perla   pearl
permiso: con su permiso   excuse me, with your permission
pedir permiso para   to ask permission to
1 pero   but
2 la persona   person
3 el perro   dog
el pescado   fish
3 la peseta   *Spanish coin normally worth about 19 cents*
3 el peso   *Mexican coin normally worth about 33 cents*
el piano   piano
Pícaro   Rascal (*used as a name for a donkey*)
1 pidiendo   *ger. of* pedir
2 el pie   foot; a pie   on foot
2 la piedra   stone, rock
la pierna   leg
3 pintar (de)   to paint
la pintura   painting
la piñata   *clay jar, decorated and filled with goodies, to be broken in a game (Mex.)*
el piso   floor, story (*of a building*)
la pizarra   blackboard
3 la planta   plant
plantar   to plant
3 la plata   silver
platicar   to chat   *144*
el platillo   saucer
el plato   plate, dish, course
2 la plaza   plaza, town square
3 la pluma   pen
4 la población   town, population
1 pobre   poor
1 poco   little (*quantity*)
poco a poco   little by little
pocos, -as   few
poquito   a very little
1 poder (ue, u)   to be able, can   *125*
1 podré   *fut. of* poder
1 podría   *cond. of* poder

1 poner (*p.p.* puesto)   to put, to place; ponerse   to put on, to become   *126*
poner la mesa   to set the table
1 ponga(n) Vd(s).   *com. of* poner
1 pongo   *1st pers. sing. pres. of* poner
1 por   by, through, for, in exchange for, throughout
la porción   portion
el pordiosero   beggar
1 porque   because
1 ¿por qué?   why?
el pórtico   arch
la posada   inn
3 poseer (*p.p.* poseído)   to possess
2 posible   possible; todo lo posible   all possible
el postre   dessert, pudding
practicar   to practice
práctico, -a   practical
la precaución   precaution
3 el precio   price
4 precioso, -a   delightful, precious
4 preferir (ie, i)   to prefer   *142*
2 preguntar   to ask
preguntón, preguntona   inquisitive
el premio   prize
la prenda   forfeit; garment
prender   to arrest
3 preparar   to prepare
2 presentar   to present, to introduce
la primavera   spring
1 primero (primer), -a   first
4 el primo, la prima   cousin
2 principal   principal, main
2 el principio   beginning; al principio   at first
4 la prisa   hurry, speed
de prisa   quickly
no hay prisa   there is no hurry
la prisión   prison

el **prisionero**   prisoner

probablemente   probably

probar (ue)   to test, to try, to prove *138*

el **producto**   product

el **profesor**, la **profesora**   teacher

la **promesa**   promise

3   **prometer**   to promise

2   **pronto**   promptly, quickly, right away

2   **propio, -a**   own

la **propuesta**   proposition

la **prosperidad**   prosperity

provecho: buen provecho   may it benefit you

4   **próximo, -a**   next

2   **público, -a**   public

1   **pud-**   *pret. stem of* **poder**

2   el **pueblo**   town;   **pueblecito**   little town

1   la **puerta**   door

1   **pues**   well, well then

1   **puesto**   *p.p. of* **poner**

el **puesto**   stall, stand

punto: en punto   exactly, sharp

2   **puramente**   purely, entirely

1   **pus-**   *pret. stem of* **poner**

Q

1   **¿qué?**   what?

1   **que**   that, which, what, who

1   **¡qué!**   *(adj.)* How ...!;   **¡qué bonito!**   How pretty!

1   **quedarse**   to remain, to stay   **quedo de Vd. atto., afmo. y S.S. (atento, afectísimo y seguro servidor)**   I remain, yours truly

4   **quejarse**   to complain

1   **querer** (ie)   to wish, to want   *127*   **querer a**   to love   **querer decir**   to mean

3   **querido, -a**   dear

1   **querré**   *fut. of* **querer**

1   **querría**   *cond. of* **querer**

el **queso**   cheese

1   **¿quién? ¿quiénes?**   who?   **¿de quién(es)?**   whose?   **¿a quién(es)?**   whom?   **a quien(es)**   whom

1   **quince**   fifteen

1   **quinientos, -as**   five hundred

1   **quinto, -a**   fifth

1   **quis-**   *pret. stem of* **querer**

2   **quitar**   to take off, to take away

1   **quizás**   perhaps

R

la **radio**   radio

4   la **rama**   branch;   **el ramito**   little bunch, bouquet

el **ranchero**   rancher;   *(adj.) applied to anyone from the country (Mex.)*

3   **rápido, -a**   rapid;   **rápidamente**   rapidly

3   **raro, -a**   rare, queer, odd

3   el **rato**   short space of time, while

el **ratón**   mouse

2   **real**   royal

la **rebaja**   reduction, discount

el **rebozo**   *shawl or scarf worn by Mexican women*

2   **recibir**   to receive

3   **recién**   recently

3   **reconocer**   to recognize   *147*

2   **recordar** (ue)   to remember   *138*

3   **recorrer**   to run through

3   el **recuerdo**   souvenir;   recollection;   **recuerdos**   regards

el **refrán**   proverb

el **refresco**   refreshment

el **refrigerador**   refrigerator

el **regalo**   present, gift

regatear   to bargain

regional   regional

3   **reír** (i)   *(p.p.* **reído**)   to laugh;   **reírse de**   to laugh at   *128*

la **reja**   window grating

3   **religioso, -a**   religious
el **reloj**   watch, clock
el **repaso**   review
repente: de repente   suddenly
2   **repetir (i)**   to repeat   *140*
3   **representar**   to represent
2   **responder**   to answer, to respond
4   la **respuesta**   answer
el **restaurante**   restaurant
3   **reunir**   to gather, to unite
revelar   to reveal
2   el **rey**   king
los **Reyes Magos**   the Wise Men
2   **rico, -a**   rich; **ricamente**   richly
3   **riendo**   *ger. of* **reír**
3   **río, ríe,** *etc., pres. of* **reír**
2   el **río**   river
el **rodeo**   round-up of cattle; Western
   riding and roping exhibition
3   **rojo, -a**   red
2   **romper(se)** (*p.p.* **roto**)   to break
3   la **ropa**   clothes, clothing
3   la **rosa**   rose
Rosario   girl's name
Rosita   Rosie
3   el **ruido**   noise

S

el **sábado**   Saturday, on Saturday
1   **saber**   to know, to know how to,
   to find out   *129*
3   **sabio, -a**   wise
1   **sabré**   *fut. of* **saber**
1   **sabría**   *cond. of* **saber**
sabroso, -a   tasty, savory
2   **sacar**   to take (out)   *144*
4   la **sala**   living room;   **sala de clase**
   classroom
1   **saldré**   *fut. of* **salir**
1   **saldría**   *cond. of* **salir**
1   **salga(n) Vd(s).**   *com. of* **salir**
1   **salgo**   *1st pers. sing. pres. of* **salir**
1   **salir (de)**   to leave; to win
   (*lottery*)   *130*

salir (muy) bien   to come out
   (very) well, succeed
la **salsa**   sauce
3   la **salud**   health;   ¡**salud!**   *said when
   someone sneezes*
la **salvación**   salvation
2   **santo**   saint, saint's day
   (*shortened to* **san** *before most
   masculine nouns*)
2   **saqué**   *1st pers. pret. of* **sacar**
el **sarape**   *blanket worn by Mexican
   Indian as an overcoat*
3   **satisfecho, -a**   satisfied
1   **se** (*reflexive*) himself, herself,
   yourself, itself, themselves,
   yourselves
1   **se** (*impersonal*) one, they, people
   se dice   it is said, one says, they
   say, people say
1   **se** (*substitute for* **le** *or* **les**)   him,
   her, you, it, them; to him, to
   her, to it, to you, to them
1   **sé** (*1st pers. sing. pres. of* **saber**)
   I know
2   el **secreto**   secret
3   **seguida: en seguida**,   at once,
   immediately
1   **seguir (i)**   to continue, to follow
   131
2   **según**   according to
1   **segundo, -a**   second
1   **seis**   six
1   **seiscientos, -as**   six hundred
4   la **semana**   week
2   **semejante**   similar
2   **sentarse (ie)**   to sit down, to seat
   oneself   *139*
1   **sentir (ie, i)**   to regret, to feel   *142*
1   el **señor** (*abbr.* **Sr.**)   gentleman, Mr.,
   sir
1   la **señora** (*abbr.* **Sra.**)   lady, Mrs.,
   madam
1   la **señorita** (*abbr.* **Srta.**)   young lady,
   Miss

1   **el señorito**   young fellow
3   **separar**   to separate
     septiembre *m.*   September
1   **séptimo, -a**   seventh
1   **ser**   to be   *132*
3   **seriamente**   seriously
     Serra, Junípero   *Franciscan priest who founded many of the missions along El Camino Real in California*
     servidor: servidor, -a de Vd.   at your service
2   **servir (i)**   to serve   *140*
1   **sesenta**   sixty
1   **setecientos, -as**   seven hundred
1   **setenta**   seventy
1   **sexto, -a**   sixth
1   **sí**   yes
1   **si**   if
1   **siempre**   always
     la siesta   afternoon nap
1   **siete**   seven
1   **siga(n) Vd(s).**   *com. of* **seguir**
1   **sigo**   *1st pers. sing. pres. of* **seguir**
1   **siguiendo**   *ger. of* **seguir**
2   **siguiente**   following; **al día siguiente**   the following day
3   **el silencio**   silence
3   **la silla**   chair
     simpático, -a   agreeable, nice
1   **sin**   without
1   **sino**   but *(after a negative)*
1   **sintiendo**   *ger. of* **sentir**
2   **sirve**   *pres. tense of* **servir**
2   **sirviendo**   *ger. of* **servir**
2   **el sitio**   place, siege
1   **sobre**   on, upon, about, over, above
3   **el sobrino**   nephew; **la sobrina**   niece
3   **social**   social
3   **la sociedad**   society
     el sofá   sofa
2   **el sol**   sun; **al sol**   in the sun
1   **solamente**   only

2   **solo**   alone, single; **solito**   all alone
2   **la sombra**   shade; **a la sombra**   in the shade
     el sombrero   hat
1   **son**   *(3rd pers. pl. pres. of* **ser***)* they are, are
     el son   tune
     la sonrisa   smile
     la sopa   soup
     sorprendido, -a   surprised
4   **la sorpresa**   surprise
1   **soy**   *(1st pers. sing. pres. of* **ser***)* I am
1   **su, sus**   his, her, your, their, its
2   **subir (a)**   to climb, to ascend
     subirán (no)   they shall (not) come up
     substituido, -a   substituted
     subterráneo, -a   subterranean
     sudamericano   South American
2   **el suelo**   floor, ground
2   **el sueño**   dream
2   **la suerte**   luck; **¡Qué suerte tan buena!**   What good luck!
2   **sufrir**   to suffer, to undergo
1   **sup-**   *pret. stem of* **saber**
3   **superior**   superior; **escuela superior**   high school
     la superstición   superstition
2   **suponer**   *(p.p.* **supuesto***)* to suppose *126*; **por supuesto**   of course
     el sur   south
     el susto   fright
1   **suyo, -a, -os, -as**   *(adj.)*   his, her, your, its, their
1   **el suyo, la suya, los suyos, las suyas**   *(pron.)*   his, hers, yours, theirs, its

T

     el taco   *popular Mexican "sandwich" made of a tortilla*

1 **tal** such; **¿Qué tal?** How goes it? (*informal greeting*)
tal vez perhaps
la **tamalada** supper of tamales (*Mex.*)
1 **también** too, also
3 **tampoco** neither, either; **ni Vd. tampoco** nor you either
1 **tan** so, as; **tan ... como** as ... as
1 **tanto, -a** so much; **tanto ... como** as much ... as
1 **tantos, -as** so many; **tantos ... como** as many ... as
2 la **tarde** afternoon
buenas tardes good afternoon
de la tarde in the afternoon, P.M.
por la tarde in the afternoon (*when no definite hour is stated*)
2 **tarde** late; **más tarde** later
la **taza** cup
el **te** tea
1 **te** thee, you; to thee, to you; thyself, yourself (*fam. sing.*)
2 el **teatro** theater
el **teléfono** telephone
3 **temblar (ie)** to tremble *139*
2 **temer** to fear
4 el **templo** temple
4 **temprano** early
1 **tendré** *fut. of* tener
1 **tendría** *cond. of* tener
1 **tener** to have *133*
aquí tiene Vd. here is
tener ... años to be ... years old
tener la bondad de + *inf.* please
tener calor to be hot
tener cuidado to be careful
tenga Vd. cuidado be careful
tener dos caras to be two-faced
tener frío to be cold

tener (mucha) hambre to be (very) hungry
tener la culpa to be to blame
tener miedo de to be afraid of
tener mucho gusto en to be very glad to
tener prisa to be in a hurry
tener que + *inf.* to have to
tener razón to be right; **no tener razón** to be wrong
tener (mucha) sed to be (very) thirsty
tener (mucha) vergüenza to be (very much) ashamed
1 **tengo** *1st pers. sing. pres. of* tener
Tenochtitlán *ancient Aztec capital of Mexico, now Mexico City*
1 **tercero (tercer), -a** third
Teresa Theresa
2 **terminar** to finish, to end
3 **terrible** terrible
4 el **tesoro** treasure
1 **ti** thee, you (*fam. sing.*) (*used after a prep.*)
1 el **tiempo** weather; time
4 la **tienda** store
1 **tiene** (*3rd pers. sing. pres. of* tener) has, he (she) has
2 la **tierra** land, earth
el **tigre** tiger
Tinita *nickname for Ernestina*
1 el **tío** uncle; la **tía** aunt
típico, -a typical
3 **tirar** to throw
3 el **título** title
2 **tocar** to play (*an instrument*) *144*
1 **todavía** still, yet
1 **todo, -a** all
el **toldo** awning
1 **tomar** to take
el **tomate** tomato
4 **tonto, -a** silly, foolish
2 **toqué** *1st pers. sing. pret. of* tocar
la **tortilla** omelet (*in Spain*); (*name

    applied to the substitute often used
    for bread in Mexico)
2 **trabajar** to work
2 el **trabajo** work
    traducir to translate *134*
    traduj- *pret. stem of* **traducir**
1 **traer** (*p.p.* **traído**) to bring *135*
1 **traiga**(n) **Vd**(s). *com. of* **traer**
3 el **traje** suit
3 **tranquilamente** tranquilly,
    peacefully
2 **tratar de** to try to
1 **trayendo** *ger. of* **traer**
1 **trece** thirteen
1 **treinta** thirty
    el **tren** train
1 **tres** three
1 **trescientos, -as** three hundred
2 **triste** sad; **tristemente** sadly
3 la **tristeza** sadness
    el **trono** throne
4 **tropezar** (**ie**) to stumble, to trip
    139, 146
    tropical tropical
1 **tú** thou, you (*fam. sing.*)
1 **tu** thy, your (*fam. sing.*)
    la **tumba** tomb, grave
    el **turista** tourist
    el **turrón** nougat
    el **turronero** nougat vendor (*Spain*)
1 **tuv-** *pret. stem of* **tener**
1 **tuyo, -a, -os, -as** (*adj.*) thy, yours
    (*fam. sing.*)
1 el **tuyo, la tuya, los tuyos, las tuyas**
    (*pron.*) thine, yours

U

2 **último, -a** last
    ultramarinos finos fine imported
    groceries
2 **lo único** the only thing
    la **universidad** university
1 **uno** (**un**), **una** one, an, a
1 **unos, -as** some

2 **usar** to use
3 el **uso** use
1 **usted, ustedes** (*abbr.* **Vd., Vds.,**
    Ud., Uds.) you
    el **utensilio** utensil
4 **útil** useful

V

1 **¿va Vd.?** (*from* **ir**) are you going?
    la **vaca** cow
    la **vacación** vacation; **las vacaciones**
    holidays
2 **valer** to be worth; **no vale nada**
    it isn't worth anything.
3 **valiente** brave
2 el **valor** value, worth
1 **¡vámonos!** (*inf.* **irse**) let's go; all
    aboard
1 **vamos a** + *inf.* we are going to,
    let's (*inf.* **ir**)
2 **varios, -as** several, various
1 **vase** (*from* **irse**) he goes out
    (*stage direction used like English*
    exit)
1 **vaya**(n) **Vd**(s). *com. of* **ir**
1 **Vd.** *abbr. for* **usted**
1 **vea**(n) **Vd**(s). *com. of* **ver**
    el **vecino** neighbor
1 **veía** *impf. of* **ver**
1 **veinte** twenty
4 la **vela** candle
    el **velo** veil
    el **venado** deer
    la **venda** bandage, blindfold
    vendar to blindfold
    el **vendedor** salesman, seller
3 **vender** to sell
1 **vendré** *fut. of* **venir**
1 **vendría** *cond. of* **venir**
1 **venga**(n) **Vd**(s). *com. of* **venir**
1 **vengo** *1st pers. sing. pres. of* **venir**
1 **venir** (**ie, i**) to come *136*
3 la **ventana** window
    la **ventilación** ventilation

1 **veo** *1st pers. sing. pres. of* **ver**
1 **ver** (*p.p.* **visto**) to see *137*; **a ver** let's see
el verano summer
4 **veras: de veras** really, truly
1 **la verdad** truth; **¿verdad?** isn't that so?
2 **verdadero, -a** real, true; **verdaderamente** really, truly
3 **verde** green
4 **vergüenza: con mucha vergüenza** very much ashamed
3 **el vestido** dress
2 **vestir** to dress (*trans.*); **vestirse** (**i**) to dress, get dressed; **vestirse de** to dress in *140*
1 **la vez** time (*pl.* **veces**)
　a la vez at a time, at the same time
　alguna vez ever, sometime
　algunas veces sometimes
　de vez en cuando from time to time
　en vez de instead of
　muchas veces often
　otra vez again
　por segunda vez for the second time
　rara vez rarely
　tal vez perhaps
　tres veces al día three times a day
　una vez once, one time, once upon a time
　varias veces several times
viajar to travel
2 **el viaje** trip; **hacer un viaje** to take a trip, to make a trip
el viajero traveler
1 **la vida** life
1 **viejo, -a** old; **viejecito, -a** little old man (lady)
1 **viene** (*pres. of* **venir**) he, she comes, is coming

el viernes Friday, on Friday (*pl.* **los viernes**)
1 **vin-** *pret. stem of* **venir**
3 **violento, -a** violent
la violeta violet
el violín violin
3 **la visita** visit
visitador, -a visiting
3 **visitar** to visit
2 **la vista** view; **hasta la vista** until I see you again
1 **visto** (*p.p. of* **ver**) seen
4 **la viuda** widow (*abbr.* **vda.**)
1 **¡viva!** hurrah for! (*from* **vivir**)
1 **vivir** to live
2 **vivo, -a** live, bright
3 **volar** (**ue**) to fly *138*
2 **la voluntad** will
1 **volver** (**ue**) (*p.p.* **vuelto**) to return; **volverse** to turn around *138, 148*
1 **vosotros, -as** you (*fam. pl.*)
1 **voy** (*1st pers. pres. of* **ir**) I go, I am going
2 **la voz** (*pl.* **voces**) voice; **en voz baja** in a low voice
1 **vuelto** (*p.p. of* **volver**) returned
1 **vuestro, -a, -os, -as** (*adj.*) your, yours (*fam. pl.*)
1 **el vuestro, la vuestra, los vuestros, las vuestras** (*pron.*) yours (*fam. pl.*)

Y

1 **y** and
1 **ya** already, now
　¡Ya lo creo! Yes, indeed! Of course!
　ya no no longer
1 **yendo** (*ger. of* **ir**) going
1 **yo** I

Z

el zaguán passage-way
la zapatería shoe store
el zapatero shoemaker
el zapato shoe

INDEX

(Numbers refer to pages.)

a
- a + el, 19
- al + infinitive, 153
- personal a, 85; footnote, 85 and 201

accents
- omission in some plurals, 19
- on past participles, 230
- *algún, ningún,* footnote, 133
- with enclitic pronouns, 144, 240
- rules for accent, 50, 477

adjectives
- absolute superlative, 242
- agreement, 18, 184
- comparison, 162–163
- describing two or more nouns, 184
- demonstrative, 83
- meaning of *gran,* 439
- of nationality, 215
- position, 2
- possessive, 26–27
- shortened forms, 133
- two adjectives describing same noun, 184
- used as nouns, 440; footnote, 166

adverbs
- formation, 153
- inverted word order, 164
- *no,* 3
- *aquí* and *acá, allí* and *allá,* 164

agreement
- of adjectives, 18, 184
- of possessive adjectives, 26–27
- of long forms and possessive pronouns, 201

al: 19
- + infinitive, 153

alphabet: 116, 478

aquí and *acá, allí* and *allá*
- distinction, 164

ártículo, definite
- forms, 17
- contractions, 4, 19
- with expressions of time, 351
- with the hour of day, 67
- with nouns in a general sense, 402
- with titles, 104
- to show possession, 184
- used in the superlative, 162
- omitted before noun in apposition, footnote, 228
- use of *el* before feminine nouns, footnote, 89
- replacing possessive adjective, 184

article, indefinite
- omission before unmodified predicate noun, footnote, 132
- omission before noun in apposition, 378

auxiliaries
- *haber,* 151–152
- *estar,* 239

capitals
- omission with some proper nouns, 11
- days of week, 60
- months, 108

cien: 440

commands
- formation, 84
- with object pronouns, 144

comparison of adjectives: 162

compound tenses: 151, 438–459

conditional tense
- regular, 428
- irregular, 429